Immigrant Entrepreneurs

Immigrant Entrepreneurs

Venturing Abroad in the Age of Globalization

Edited by
Robert Kloosterman and Jan Rath

Oxford • New York

First published in 2003 by
Berg
Editorial offices:
1st Floor, Angel Court, 81 St Clements Street, Oxford OX4 1AW, UK
838 Broadway, Third Floor, New York, NY 10003–4812, USA

Berg is the imprint of Oxford International Publishers Ltd.

Library of Congress Cataloging-in-Publication Data
Immigrant entrepreneurs : venturing abroad in the age of globalization
Robert Kloosterman and Jan Rath (editors).
     p. cm.
Includes bibliographical references and index.
     ISBN 1-85973-634-3 (Cloth) – ISBN 1-85973-639-4 (Paper)
1. Minority business enterprises. 2. Entrepreneurship. 3. Emigration
and immigration—Economic aspects. 4. Globalization—Economic aspects.
5. Immigrants—Economic conditions. 6. Immigrants—Social conditions.
7. Multiculturalism. I. Title: Immigrant entrepreneurship in the
global economy. II. Kloosterman, Robert. III. Rath, Jan, 1956–
HD2358.I46 2003
338′.04′086912—dc22

                                                              2003018396

British Library Cataloging-in-Publication Data
A catalogue record for this book is available from the British Library.

ISBN   1 85973 634 3 (Cloth)
       1 85973 639 4 (Paper)

Typesetting by Avocet Typeset, Chilton, Aylesbury, Bucks.
Printed in the United Kingdom by Biddles Ltd, Guildford and King's Lynn

www.bergpublishers.com

Acknowledgements

Acknowledgement of outside financial support:

European Commission DG XII, Brussels
European Science Foundation, Strasbourg
Institute for Migration and Ethnic Studies (IMES), University of Amsterdam
Netherlands Organization for Scientific Research (NWO), Fund for
Internationalizing the Social Sciences, The Hague

Contents

List of Tables and Figures

List of Tables

Notes on Contributors

Giles A. Barrett is Lecturer in Human Geography at Liverpool John Moores University. His degrees are from Liverpool Polytechnic and Liverpool John Moores University. From 1998 to 2001 he has co-ordinated the British contribution to the European Union 'Working on the Fringes' Targeted Socio-economic Research Network. He has a particular interest in the financing of African-Caribbean small business in Britain and African American enterprise in the United States. He has been a visiting scholar at Hunter College of the City University of New York. He has published in *Urban Studies, Journal of Ethnic and Migration Studies*, and in two edited collections, *Enterprise and Small Business*, ed. Carter, Jones and Evans, Pearson, 2000, and *Immigrant Businesses*, ed. Rath, Macmillan, 2000. He is currently engaged in a study of housing policy in Merseyside.

Mehdi Bozorgmehr is Associate Professor of Sociology at the City University of New York (CUNY) and Co-Director of the Middle East and Middle Eastern American Center at the Graduate Center, CUNY. His research interests include immigration, ethnicity, urban and economic sociology. He has focused on Middle Easterners, who rank among the most entrepreneurial immigrant groups in the United States. He is the co-editor of the award-winning *Ethnic Los Angeles* (Russell Sage 1996). His articles on immigrant entrepreneurship have appeared in *Social Problems, Ethnic and Racial Studies, International Migration Review* and *Revue Européenne des Migrations Internationales*, among others. In addition, he has contributed numerous chapters on the topic to edited volumes.

Jock Collins is Associate Professor of Economics at the University of Technology, Sydney (UTS), Australia, where he has taught for twenty-four years. Jock Collins has been writing on issues related to Australian immigration, multiculturalism and racism and the Australian labor market since 1973. He is the author of *Migrant Hands in a Distant Land: Australia's Post-war Immigration* (1988, 1991) and co-author of *A Shop Full of Dreams: Ethnic Small Business in Australia* (1995), *Cosmopolitan Sydney: Explore the world in one city* (1998) and *Kebabs, Kids, Cops and Crime: Youth, Ethnicity and Crime* (2000). Pluto Press, Sydney, published all these books. He is also co-editor (with Scott Poynting) of *The Other Sydney: Communities, Identities and Inequalities in Western Sydney*

(Common Ground Publishing, Melbourne, 2000). Jock Collins has held consultancies with the NSW Department of Treasury, the NSW Ethnic Affairs Commission, the Office of Multicultural Affairs, the Department of Immigration and Multicultural Affairs and the Council of Small Business Organizations of Australia. He has been a Visiting Fellow at universities in Britain, Canada and the United States.

Regina Haberfellner is the Head of the Department 'Equal Opportunities-Integration' at the Centre for Social Innovation in Vienna, Austria, and Member of the Board. She studied sociology at the University of Vienna and her work focuses mainly on immigrant business as a pathway to socio-economic integration. The impact of the knowledge-based society and ICT on immigrants' opportunities for participating in economic and political life is another important aspect of her work. She is involved in a number of international networks, and linking up basic research with applicable solutions is a main feature of her work. Her publications include *Ethnische Ökonomien: Integration vs. Segregation* (Vienna, Centre for Social Innovation, 1997, with M. Böse) and articles in *SWS-Rundschau* and *Isotopia*.

Daniel Hiebert is Professor of Geography at the University of British Columbia and a research co-ordinator at the Centre for Excellence for Research on Immigration and Integration in the Metropolis (RIIM) in Vancouver, Canada. His research focuses on several aspects of immigrant settlement in Canada, including the emerging social geography of immigrant neighbourhoods in Canadian cities, immigrant integration in the Canadian labour market, and the rise of immigrant entrepreneurship. Papers on all these topics can be found at the RIIM Internet site (www.riim.metropolis.net), as well as in more traditional academic publications, such as the *Annals of the Association of American Geographers*, *The Canadian Geographer*, *The Canadian Journal of Regional Science*, *Economic Geography*, and *Progress in Planning*.

Trevor P. Jones was formerly Reader in Social Geography at Liverpool John Moores University. He continues part-time research at that university and is Visiting Professor at De Montfort University. He studied at the London School of Economics and worked previously at Huddersfield Polytechnic. His collaboration with David McEvoy and others on ethnic minority business and on ethnic segregation has produced papers in *Area, Annals of the Association of American Geographers, New Community, New Society, Social Forces, Sociological Review, Revue Européenne des Migrations Internationales, New Economy, Urban Studies, Work, Employment and Society*, and the *Journal of Ethnic and Migration Studies*. Numerous essays in books have also appeared. He was senior author of

Geographical Issues in Western Europe (Longman, 1988) and *Social Geography* (Edward Arnold, 1989).

Robert C. Kloosterman is Professor of Economic Geography/Planning at the University of Amsterdam. His research activities centre on processes of dualization, polarization and informalization in urban environments, business formation (especially immigrant businesses) and polycentric urban configurations in advanced economies. Most of this research is undertaken from an explicitly international comparative perspective. A connecting theme concerns the way different (national or local) institutional environments filter, shape, reinforce or block more general trends. He recently started a new project on cultural industries and urban economies where the focus will be on spatial patterns of cultural industries and their interrelationship with social networks, in polycentric and monocentric urban configurations.

Thomas Lacroix is preparing a doctoral thesis at MIGRINTER, University of Poitiers (Dir. Patrick Gonin) and CERI, IEP of Paris (Dir. Catherine Wihtol de Wenden). His work focuses on how Moroccan migrants affect the development of their country of origin, with a particular emphasis on the transnational networks and the state policies toward these transnational activities. He is the co-author of *Les Motifs de l'Altérité, Quand l'Autre se Fait En-Jeux* (l'Harmattan, 2002). He is co-organizer of a conference on 'The Migrant: Agent of Change on the Two Banks of Sahara', held at the University of Agadir, Morocco, September 2002.

Emmanuel Ma Mung is a geographer and Director of Research at the CNRS (the French National Centre for Scientific Research). He has carried out studies of ethnic economy and entrepreneurship, the mobility of international migrants, and the Chinese diaspora. Since 1995, he has been in charge of MIGRINTER (International Migrations, Spaces, and Societies), Unit of Research of the CNRS at the universities of Poitiers and Bordeaux. He is author of *Commerçants Maghrébins et Asiatiques en France* (Paris: Masson 1990), *Mobilités et Investissements des Emigrés, Maroc, Tunisie, Turquie, Sénégal* (Paris: L'Harmattan 1996), *La Diaspora Chinoise, Géographie d'une Migration* (Paris: Ophrys 2000), and editor of the 'Entrepreneurs entre Deux Mondes' (1982) and 'La Diaspora Chinoise en Occident' (1992), special issues of the *Revue Européenne des Migrations Internationales*.

Mauro Magatti took a PhD in sociology at the University of Kent at Canterbury (UK). Currently he is Associate Professor at the Catholic University of Milan, where he teaches economic sociology and sociology of labour. He is interested in how social forces shape markets and particularly focused on ethnic entrepreneurship in Italy.

David McEvoy is Emeritus Professor of Urban Geography at Liverpool John Moores University. He was Director of the School of Social Science in that university from 1991 to 1998. He graduated from Manchester University and previously worked at Sheffield University, Durham University and North East London Polytechnic. His research on ethnic minority residence and on ethnic minority business in Britain and Canada stretches over 20 years. His collaboration with Trevor P. Jones and others, including Giles A. Barrett, has been funded by the Social Science Research Council (UK), the Economic and Social Research Council (UK), the Commission for Racial Equality (UK) and the Canadian High Commission in London. He was awarded the TIEM Canada prize for best paper at the 32nd World Conference of the International Council for Small Business.

Pyong Gap Min is Professor of Sociology at Queens College and the Graduate Center of the City University of New York. His areas of research are immigration, ethnicity, ethnic businesses, women's gender roles, and immigrants' religions, with a special focus on Asian Americans. He is the author of three books, including *Caught in the Middle: Korean Communities in New York and Los Angeles* (1996), the winner of two national book awards. He is the editor or co-editor of five books, including *The Second Generation: Ethnic Identity among Asian Americans* (2002) and *Mass Migration to the United States: Classical and Contemporary Periods* (2002).

Ching Lin Pang was postdoctoral researcher at MERIB (Migration and Ethnicity Research Institute Brussels), Catholic University of Leuven, Belgium, and is now at the Centre for Equal Chances and against Racism, Brussels. In the past, she has done research on Japanese and Chinese immigrants in Belgium with a particular emphasis on their ethnic identity and social position in both receiving and host societies. Recently she has also started to study (female) immigrant entrepreneurship and new migrations. She is the author of *Negotiating Identity in Contemporary Japan: The Case of Kikukoshijo* (2000) and co-editor of *Structure, Culture and Beyond* (1999) and *Cultuur, etniciteit en migratie* (1999). She was a member of the TSER Thematic Network 'Working on the Fringes'.

Sally Peberdy is the Project Manager for the Southern African Migration Project (SAMP) and an Honourary Lecturer in the Department of Geography and Environmental Studies at the University of the Witwatersrand. She is continuing to pursue research on migrant entrepreneurs and cross-border trade in Southern Africa and is a regular contributor to policy debates on the issue. As Project Manager for SAMP she is also involved in collaborative studies on regional migration issues, including repatriation, women's migration and borders with researchers in the region.

Fabio Quassoli got his PhD in sociology at the University of Milan. He is a researcher at the Department of Sociology of the University of Milano-Bicocca. He has done comparative research on different aspects of foreign immigration, with particular emphasis on immigrants' incorporation in the Italian labour market, self-employment, access to welfare state provisions and exclusion. He has published several papers on these topics and he contributed with essays in edited books. He is currently writing a book on the social construction of immigrant crime. He was a member of the TSER Thematic Network 'Working on the Fringes'.

Jan Rath is an Associate Professor and Co-Director of the Institute for Migration and Ethnic Studies (IMES) at the University of Amsterdam, The Netherlands (http://users.fmg.uva.nl/jrath). An anthropologist, he is also active in urban and economic sociology. He co-founded an international network of experts on immigrant entrepreneurship. He is the author of numerous articles, book chapters and reports on the sociology, politics and economics of post-migratory processes. He edited *Immigrant Businesses: The Economic, Political and Social Environment* (Macmillan, 2000), the 'Immigrant Entrepreneurship' issue of the *Journal of Ethnic and Migration Studies* (with Robert Kloosterman, 27(2), April 2001), and *Unravelling the Rag Trade: Immigrant Entrepreneurship in Seven World Cities* (Berg 2002).

Christian M. Rogerson is Professor of Human Geography, School of Geography, Archaeology and Environmental Studies, University of the Witwatersrand, Johannesburg. His research interests are focused on issues of local economic development, spatial change and small-enterprise development. He is the author of more than 100 scholarly articles and publications concerning these themes, including the co-edited book *South Africa's Informal Economy* (1991) and *Rethinking the Informal Economy of South Africa* (1996).

Czarina Wilpert is a sociologist, and has worked at the Science Centre Berlin, the Bundesinstitut für Berufsbildung (National Institute for Vocational Training Research) and the Berlin University of Technology. In this capacity she was a member of the TSER Network 'Working on the Fringes'. She has published books and numerous articles on research regarding the descendants of migrants, transitions from school to work, intercultural competence, the informal labour market, the social organization of the migrants from Turkey to Berlin. Currently she is studying intervention strategies of federally financed projects to counteract racism and xenophobia in Germany. Her latest book is *Challenging Racism in Britain and Germany* (co-edited with Zig Layton-Henry, Palgrave, 2001). She is founding member and head of the Board of the *Initiative Selbständige Immigrantinnen*, an association established to counsel, train and support immigrant women who desire to become self-employed.

Preface

Entrepreneurs from less-developed countries have set up shop all over the Western world. A Pakistani wholesaler supplying confectioners, tobacconists and newsagents in London, a Taiwanese IT specialist in Silicon Valley, a Turkish cook selling kebabs in Berlin, and an Iranian couple running a beauty salon in Rotterdam are all examples of immigrants who start their own businesses. In doing so, they articulate their sets of resources and limitations with the local opportunity structure for businesses in advanced economies. Immigrant entrepreneurship is on the rise in virtually all the advanced economies and has been the focus of multifarious academic studies.

By presenting an overview of contemporary immigrant entrepreneurship in North America, Europe, Australia and South Africa, this book makes a substantial contribution to this burgeoning field of research. Each chapter gives an overall picture of the trends, policies, and academic perspectives on immigrant entrepreneurship in one country. With the exception of South Africa, the countries are all advanced economies in the sense of being members of the OECD. South Africa is included because a significant part of its economy can also be qualified as advanced and it is an important destination for migrants from much less developed parts of Africa. We are well aware of how many other countries could have been included in our international survey. However, as is amply illustrated, the study of immigrant entrepreneurship has barely begun in many of these countries and many of the researchers in the field are isolated from international research networks and limited to their own national stage. We hope that this book will serve as a source of inspiration for these researchers and that, at some point, their studies on immigrant entrepreneurship will be accessible to a larger international audience.

In this book, we confine ourselves to immigrants from less developed economies, countries that are not members of the OECD, though obviously migration flows are not solely from these countries. Immigrants from developed economies constitute a considerable part of the international migration flows, since multinationals have expanded the spatial scope of their operations and national immigration agencies tend to specifically target highly skilled immigrants. Increasingly, highly skilled immigrants come from developing countries such as India, China and Ghana. There is thus far less of a simple dichotomy between highly skilled immigrants from advanced economies and unskilled ones from less developed countries than two or three decades ago. However, most of the unskilled immigrants still come from less developed countries. If they want to start their own businesses, they are faced with quite different opportunity structures than highly skilled immigrants such as Indian or Chinese software engineers starting a firm in Silicon Valley. By focusing on immigrants from less developed countries, we highlight the incorporation processes of this particular category of immigrants in advanced economies.

The study of immigrants who set up their own businesses in various advanced economies is not new. The most important landmark in this respect is *Ethnic Entrepreneurs: Immigrant Business in Industrial Societies* by Roger Waldinger, Howard Aldrich, Robin Ward and Associates (1990a). Our book, intended in part to be its successor, systematically updates the developments in immigrant entrepreneurship in advanced economies. Since the past decade has witnessed a significant rise of immigrant entrepreneurship in advanced economies, the need for an update was pressing. With eleven countries, a much broader international overview is given, focusing attention on general developments and national specifics alike. The book analyses how immigrant entrepreneurship is approached theoretically by social scientists in each country. It incorporates some of the more recent theoretical developments pertaining to immigrant entrepreneurship. The emergence of social capital and class or ethnic resources as the major theoretical tools for interpreting and explaining immigrant entrepreneurship is perhaps the most notable of the shifts in theoretical perspective since the publication of *Ethnic Entrepreneurs*. However, too narrow a focus on social capital and class or ethnic resources fails to appreciate the macro-economic and regulatory structures as important factors in determining the extent and incidence of immigrant entrepreneurship in various countries. These factors invariably emerge when countries with extensive welfare systems such as many European countries are compared with countries with a lean welfare system such as the United States. In short, the book is not only an up-to-date reference book on immigrant entrepreneurship in advanced economies, it also makes a significant contribution to business studies, migration studies, urban studies, economic sociology, economic geography and institutional economics.

The book evolved from the activities of the interdisciplinary and international Thematic Network 'Working on the Fringes: Immigrant Businesses, Economic Integration and Informal Practices' that has been active since 1999. All but one of the chapters have been presented as papers at Network conferences. The Network operated under the Targeted Socio-Economic Research Programme of the European Commission DG XII (1997 edition, area III.2). The European Science Foundation under the SCSS Exploratory Grant Scheme, the Fund for Internationalizing the Social Sciences of the Netherlands' Organization for Scientific Research and the Department of Economic Affairs of the City of

Amsterdam have also supported the network (for further information, see http://users.fmg.uva.nl/jrath/imment/tser.htm).

We would like to express our gratitude for this support. We would also like to thank the other participants in the Network conferences for their contributions to the discussion, Sheila Gogol for her linguistic editing, and Joost Penninx, Hulda Rútsdóttir and especially Heleen Ronden for completing the editorial process.

Robert Kloosterman
Jan Rath

Introduction

Robert Kloosterman and Jan Rath

Immigrants as Entrepreneurs

Many advanced economies, especially their larger cities, acquired a more cosmopolitan outlook in the closing decades of the twentieth century. This is reflected in an ever-broadening product range, which now not only includes such obvious items as Coca Cola, hamburgers and Levi's but also Thai food, North African musical instruments and Indian saris. It is not just the appearance of these 'exotic' products in shops in Berlin, Liverpool, Paris, Sydney or Los Angeles that reveals the deepening links between less-developed and advanced economies. The demographic make-up of many advanced economies has also significantly changed as flows of long-distance migration from ever more locations increased in the second half of the twentieth century. Immigrants from less-developed countries moved to advanced economies, embodying the complex process of globalization in a very palpable sense. These two highly visible aspects of globalization are often directly related as immigrants themselves introduce their products to far-off places. They start businesses in their countries of settlement and become 'self-employed' or 'immigrant entrepreneurs'.[1]

Notwithstanding increasing numbers of immigrant entrepreneurs from less-developed countries who set up shop, they have long remained unsung heroes, especially in Europe.[2]

In socio-economic terms, for a long time these immigrants were largely viewed as *workers*. Immigrants were predominantly depicted as suppliers of cheap low-skilled labour in advanced economies. More recently, attention has shifted toward immigrants from less-developed countries who start their own businesses.

By becoming self-employed, immigrants acquire roles quite different from these of immigrants who become workers and also different from those of mainstream entrepreneurs. By starting their own businesses, immigrant entrepreneurs create their own jobs. This enables them to circumvent some of the barriers they may encounter in looking for a job. Immigrants from less-developed countries are especially likely to come up against these barriers. They may lack or be felt to lack educational qualifications, they may not have sufficient access to relevant social networks for transmitting information on vacancies, or local employers may simply discriminate against them. Becoming self-employed does not mean that all these barriers have become irrelevant – banks may still discriminate against immigrants when they ask for business loans – but entrepreneurs are less vulnerable (Watson et al. 2000).

If they are successful, immigrant businesses can create jobs for others as well. This can benefit relatives, friends and acquaintances and, more generally, co-ethnics as social networks are often interfaces for information on the recruitment of new workers by small firms (cf. Waldinger 1986a). Creating jobs then helps alleviate unemployment among immigrants.

Immigrant entrepreneurs can also contribute different forms of social capital than immigrant workers to the immigrant communities.[3] Because of their links to suppliers and customers, immigrant entrepreneurs can be useful in constructing bridges to other networks outside the inner circle, thus improving chances of upward mobility (Putnam 1998, 2000). Moreover, immigrant entre-preneurs often act as self-appointed leaders for their communities (Minghuan 2000).

Most important they show that immigrants from less-developed countries are not necessarily restricted to filling vacancies on the job market, they can be active agents and shape their own destinies by setting up their own businesses (Kumcu 2001). Even if they are confined to lines of businesses with little promise, they are still actors in a very literal sense.[4]

Immigrant entrepreneurs not only differ from immigrant *workers*, but also from *indigenous* entrepreneurs. They may provide goods and services indigenous entrepreneurs are not very likely to offer. Immigrant entrepreneurs may have expert knowledge on specific demands or specific sources of supply relating to foreign products as in the case of foodstuffs (e.g. spices from Indonesia), music (e.g. rai music from North Africa) or videos (e.g. Bollywood movies from India). In many cases this hard-to-copy expertise can be based on first-hand knowledge from back home or it can be generated through transnational networks that bridge the country of origin and the sometimes extensive diaspora of a specific group of immigrants (Faist 1997; Portes 1995). By introducing new products and new ways of marketing, even immigrant entrepreneurs at the bottom end of a market can be innovators – Joseph Schumpeter's 'new men', albeit in a more modest form (cf. Engelen 2001; Hall 1998). One example is the introduction of Döner Kebab by Turkish entrepreneurs in Germany (see the contribution by Czarina Wilpert, Chapter 12 in this book). Or indigenous entrepreneurs might lack the credibility for specific kinds of businesses, as in the case of Chinese restaurants where the owner and staff need at least a Chinese appearance. Or preferences may keep indigenous entrepreneurs out of certain lines of business that require long hours of hard work at low pay that only immigrants are prepared to put up with (cf. Waldinger 1996). Migrant entrepreneurs may thus broaden the range of goods and services in a country and hence expand the consumers' choice. In an indirect sense, this may even allow indigenous entrepreneurs to focus more on activities where they can exploit their own specific comparative advantages (*The Economist* 2002).

From a geographical perspective, migrant entrepreneurs can add vitality to particular streets or even neighbourhoods in cities (Rath 2002d, and in this book Chapter 9 by Emmanuel Ma Mung and Thomas Lacroix). If streets are deserted by indigenous businesses and replaced – in an invasion-and-succession sequence – by foreign entrepreneurs, deterioration can be reversed (Kloosterman and van der Leun 1999). As owners of local businesses, they have a clear stake in the prosperity, accessibility and safety of the street or neighbourhood. In many cases, these businesses are also where members of local social networks gather (Davies and Herbert 1993: 137; Kumcu 2001). They are thus an important component of the social fabric sustaining civic society at the grass-roots level.

Analogous to the last point, immigrant entrepreneurs can be instrumental in giving certain sectors a new lease on life.[5] In some industries, because of their specific skills, knowledge or social capital immigrant businesses can be at a comparative advantage (cf. Waldinger 2001). The garment industry is a case in point (cf. Rath 2002c). In this sector, immigrants bring skills no longer reproduced on a sufficient scale in most advanced economies. In addition, they are willing to work long hours and use their social capital and networks to reduce production and transaction costs.

The Institutionalization of Research on Immigrant Entrepreneurship

Immigrant entrepreneurs are thus an important research topic from any number of perspectives, but it took some time for this view to become widespread. This interest is partly driven by the rise in immigrant entrepreneurship itself. This rise was first observed in the United States and somewhat later in the United Kingdom; the sequence of the scientific research on contemporary immigrant entrepreneurship reflects this pattern. The first significant publications appeared in North America in the early 1970s, closely followed by similar work in the United Kingdom.[6] Soon after, researchers in Australia and Europe followed suit. Together, these researchers have created an impressive body of literature consisting of more than 1,700 books, reports, monographs, chapters, journal articles and special issues on aspects of immigrant entrepreneurship.[7] Immigrant and ethnic entrepreneurship has become a recurrent theme at international conferences of anthropologists, historians, sociologists or geographers. Researchers have established international networks and exchange information by electronic and other means. Last but not least, in their capacity as university teachers they give a variety of courses on immigrant and ethnic entrepreneurship that help foster researchers' continued interest. Looking back on more than three decades of research, we can safely conclude that immigrant entrepreneurship has not only been incorporated in the corpus of topical social science subjects, it has become a kind of growth sector itself.[8]

Notwithstanding the institutionalization of research on immigrant entrepreneurship in many countries, cross-border comparisons have been scarce (see Rath 2002a). This is partly due to a dearth of relevant statistical data. Information on immigrant entrepreneurship is hard to come by in many countries and even harder to compare. How 'immigrants' or 'ethnic' minorities are defined is contingent on the specific national incorporation regime and differs from country to country (cf. Hollifield 1992; Soysal 1994). Immigrants in France are largely statistically invisible since they have acquired French citizenship, whereas immigrants from Turkey in Germany are still considered foreigners and registered as such, and immigrants from Eastern Europe who are of German ancestry (*Aussiedler*) can get citizenship right away (see Wilpert in Chapter 12). Immigrants who have the same backgrounds but settle in different countries can end up as very different statistical categories. Somewhat analogous to the first point, the definition of entrepreneurship or self-employment also differs from country to country depending on the regulatory regime. According to Blanchflower (2000: 478), it is anything but a 'simple matter to determine whether an individual is actually self-employed or not' and this holds even more true if one wants do this in a consistent way across countries. In some countries, very small firms are not counted as official businesses and thus remain part of the underground or informal economy. As Regina Haberfellner shows in Chapter 11, after a change in the official definition of businesses to include very small ones, the number of self-employed in Austria suddenly mushroomed. The statistical category 'immigrant entrepreneurship' is at the crossroads of these two conceptual interpretations, resulting in large disparities between countries. In some countries (e.g. France), the whole official statistical concept of 'immigrant' as such is non-existent, whereas in others (such as the United States) the official Census data allow for a combination of country of birth and/or nationality with socio-economic status. Even if official quantitative data are available, time series of immigrant entrepreneurship are often difficult to construct. Figures on employment and unemployment are published quarterly or even monthly, and in many cases they can be broken down according to sex, age group, ethnic category and region. Data on self-employment are not subjected to this rigid (OECD) format and can have very different time intervals. Census data tend to be collected once a decade. The construction of the very concept of 'immigrant entrepreneurship' and its particular way of statistical explicitation is located, hence, at the intersection of partly idiosyncratic *national* processes of the social construction of immigrants, and the social construction of self-employment. This fundamental lack of a sound uniform conceptual and statistical base of immigrant employment that can be applied across countries also implies that truly international comparative research on this topic is still not feasible. [9]

In this volume, researchers have therefore, sometimes painstakingly, constructed quantitative immigrant entrepreneurship trends in their countries by using such sources as national statistical time series, the Census, and Chambers of Commerce databases. Still, the underlying diversity of the data does not allow for a refined statistical comparative analysis of national trends.

In addition to the data issue, there is another explanation for the relative lack of international comparative work on immigrant entrepreneurship. Research on immigrant entrepreneurship has taken its own theoretical path in the past three decades and has usually been national or local in focus. There has been a strong emphasis on the supply side with the focus on the entrepreneurs themselves and not the broader context. To economists such as Borjas (1990) and Bates (1997), human capital has been the crucial explanatory variable of entrepreneurial success. According to sociologists, however, this neoclassical view with atomistic individuals pursuing the narrowly defined goal of profit maximization fails to explain variations among different categories of immigrant entrepreneurs and immigrant entrepreneurship more generally (cf. Light and Gold 2000; see also Power 2001). They tend to stress the role of social capital, the resources that characterize a whole group and not just its isolated members. Although these perspectives can make it easier to explore immigrant entrepreneurship in a number of cases, they do not suffice if one wants to compare immigrant entrepreneurship in different settings; they leave out the demand side or opportunity structure. Immigrant entrepreneurs do not operate in a vacuum, they have to operate in virtual socio-economic spaces where there are specific opportunities for businesses, especially small ones. The shape of these spaces is contingent on multifarious factors such as sectoral and income distribution, financial system, available technology, welfare system, and rules and regulations. To understand national trends in immigrant entrepreneurship, these opportunity structures have to be taken into account in order to put the actors into a proper perspective (cf. Aldrich et al. 1984; Rath 2002a).

Actors and Opportunity Structures

This book is a successor to *Ethnic Entrepreneurs: Immigrant Business in Industrial Societies* by Roger Waldinger et al., published by Sage in 1990. This first more comprehensive international overview of immigrant entrepreneurship also made an effort to move beyond actors' perspectives and address cross-border differences. The authors believed that in order to understand and explain ethnic entrepreneurial strategies, ethnic and socio-cultural factors should be combined with politico-economic factors. In their opinion, the set of politico-economic factors includes access to ethnic and non-ethnic consumer markets and to owner-ship in the form of business vacancies, competition for vacancies, and govern-ment policies. Many researchers still consider this *interactive model* an impor-tant step toward a more comprehensive theoretical approach, even though it is more like a classification than an explanatory model. After its publication, various researchers observed shortcomings in the interactive model. Light and Rosenstein (1995) stressed a number of methodological flaws. Morokvasic (1993) and Collins et al. (1995a) felt insufficient attention was devoted to gender issues, whereas the latter also deplored the absence of processes of racialization. Rath and Kloosterman (2000b) criticized the a priori categorization of immi-grants as ethnic groups and the concomitant assumption that as ethnic entrepre-neurs, immigrants act differently by default than mainstream entrepreneurs. Bonacich (1993) and Rath (2000b, 2002a), disapprove of the model's narrow and static approach of economic and regulatory factors. The authors view market conditions in terms of the ethnicization or de-ethnicization of consumer markets, and confine regulatory factors to a short list of laws and regulations that specif-ically apply to immigrants.

Partly due to this criticism, the debate went into another direction after the publication of *Ethnic Entrepreneurs*. Again the focus moved to the supply side or the entrepreneurs themselves. Light and Gold (2000), and Yoon (1997) gave ethnic and class resources a central role in their analyses. In their view, immi-grant entrepreneurship is the product of the mobilization of a combination of resources. Broader contextual characteristics still matter, particularly with respect to the fit between a specific set of resources and contextual characteris-tics, but they do not theoretically elaborate upon the latter. Other researchers have followed mainstream economic sociologists such as Granovetter (1995), and focus on the entrepreneurs' social networks and their impact on entrepre-neurship (e.g. Lee 1999; Light 2000; Waldinger 1996; Yoo 1998; Zhou 1992). To put it bluntly, many researchers confine themselves to exploring and refining agency matters, in particular regarding the significance of social networks, instead of elaborating upon the interplay of agency and structure.

There have also been efforts to address immigrant entrepreneurship from structural perspectives. Various authors posit that immigrants gravitate toward self-employment because there are so few alternatives. Blocked-mobility – an inability to find a job that fits their skills, interests and ambitions due to racist practices (Saxenian 1999) – pushes immigrants toward self-employment. This perspective has always been popular in the United Kingdom and some of the leading scholars have embraced it since the early 1980s. Trevor Jones and David McEvoy in particular have gone to great lengths to shift theoretical attention from internal processes to the external environment where businesses operate (see their Chapter 6 in this book). Their work is grounded in a political economy perspective and emphasizes the negative influence of contemporary structural changes in advanced economies on immigrant business development.

Saskia Sassen also emphasizes the role of structural forces, albeit in a more positive way. In her view, immigrants are pulled rather than pushed into self-employment. Her book *The Global City* (2001) describes the decline of manufacturing industries and the growth of the service economy. These processes are particularly salient in 'global cities', where capitalism is at a peak. The high end of the service sector in these global cities creates a demand for low-end activities by outsourcing directly (producer services) and indirectly (consumer services). Immigrants engage in these activities, intimately associated with processes of flexibilization and informalization, and their expansion serves as a magnet for new immigrants.[10] Thus opportunities are created for people who have no access to the primary segments of the labour market. Sassen's perspective also underscores that economic restructuring can be a driving force behind immigrant entrepreneurialism, even though many of these micro-entrepreneurs never transcend the level of the *Lumpen-bourgeoisie*.

Taking Sassen's view as a point of departure, one could even argue that immigrant entrepreneurship is the logical outcome of two structural processes of change in advanced economies. The first process of change has affected the supply side. The general increase in immigration from less-developed countries to advanced economies expanded the *supply* of potential immigrant entrepreneurs after 1950 and increasingly so after 1975.[11]

The second process of change involves the post-industrial transition after 1970 which has tilted the *demand side* more toward small firms by eroding the dominance of large-scale, Fordist modes of production. This phase of drastic economic restructuring not only entailed the end of many manufacturing activities and a rapid expansion of the service sector (high- and low-end), but it also shed new light on the role of small businesses and, hence, of the self-employed. Economies of scale, very dominant in the first decades after the Second World War, lost their hitherto seemingly incontestable economic logic in at least some activities, and small-scale production appeared to be the wave of the future. Saturation of industrial markets and the long-term diversification of taste fragmented markets on the one hand, and created new markets for which the demand was too unstable to use the traditional equipment profitably on the other. Small-scale production or flexible specialization seemed to be the answer (Piore and Sabel 1984: 206–7). The opportunities for small businesses also expanded as a result of the increase in subcontracting by firms and private households and hierarchies were replaced by networks of small firms.[12] Deregulation, part of the neoliberal political programme many countries adapted after 1980, also increased the possibilities for small firms in low-value added activities (OECD 1992, 2000).

Especially in larger cities with a significant immigrant population, crossing the second industrial divide, to use a phrase coined by Piore and Sabel, would hence inevitably result in a marked rise of immigrant entrepreneurship. The relation between agency and structure, however, is much less clear-cut and more open. It is not just that the post-industrial transition (although it does involve more opportunities for small firms) is far more complex than many observers first noted.[13] The match between potential entrepreneurs and opportunities for small firms is seldom as straightforward as it seems to be in the chapters of this book. Mechanistic structural perspectives not only underestimate the role of agency by assuming that immigration is a homogenous phenomenon, they also run the risk of taking too much of the broader context for granted. They tend to overlook such issues as government regulation, which may be very different in other countries.

More recently, we have tried to combine agency and structure perspectives in our concept of *mixed embeddedness* (Kloosterman and Rath 2001b; Kloosterman et al. 1999; Rath 2002a). We want to go beyond the social embeddedness of the actors themselves and take into account the wider societal context in which immigrant entrepreneurs are starting their business. Mixed embeddedness clearly means putting the opportunity structure back in again, but this time strongly influenced by Esping-Andersen (1990, 1998). He demonstrated how different national institutional frameworks, even if they are confronted with a similar structural change in the shape of the post-industrial transition, help to create divergent *post-industrial employment trajectories* by way of path-dependent processes. To paraphrase Esping-Andersen, one could also argue that various institutional frameworks also bring about divergent post-industrial *self-*employment trajectories and hence different opportunity structures for entrepreneurs, local and immigrant alike. First, the national institutional framework influences the division between market, public and familial provision. If the public sector takes care of a whole range of low-wage activities or if the familial domain is relatively large, the scope for small businesses is accordingly smaller than in the case where the market is the main provider for all kinds of household services (e.g. childcare, housecleaning, etc.) or municipal services (e.g. maintenance of public gardens, catering, etc.). This division is partly related to the role of a legal minimum wage. If a relatively high legal minimum wage exists (especially in conjunction with a strongly developed welfare system), the profitability of the market provision of labour-intensive, low-value added services is seriously undermined. In this case, the public sector, the family or informal provision will take place or these services will not be provided at all. A relatively high legal minimum wage may also impede those types of low-value-added manufacturing – such as the garment industry – that have a strong inclination to be in close proximity to large consumer markets and are, hence, less able to opt for locating in low-wage places in developing economies. These 'background institutions' that diverge from country to country determine to a significant extent the shape of the opportunity structure for small businesses and, accordingly, the set openings that aspiring immigrant entrepreneurs face in a particular context.

Secondly, a whole host of formal and informal institutions may regulate in a more concrete way if openings for small businesses occur and if they are accessible for immigrant entrepreneurs. In corporatist countries with a thick institutional context (a plethora of rules and regulations, both formal and informal), obstacles may arise in the form of the requirement of permits to start a particular line of business or even any business as in Germany (see Wilpert's Chapter 12 in this volume), or in the form of exclusionary rules that protect insiders by allowing, for example only a limited number of bakeries. In addition, institutions that determine or even foster the accessibility to, for instance, financial resources or the availability of commercial properties with regard to newcomers can also be crucial in shaping the opportunity structure for immigrant entrepreneurs. Regulation, to be sure, is not just a matter of repression and constraining, but also of enabling.

The mixed-embeddedness approach is intended to take into account the characteristics of the supply of immigrant entrepreneurs, the shape of the opportunity structure, and the institutions mediating between aspiring entrepreneurs and concrete openings to start a business in order to analyse immigrant entrepreneurship in different national contexts. The concept of mixed embeddedness still requires further elaboration and operationalization and has only guided the chapters of this book in a very broad manner.[14]

The authors examine trends in immigrant entrepreneurship, and address (national) dimensions of (potential) variation in eleven countries, migration history (i.e. supply side), the opportunity structure (the demand side), and the impact of government policies and regulation on the demand and supply of the entrepreneurial market. The emphasis, given that the focus is on *national* developments, is on the structural side of the equation, although actor perspectives are also addressed. In addition, involvement in informal activities is included since they may constitute an important refuge for immigrant entrepreneurs (Held et al. 1999: 325; Waldinger 1996). The authors analyse how contemporary immigrant entrepreneurship is perceived by social scientists in the different countries, reflecting the state of research on this topic.

A Brief Overview

A first general finding is anything but startling. All the countries had growing numbers of immigrants from an increasing number of more and more distant countries. Immigrants from Asia, Central Africa and Latin America show up all across the globe. Even Italy, long a country of *emigration*, as Mauro Magatti and Fabio Quassoli show in their Chapter 8 of this volume, has become an immigration country. This new phase in immigration has significantly changed the demographic make-up of the world's larger cities. In other words, the supply of potential immigrant entrepreneurs has expanded.

International trends in immigrant entrepreneurship are the subject of this book's second general finding. Although the paucity and diversity of the data do not permit the construction of a cross-border quantitative overview, on the whole immigrant entrepreneurship is clearly increasing in all eleven countries discussed in this volume. From the United States to South Africa and Austria to Canada, immigrants are increasingly self-employed. In the Netherlands (see Chapter 7 by Jan Rath and Robert Kloosterman) and the United States (Pyong Gap Min and Mehdi Bozorgmehr in Chapter 2) immigrant self-employment has mushroomed.

Although it is not the explicit topic of this book, we also note the emergence of post-industrial economies in the selected countries. South Africa is somewhat the odd one out, as Sally Peberdy and Christian Rogerson note in Chapter 5. The other countries clearly show a declining manufacturing base, a growing service sector and an increasing number of small businesses and self-employed people. Germany, with its traditionally strong manufacturing base, has not escaped this trend. After a drop in self-employment between 1950 and 1980, German growth in self-employment, particularly in the service sector, picked up (see Chapter 12 by Czarina Wilpert).

The intersection of rising immigration and the post-industrial transition in the advanced economies in the last quarter of the twentieth century did indeed apparently result in growing immigrant entrepreneurship. Social reality in each of the eleven selected countries is, however, much more complex.

The post-industrial transition implies a rise of small businesses as a result of the shift to flexible specialization modes of production in manufacturing and multifarious forms of outsourcing and subcontracting in manufacturing and services. We would thus expect to find immigrant entrepreneurs in what Allan Scott (1998: 21) calls the leading edges of capitalist development: high-tech manufacturing, consumer-oriented industries (resolutely focused on niche markets), and personal and business services. The dominant pattern of immigrant entrepreneurship that emerges in this book is however somewhat different. Most authors note that immigrant entrepreneurs are concentrated in lower-end retailing, wholesaling and restaurants and catering. These openings are closely linked to the vacancy chains where the most recent immigrant entrepreneurs replace earlier ones at the lower end of market, the rise of ethnic markets or markets of immigrants sharing the same kind of background, and offer immigrant entrepreneurs captive markets (Kloosterman 2002; Kloosterman and Rath 2001b). In France, as is noted by Ma Mung and Lacroix in Chapter 9, shopkeepers from North Africa have partly replaced local French businessmen. The same can be said of Turkish bakeries and grocery stores in the Netherlands (Rath and Kloosterman in Chapter 7) and Asian confectioners, tobacco shops and newsagents in the United Kingdom (see Chapter 6 by Giles Barrett, Trevor Jones and David McEvoy). The rise of consumer markets of Eastern European immigrants until 1993 in Austria is an example of an ethnic market process creating openings for small businesses (see Chapter 11 by Haberfellner). The spatial concentration of immigrants favours the emergence of these ethnic markets. In Germany (see Wilpert' Chapter 12), Turkish shops have clearly benefited from being concentrated in certain neighbourhoods.

National differences in the opportunity structure may result from the rate of replacement in vacancy chain businesses, which is related to general upward social mobility. It may also result from the creation or decline of ethnic markets in a process contingent on the rate and composition of immigration and the spatial distribution of groups of immigrants. More generally, the institutional framework also impacts the opportunity structure by regulating the access of immigrants to self-employment in some sectors or even in a wide range of activities. In Austria and Germany, aspiring immigrant entrepreneurs run into difficulties because the corporatist rules and regulations explicitly limit access to self-employment for non-EU immigrants. Although backed by the state, in some cases non-state bodies such as the Chambers of Commerce are involved as gatekeepers. The viability and profitability in these market segments is also dependent on the supply of aspiring entrepreneurs or, in other words, on the strength of the push factor. In part the push factor is a function of structural unemployment. In European welfare states, unskilled immigrants have a hard time in finding a job because the expansion of the (private) service sector is hampered by high minimum wages (Kloosterman 2000).

The openings resulting from vacancy chains and ethnic markets are relatively accessible; they often, although not always, require only low start-up costs and little or no specific educational qualifications and tend to rely on hard (and cheap) labour. Profit margins are squeezed because of the easy entry and many markets at the lower end are near saturation as is the case in the United Kingdom. Social capital and ethnic resources are needed to survive in these cut-throat markets. The combination of hard work and low pay means these openings are not very attractive. Many immigrant entrepreneurs are not so much pulled as pushed toward these openings. Unemployment is an important driving force behind the push toward entrepreneurship. Especially in Europe, where unemployment, particularly among immigrants from less-developed economies, has been high since 1980, immigrants have been partly pushed toward self-employment in these less-promising market segments. However, if the countries of settlement do not fully recognize immigrants' educational qualifications or if discrimination blocks their upward mobility on the regular labour-market, they may be pushed toward self-employment. In Australia, as Jock Collins shows in his contribution, there is an *accent ceiling* that limits the social mobility of non-English-speaking immigrants and operates as a push toward self-employment.

The prevalence of this traditional pattern of immigrant entrepreneurs working hard in sweat shops should not, however, be interpreted to mean that there is no relation at all between the post-industrial transition and the rise of immigrant entrepreneurship. First there is the mobility of immigrant entrepreneurs: those who start in vacancy chain or ethnic market openings are embedded in societies where post-industrial transformations are taking place. This means that in principle, they can start by exploiting a vacancy chain or ethnic market opening and then move to another, expanding segment. This 'breaking-out' (cf. Engelen 2001) is difficult, though there are examples of immigrant entrepreneurs successfully pursuing this strategy. In many countries, immigrant entrepreneurs in the restaurant sector who started by catering primarily to a clientele of immigrants with the same background profit from an expanding taste repertoire in the host societies linked to the cultural shrinkage of the world.[15] Ching Lin Pang, in Chapter 10 on Belgium, notes how Chinese, Greek and Turkish food has been 'creolized' or adapted to the culinary tastes of a broader clientele. This kind of strategy requires cultural capital or knowledge that straddles the products of the country of origin as well as of the consumer tastes in the country of settlement.

Secondly, there is the continuing presence of immigrant entrepreneurs in the garment industry (Dicken 1998; Rath 2002c) and in some countries (such as Italy) in construction (Rath 2002f). Although almost proverbial activities, they have been fundamentally affected by processes of outsourcing and subcontracting. In the United States, as Min and Bozorgmehr note in Chapter 2, large firms have been outsourcing to sweatshops run by immigrants to circumvent rules and regulations on minimum wages and working hours (cf. Klein 2000). In this case, *regulations* and the drive to get around them drive the creation of opportunities for small businesses. The Italian case is intriguing in this respect. Italy, once an industrial laggard because of its plethora of small firms, became the prime example of flexible specialization in the 1980s (Weiss 1988). Given that, according to Magatti and Quassoli in Chapter 8 of this volume, indigenous Italians already filled almost all the openings for small businesses, the scope for immigrant businesses was limited.

Thirdly, a new kind of immigrant entrepreneur from less-developed countries seems to be emerging that connects directly to the post-industrial society. These immigrant entrepreneurs are highly educated (undergraduates and graduates), thereby reflecting the higher education level in many less-developed countries and the increasing access of these immigrants to educational facilities in advanced economies (itself a form of globalization). Min and Bozorgmehr (Chapter 2) note the role of highly skilled Iranian, Iraqi, Taiwanese, Indian and Chinese entrepreneurs in professional businesses (e.g. financial services) in the United States. Their businesses in rapidly growing post-industrial markets differ from the more traditional immigrant businesses in that they are often gazelles (with strong growth potential) and that they rely more on class resources.

Although these highly educated immigrants can also be found in Europe, especially among second-generation immigrants (cf. van der Leun and Rusinovic 2001) they are predominantly attracted to the United States. Their average return on human capital is considerably higher there than in most European countries (cf. Borjas 1994; Brücker 2002). Immigrant entrepreneurs who are rich in individual resources also favour Canada and Australia, and even constitute a transnational category of *astronauts* who link Asia, Australia and Canada (see chapters 4 by Collins and 3 by Daniel Hiebert). African immigrant entrepreneurs in South Africa are also relatively well educated and capitalized. To a certain extent, the larger opportunity structure in a country preselects the composition of the incoming immigrant population with respect to skills and education.

A Continuing Venture

For quite some time, American researchers have dominated immigrant-entrepreneurship research. In light of the rapid growth of immigrant entrepreneurship there, this leading role is hardly surprising. But many American approaches, although fruitful and inspiring, tend to take the American economy and its specific regulatory setting too much for granted. This volume presents a much wider array of contributions on the subject of immigrant entrepreneurship. Not only is immigrant entrepreneurship contingent on the national institutional context, so are the perception, definition and conceptualization of it and also the ways of conducting research. Researchers communicate in different languages and are informed by national ideologies and debates. Furthermore, national research agendas obviously do not take the same routes, and modes of research funding differ. Consequently, researchers in different countries, albeit connected via conferences, international networks and journals, produce different kinds of knowledge, pursue different avenues of research, and apply different concepts and methods. The reflections in this book on the state of research in the selected countries provide ample evidence of these different traditions. These differences still stand in the way of more thorough comparative research on immigrant entrepreneurship. The dearth of comparable data and the complexity are still obstacles to the construction of a more comprehensive model and it does not seem likely that in the foreseeable future much progress will be made with making the database more uniform. Notwithstanding this lack of cross-border data, one the aims of this book is to open up a new phase of more intensive international research on immigrant entrepreneurs by providing a sound base for further explorations in other countries and for research on more specific themes such as female entrepreneurs, the emergence of highly educated immigrant entrepreneurs in specific lines of business, or the role of the one-and-a-half (born in the sending country but raised in the country of settlement) and second-generation immigrant entrepreneurs. Or the focus may turn toward the wider context of immigrant entrepreneurship with regard to the emergence of new regulation frameworks that accommodate small businesses in a much more sophisticated way (cf. Hudson 2001: 310) or the changing socio-political context regarding immigration and its impact on immigrant businesses.

Notes

1. We use the terms 'self-employed' and 'entrepreneurs' interchangeably. Although in the true Schumpeterian sense, there is a crucial difference between the self-employed and people who introduce innovations – the 'real' entrepreneurs who 'reform or revolutionize the pattern of production' (Schumpeter 1974: 132) – we use both terms to denote people who own and run their own businesses. This is very much in line with the common usage in literature on immigrant businesses.
2. See the cover story in the European issue of *Business Week* (2000).
3. '… the connections that bind the newcomers together and the resources generated by the contacts that crisscross the immigrant communities. These ties constitute a source of "social capital", providing social structures that facilitate action, in this case the search for jobs and the acquisition of skills and other resources needed to move up the economic ladder' (Waldinger 2001: 300).
4. Storper (1997: 25) emphasizes the actor perspective as he states that immigrants, even without much pull from any labour-market demand structure in the cities of arrival, create their own niches.
5. 'Through the immigrant community, immigrants become agents actively engaged in rehabilitating both spatial and economic sectors of the city. The immigrant community can be seen as representing a small-scale investment of direct labour (through neighbourhood upgrading) and of capital (through neighbourhood commerce) in city's economy' (Sassen 2001: 321).

6. 'Small business had always been an immigrant and ethnic specialty, but too insignificant to get more than the passing academic nod, until Ivan Light wrote his seminal *Ethnic Enterprise in America*', according to Roger Waldinger (2001: 302).

7. To mention only a few of these special issues: *Kroniek van het Ambacht, Klein- en Middenbedrijf* (see Kroniek 1984), *International Small Business Journal* (see Ward 1986), *Focaal* (see Vermeulen 1991a), *Prokla, Zeitschrift für kritische Sozialwissenschaft* (see Schmidt 2000), *Revue Européenne des Migrations Internationales* (see Body-Gendrot and Ma Mung 1992), *Hessische Blätter für Volksbildung* (see Apitzsch 2000b), *Journal of Ethnic and Migration Studies* (see Kloosterman and Rath 2001a), *Pacific Migration Journal* (see Fong and Lee 2001), *Entrepreneurship and Regional Development* (see Ram 2002), and *International Journal of Urban and Regional Research* (see Kloosterman et al. 2003). For details go to the ImmEnt Bibliography on http://users.fmg.uva.nl/jrath.

8. Immigrant entrepreneurship has also been the subject of 'Working on the Fringes', an international research project funded by the European Union under the Targeted Socio-Economic Research programme. The research team includes social scientists (sociologists, geographers, anthropologists, economists and historians) from Australia, Austria, Belgium, Canada, France, Germany, Israel, Italy, the Netherlands, South Africa, the United Kingdom and the United States. The aims of this project are to get an overview of the recent developments regarding immigrant entrepreneurship in various countries, to review the research on the subject, to improve our understanding of the significance of immigrant entrepreneurship for immigrants themselves and society at large and to explore the policy implications. As already indicated in the preface, this volume is largely a product of this project.

9. Data on subcategories of immigrant entrepreneurs – such as women, young or, say, Moroccan – that can be used in cross-border settings are even much harder to come by, if available at all. The difficulties of comparison are significantly reduced if just one specific sector (e.g. the rag trade, Rath 2002a) is compared. Even these international comparisons are, however, scarce.

10. 'The expansion in the supply of low-wage jobs generated by major growth sectors is one of the key factors in the continuation of ever-higher levels of the current immigration' (Sassen 2001: 321).

11. According to Held et al. (1999: 310): 'The key feature of the contemporary era is economic immigration to OECD countries. In Western Europe these began, primarily, as intraregional migrations from Southern Europe to Northern and Western Europe. These movements were soon surpassed by

migrations from ex-colonial possessions and states beyond Europe. For the first time significant incoming migratory flows were established between Western Europe and the Caribbean, the Middle East, North Africa, Latin America and South Asia. Similarly, in North America and Australia, where these migratory flows began later, the already global flows from Europe to the New World of the nineteenth and early twentieth century were accompanied and eventually superseded by flows from Latin America, the Caribbean, the Middle East, North Africa, Latin America and South Asia.'

12. 'Organised subcontracting opens up opportunities for small business formation, and in some instances permits older systems of domestic, artisanal, familial (patriarchal), and paternalistic ("god-father", "guv'nor" or even mafia-like) labour systems to revive and flourish as centrepieces rather than as appendages of the production system', according to David Harvey (1990: 152).

13. See for instance Cooke and Morgan (1998: 17): '... the organizational menu is very large: hence it is not hierarchies or networks per se that are important, but rather how well these forms operate given the nature of the product market and the scope for the presence of economies of scale (there are no networks of small firms producing memory chips, aircraft, or digital switches, for example).' See also Whitley (2000).

14. There will be a further elaboration upon mixed embeddedness in a large multidisciplinary project on immigrant entrepreneurs in the four largest Dutch cities.

15. We owe this phrase to Ivan Light.

United States:
The Entrepreneurial Cutting Edge

Pyong Gap Min and Mehdi Bozorgmehr

Introduction

A century ago, a record number of immigrants from southern and eastern Europe immigrated to the United States.[1] A relatively small but significant number of Asians also settled on the United States West Coast. At least four of the turn-of-the-century immigrant groups, two from Europe (Jews and Italians) on the East Coast and two from Asia (Chinese and Japanese) on the West Coast, were highly entrepreneurial (Bonacich and Modell 1980; Kessner 1977; Light 1972; Lowen 1971). The concentration of these immigrant groups in small business was partly due to discrimination and other labour-market disadvantages. Aggregate data from the US decennial census reports show that on the whole the foreign-born have historically had a higher self-employment rate than the native-born. The reversal in the steady decline of the self-employment rate of the US population in the 1980 census, partly as a result of the influx of immigrants (Light and Sanchez 1987), revived research on immigrant and ethnic entrepreneurship. As is clear from the long list of references, a dozen books and numerous articles and chapters have been published on immigrant and ethnic entrepreneurship. Three decades of research on the topic contributed to the conceptual clarifications and theoretical refinements, some of which will be reviewed here.

In line with other chapters in this volume, this chapter consists of four major sections. The first briefly examines immigration to the United States, with a focus on the last four decades of the twentieth century when large-scale immigration resumed, and the socio-economic status of immigrants. The second reports on trends in immigrant entrepreneurship in the United States based on a review of major empirical studies. The third reviews research on immigrant entrepreneurship in the United States, with a focus on conceptual and theoretical developments. Social scientists in the United States have tried to explain the causes and effects of immigrant entrepreneurship. However, due to limited space, we confine our review of the research on immigrant entrepreneurship in the

United States to its causes. The final section examines the role of the US policies.

Background

Most of the immigrants who came in the 'mass migration' period (1880–1930) were from southern and eastern Europe (see Table 2.1). The three-decade period following the mass migration witnessed the lowest immigration flows to the United States. The immigration flows to the United States began to rise again in the late 1960s when the Immigration Act of 1965, abolishing the national-origins quota system, went into full effect. Immigration continued to expand in the next three decades, with the annual figures reaching approximately 450,000 in the 1970s, and increasing to 730,000 in the 1980s and to over 900,000 in the 1990s (see Table 2.1). Douglas Massey (1995) refers to the turn-of-the-century mass migration period as the 'classical mass migration' era to distinguish it from the contemporary mass migration era. In the peak decade of the classical mass migration period (the 1900s), 8,700,000 immigrants were admitted. More than 9 million immigrants were admitted in the 1990s, exceeding the figures of the first decade of the twentieth century.[2] According to the census data, the percentage of the foreign-born in the total US population increased steadily after 1970 when it was 4.7 per cent, though it has not reached the 1910 level (14.6 per cent). The 2000 US Census shows that 31 million out of 281 million or 11 per cent of the US population is foreign-born.

The vast majority of the post-1965 immigrants came from non-European, Third World countries, mostly from Latin America, Asia and the Caribbean (Massey 1995, 2000; Rumbaut 1995), but also from Africa and the Middle East (see Table 2.1). While nearly 90 per cent of the immigrants admitted to the United States in the classical mass migration period came from Europe, only about 15 per cent of the post-1965 immigrants are from there (see again Table 2.1). Latino immigrants constitute about 35 per cent of all the immigrants admitted since 1970s, with Mexican immigrants alone accounting for approximately a quarter of the total number of immigrants (Rumbaut 1995: 28). In addition to Mexico, the Dominican Republic, El Salvador, Cuba, Haiti, the Philippines, China, India, Vietnam and South Korea are major source countries of contemporary immigrants.

The differences in the immigrants' socio-economic status between the two mass migration periods are even more striking than the regional differences. The majority of the earlier southern and eastern European immigrants were illiterate peasants and unskilled workers, although Jewish immigrants came from urban origins and were skilled (Kraut 1982). Most of them, with the exception of the Jews, who often had urban and higher-educational

Table 2.1 Immigration to the United States by Decade and Region of Origin, 1841–1996

Decade	Total (N in 1000s)	Region of origin (%)					
		North & Western Europe	South & Eastern Europe	Canada	Total Europe & Canada	Latin America & Caribbean	Asia & Middle East
1841–50	1,713	93.0	0.3	2.4	95.7	1.2	0.0
1851–60	2,598	93.6	0.8	2.3	96.7	0.6	1.6
1861–70	2,315	87.8	1.5	6.7	96.0	0.6	2.8
1871–80	2,812	73.6	7.7	13.6	94.9	0.7	4.4
1881–90	5,247	72.0	18.2	7.5	97.7	0.7	1.3
1891–00	3,688	44.6	51.9	0.1	96.6	1.0	2.0
1901–10	8,795	21.7	69.9	2.0	93.6	2.1	3.7
1911–20	5,736	25.3	50.0	12.9	88.2	6.0	4.3
1921–30	4,107	32.5	27.5	22.2	82.2	14.4	2.7
1931–40	528	38.7	27.2	20.5	86.4	9.7	3.0
1941–50	1,035	49.9	10.1	16.6	76.6	17.7	3.1
1951–60	2,516	38.2	14.5	15.0	67.7	24.6	6.1
1961–70	3,322	18.3	15.5	12.4	46.2	39.3	12.9
1971–80	4,493	11.6	10.0	23.8	45.4	40.3	35.3
1981–90	7,338	4.6	5.2	1.8	11.6	46.8	38.0
1991–2000	9,095	4.5	10.5	2.1	17.1	47.2	30.7

Sources: US Bureau of the Census, 1960, 1975; US Immigration and Naturalization Service, Statistical Yearbook, 1950–1978, 1979–2001.

backgrounds (Steinberg 1981), were at the bottom of the occupational ladder in American society. Post-1965 immigrants are socio-economically heterogeneous, even polarized. The majority of the Asian, Middle Eastern and African immigrants have professional and middle-class backgrounds, and the majority of the Latino and Caribbean immigrants come from working-class and farming backgrounds.

Immigrant Entrepreneurship in the Post-1965 Era

Self-employment Rates of Immigrant Groups

In the introduction, we note that due to labour-market disadvantages, such as discrimination, language barriers and job-information deprivation, immigrants have historically had a greater tendency to turn to entrepreneurship. The 1980 and 1990 US censuses both show that this is true of the post-1965 immigrants. Light and Rosenstein (1995: 39) report the self-employment rates of the US population by ethno-racial group and native-born vs foreign-born status. They show that as a whole the foreign-born population in the United States had a higher self-employment rate (8.5 per cent) than the native-born population (7.0 per cent) in 1980. If the population is divided into four major ethno-racial groups, the foreign-born population consistently exhibits a significantly higher self-employment rate than the native-born for every group.

Table 2.2 presents data on the self-employment rates for the 35 largest immigrant groups in 1990 (the most recent available census data). Table 2.2 also reports the rate for all foreign-born (11.6 per cent) and all native-born (10.5 per cent) in the United States as points of reference. These 35 largest groups range in size from 0.5 per cent to 4.5 per cent of all immigrants, with the exception of Mexicans who make up roughly one-fourth of all immigrants in the United States. The groups are categorized into above, near and below US average, which is roughly the same for all foreign- and native-born. As can be seen, there is a wide variation in self-employment rates by nationality (ranging from 3.4 per cent for Laotians to 32.1 per cent for Greeks, a tenfold gap). In general, Asian immigrant groups (Koreans, Iranians, Taiwanese, Chinese and Indians) have above average rates of self-employment, with the exception of Vietnamese, Filipinos and Laotians who are below average – Japanese and Hong Kong Chinese are near average. Several European groups (Greeks, Italians, Germans, Yugoslavs, French, Irish, English and Polish) also have above average rates of self-employment. Latin Americans (Ecuadorians, Nicaraguans, Hondurans, Mexicans and Guatemalans and Salvadorians), with the exception of Argentines and Cubans, generally fall below US average – only Colombians are near average. Similarly, Caribbeans (Dominicans, Jamaicans, Haitians, Trinidad and Tobago nationals and Guyanese) fall below the US average.

Table 2.2 Self-employment Rates for 35 Largest Immigrant Groups, 1990

Country of origin	Self-employment rate (%)
All foreign-born	11.6
All native-born	10.5
Above USA average	
Greece	32.1
Korea	30.7
Iran	23.7
Italy	20.7
Argentina	20.7
Germany	17.0
Cuba	16.9
Taiwan	16.5
Yugoslavia	16.2
Canada	15.9
France	15.9
China	15.5
Ireland	13.5
UK	13.0
Poland	12.7
India	12.3
Near USA average	
Colombia	11.3
Japan	10.8
Peru	10.8
Hong Kong	10.4
Portugal	10.0
Below USA average	
Vietnam	8.9
Dominican Republic	8.6
Jamaica	7.3
Haiti	7.3
Ecuador	7.2
Trinidad & Tobago	7.2
Nicaragua	6.9
Honduras	6.9
Mexico	6.1
Guatemala	5.9

Table 2.2 *(cont.)*

Country of origin	Self-employment rate (%)
Philippines	5.6
El Salvador	5.2
Guyana	4.6
Laos	3.4
Sample size	260,598

Notes: The sample consists of nonagricultural workers who are at least 16 years old and worked at least 15 hours per week for at least 20 weeks in 1989. The self-employment rate is the percentage of all those working who are self-employed. All self-employment rates are calculated using weights provided by the 1990 Census. The native-born self-employment rate is for the largest 132 Metropolitan Areas in the USA, which represent about 68.5 percent of the native non-black population.
Sources: Adapted from Robert Fairlie. 'Immigrant Self-Employment', University of California, Santa Cruz: Working Paper, 2001, and 'The Effect of Immigration on Native Self-Employment', National Bureau of Economic Research: Working Paper 7561, 2000.

Light and Roach (1996) note that in 1990, five ethnic-immigrant groups had higher self-employment rates than the native-born white population in Los Angeles. Their self-employment rates, in rank order, were: 35 per cent for foreign-born Koreans, 28 per cent for foreign-born Iranians (excluding Armenians from Iran), 27 per cent for foreign-born Armenians (including Armenians from Iran), 23 per cent for native-born Russians, and 17 per cent for foreign-born Chinese, compared to 13.3 per cent for other native-born white Americans (excluding individuals of Russian ancestry) (ibid.: 199). Of the five top entrepreneurial groups in Los Angeles, Russians are the only native-born group who are predominantly Jewish Americans.

Light and Roach (1996) show that the self-employment rates of most entrepreneurial immigrant groups substantially increased from 1970 to 1990. The self-employment rate of Korean immigrants in Los Angeles rose from 3.6 per cent in 1970 to 24.8 per cent in 1980 and 34.6 per cent in 1990. By contrast, the rest of the native-born white population in the city only experienced a slight increase in self-employment from 10.1 per cent in 1970 to 12.0 per cent in 1980 and 13.3 per cent in 1990. This suggests that for some highly entrepreneurial immigrant groups the increase in the self-employment rate was not only caused by the national trend of an increasing self-employment rate over time, but also by other factors specific to the immigrant groups. As is clarified elsewhere by Min (1996), the Korean immigrants who came in the 1960s and the early 1970s and were from solid professional backgrounds were more successful at finding professional jobs in keeping with their educational level in the general economy than the more recent Korean immigrants. This is why most of them did not need to turn to self-employment, especially in small business with long working hours. Moreover, the pioneering Korean merchants in the early stages of Korean immigration had difficulty accumulating business capital and getting business training and information. However, recent Korean immigrants can start their own businesses much more easily, partly because many of them bring enough for start-up capital, and partly because they are given training and information by established Korean entrepreneurs.

Types and Sizes of Immigrant Businesses

Chinese immigrants in the first half of the twentieth century specialized in laundry and restaurants, while Japanese immigrants were heavily concentrated in farming and the wholesale and retail trade in farm products in California (Bonacich and Modell 1980; Light 1972). The business specialization of contemporary immigrant groups is much more varied than at the turn of the century. There are significant inter-city differences in the business patterns of particular groups, partly caused by the inter-city differences in industrial and urban structure and partly by differences within the groups. Razin and Light (1998) report great variations in the self-employment rates of the same immigrant groups in the largest metropolitan regions of the United States.

There are significant inter-group differences in terms of how many branches of business each entrepreneurial group specializes in. At one extreme, the Cuban immigrant entrepreneurs in the Cuban enclave in Miami engage in diverse businesses: retail and wholesale trade, manufacturing, construction, professional services, finance/insurance/real estate services, and entertainment and recreation services (Portes and Bach 1985: 205–8). At the other extreme, the Chaldeans (Iraqi Christians) in Detroit mainly specialize in the grocery retail business in black neighbourhoods (Sengstock 1982) and Palestinians in New York and other cities are heavily concentrated in retail businesses (Cohen and Tyree 1994). In between the two extremes, most entrepreneurial immigrant groups operate in a number of lines of business. Chinese immigrants in New York are concentrated in garment subcontracting, Chinese restaurants and gift shops (Kwong 1987; Zhou 1992), and Indian immigrants in New York are specialized in retail warehouses, gas stations and taxicab services (Sheth 1995).

Korean immigrants in Los Angeles, New York and other major cities have monopolized several labour-intensive business specialties serving non-Korean customers: the grocery and liquor retail trade, dry cleaning, the wholesale and retail trade in Asian-imported manufactured goods, and garment subcontracting (Light and Bonacich 1988; Min 1988, 1996; Yoon 1997). Yet Koreans are a good example of an immigrant group in different cities that has developed different types of business. Grocery stores are probably the most widely known Korean businesses in New York, of which there are about 2,000 (Min 1996: 54). But no other Korean community in the United States has gone into this business niche. The Korean immigrants' clustering in the produce retail business in New York City has to do with its unique spatial patterns (ibid.: 61). Due to the scarcity of space in New York City, residential and commercial zones are compressed together. Green grocers are popular in New York because people buy fruit and vegetables on their way home from bus stops and subway stations.

The traditional literature on immigrant and ethnic entrepreneurship gives the impression that immigrant-owned businesses are all small and largely based on unpaid family labour. However, contemporary immigrant businesses in the United States are not all that small; they include medium-size businesses with a dozen or more employees, such as supermarkets and fast-food franchise stores. Indeed, immigrant businesses in one and the same ethnic niche differ significantly in size. For example, Chinese restaurants bring to mind the small family-run take-away so aptly described by Song (1999). Although most Chinese restaurants fit this pattern, some of the ones in New York's Chinatown are stylish and have chefs recruited from Hong Kong and Taiwan who serve high-income professionals, managers and white-collar workers from Wall Street (Kwong 1987: 34). Cuban-owned businesses in Miami as well as Asian-owned ones in Los Angeles, New York and other cities also include numerous import and export companies based on international trade between American cities and Latin American or Asian countries (Min 1984b, 1996: 55–7; Portes 1987; Yoon 1997: 114–18).

Taiwanese, Indian and Iranian immigrants have exceptionally high educational levels; the majority of the adults have a college education and nearly half the male adults have Master's degrees. Many members of these groups have completed undergraduate or graduate studies in the United States (Min and Bozorgmehr 2000). Their high educational level has enabled them to develop professional businesses[3] to serve a white clientele as well a co-ethnic one. According to the 1990 US census, 15 per cent of the self-employed Taiwanese immigrants in Los Angeles were engaged in professional businesses, with medical and engineering services accounting for the majority (Tseng 1995: 48). The survey of Iranian immigrants in Los Angeles in the late 1980s revealed that about 17 per cent of the self-employed Iranian immigrants were professionals (e.g. medical and accounting services) (Bozorgmehr 2003). It is also widely known that many Asian immigrants – especially Taiwanese and Indians – in Silicon Valley, California have developed highly lucrative professional businesses based on innovative software technology (Saxenian 1999). It is hazardous, however, to overstate the success of immigrant professionals simply based on their presence (e.g. the number of physicians in a group).

Other contemporary middle-class immigrant groups, Koreans, Chinese from China and Hong Kong, Israelis, Lebanese, Cubans and Russian Jews, do not have as many professional businesses as the above-mentioned immigrant professional groups. Yet they too have numerous self-employed professionals and semi-professionals who largely serve a co-ethnic clientele. For example, the 1994 Korean business directory of Southern California listed 400 accounting and law firms, 640 medical and dental offices, and 1,075 real estate, insurance and travel agencies (Min 1996: 64). Korean immigrants, especially recent arrivals, tend to prefer having fellow Koreans perform these professional and semi-professional services. Korean professional businesses have thus emerged to meet the needs of this so-called protected market (Auster and Aldrich 1984; Min 1987).

Reasons for Starting Businesses

The disadvantage thesis, as is discussed below, posits that immigrants are more motivated than the native-born to start their own businesses because of general labour-market disadvantages such as discrimination, the language barrier and the fact that their educational credentials are not recognized (Ladbury 1984; Light 1979; Light and Gold 2000: 200). Some survey studies that directly test the disadvantage hypothesis exhibit mixed results. As Koreans best fit this model due to their language barrier, two studies of Koreans are cited here to support the disadvantage hypothesis. According to a survey of Korean immigrant entrepreneurs in Atlanta (Min 1984a, 1988: 67), 90 per cent of the respondents cite general labour-market disadvantage as the major reason for their entry into small business. The vast majority of the respondents had professional and white-collar jobs in Korea, but their initial jobs in the United States were largely low-level blue-collar and service-related jobs. They started their own businesses as an alternative to the lower-level jobs available to them in the United States. Dividing the sample into three groups: non-college graduates, US college graduates, and home-country college graduates, Kim et al. (1989) examined the probability of Chinese, Indian and Korean immigrant workers engaging in self-employment. They found that home-country college graduates are much more apt to start a business than the other two groups. The authors conclude that college graduates with more class resources have more advantages for establishing their own busi-nesses than non-college graduates, and that home-country college graduates have a greater probability to start a business than US college graduates because of their language barrier and other disadvantages. A study of Asian and Latino immigrants in New York and Los Angeles based on the 1980 US census data also reveals that the number of years of school in the United States is negatively related to self-employment (Sanders and Nee 1996).

Studies of professional and large businesses have shown that immigrants' perceived labour-market disadvantages are not as important as other factors in their decision to start their own businesses. For example, very few of the Iranian respondents in Los Angeles mentioned labour-market disadvantages as their reasons for going into business. Many of them gave 'good income', 'higher income' and 'opportunity for advancement' as the main reasons for starting their own businesses (Bozorgmehr 2003). In addition, as classic trading minorities, most Jewish Iranian and many Armenian Iranian respondents ran businesses in Iran, and their business know-how and starting capital helped them get into business in the United States (Bozorgmehr 1998).

The labour-market disadvantage thesis also fails to apply to the new Japanese business owners in New York (Hosler 2000). Despite their high levels of education, Japanese immigrants have a severe language barrier because most of them completed their education in Japan. Yet, the language barrier is not a labour-market disadvantage because the local branches of Japanese firms create many high-paying managerial and professional jobs. For Japanese immigrant entrepreneurs, 'opening a business is the realization of their training and previous career, and not a situational adaptation due to their disadvantage' (ibid.: 86).

Ethnic versus Class Resources for Business Capitalization and Operation

In this subsection, we devote special attention to the extent to which contemporary immigrant entrepreneurs utilize ethnic resources for business capitalization and operation. Lacking class resources such as human capital and business experience, the earlier immigrant entrepreneurs largely established mom-and-pop businesses in the retail, agriculture, manufacturing and service sectors, usually depending upon unpaid family and co-ethnic labour (Bonacich and Modell 1980; Light 1972). However, contemporary self-employed immigrants include many affluent entrepreneurs and professionals who mainly rely on class resources for the establishment and operation of businesses (Bozorgmehr et al. 1996; Marger and Hoffman 1992; Min and Bozorgmehr 2000).

Not surprisingly, the traditional literature emphasized ethnic resources as central to the establishment and operation of immigrant and ethnic businesses (Bonacich and Modell 1980; Light 1972). Ethnic resources are less important for contemporary immigrant businesses, especially professional businesses, although they are very important for the ones located in an ethnic enclave. Contemporary immigrant businesses in the United States are diverse in terms of size and type. They include non-professional and professional businesses alike, an overlooked distinction that we believe is as important as the one between employment in professional and non-professional wage and salaried jobs.

Accumulating capital is essential in order to set up a business. Light (1972) argues that Chinese and Japanese immigrants have been far more successful in establishing small businesses than African Americans because they have a tradition of using rotating credit associations (RCA) to raise business capital. The

RCA is a close-knit association of people that lends money to each member on a rotating basis.

Many researchers have since emphasized the role of rotating credit associations, private loans and other ethnic sources of capital. Several studies show that some recent immigrant groups continue to use rotating credit associations (Bonnet 1980; Light and Bonacich 1988: 247–59; Light et al. 1990; Min 1988, 1996; Yoon 1997: 147). Yet with the exception of a study by Light et al. (1990), these studies generally note that rotating credit associations are no longer often utilized as a means of amassing business capital due to the higher-class background of entrepreneurs. Min's surveys show that only 4 of the 159 Korean business-owners in Atlanta and 3 of the 86 Korean business-owners in New York City used money from RCAs as their major business capital (1988: 80, 1996: 102). Instead, Korean immigrants mainly depend upon money brought from Korea and savings accumulated in the United States for business capitalization.[4]

A study of Taiwanese entrepreneurs in Los Angeles also shows that most of the respondents brought their start-up capital from their homeland (Tseng 1995). In addition, none of the 194 respondents in the study of Japanese immigrant entrepreneurs in New York, mentioned earlier, utilized RCAs for business capitalization; most of them depended on their own savings or money brought from their homeland as their main source of capital (Hosler 2000: 94). Refugees usually do not bring much cash or assets, but the class resources of the first wave of Cuban refugees were critical to the development of Cuban businesses in Miami (Portes 1987). These studies support the view that contemporary middle-class and professional immigrant groups depend on class resources far more than traditional ones.

The traditional literature gives the impression that immigrant and ethnic entrepreneurship mainly depend on unpaid family or co-ethnic labour (Bonacich and Modell 1980; Light 1972; Lovell-Troy 1980). Studies of contemporary immigrants also show that family ties correlate strongly with the probability of self-employment or business success (Der-Martirosian 1996; Min 1988; Sanders and Nee 1996; Wong 1998: 66–81). However, various case studies of post-1965 immigrant groups show that professional and non-professional entrepreneurial groups differ significantly in the extent to which they depend upon unpaid family labour. For instance, Korean immigrants are heavily involved in non-professional, labour-intensive businesses, and Korean business owners are heavily dependent on unpaid family labour. A study of Korean entrepreneurs in Atlanta shows that among 62 per cent of married couples (58 per cent of all the respondents), both spouses worked at the same business, and the husband-wife co-ordination was essential to their business success. Furthermore, most of the respondents with adult children (22 per cent of all the respondents) were helped by their children for ten or more hours a week, usually after school or on the weekends (Min 1988: 113–15). In contrast, professional and large Japanese immigrant businesses depend on unpaid spousal labour much less, and only 38 per cent of the Japanese respondents reported that their spouses were involved in the business (Hosler 2000: 126).

The assumption that an immigrant business, typically family-operated, has no paid employees is also challenged by data on new immigrant groups. Heavily labour-intensive, Korean immigrant businesses rely more on unpaid family labour than other immigrant businesses, but even they usually have at least one paid employee. For example, a 1986 survey indicated that 72 per cent of the Korean businesses in Los Angeles had one or more paid employees (Min 1989: 93). Survey studies of Korean businesses in other cities show that even higher percentages of Korean businesses have paid employees (Min 1996: 114; Yoon 1997: 154). An even higher percentage of Japanese immigrant businesses (86 per cent) have one or more paid employees (Hosler 2000: 126). About two-thirds of the self-employed Iranians in Los Angeles had at least one paid employee (Der-Martirosian 1996, Table 6.1). Some people who work for their co-ethnics manage to eventually become self-employed by working hard, saving their money and using their jobs as a 'training system' for future self-employment (Bailey and Waldinger 1991).

The traditional literature depicts immigrant and ethnic entrepreneurs as rarely hiring non-ethnic employees (Bonacich and Modell 1980; Light 1972). Again, the findings from studies of contemporary immigrant entrepreneurs in the United States challenge this stereotype. These findings show that at least half the paid employees in immigrant-owned businesses are not co-ethnic, although the percentage differs significantly for different immigrant groups and types of busi-nesses. More than 40 per cent of the paid employees of the self-employed Iranian respondents in Los Angeles were non-Iranian (Light et al. 1993: Table 4). Among the Koreans in Los Angeles, co-ethnics only accounted for 31 per cent of the paid employees and Mexicans almost half (Min 1989: 93). Korean business-owners in New York also rely largely on Latino workers, with co-ethnic employees accounting for less than 40 per cent (Kim 1999; Min 1996: 114). The businesses owned by Chinese-Vietnamese refugees in Southern California also rely largely on Latino employees (Gold 1994). Light et al. (1999) refer to the Los Angeles garment businesses, with their immigrant owners and non-ethnic immigrant employees, as an 'immigrant economy' as opposed to an 'ethnic economy'. As the cheapest source of labour, Latinos are the most commonly employed workers in the majority of businesses in immigrant cities, irrespective of the ethnicity of the owners.

Conceptual and Theoretical Developments on Causes of Immigrant Entrepreneurship

Status Gap and Middleman Minority Theory

The concept of middleman minorities was introduced in the US social science literature, especially in ethnic stratification, in the late 1960s and early 1970s. Middleman minorities are the minority groups that play an intermediary economic role linking dominant-group producers and minority-group customers (Blalock 1967: 79–84; Bonacich 1972; Eitzen 1971; Lowen 1971; Palmer 1957; Rinder 1959; Zenner 1991). As classic examples, they cite the Jews in Europe, the Chinese in Southeast Asia, the Indians in Africa and the Parsis in India. The intermediate economic role, i.e., concentration in trading and money lending between elite producers and lower-class or minority customers, subjects the middleman minorities to host hostility, thereby further enhancing their ethnic solidarity (Bonacich and Modell 1980).

Most early middleman-minority theorists emphasize structural factors, especially the status gap, in the host society as the major determinants of the unique economic, social and political position of middleman minorities (e.g. Rinder 1959). Rinder argues that 'although strata boundaries are continuous and flexible in American society a status gap is apparent in the margin of white-Negro relations' (ibid.: 257). Lowen (1971) later extrapolates from this black-white status gap to explain the concentration of Chinese immigrant families in the Delta region of Mississippi. In his view, the social structure of the Delta, which is characterized by strict segregation, a large status gap and a sizeable social distance between blacks and white, is mainly responsible for the Chinese immigrants' concentration in the black-oriented grocery business.

Other researchers have also emphasized the status gap between whites and blacks in the United States to explain the concentration of the Chaldeans, Jews and Chinese in small businesses in black ghettos (Capeci 1985; Sengstock 1982; Shibutani and Kwan 1965: 191–7). Since the 1970s, Korean immigrants have concentrated in retail businesses in low-income black and Latino neighbourhoods since large corporations and independent white business owners are reluctant to invest in minority neighbourhoods with high crime rates and a low spending capacity. Several researchers view Korean merchants in black neighbourhoods as middlemen, bridging white suppliers and minority customers (Kim 1981; Min 1990, 1996; Min and Kolodny 1994; Waldinger 1989).

Bonacich (1972) is the only one of the earlier theorists to posit that it is the middleman minority groups' sojourning orientation, rather than the status gap of the host society, that is the fundamental cause of the middleman-type adjustment. The economic effects of sojourning include a tendency toward thrift to hasten the return home, and the concentration in occupations that are easily liquidated or transportable such as commerce and trade. In her later writings, she does not confine the middleman minorities to the minorities that bridge the status gap, but also includes other minority groups with high self-employment rates (Bonacich and Modell 1980; Turner and Bonacich 1980). Bonacich and Modell (1980) treat Japanese truck farmers as well as wholesalers and retailers of farm products in California as a middleman minority.

Probably influenced by Bonacich's writings, some other researchers continue to refer to immigrant and ethnic groups with high concentrations in commercial occupations as 'middleman minorities' (Cobas 1985; Cobas and Duany 1997: 10–20; Light 1980; Light and Bonacich 1988: 17–18; Light and Gold 2000: 6–7). Light and Bonacich (1988: 17) define middleman minorities as 'entrepreneurial ethnic minorities that cluster in commercial occupations, especially in Third World societies'. However, we believe that the term 'trading minorities' should be used to refer to immigrant and minority groups that concentrate in commercial occupations in various societies, and that 'middleman minorities' should be reserved for the immigrant and ethnic-minority groups that play an intermediary economic role in ethnically stratified societies. This way, the concept of middleman minorities is consistent with the meaning which the above-mentioned original theorists intended it to convey.

The Disadvantage Thesis

Very few immigrant and minority groups play a middleman-minority role, but numerous immigrant groups are active in small business because, compared to the native-born population, they have general labour-market disadvantages (e.g. language barrier). Light (1979) argues that labour-market disadvantages stimulate all minority members and immigrants to become self-employed, but only the ones with cultural advantages such as an ability to raise capital can successfully start a small business. He suggests that minority members without the cultural resources for a business in the formal economy often become self-employed in peddling, illegal enterprises and predatory crimes.

The disadvantage thesis is the key to the question 'Why do immigrants become self-employed?' European scholars seem to place a greater emphasis than US scholars on the labour-market disadvantage as the major determinant of immigrants' decision to start businesses, probably because immigrants encounter more restrictive regulation in Europe than in the United States (Auster and Aldrich 1984; Jones et al. 1994; Ladbury 1984).

The Group (Ethnic and Class) Resources Thesis

Although all immigrant groups have disadvantages when it comes to employment in the general labour-market, there are still significant inter-group differentials in the self-employment rate among various immigrant groups. So the disadvantage thesis alone cannot explain the inter-group differentials in the self-employment rate. These differentials are largely determined by differences in resources among various groups in establishing and operating small businesses. The business resources of each group are referred to as 'cultural resources', 'social capital' or 'organizational ability'. To explain the group differentials in business development, US-based scholars seem to place a greater emphasis than European scholars on group resources.

Ivan Light (1972) originally developed the concept of 'ethnic resources' to explain the overrepresentation of Chinese and Japanese immigrants and the underrepresentation of African Americans in small business prior to the Second World War in terms of advantages in ethnic resources. These Asian groups relied on the institution of rotating credit associations brought from their home countries as a means of acquiring business capital, whereas African Americans had lost these practices during slavery. These Asian immigrant groups had an additional advantage over African Americans for small business by virtue of their traditions of extended kinship and filial piety.

Since some contemporary immigrant groups in the United States are more reliant on class than ethnic resources for business development, Light (1984) draws a further distinction between ethnic and class resources (see also Light and Bonacich 1988, Chapter 7). Class resources derive from the class background, while ethnic resources derive from participation in the ethnic community across all the classes. Class resources are material (property, human capital and money to invest) and cultural (bourgeois values), both of which are important for business development (Light 1984).

An emphasis on ethnic resources leads one to interpret immigrant entrepreneurship as collectivistic, and a focus on class resources leads one to view it as more or less individualistic. The collectivist orientation is more in line with the sociological approach, at least in the United States. Although they recognize the role of class resources, sociologists in the United States emphasize ethnic resources as the major contributing factor for establishing and operating immigrant and ethnic businesses. By contrast, economists stress human capital (education and work experience) and financial capital as determinants of the development of immigrant and minority businesses (Bates 1987, 1994, 1997; Becker 1995; Borjas 1996).

Responding to the debate about whether ethnic or class resources are more central to immigrant and ethnic business, we argue that the relative utilization of ethnic versus class resources depends on the patterns of immigrant and ethnic businesses rather than on their development in the first place (Min and Bozorgmehr 2000). Immigrant and ethnic businesses which are heavily dependent on ethnic resources, are generally small and family-oriented and more likely to be located in an ethnic enclave or minority neighbourhood. By contrast, immigrant and ethnic enterprises that are more reliant on class resources are usually large-scale and located in white middle-class neighbourhoods. Yoon (1991) suggests that the relative use of ethnic versus class resources also varies according to different stages of business development. His study shows that ethnic resources are very important for Korean immigrant businesses in Chicago in the initial establishment stage, but class resources become more important later for the expansion of businesses.

Opportunity Structure

Ward and Jenkins (1984) have compiled the results of research on ethnic and immigrant businesses in Great Britain. In the introductory chapter, Mars and Ward (1984) emphasize the importance of the interaction of resources and opportunities to an understanding of the development of minority businesses. In another chapter, Aldrich et al. (1984) compare Asian and white shopkeepers in three English cities (Bradford, Ealing, and Leicester) as regards their business resources and competitive practices. They find very few differences in socio-economic characteristics and access to informal resources between Asian and white entrepreneurs, but significant business-environment differences among the three cities. Based on these findings, they conclude that 'the opportunity structure of the receiving society outweighs any cultural predisposition toward entrepreneurship' (ibid.: 205). The book sets the tone for European, especially British, scholars' emphasis on the opportunity structure.

Probably influenced by Howard Aldrich and European scholars,[5] Roger Waldinger devotes greater attention to the interaction model than any US scholar. In a series of articles published since the mid-1980s (1984, 1985, 1986b) and his book (1986a), he criticizes the one-sided emphasis on 'ethnic resources' by US scholars, and emphasizes 'opportunity structure' or 'the congruence between the characteristics of industry and immigrants' economic orientations' as an important determinant of immigrant and ethnic businesses. Waldinger and other researchers have specified three major demand or structural factors that create opportunity for immigrant businesses in advanced economies, with industrial structure probably being the most important of the three. Small firms with flexible work schedules are more efficient than large ones in some industrial sectors, thus stimulating the emergence of immigrant businesses (Boissevain 1984; Bonacich et al. 1994; Waldinger 1984, 1985, 1986a, 1986b). For example, given the short nature of fashion cycles, small garment firms can execute orders more rapidly. Access to cheap labour rather than a large amount of capital is more essential to the operation of small garment firms. These conditions make it easy for new immigrants to start garment firms with relatively simple technologies. Based on his study of Hispanic garment businesses in New York, Waldinger (1985: 336) observes: 'Because production technology is organized around the social relationships of kinship, friendship, and nationality, the immigrant firms gain the flexibility needed to maneuver in markets with quick turnaround times and rapidly fluctuating product flows.' For similar reasons, small immigrant firms are more efficient than large corporations in retail food and food service businesses as well as the taxicab industry (Bailey 1987; Waldinger 1984, 1986b).

Residential succession and racial segregation are two other related structural factors that facilitate immigrant and minority businesses. Aldrich and Reiss (1976) indicate that when blacks and Puerto Ricans move into areas previously occupied by whites, this leads to a transfer of business ownership from whites to members of these minorities. They suggest that blacks and Puerto Ricans are slow to take over white-owned businesses, or establish new businesses in racially changing areas because of their lack of capital and business experience. As a result, residential succession increases the number of vacant sites as well as black and Puerto Rican business ownership. This situation provides new immigrants with business opportunity in inner cities and newly established black areas.

Immigrants can establish and run small grocery and liquor businesses in low-income minority neighbourhoods without much competition, mainly because large corporations and independent white business owners are reluctant to invest there. Indeed, many of them are disinvesting from these areas due to the high crime rates and low spending power of the residents (Light and Bonacich 1988; Light and Rosenstein 1995; Min 1996; Sengstock 1982). Low-income minority customers have no choice but to patronize immigrant-owned neighbourhood grocery and liquor stores that often charge higher prices, partly because most of them do not have the means of transportation to go to chain grocery stores or supermarkets. As long as racial inequality and racial segregation are not moderated, immigrants will continue to find business opportunities in low-income minority neighbourhoods. This is why we shall now address the possible effects of government policies on immigrant and minority businesses in the United States, as well as the policy implications of immigrant entrepreneurship.

The Role of Government Policies

American scholars have relegated the role of government policy to a background variable. Waldinger et al. (1990a), many of whom are European, are exceptions since they consider government policies that encourage or restrict small businesses to be a component of the opportunity structure. European scholars, however, have privileged the role of government policies. This is understandable, since many European countries have strong governments whereas the United States has a strong economy. Elsewhere, the editors of this volume argue that we need to develop a new theoretical framework for immigrant entrepreneurship that 'will take into account the institutional framework of the welfare state within which entrepreneurs operate' (Rath and Kloosterman 2000a: 657). They indicate that such a framework is especially necessary for comparative international research on immigrant entrepreneurship.

There is a general consensus that government policy can either facilitate or impede the development and survival of minority business (Kloosterman and Rath 2000; Light and Gold 2000; Min 1987; Waldinger et al. 1990a). Although countries on both shores of the Atlantic have increasingly tried to serve as the facilitators of immigrant and minority businesses, this facilitating role seems to be more pronounced in the United States than in Europe.

The federal policies to promote minority businesses in the United States emerged in response to the black civil rights movement and the black riots in the 1960s (Waldinger et al. 1990a: 188). Both the Small Business Administration (SBA), established in 1953, and the Office of Minority Business Enterprise (later called the Minority Business Development Agency – MBDA), founded in 1969, have tried to encourage greater participation on the part of black and other minority members in small business since the 1960s (Doctors and Huff 1973; Gold and Light 2000; Yancy 1974). The SBA focuses on providing low-interest loans for prospective minority business owners, and the MBDA provides management and technical assistance (Woodard 1997). The SBA loans were mainly created to revive black businesses, although other minority members and women can also apply for them. But these government-initiated loan programmes are characterized by exceptionally high failure rates, and do not significantly increase black business ownership (ibid.). However, Gold and Light (2000) suggest that some immigrants, such as Koreans in Los Angeles, have benefited from the government-loan funds in establishing their businesses.

The federal government has also tried to encourage the growth of minority-owned businesses by providing minority members with access to government procurement. There are two government procurement programmes (ibid.). Starting in 1969, the SBA 8(a) 'set-aside' has awarded a large amount of money in contract to disadvantaged businesses. The Public Works Employment Act of 1977 requires that the state and local governments use at least 10 per cent of the federal funds allocated to them for public works contracts to pay for the services or merchandise of minority-owned businesses. These government procurement programmes have had greater positive effects than the government-loan programmes on promoting black and other minority businesses (Woodard 1997). However, attacks on the set-aside programmes by conservative lawmakers and judges at all levels of govern-ment since the late 1980s have significantly reduced the amounts of government procurements by minority-owned businesses (Gold and Light 2000).

Researchers (Auster and Aldrich 1984; Waldinger et al. 1990a) conclude that on the whole, the US government policies to facilitate minority business owner-ship have failed to achieve the intended goal. Waldinger et al. (1990a) argue that the government policy model is incongruent with their interactive model, since it only addresses half the equation – i.e., the demand side of businesses (opportunity structure) – and leaves out the supply side (group characteristics). If minority business ownership is a supply-side problem, as is the case when explaining the very low self-employment rates of African Americans, Mexicans and Puerto Ricans, then government policies are inappropriate. Moreover, sheltered markets, networks and mutual trust among ethnic communities cannot be created by government policies. As minority members, non-white immigrants are eligible for the SBA loan. But research shows that very few immigrant entrepreneurs rely upon the SBA loan for their initial business capitalization, although some do use it to expand their ongoing businesses (Hosler 1998: 97; Hurh and Kim 1985; Min 1988: 80; Tseng 1995).

In addition, government policies can hinder the activities of small-business owners in the United States, including immigrants. There are many local and federal government regulations on small-business activities pertaining to licensing, commercial parking, commercial leases, the disposal of commercial waste, sidewalk obstruction, the protection of the environment, sanitary conditions at stores and so forth. No doubt these regulations have negative effects on small businesses. An Arthur Anderson survey (Arthur Anderson Enterprise Group and National Small Business United 1994) reports that more than 40 per cent of the businesses surveyed ranked government regulations as 'one of the most significant challenges to the survival of their business'.

Federal and local governments both can indirectly support small immigrant businesses by moderating the monopoly of corporations through anti-trust measures and tight labour regulations and standards. Strict labour regulations and heavy tax obligations lead big corporations to decentralize, a trend that is pronounced in the garment industry. The vast majority of immigrant owners of small garment firms are sub-contractors working for large manufacturing companies (Loucky et al. 1994; Min 1996: 60; Morokvasic et al. 1990: 166–7). Large garment firms sub-contract the production of specialized items to immigrant-owned small sweatshops to avoid labour-union and government scrutiny regarding such matters as taxation, pollution and working conditions (Light and Bonacich 1988: 333–47; Loucky et al. 1994).

Conclusion

In this chapter, we have reviewed the trends, empirical research, conceptual and theoretical developments, and government policies in the ever-growing field of immigrant entrepreneurship. It is impossible to cover everything in one chapter, so the focus has been on the causes of self-employment, since this is the most heavily theorized aspect of this literature. There was no space to address the effects of immigrant entrepreneurship such as upward mobility, the ethnic enclave economy debate or ethnic attachment and solidarity. We have included a brief discussion of immigration trends and the characteristics of the post-1965 immigrants for a broad international audience who may not be familiar with the American situation.

One of the unintended consequences of the milestone Immigration Act of 1965 was a shift in the origins of US-bound immigrants from Europe to the Third World. The massive influx of Asians and Middle Easterners ever since has ushered in numerous prospective entrepreneurs. In addition, the exodus of refugees, many with entrepreneurial know-how, from socialist countries such as Cuba or Vietnam has further expanded the supply of entrepreneurs. At the same time, sizeable immigration from Latin America and to a lesser extent the Caribbean has created a large source of cheap labour for the new entrepreneurs.

A central theme in this chapter has been the distinction between post-1965 and turn-of-the-century immigrant entrepreneurs. The new immigrant entrepreneurs have far more class resources in the form of human and financial capital than their predecessors. These class resources have facilitated the development of immigrant entrepreneurship and led to different business types, sizes and patterns than the typical mom-and-pop business. Many of the earlier generalizations about immigrant and ethnic entrepreneurship and entrepreneurs pertaining to labour-market disadvantage, the reliance on rotating credit associations for raising business capital, and the dependence on unpaid family labour and co-ethnic employees are much less applicable to the new immigrant entrepreneurs.

Since the mid-1980s, researchers in the United States and Europe have agreed that immigrant and minority groups' labour-market disadvantages, group resources and the opportunity structure of the host country or city are the three major contributing factors to the development of immigrant and ethnic entrepreneurship. However, US-based scholars stress the importance of group resources, while European ones put more emphasis on the other two variables. We think that this difference is due to two factors. First, there have been significant group differentials in the self-employment rate in the United States. Some immigrant and ethnic groups, regardless of where they settle, have maintained exceptionally high self-employment rates. To explain these group differentials, American scholars emphasize differentials in ethnic and class resources for business development. Second, immigrants in Europe seem to have encountered more government restrictions pertaining to the general labour market and to the establishment and operation of businesses. The chapters on Europe in this volume elaborate on this issue.

Notes

1. We would like to express our gratitude to Jan Rath, Ivan Light and Steve Gold for their useful comments on an earlier draft of this chapter.
2. As a result of the amnesty programme, a provision of the Immigration Reform and Control Act of 1986, several million illegal aliens who had illegally entered the United States in 1982 or before adjusted their status to that of permanent residents, mostly between 1989 and 1993. The vast majority of the legalized residents were Latinos, especially Mexicans. The addition of these status adjusters inflated the total number of immigrants in the 1990s.
3. Some immigrant entrepreneurship researchers include self-employed immigrant professionals in the category of immigrant entrepreneurs (Light et al. 1994; Min 1996), while others do not (Hurh and Kim 1985). We feel that self-employed professionals should be considered entrepreneurs because professional businesses involve business management. However, immigrant professional businesses basically differ from other labour-intensive immigrant businesses in that professional qualifications and skills are central. We therefore argue that a distinction should be drawn between professional and non-professional businesses and that the two should be analysed separately.
4. However, Light et al. (1990) point out that survey studies underestimate the extent to which Korean immigrants utilize rotating credit associations for business capitalization.
5. Waldinger collaborated with European scholars on several chapters in his edited volume *Ethnic Entrepreneurs: Immigrant Businesses in Industrial Societies* (Waldinger et al. 1990a).

–3–

Canada: A False Consensus?

Daniel Hiebert

Introduction

As the long post-war boom ended, commentators in Canada, as in other Western countries, began to notice two trends that surprised them. First, contrary to the expectation that large corporations would continue to capture ever larger shares of the economic activity, small- and medium-sized enterprises (SMEs) were apparently better equipped to survive the turbulence associated with the energy price shocks and rapidly fluctuating consumer demand characterizing the 1970s. Secondly, researchers began to document particularly high rates of small-business creation among immigrants and members of certain minority groups. In academia, these emerging patterns were initially noticed in the United States, but scholars in Canada quickly followed suit. It will surprise many, however, to learn that Canadian policy-makers saw connections between immigration and small-scale entrepreneurship well before academics on either side of the border. In the late 1960s, the Canadian government established a new immigration category to facilitate the entry of individuals who would quickly become self-employed. The prevailing wisdom was that these immigrants would create their own economic opportunities and were likely to hire others as well. During the next two decades, other categories of 'business immigrants' were introduced as the government became increasingly convinced that immigrants could play a catalytic role in economic expansion. During these years, Canadian academics turned their attention to documenting the degree of entrepreneurial activity among ethnic minorities and immigrants. A consensus quickly emerged that these groups, which were generally marginalized in the regular labour-market, were especially prone to self-employment.

In this chapter, I begin by outlining Canada's immigration system, devoting particular attention to the development of the business-immigration programmes noted above. I then turn to the question of minority and immigrant self-employment, first by summarizing the Canadian literature on the subject, and then exploring 1996 census data. The data survey is focused on a seemingly simple but in reality quite complex question: are immigrants and cultural minorities more prone to self-employment than the native-born or European-origin population? This may appear a redundant issue, given the widespread conclusion that immigrants and minority groups have higher rates of self-employment than the mainstream population. However, I attempt to show that the prevailing view requires considerable qualification, since it appears that the degree of immigrant and minority entrepreneurialism in Canada, relative to the dominant group, slipped substantially during the recession of the early 1990s. Also, comparisons between immigrants and the native-born shift as different data sets are explored. After charting the extent and character of minority and immigrant self-employment, I use tax records to examine the rather more sparse evidence of entrepreneurship among business immigrants. I conclude on a pessimistic note. It seems that business immigrants have not achieved the degree of entrepreneurial success that was anticipated by policy-makers.

The Canadian Immigration System

The Canadian Immigration Act specifies three main categories of entry, i.e. refugee, family, and independent immigrant programmes, and a number of minor ones such as the Domestic Caregiver Program, and a special programme for people who wish to retire in Canada. The refugee and family programmes are designed, respectively, to fulfil Canada's moral obligations to oppressed people around the world and to allow for the reunification of family members. Both are primarily driven by humanitarian concerns, but economic issues are not entirely absent; for example, the Canadian government gives priority to refugee applicants deemed able to become self-supporting once they arrive, i.e. those with skills or capital (Nash 1987, 1996). The rationale for independent immigrants, however, has always been strictly economic, and admission criteria are set in accordance with the perceived needs of the Canadian economy. There are several sub-groups within this broad category. First and foremost in programme design, and the largest single form of entry into Canada, is the skilled-worker programme. Prospective immigrants applying under this category are assessed according to a system where points are assigned for specific characteristics deemed desirable in the labour market (e.g. educational attainment, specific educational qualifications, facility in one or both of Canada's official languages, work experience). Interviewing officers also assign a number of points based on their determination of the personal suitability of the applicant. Those who accumulate a sufficient number of points (typically 70 out of a possible 105) are granted landed-immigrant status. Individuals who are not quite able to pass this test can gain a small number of additional points if they have a relative in Canada willing to support them; such an application falls under the 'assisted relative' category. Finally, the Canadian government has increasingly come to value immigrants who have a business track record or are willing to invest capital in a Canadian business. Three sub-categories of 'business immigrants' have been introduced over the past thirty years or so. In 1967, the 'self-employed' category was established to facilitate the entry of small-scale business persons who would, effectively, take care of their own needs in the labour market. This programme has declined in significance over the years, in terms of numbers admitted. The second business-oriented programme was introduced in 1978, also targeting mainly small-scale entrepreneurs. To enter Canada under this category (as 'entrepreneur immigrants'), applicants must show that they have a track record in business, intend to operate a business in Canada that will either save one Canadian job or create a new one, have a plausible business plan, and have sufficient capital to implement their plan. In a more recent shift in emphasis, the federal government established the 'investor' immigrant programme in 1986; applicants to this category must agree to invest a sum of money (the amount varies according to the intended provincial destination from CDN$150,000 to CDN$500,000) for at least three years in a venture-capital fund, but are not required to establish their own business (Gutstein 1990; Ley 2000; Nash 1987).

Within these business programmes, the government is especially eager to admit immigrants who have experience in manufacturing. This is a chronically laggard part of the Canadian economy and many believe that highly motivated, experienced immigrants from Europe, the United States, and newly industrializing economies could add vital technical knowledge and capital to it (Froschauer 1998). The desire to attract entrepreneurial and investor immigrants, however, has recently become more difficult to fulfil, for several reasons: the downturn of the Asian economy has reduced the potential for capital to flow outside the region; the relatively calm transfer of Hong Kong to Chinese jurisdiction has lessened fears of political instability in eastern Asia (the source region of most business immigrants to Canada during the 1980s and 1990s); the weak recovery of the Canadian economy since the recession of the early 1990s has dampened enthusiasm among potential immigrants; the creation of business-immigration programmes elsewhere – e.g. Australia – has intensified the 'competition' for footloose entrepreneurs; and, as will be explored later, the general lack of economic success of business immigrants in Canada appears to have given many potential applicants second thoughts about transferring their businesses to Canada. As a result, the number and proportion of business immigrants has fallen somewhat in recent years (see Table 3.1; from over 9 per cent including applicants and their spouses and dependants during the mid-1990s to under 7 per cent in 1999). Moreover, business immigrants who come to Canada have shown little interest in establishing factories, and instead are drawn to real

Table 3.1 Immigration to Canada by Class, 1995–1999

	1995		1996		1997		1998		1999	
	N	%	N	%	N	%	N	%	N	%
Family	77,227	36.3	68,330	30.2	59,956	27.8	50,880	29.2	55,216	29.1
Immediate family	44,112	20.7	43,712	19.3	39,741	18.4	36,681	21.1	40,753	21.5
Parents and grandparents	33,115	15.6	24,618	10.9	20,215	9.4	14,199	8.2	14,463	7.6
Economic	100,911	47.4	120,291	53.2	125,493	58.1	94,967	54.5	105,404	55.5
Skilled worker, principal app.	34,550	16.2	42,095	18.6	44,913	20.8	35,903	20.6	41,482	21.9
Skilled worker, spouse & dep.	46,907	22.0	55,734	24.7	60,656	28.1	45,288	26.0	50,912	26.8
Business, principal app.	5,304	2.5	6,209	2.7	5,582	2.6	3,818	2.2	3,638	1.9
Business, spouse & dep.	14,150	6.6	16,253	7.2	14,342	6.6	9,958	5.7	9,372	4.9
Refugees	27,761	13.0	28,351	12.5	24,101	11.2	22,700	13.0	24,367	12.8
Government assisted	8,194	3.8	7,872	3.5	7,663	3.5	7,397	4.2	7,442	3.9
Privately sponsored	3,249	1.5	3,067	1.4	2,593	1.2	2,169	1.2	2,331	1.2
Refugees landed in Canada	12,797	6.0	13,456	6.0	10,622	4.9	10,790	6.2	11,790	6.2
Dependents abroad	3,521	1.7	3,956	1.7	3,223	1.5	2,956	1.7	2,804	1.5
Other	6,970	3.3	9,099	4.0	6,489	3.0	5,415	3.1	4,767	2.5
Live in caregivers	5,458	2.6	4,756	2.1	2,723	1.3	2,868	1.6	3,259	1.7
Other	1,512	0.7	4,343	1.9	3,766	1.7	2,547	1.5	1,508	0.8
Total	212,869		226,071		216,039		174,159		189,816	

Source: CIC, Facts and Figures, 2000 (C&I-291-07-00E).

estate and commerce (Froschauer 1998). There is one other major trend related to Canada's immigration system worth noting at the outset of this chapter: as in many other immigrant-receiving countries, an overwhelming proportion of immigrants to Canada settle in large metropolitan areas, especially Toronto and Vancouver; this tendency is especially true of business immigrants (Hiebert 1994).

Canadian Research on Immigrant and Minority Self-employment

Modern scholarship on the relationship between ethnicity and the Canadian economy began, essentially, with the publication of John Porter's *The Vertical Mosaic* in 1965. Porter challenges a number of widely-held views about Canadian society, especially the myths that most Canadians are middle-class, that all groups enjoy equal opportunity, and that ethnic identities flourish because of a pervasive openness to diversity. (At the time, and still today, many Canadians differentiate between what they see as the American expectation of cultural conformity, the proverbial melting pot, and a pluralist 'mosaic' of cultures in Canada that are separate but equal.) Porter instead argues that minority ethnic groups in Canada have a stronger identity than those in the United States because, in Canada, they face stronger economic barriers. Thus, where most commentators see the idea of a cultural mosaic in a positive light, Porter asserts that minority groups experience structural disadvantage, reproduced across generations. Porter's work touched off more than a decade of research designed to affirm or deny the validity of his thesis. In particular, scholars have shown substantial upward mobility among several minority groups, but have never been able to show economic equality between all groups (Lautard and Guppy 1990; Reitz 1980).

While sociologists, following in the tradition of Porter, approach these questions statistically (using census data), another research tradition emerged in the 1970s, largely led by historians. Inspired by a major government investigation into the nature of ethnic relations in Canada, a series of monographs about Canada's immigrant groups was published. Typically, each of these contains at least one chapter on the economic participation of the group in question. Brunet and Palmer (1988: 77) offer a succinct summary of these narrative accounts: 'When members of various Canadian ethnic groups tell their story, in its economic aspects it is almost without exception a story of initial hardship, long struggle, and eventual success, limited, however, by exclusion from the topmost ranks.' Throughout these studies, there are frequent references to immigrant entrepreneurs but no systematic analysis of this phenomenon. The lack of a sustained treatment of entrepreneurship was characteristic of both research traditions in the 1970s: the statistical studies of sociologists and the more descriptive ones produced by historians.

There were two other areas of research where the subject of ethnic business arose, at least tangentially. First, with an eye toward the American assimilation debate, Canadian scholars began to consider the circumstances that enabled ethnic affinity to be maintained across generations. The formative contribution to this body of work was Raymond Breton's (1964) theory that 'institutionally complete' ethnic groups – those with elaborate internal economies and social institutions – are most likely to hold the loyalty of their populations. The existence of a petite bourgeoisie, and an accompanying commercial landscape, are seen as integral to the development of an ethnic economy. Second, in the 1970s, social scientists turned their interest both theoretically and empirically to the intersection between class and ethnicity (e.g. Harney 1977; Li 1988; McAll 1990; Thompson 1979). In this case the growth of a minority middle-class is interpreted as a turning point in which 'modern' class relations transform 'pre-modern' ethnic communities. Again, this middle-class emerged through small-scale entrepreneurship, and its social position solidified along with its material success. While these ideas gained momentum, there was little interest in the general theories of ethnic and minority entrepreneurship that had begun to animate scholarship in the United States.

It was only in the 1980s that Canadian researchers began to examine ethnic enterprise in more systematic ways, a decade later than the pioneering work on this subject in the United States. Given the head start taken by American researchers, Canadian scholars on this subject essentially adopted the theoretical ideas and methods developed by their US counterparts. This is not to say Canadian research on self-employment and entrepreneurship among immigrants is simply derivative. In fact, there are examples of authors who take little notice of emerging US trends, such as Kallen and Kelner (1983) in their large study of ethnic entrepreneurship in Toronto, which is designed to evaluate Weber's conceptualization of the Protestant work ethic. But in the main, the growing body of American work provides inspiration for new research directions. Peter Li (1976, 1979), who first studied the rise of Chinese-American entrepreneurs in the United States, was an early proponent of these ideas in Canada. In particular, Li attributes the rise of small businesses among the Chinese-Canadian population to problems of racism and discrimination in the regular labour-market. Chan and Cheung (1985), also working within an American theoretical framework, agree with Li's contention that blocked-mobility is important in the case of Chinese-Canadian entrepreneurship. However, drawing on ideas advanced by Ivan Light (who shows variable rates of self-employment among groups similarly marginalized in the United States), Chan and Cheung add cultural and individual factors to their analysis, and conclude that the high rate of self-employment among Chinese-Canadians reflects a combination of class resources (i.e. human capital) held by individuals and the ethnic resources of the group, and that it is also a response to discrimination.

In the mid-1980s, the Canadian government commissioned two studies to investigate the contribution of immigrants and minority groups to the growing small-business sector (Multiculturalism Canada 1986; Tepper 1988). Both of these reports show a higher rate of self-employment among immigrants than among the native-born, a 'fact' that is taken for granted within virtually all Canadian scholarship on the subject, but one which may no longer be true, as discussed below. Also, both studies reveal wide variations in entrepreneurial behaviour between ethnic groups. These variations appear unsystematic. For example, few individuals of Black and Latino ethnic origins are self-employed, while those of Jewish, East Asian, and Arab descent have higher-than-average rates. Yet all these groups are classified in Canada as 'visible minorities'[1] and all have suffered discrimination in one form or another. Unfortunately, these studies do not engage theoretical work that would have helped explain these differences. Still, the fact that they were commissioned reflects the growing interest on the part of government in immigrants as entrepreneurs (particularly after the introduction of the entrepreneurial-immigrant programme discussed earlier). They also show that the federal government was eager to collaborate with academics in research on immigrant entrepreneurship, a process that accelerated in the 1990s.

Returning to the specifically academic literature, approaches developed in the United States were fully integrated into Canadian research by the late 1980s. Since then, scholars have devoted particular attention to the causes of self-employment; most now adopt an interactive approach based on a combination of 'push' (i.e. blocked-mobility in the regular labour market) and 'pull' (e.g. group histories of entrepreneurship) factors, as well as the nature of metropolitan economies (Beaujot et al. 1994; Lo et al. 1999; Razin and Langlois 1996; Reitz 1990). Several researchers have explored the relations between class and ethnic resources in supporting entrepreneurship. Marger (1989), in an interview-based project examining South Asian entrepreneurs, concludes that class resources are decisive in the process of business formation. That is, there is no substitute for capital, education, skills and experience in determining who will be able to establish a business. Based on his study of Chinese and Black immigrants in Toronto, Uneke (1996) agrees that class resources are crucial in the transition to self-employment, but argues that the socio-economic structure of the ethnic community is a critical determinant of entrepreneurial *success*. Groups with elaborate sub-economies including available labour, access to capital, and demands for distinctive cultural products provide a fertile ground for entrepreneurial activities (also see Brenner and Toulouse 1990; Dana 1993; Marger and Hoffman 1992; Walton-Roberts and Hiebert 1997). Given the many inter-group differences, in terms of their immigration histories, population sizes, internal economic organization levels, and the metropolitan economies within which they are located, we should expect to find pronounced variations in self-employment rates. Under these circumstances, generalizations about entrepreneurial behaviour are difficult.

The cost/benefit balance for immigrants who turn to self-employment has also preoccupied researchers. As in the US literature, opinions differ. Maxim (1992), in a census-based study in which many variables are held constant, finds that members of minority groups and immigrants both face income penalties in the regular labour market. However, these gaps in income are reduced to the point of statistical insignificance for those who are self-employed. According to his study, therefore, self-employment is an obvious route to material advancement. While this may be the case generally, Reitz (1990) adds a valuable qualification: the returns to self-employment vary widely between groups. Some have much to gain through entrepreneurship while others do not. Li (1994, 1997) explores this complexity by distinguishing on the one hand between visible minorities vs members of European ethnic groups, and on the other by considering the variable rewards received by entrepreneurs working in different industrial sectors. Using 1986 census data, he finds that a high proportion of immigrants from non-European backgrounds become self-employed by establishing small firms in accommodation/food services and retailing. In these fields, entrepreneurs receive modest incomes relative to their human capital, regardless of their ethnic origin. However, members of visible-minority groups are far less prevalent in sectors of the economy where the gains from self-employment are substantial but where start-up costs are high (also see Langlois and Razin 1989). As a result, immigrants *in general* may receive economic benefits from self-employment, but these are significantly less for visible-minority immigrants (McEvoy and Jones 1993). This point coincides with Teixeira's (1998) argument that visible minorities are usually propelled into self-employment by discrimination, while European groups (in his case the Portuguese) gravitate to entrepreneurialism as a means of upward mobility.

On one level, a clearer portrait of ethnic and immigrant self-employment can be obtained by focusing on a single group. Given that it is, by far, the largest visible-minority population in the country, researchers have investigated the case of Chinese-Canadians in the greatest detail. The sheer size of the population, especially in Toronto and Vancouver (in the two cities combined, Chinese-Canadians numbered 650,000 in 1996), provides a vast internal market for small- and medium-sized firms (Lo et al. 1999). There have been a few remarkable success stories in each of the cities, in Toronto in the computer-manufacturing sector and in Vancouver in real estate development. In these cases, entrepreneurs began their operations in the ethnic economy but were eventually able to 'break out' and market their products or services to the population at large. A few, in fact, have established firms of global significance (Lo et al. 1999; Wong 1993,

1995). Li (1992), in a thoughtful reconsideration of the blocked-mobility thesis he had advanced in the 1970s, argues that the increasing scale of Chinese-Canadian entrepreneurship has occurred in the context of reduced exclusionary barriers against the group. Moreover, a much larger number of Chinese-Canadians have been able to obtain professional and managerial jobs, another sign that discriminatory behaviour has declined. While the blocked-mobility hypothesis may have held a generation or two ago, it is no longer valid in the case of Chinese-Canadians. Instead, Li believes, the level of entrepreneurship within this group reflects a rapidly growing market (as noted) and also a dramatic transfer of capital from East Asia to Canada. While a sustained focus on the entrepreneurial activities of a single group helps bring larger processes into focus, it also reveals complexities that render generalization suspect. Thompson (1989), surveying the socio-economic situation of Toronto's Chinese population, shows significant differences between earlier waves of migrants, who arrived poor, and those who came under more recent immigration programmes (especially business programmes), and are often wealthy. Taken as a whole, it is as easy to discern differences within the Chinese-Canadian population as it is to find similarities.

Researchers have also begun to investigate the case of business immigrants in greater detail. Initial assessments, which generally strongly endorsed these programmes, were based on the intended transfers of capital and business plans provided by prospective immigrants on their application forms. The reported statistics were indeed impressive. An official report noted that entrepreneur immigrants landing in Canada between 1992 and 1995 intended to create or maintain some 24,000 jobs (CIC 1996). Those who were selected as investor immigrants between 1986 and 1996 anticipated adding over CDN$3 billion of additional venture-capital to Canada. These figures more than justified the government's decision to establish the entrepreneurial and investor programmes. Early academic research generally reached similarly positive conclusions about the economic impacts of the programme (e.g. Li 1992, 1993; Wong and Netting 1992).

More recently, commentators have begun to question these results. In a discussion of the moral implications of the business programme, Nash (1987) questions the validity of statistical studies based on intentions, though concludes that, on balance, the programmes make a positive contribution to Canada's economy. Given the absence of quantitative statistics on business immigrants, in the 1990s researchers began to initiate interview-based studies. While these studies are all based on relatively small samples, their results are sobering. Froschauer (1998) contrasts the behaviour of European and Asian immigrants who entered Canada under the entrepreneurial programme, showing that the former are more active in the manufacturing sector (as intended by the programme) than the latter.

According to Froschauer, this important difference reflects pre-migration circumstances. Entrepreneurial immigrants from European countries have a better grasp of English and typically have had rigorous apprenticeship training in factories. In contrast, most of the East Asian entrepreneurs in his sample did not have shopfloor training and had a lower level of language competence. The Europeans he interviewed were able to start small manufacturing firms, while those from Asia were limited by their inadequate mastery of the language and their lack of basic knowledge about production systems.

In a study of Chinese-origin entrepreneur immigrants living in Vancouver, Wong and Ng (1998) also report problematic results. As is generally common in studies of ethnic entrepreneurship, their interviewees speak of kinship and co-ethnic capital and labour resources. They work long hours and achieve low profit rates, and in fact many of their businesses are in precarious circumstances. While these findings are typical of research on ethnic enterprise, they are surprising in light of the objectives of the business programme. Entrepreneur immigrants are selected on the basis of their previous business record and the credibility of their future plans, and one would expect more successful outcomes. In another inter-view-based study, Woo (1997) confirms Froschauer's conclusion that immigrants from Hong Kong are reluctant to enter the manufacturing sector. In contrast to Froschauer and Wong and Ng, Woo includes investor immigrants in his sample. They complain bitterly about losing money in the venture-capital investments they are required to make as a condition for coming to Canada. According to Woo, these funds are often poorly managed. Ley (2000) combines interviews and statistical data from the Longitudinal Immigrant Data Base (see below) to examine the case of business immigrants in British Columbia. He also observes expectations that were not met, and a great reluctance among investor immigrants to invest money in new ventures after their first business failure. Ultimately, many have begun to see Canada in general, and Vancouver in partic-ular, as a poor place to conduct business – with high tax rates, high wages, powerful unions and too much regulation – but a pleasant place to live ('Hong Kong for money; Canada for quality of life'). Ley concludes that the individuals he interviewed were unprepared for the economic climate they encountered, and questions the assumption that business skills can be transferred from one cultural or economic and regulatory setting to another. Yet this assumption is at the core of the business-immigration programme.

Several of the authors cited in this discussion of Canada's business programme have noted, mostly in passing, an important strategy used by many of the entre-preneurs and investors they interviewed: operating a business in their source country while living in Canada or commuting across the Pacific on a regular basis (Ley 2000; Wong and Ng 1998; Woo 1997). These 'astronaut families', as they are known locally, reveal a key aspect of immigrant entrepreneurialism that is under-represented in the literature, the growing significance of transnational networks of small- and medium-sized businesses associated with diasporic groups. While there is an extensive literature on Chinese overseas business networks, few authors have connected this complex set of business practices with immigration and ethnic entrepreneurialism (though see Olds 1996, and Olds and Yeung 1999). Virtually all the studies of ethnic enterprise are conducted in local settings (usually in single settings, with single groups), but many entrepreneurs obtain capital, recruit labour and conduct trade across national borders.

Summarizing the Canadian literature on immigrant and minority enterprise, most Canadian scholars have looked to the United States and, to a lesser extent, to Britain for models to help explain particular patterns. Empirical studies based on tabulations of data from the 1971–1991 censuses have shown that the rate, success and economic structure of entrepreneurship varies dramatically between groups. Immigrants are more likely than the native-born to be self-employed, though analysts are not agreed on whether this is the result of blocked-mobility or other factors. European-origin immigrants are apparently more able to become self-employed in sectors of the economy that offer higher returns to human capital. Visible-minority groups have higher rates of entrepreneurship in labour-intensive sectors associated with narrow profit margins. Researchers have recently turned their attention to the economic impacts of Canada's business-immigration programme. While early studies tended to portray the self-employed, entrepreneurial and investor classes in positive terms, in the past few years analysts have generated more cautious and, in some cases, quite negative conclusions about this form of immigration. In general, while several topics have been well explored in the Canadian literature, there are conspicuous gaps, notably discussions of the role of family members and women in immigrant firms (see Walton-Roberts and Hiebert 1997), the role of the state in supporting immigrant and minority entrepreneurs, and transnational systems of entrepreneurship.

I have noted in a few passing comments that the Canadian government has commissioned academic research on immigrant entrepreneurship. More broadly, how have the studies produced by academics been received by policy-makers? Have they been instrumental in policy developments during the past few decades? On the subject of immigrant and ethnic enterprise, university researchers have had little apparent policy influence.[2] As mentioned in the introduction, the self-employed immigrant class was launched long before Canadian academics had turned their attention to immigrant entrepreneurship. Even the entrepreneur-immigrant-programme, established in the 1970s, predated the bulk of scholarship on the subject. And, finally, the investor programme, designed to foster transnational investment and trade, was introduced in the mid-1980s, well before the current fascination with the concept of transnationalism. These policy developments were generated with little input from university-based research. However, as academics turned their attention to entrepreneurship among visible minorities and immigrants, bureaucrats began to take note. As discussed, an initial step toward engagement was to commission contract research on the subject. In the 1990s, though, a convergence between academic and policy-based activities began to take place, largely through the Metropolis Project. The original vision for Metropolis, which was an effort to create a collaborative system of research involving policy-makers, academics and researchers from community-based organizations, arose within the bureaucracy. In 1996, the federal government funded at Canadian universities four new centres of excellence that focused on immigration research. A great deal of attention has been devoted to the broad subject of immigrant incorporation in the economy, and self-employment has been a significant theme within this body of work. In fact, several of the studies discussed in this chapter were written by scholars associated with the Metropolis Project. So far, the policy impact of this effort has been general rather than particular. There are echoes of this recent scholarship in the latest proposal to revise Canadian immigration law (under debate in the House of Commons in 2001), for example, but so far its role in altering the basic rules of the immigration programme has been limited. Given the closer connections between policy-makers and university researchers that are being built through the Metropolis Project, this is likely to change.

Measuring Immigrant Entrepreneurship in Canada

A consensus has thus emerged among Canadian researchers that immigrants and certain ethnic-minority groups have higher rates of self-employment than the native-born, dominant population, and that entrepreneurship is an important means of economic advancement for marginalized groups. This positive view has been established by researchers using census data from the 1970s up to 1991. In this section, I examine more recent census information (1996) as well as the administrative database of Citizenship and Immigration Canada to see whether the optimistic generalizations about minority and immigrant self-employment in Canada continue to be true. These data confirm some aspects of the prevailing view but challenge others. In particular, conclusions about the relative rates of immigrant vs non-immigrant entrepreneurship depend on how the census information is organized and the scale of analysis. Census data can be used to establish quite different and indeed conflicting conclusions about self-employment rates. The selection of census data is thus crucial in entrepreneurial research, and this fact is not sufficiently debated or even acknowledged in most research on the subject. To explore this issue further, I begin by summarizing the statistics on immigrant self-employment in Canada, posing two seemingly straightforward questions: is the rate of self-employment among immigrants different from that of non-immigrants, and how does the level of earnings of self-employed immigrants compare with that of non-immigrants?

The most comprehensive source of information on these topics is the census, but unfortunately the characteristics of immigrant self-employment differ depending on the particular data we examine and the scale of analysis. Studies of immigrant self-employment are frequently conducted on the basis of public use samples drawn from the census (in Canada, they are called Public Use Microdata Files, or PUMFs). In Canada, they are released three years after each census and provide nearly complete information for approximately 2.8 per cent of the total population. The relevant variable for our purpose is 'class of worker', where each individual over fifteen years old who is in the labour market is classified as someone who earns a wage or salary, someone who is self-employed, or someone who works without payment (e.g. a family member). These are discrete categories and the allocation is based on one's 'primary' form of work in terms of hours and income in the sixteen months prior to the census (but focused on the prior week if the individual was actively employed at the time). According to this variable, immigrants are more prone to self-employment than non-immigrants (15.1 vs 11.8 per cent), a common conclusion in immigrant entrepreneurship studies. However, I have also obtained a special tabulation of the complete census using a more stringent definition of self-employment. This variable, labour-force activity, includes only those who were working in the week prior to the census. Using this information base, it is shown that immigrants have only a slightly higher rate of self-employment than non-immigrants (8.8 vs 7.7 per cent; see Table 3.2). There is a clear relation between duration of residence in Canada and self-employment: immigrants who have been in the country longer have much higher rates of self-employment than recent arrivals. While this finding is logical in that individuals with a longer history in Canada are likely to have more capital to invest as well as a better knowledge of the market conditions, it also reflects another influence: in general terms, the rate of self-employment increases with age (Statistics Canada 1997), and immigrants who have been in Canada longer are likely to be older.

Shifting the focus to income, however, yields a different set of results. In the same census, individuals listed all their sources of income, and this information is coded in a non-mutually exclusive variable. The income variable is more universal than the work activity one: while 14.8 million of Canadians over fifteen years old were in the labour market in the week preceding the census, 20.9 million received some form of income at some point in 1995. Also, the income variable allows multiple classifications. In the work-activity variable, a person who works for an employer five days a week and engages in self-employment to earn extra money would be simply classified as an employee, whereas in the

Table 3.2 Self-employment by Immigration Status, Canada, 1996

	Total Labour force	Self-employed			
		Total		Without paid help	
		N	%	N	%
Total – Immigrant Status	14,812,700	1,172,910	7.9	822,685	70.1
Non-permanent residents	63,850	2,885	4.5	2,090	72.4
Non-immigrants	11,909,710	919,890	7.7	655,260	71.2
Immigrants	2,839,145	250,130	8.8	165,335	66.1
Before 1961	393,425	56,095	14.3	38,950	69.4
1961–1970	528,120	53,225	10.1	34,460	64.7
1971–1980	743,390	61,610	8.3	39,070	63.4
1981–1985	264,410	21,255	8.0	13,945	65.6
1986–1990	409,745	28,260	6.9	19,005	67.3
1991–1996	500,050	29,690	5.9	19,905	67.0

Source: CIC 1996 tabulations, table 6.

income variable, he or she would be classified as having both types of income. Thus the number of self-employed people is far larger if we use the income variable (1.67 million as opposed to 1.27 million), indicating a substantial degree of part-time self-employment in combination with other types of work. Using this logic, immigrants are slightly *less* prone to self-employment than non-immigrants (7.9 vs 8.0 per cent; see Table 3.3). That said, self-employed immigrants tend to be more financially successful than their non-immigrant counterparts. Their average earnings through self-employment are respectively CDN$19,800 and CDN$17,000 in 1995. The gap between these groups in total incomes, however, is less (about CDN$1,400), implying that self-employed immigrants rely to a larger extent on their business earnings. The most interesting finding here, I believe, is the shift in the direction of the income gap between immigrants and non-immigrants among the total working population vs the self-employed. On average, immigrants have smaller incomes than non-immigrants, though the difference is not that large. However, among the self-employed, immigrants earn more than non-immigrants, suggesting that self-employment is a vital opportunity for economic advancement.

Since most immigrants settle in Canada's largest cities, are the same basic patterns evident there? The simple answer is no. If we isolate the four largest immigrant-reception metropolitan areas of Canada, Toronto, Montreal, Vancouver and Calgary, we find that they alone house some 62 per cent of all the immigrants living in the country (compared with 27 per cent of the Canadian population). Immigrants gravitate to these places to follow their family members and friends, and in an effort to achieve rapid economic mobility. Rates of self-

Table 3.3 Self-employment Income by Immigration Status, Canada, 1995 Tax Year

	Total		Individuals with self-employment income			
	#	$avg-total	#	%	$avg-SE	$avg-total
Total – Immigrant Status	20,916,755	25,196	1,666,950	8.0	17,554	32,569
Non-permanent residents	115,475	17,103	4,165	3.6	20,270	29,816
Non-immigrants	16,509,765	25,308	1,325,340	8.0	16,983	32,289
Immigrants	4,291,515	24,980	337,450	7.9	19,759	33,706
Before 1961	1,030,105	27,490	78,445	7.6	18,779	37,534
1961–1970	755,510	31,538	71,250	9.4	22,906	38,382
1971–1980	952,665	27,690	82,390	8.6	22,763	35,756
1981–1985	356,275	22,873	28,655	8.0	19,724	31,858
1986–1990	537,105	19,720	38,505	7.2	15,719	25,653
1991–1996	659,850	15,058	38,210	5.8	13,528	22,211

Source: CIC 1996 tabulations, table 10.

employment vary considerably between the four cities, from 5.4 per cent in Montreal to 8.6 per cent in Calgary (see Table 3.4), reflecting the specific characteristics of each urban economy. This issue is explored, using 1981 data, by Langlois and Razin (1989), and using 1991 data by Razin and Langlois (1996).

Shifting the focus from the national to the urban level shows that immigrants still achieve financial gains via self-employment, since the total income of self-employed immigrants is, on average, nearly 40 per cent higher than the average income of all immigrants. Significantly, though, non-immigrants witness almost exactly the same rise in income via self-employment, and the relative income gap between immigrants and non-immigrants remains constant. Returning to the questions posed at the outset of this section, in metropolitan areas, where the bulk of Canada's immigrants reside, they have a slightly *lower* propensity to self-employment than non-immigrants and have lower incomes regardless of their employment status. Self-employment is thus a means to upward mobility but not, in aggregate, a way to close the income gap between immigrants and the host society.

A number of more detailed patterns become visible if we examine the population of self-employed immigrants. While the level of self-employment among immigrant women is rising rapidly, approximately two-thirds of the immigrant entrepreneurs are men. There is a good economic reason for this pattern: women have less to gain by engaging in self-employment. At the aggregated scale examined here, the total income of self-employed women is 18 per cent above that of all women with an income, compared with a 22 per cent increase for men. There are equally marked differences in entrepreneurial behaviour between different ethnic groups. According to the census, the rank order of the population groups in terms of the percentage of adults who are self-employed is: Korean (20.4 per cent), Japanese (11.1 per cent), Arab/West Asian (9.2 per cent), White (9.0 per cent), Chinese (6.8 per cent), South Asian (6.4 per cent), Latin American (5.2 per cent), Southeast Asian (4.4 per cent), Black (4.3 per cent), and Filipino (3.4 per cent). Surprisingly, among these groups, there is no clear relation between the propensity to become self-employed and the level of income from self-employment ($r = 0.101$).

Unfortunately, there are no questions in the Canadian census that allow us to monitor the economic performance of the immigrants who have come to Canada through the various programmes of entry. Entrepreneurial and investor immigrants who have been admitted to Canada because of their business experience and capital might be expected to exhibit particularly high rates of self-employment, and refugees and perhaps family-based immigrants particularly low rates. However, several qualitative studies suggest that business immigrants are experiencing difficulty. To investigate this issue, I turn to the newly operational Longitudinal Immigrant Data Base (IMDB), a noteworthy resource for

Table 3.4 Self-employment Income in Canada and Selected Metropolitan Areas, 1995

		Total		Individuals with self-employment income			
		Number self-employed	*$avg-total*	*Number self-employed*	*%*	*$avg-SE*	*$avg-total*
Canada	Non-immigrants	16,509,765	25,308	1,325,335	8.0	16,983	32,289
	Immigrants	4,291,515	24,980	337,445	7.9	19,759	33,706
Montreal	Non-immigrants	1,915,825	25,525	101,760	5.3	21,615	35,977
	Immigrants	494,295	21,755	27,970	5.7	20,731	33,123
Toronto	Non-immigrants	1,553,550	32,521	119,030	7.7	29,384	47,401
	Immigrants	1,504,800	25,548	101,485	6.7	22,792	35,984
Calgary	Non-immigrants	447,020	30,195	39,370	8.8	17,020	36,137
	Immigrants	149,900	25,387	12,360	8.2	15,196	29,604
Vancouver	Non-immigrants	816,310	29,832	68,855	8.4	20,547	36,561
	Immigrants	533,480	24,153	44,175	8.3	18,551	31,133

Source: CIC special tabulations, table 10.

researchers in Canada that has been created by merging two complex data files (Langlois and Dougherty 1997). The first is the Landed Immigrant Database System (LIDS), based on the forms immigrants fill in when they formally land in Canada, which specify their place of birth, place of last permanent residence, citizenship, marital and family status, first language, intended occupation, educational qualifications and intended destination. Immigration officers add a series of administrative codes, including language ability in English and French and class of entry. These data have been available to researchers in Canada for a number of years. In the IMDB, LIDS information is linked with the annual tax forms immigrants submit to Revenue Canada after they land. For example, an immigrant landing in Canada in 1980 (the first year of the database) would have filled in a form that year and tax forms every year since then. So far, data has been coded up to 1995, so for the individual in question, there could be sixteen tax returns in the data base. There is a substantial amount of information on Canadian tax forms, especially related to a minute breakdown of income from all sources, occupation, place of employment and, of course, residential location.

So far, only a fraction of the IMDB has been fully processed and released to researchers in the form of special compendium tables. At this point, the tables are only available at the provincial and national levels. In addition, the definition of self-employment is not the same on the census and the IMDB, so neither the number of self-employed individuals nor their incomes can be compared across the two data bases. Here I am only interested in comparing, within the IMDB, the labour-market behaviour of immigrants who enter Canada through different immigration categories. There is one other important limitation of the IMDB data as it is currently released. This is also true of census data, but is particularly relevant when discussing the economic participation of business immigrants. The compendium tables include income from four major sources: employment, self-employment, investment and unemployment.[3] This is perfectly reasonable in most cases. However, in some cases individual entrepreneurs set up firms and then pay themselves a salary. In these cases, the income they receive, although it is the result of entrepreneurship, will show up in the data as employment income. Thus, the extent of self-employment and the level of self-employment income are likely to be under-represented in the IMDB. However, the total income figures are reliable.

As expected, independent immigrants who are assessed according to economic criteria have the highest propensity for self-employment (see Table 3.5), followed by refugees and those who have come to reunite families. Within the economic category, predictably, principal applicants are much more entre-preneurial than spouses and dependants. Skilled workers are almost twice as likely to be self-employed as immigrants. Business immigrants have the highest rates of self-employment, reaching over 40 per cent of all the adults who filed a

Table 3.5 Class of Entry by Self-employment and Income, 1980–1995 Immigrants to Canada, 1995 Tax Year

	Total		With self-employment income			
	N	Avg total income	N	Percent SE	Avg SE income	Avg total income
Total	1,272,200	15,138	137,350	10.8	8,195	20,575
Family	500,365	12,685	41,485	8.3	7,735	18,497
Economic	442,080	18,898	61,910	14.0	9,867	24,140
Principal applicants	245,465	24,213	42,205	17.2	10,954	27,410
Entrepreneur (abroad)	17,850	11,789	3,750	21.0	4,714	10,857
Self-employed (abroad)	8,550	18,309	3,645	42.6	9,919	17,563
Investor (abroad)	6,820	14,662	1,010	14.8	4,328	15,733
Skilled worker (abroad)	116,200	30,845	21,120	18.2	13,785	35,763
Assisted rel (abroad)	52,525	20,344	6,210	11.8	6,451	19,433
Other economic (C+abroad)	43,520	18,926	6,470	14.9	11,271	24,762
Spouses & dependents	196,615	12,263	19,705	10.0	7,538	17,136
Business (abroad)	49,570	8,834	5,650	11.4	6,430	12,674
Skilled workers (abroad)	85,120	13,934	9,170	10.8	8,561	20,148
Assisted relatives (abroad)	46,680	12,736	3,435	7.4	5,560	15,568
Other economic (C+abroad)	15,245	12,635	1,450	9.5	10,066	19,191
Refugees	210,580	13,693	24,075	11.4	6,250	17,599
Principal applicants	148,800	15,038	19,240	12.9	6,305	18,121
Spouses & dependents	61,780	10,454	4,835	7.8	6,032	15,523
Live in caregivers	36,675	15,893	2,265	6.2	3,472	14,190
ADR and backlog	60,175	14,385	6,480	10.8	4,644	14,096
Retired & other	22,260	10,188	1,190	5.3	4,833	15,110

Note: C=applications submitted in Canada; abroad=applications submitted abroad.
Source: IMDB Compendium tabulation M101S9.ivt.

tax return among the principal applicants in the self-employed category. Entrepreneur immigrants also enter self-employment in large numbers, although the rate for investor immigrants is not much higher than the average. However, one could easily refute this apparently positive picture. In the first place, business immigrants are deliberately selected for their experience, capital, and plans to set up independent firms in Canada; in that sense, higher than average rates of self-employment are expected, and the fact that only one in five of the entrepreneurial immigrants is self-employed may indicate a failure of the programme rather than its success. Surprisingly, too, the principal applicants who entered Canada as refugees are almost as inclined toward self-employment as investor immigrants (11.4 vs 14.2 per cent). Secondly, business immigrants who do become self-employed do not realize very high incomes compared to other types of immigrant. In fact, the average total income reported by refugees (principal applicants) and reunited family members who engage in entrepreneurial activities is actually *higher* than that of each of the three specifically defined categories of business immigrant. The most successful category of immigrants, in terms of entrepreneurial income, is the skilled-worker category. These statistics are not yet widely known in Canada; as they are presented to the public, they are sure to spark additional debate on the relative merits of business-immigration programmes.

Conclusion

Canadian scholars have generated a considerable literature on the participation of immigrant and minority groups in the economy. Early interest in the entrepreneurial activities of these groups was dominated by narrative accounts by historians and statistical studies, mainly by sociologists. Theories and models developed in the United States gradually came to the fore in Canadian research, as they did throughout the Western world. Since the 1980s, this has meant most researchers adopt an interactive view of immigrant entrepreneurship. In recent years, however, Canadian analysts have begun to concentrate on specifically Canadian issues, especially the outcomes of the business-immigration programme. Documenting the nature and extent of transnational business networks is also an emerging trend in Canadian research.

Throughout the past few decades, scholarship on immigrant entrepreneurship in Canada as elsewhere has emphasized the immigrant propensity to become self-employed. In this literature, immigrants are portrayed as more entrepreneurially inclined than the native-born. Data surveyed here from the 1996 census challenge this prevalent view. At the national level, especially if the PUMF data are used, immigrants have higher self-employment rates than those of the population at large. However, refining the data by removing individuals unemployed in the week prior to the census and concentrating on the metropolitan scale where the majority of immigrants live presents a different picture. Incomes *in general* are higher in metropolitan areas, and most immigrants live in large cities; the combination of these factors means the degree of immigrant economic success appears high when national-scale data are analysed. In metropolitan areas, immigrants are slightly less likely than non-immigrants to become self-employed and both groups experience roughly the same rise in income through entrepreneurship.

Unfortunately, the empirical portion of this chapter is entirely based on the 1995/6 data. I am therefore unable to provide a definitive answer to the question: have other researchers been 'mistaken' in their portrayal of high rates of self-employment among immigrants, or have historical circumstances changed? I suspect the latter. For most of the post-war period, immigrants have been more likely than the native-born to engage in entrepreneurial activities, but the scope for self-employment declined in the recession of the early 1990s. The results of the 2001 Canadian census, which probably coincide with a more robust economy, will be extremely important in enabling us to see whether this is a temporary or a long-term trend.

I have presented a brief glimpse into the economic performance of business immigrants, using information from a new Canadian database. The statistics reported here confirm the results of recent qualitative research and the British Columbia data surveyed by Ley. In essence, individuals who come to Canada as skilled workers outperform business immigrants in terms of total income, and have similar and in some cases higher rates of entrepreneurship. There are several possible explanations for these unexpected results. Of course, the data may be wrong: perhaps business immigrants under-report their incomes more than others when filling out their tax forms, or perhaps the methods used to link landing records and tax forms in the IMDB are faulty. I suspect the latter explanation is erroneous and have no way of assessing the validity of the former. It is also possible, as Wong and Ng (1998) suggest, that entrepreneur immigrants face racism in Canada that inhibits their success. While I have sympathy with this view, and in fact have written about the subtle forms of racism encountered by minority entrepreneurs (see Walton-Roberts and Hiebert 1997), I am not convinced that business immigrants face more hostility than those who come to Canada as skilled workers. Instead of concluding that the data are erroneous, or that entrepreneur and investor immigrants experience heightened levels of racism, I am more drawn to a third explanation, which largely coincides with the views expressed by Ley: the assumption that individuals can reproduce their entrepreneurial success in a different economic and cultural setting may be wrong.

In this chapter I show that the rate of entrepreneurship among immigrants to Canada is not as high as we have been led to believe. The individuals selected to come to Canada as entrepreneurs and investors may be less successful than expected. However, these critical points should not obscure the larger picture. In general, even during a crushing recession, the immigrant rates of entrepreneurship and incomes from self-employment are approximately the same as those of the native-born. This, I believe, reflects immense effort on the part of immigrants and should be acknowledged as a significant achievement.

Notes

1. In general, in this chapter I employ terms commonly used in Canada to describe various groups. Immigrants are individuals who were born outside Canada but have permanent residence status; they may have arrived one month or many decades ago. All the groups except Aboriginals and those who are descendants of the original colonial powers, the British and the French, are collectively referred to as 'minorities'. The term 'visible minorities' is used to refer to non-European minorities and is roughly equivalent to the term 'people of colour' widely used in the United States.
2. I am careful to use the term 'university researchers' in this sentence. It is important to keep in mind that in the post-war period, the Canadian government had its own extensive research capacity. Until the recent past (see below), the dialogue between researchers in university and bureaucratic settings was minimal.
3. Total income in the compendium tables is simply the aggregate of these four types of income, and is not necessarily the same as the actual total income indicated by the person filing the tax form. Income from social assistance (welfare), for example, is not included in the compendium tables.

Australia:
Cosmopolitan Capitalists Down Under

Jock Collins

Immigrants in Australian Society

Cosmopolitan Australia

Australian society has been shaped more by immigration and immigrants than most countries in the world today. After Israel and Luxembourg, Australia has the greatest proportion of permanent immigrants of all contemporary Western societies. In 1996, for example, 21.1 per cent of Australia's population were first-generation immigrants (that is, were born overseas), compared to Switzerland (19 per cent) and Canada (17.4 per cent). This greatly exceeds the immigrant presence in Germany (8.9 per cent), the United States (9.3 per cent), France (6.3 per cent) and the United Kingdom (3.4 per cent) (SOPEMI 1998: 31). Immigration has been a major source of the Australian labour force and population growth for all its white history. Australia's immigrants have come from all corners of the globe, with people of more than 180 nationalities caught in the Australian immigration net. These first-generation immigrants, together with their Australian-born children – the second generation – comprise over half the population of Australia's largest cosmopolitan cities of Sydney, Melbourne, Adelaide and Perth (Collins 1991: 38–9).

While most post-war immigrants are employees in factories, building sites and offices, some immigrants have established their own business enterprises. Indeed, in Australia 25.8 per cent of all the self-employed are foreign-born, a higher proportion than in all the major OECD countries other than Luxembourg (SOPEMI 1998: 36). These Australian immigrant entrepreneurs are the subjects of this chapter. The chapter first outlines the major dimensions of recent Australian migration trends, the ways in which migrants are incorporated into the Australian labour market and the socio-economic position of immigrants in multicultural Australia. It then presents an overview of self-employment in Australia in general, and among immigrant groups in particular. The chapter then presents a summary of research into immigrant entrepreneurship in Australia.

The final section briefly reviews the policy responses to immigrant entrepreneurship.

Recent Migration Trends

Prior to 1947, most immigrants to Australia came from Britain and Ireland. This was partly because of Australia's history as a British colony and partly because of the racist immigration policy. The 'White Australia' policy, which excluded Chinese and other 'coloureds' from taking part in subsequent immigration, was introduced at the birth of the Australian nation in 1901 (Markus 1994; Price 1974). In 1947, when the Australian population was about seven and a half million, 744,000 people, or just under 10 per cent of the Australian population, were born overseas. Only one-third of these immigrants came from a non-English-speaking background (hereafter referred to as NESB immigrants) (Collins 1991: 20–2).

In 1945 the Australian government embarked on an ambitious settler-immigration programme that was planned to add 1 per cent a year to the rate of Australia's population growth. The intention to maintain a white Australia in the second half of the twentieth century (Australian Institute of Political Science 1953) failed: only 40 per cent of Australia's post-war immigrant intake were to come from Britain and Ireland, with the remainder drawn from all corners of the globe.

In the first three post-war decades, the Australian immigration net was mainly thrown over Britain and Ireland, as well as Eastern, Northern and Southern Europe. The high-water mark of post-war Australian immigration was in the late 1960s, when some 180,000 immigrants entered Australia each year (Collins 1991: 20–32). In the past three decades, Australian immigration has changed in terms of numbers and ethnic composition. With the formal end of the White Australia policy in the early 1970s, the Australian immigration net was cast over Asian countries for the first time in nearly 100 years. Since then, Asian countries have been very prominent among the 'top ten' Australian immigration countries (Coughlan and McNamara 1997; Inglis et al. 1992). Net annual permanent immigration to Australia declined in these decades, averaging 110,000 in the 1980s and 92,000 in the first half of the 1990s (Castles et al. 1998: 6).

The characteristics of Australia's immigrants have also changed. People with little formal education and poor English-language skills, such as those from Southern Europe who came as family migrants in a chain migration process in the first three decades after the Second World War, are now largely missing out on immigration selection. Like Canada (Hawkins 1989), Australia has geared immigration to meet more direct economic needs and now uses a floating points system to cream off the 'best' until the quotas are filled. Immigration flows in recent years have been increasingly comprised of highly educated and highly qualified people with good English-language skills, with family-reunion migration declining in relative terms. Of course, it helps if you are rich. In the past two decades a business-migration scheme has been introduced in Australia (Borowski and Nash 1994; Pe-Pua et al. 1996) for millionaire immigrant entrepreneurs who go straight to the top of the immigration queue.

Labour-market Trends

Australian immigration has always been linked to the Australian labour-market needs, with intakes increasing during economic booms and declining during periods of economic downturn. But the labour-market experience of Australia's immigrants has not been uniform. The Australian labour market is segmented along (changing) lines of class, gender, ethnicity and Aboriginality. Workers born in Australia and ESB immigrants have been over-concentrated in the best, highest-paid jobs in the male and female labour markets, while NESB immigrant males and females have tended to be over-concentrated in semi-skilled and unskilled jobs in the blue-collar sector or 'secondary' labour market. These NESB immigrants in Australia were employed as *factory fodder* in much the same way as immigrant workers in many other countries (Castles and Miller 1993: 168–78). Finally, indigenous people are so disadvantaged relative to the rest of the Australian population that they are a segment with unique characteristics (Taylor 1992).

This rigid labour-market segmentation seemed deeply rooted, with the key finding that once in the secondary sector of the labour market, NESB immigrants tended to be stuck there, regardless of their Australian education and training (Turpin 1986: 22). However, data from the 1996 Australia census show that these patterns of labour-market segmentation have in fact changed considerably. Some groups of NESB immigrants have broken into the primary labour market in Australia: immigrants from Northeast Asia and South Asia had a relatively higher presence in the primary labour-market occupations of 'professionals' and 'managers and administrators' compared to the Australian-born (Collins 2000). On the other hand, NESB immigrants from the Middle East and Indo-China are still over-represented among the unemployed and the unskilled and semi-skilled workforce.

Employment status is perhaps the most important influence on the standard of living in Australia. While NESB immigrants had to bear the greatest burden of unemployment in Australia's three post-war recessions (Ackland and Williams 1992), they did not gain their fair share of jobs during the subsequent years of economic recovery, with unemployment rates for Vietnamese, Lebanese and Turkish immigrants, particularly for youth, running at between three and four times the national average for more than a decade and a half.

Many of those NESB immigrants who do get jobs in the primary labour market are often employed at levels below their capacity because the Australian labour market more often penalizes than rewards *cultural capital*, defined here as relating to an immigrant's linguistic diversity and knowledge of cultural practices and modes of business practice in other countries or in ethnic communities other than the mainstream Anglo-Celtic society. As a consequence an *accent ceiling* has developed which keeps many NESB immigrants from reaching the highest levels of the corporate structure. The evidence suggests that the Australian labour market failed to adequately respond to or reward cultural diversity, with strong evidence supporting the existence of racial discrimination (Collins 1996; Foster et al. 1991).

Racism shapes the lives of most NESB immigrants once they are in Australia, though in changing and uneven ways (Human Rights and Equal Opportunity Commission 1991). Many individuals and institutions in Australia still interact with NESB immigrants in a way that is based on negative stereotypes about ethnic, cultural, linguistic or religious groups. One such institution is the Australian labour-market. For example, one study of British and Middle Eastern engineers in Australia found that all the British immigrant engineers had jobs whereas none of the Middle Eastern immigrant engineers could get a job, despite the fact that the Middle Eastern immigrant engineers had British university qualifications in engineering (Hawthorne 1994).

Socio-economic Trends

To understand what has happened to immigrants in Australian society is to investigate how ethnicity intersects with class, gender and culture (Bottomley et al. 1991). The major point is that while immigrants from an ESB background demonstrate much the same patterns of wealth, occupational distribution, unemployment and poverty as the Australian-born, many NESB immigrants are worse off than the Australian-born. Some NESB immigrants have nonetheless done very well in Australia according to the standard socio-economic characteristics.

One of the constants of Australian socio-economic life is that as the rich get richer the poor get poorer. This is clear in Australian poverty research. Saunders (1994: 270) found that in the 1980s, when the number of income units in poverty nearly doubled in Australia, poverty among the Australian-born increased by 16 per cent but for first-generation immigrants it increased by 50 per cent (Williams and Batrouney 1998: 263–5). Studies of income distribution suggest that recently arrived immigrants, particularly NESB immigrants, are 'more heavily concentrated in the lower reaches of the distribution than other immigrants or the Australian-born' (Saunders and King 1994: 90).

But not all NESB immigrant groups are over-represented among the *have nots* of Australian society. Possessing higher levels of education and better language skills, many recent South and Northeast Asian immigrants, including those born in India, Sri Lanka and Malaysia, have sought and found jobs in the attractive primary labour market. They exhibit unemployment rates similar to or lower than these of the Australian-born and have *higher* incomes than the national average. On the other hand, Southeast Asian immigrants such as the Vietnamese, whose roots were in refugee and family migration, have the lowest incomes and the highest unemployment rates in Australia for non-indigenous peoples.

But not all NESB immigrants are limited to wage labour. More than one in four of the wealthiest people and families in Australia are NESB immigrants (Collins et al. 1995a: 58–76; Ostrow 1987). In addition, many immigrant millionaires, mostly from the Asian region (McNamara 1997: 49), are arriving in Australia as business migrants. Moreover, an increasing number of NESB immigrants have moved into entrepreneurship. The key point here is that Australia's post-war immigrants are spread across all the social classes with complex, changing patterns of ethnicity, class and gender emerging.

Australian Multiculturalism and Immigrant Minorities

Immigrants in Australia can become entitled to citizenship after two years and the federal government encourages them to do so. Today, all new immigrants other than refugees have to wait two years before they are eligible for welfare payments such as Medicare, unemployment benefits, and sickness and old-age pensions. Their place in Australian society is shaped by the policy of multiculturalism that was introduced to replace the assimilation policy in the mid-1970s. The assimilation policy was based on the central assumption that new immigrants should shed their differences (cultural, linguistic, religious, dress, food) and become the same as Australians (Castles et al. 1988; Martin 1978). Under the assimilation policy, no initiatives were introduced to respond to different immigrant needs in the areas of education, health, welfare, the law and the labour market (Collins 1991: 228–30).

The Whitlam Labor government (1972–1975) rejected the assimilation philosophy and sought a more inclusive approach to immigrants that would respond more positively to cultural differences. But it was the Conservative Fraser government (1975–1983) that entrenched multiculturalism in Australia, borrowing the term and many policy approaches from the Canadian experience. Under multiculturalism, the cultural backgrounds of Australia's immigrant communities became objects of celebration, not shame. Many programmes and services for new immigrants – including the Special Broadcasting Service (SBS) to broadcast television and radio to 'ethnic' audiences in Australia, as well as child and adult migrant education programmes – were introduced by the Fraser government as part of the institutional fabric of Australian multiculturalism (Collins 1991: 234–6).

The Hawke (1983–1993) and Keating (1993–1996) Labor governments supported and redefined multiculturalism as a policy based on cultural identity (the right to maintain cultural, religious and linguistic freedom in Australia), social justice (the right of all Australians to equality) and economic efficiency (the economic advantages of immigration and cultural diversity if this productive diversity is recognized and rewarded). The 1996 Conservative Howard government's attitude to multiculturalism was at best lukewarm. Howard retained a reputation of being very uncomfortable with multiculturalism.

The introduction of multiculturalism should have reduced some of the barriers faced by new immigrant minorities. However, all the Australian governments in the past two decades have embraced economic rationalism and globalization, which undermined the opportunity structures for many immigrant minorities.

The Australian research community has debated economic rationalism in general (Rees et al.1993) and the merits of immigration and multiculturalism in particular (Castles et al. 1998; Wooden et al. 1994). The Australian Labor government established a Bureau of Immigration Multiculturalism and Population Research (BIMPR) in the late 1980s, commissioning research that supported the conclusion that the impact of immigration on the Australian economy was either positive or benign (Wooden et al. 1994). However, this finding was limited by the neoclassical framework employed by many of the commissioned researchers, and by the fact that most of the economic studies ignored the impact of ethnic entrepreneurs in econometric models or general studies of the economic impact of immigration (Collins 1991: 103–7). This meant the positive economic impact of immigration has not been fully recognized. In addition, conservative theoretical frameworks have dominated the assessment of the contribution of multiculturalism to Australian society, with right-wing critics (Blainey 1984; One Nation 1998; Rimmer 1991) stressing that multiculturalism divides the nation into 'many tribes' and will lead to ethnic conflict. The Conservative Howard government (1996–) has been less than enthusiastic about immigration and multiculturalism. One of its earliest decisions was to axe the BIMPR and to severely downgrade the Office of Multicultural Affairs.

Self-employment Trends in Australia

Overall Trends

Despite the predictions by social theorists from Marx to Weber to Schumpeter (Light and Rosenstein 1995), self-employed entrepreneurs and those in small business[1] are now growing in number and in economic importance in almost all capitalist societies (Sengenberger et al. 1990). Australia is no exception. The past two or three decades have witnessed a renaissance of small business in Australia.

A study of self-employment in the OECD countries found that Australia experienced the largest growth in self-employment of all the OECD countries, with self-employment in the non-agricultural sector increasing by a third in the fifteen-year period from 1969 (9.3 per cent) to 1984 (12.4 per cent) (OECD 1985: 44). The OECD calculated that most (87 per cent) of this increase in self-employment resulted from an increase in what it calls 'own account' workers, that is, the self-employed who do not have paid employees (ibid.: 58).

In 1989/90 there were 692,700 non-rural small businesses that provided 48 per cent of the private-sector employment and gave jobs to over two million people in 1989/90 (Revesz and Lattimore 1997). By 1994/5, there were 887,000 non-rural small-businesses and 1,252,100 small business operators in Australia. These small businesses employed 2.9 million people or just over half (51 per cent) of all the private-sector employees and created about a third of Australia's gross domestic product (Small Business Deregulation Task Force 1996: 151, 153). There were also 428,000 non-employing business operators in Australia at the time (ibid.: 13). Over the period 1985–1996, employment in Australian small business grew at an annual rate of 3.6 per cent. This figure contrasts sharply with the slow employment growth – 0.7 per cent per annum over the same period – in Australia's big-business sector (Burton et al. 1995; see also Chapter 11 on Austria in this book).

Women own an increasing number of these new small businesses in Australia (Roofey et al. 1996), as in many other Western countries (Allen and Trueman 1993). At present, about one in three small-business entrepreneurs in Australia are female. It is estimated that female entrepreneurs in small businesses contribute 10 to 15 per cent of the Australian non-government output and contribute 20 per cent of the private-sector net employment in Australia (Small Business Deregulation Task Force 1996: 13). Many of these new female entrepreneurs in Australia are immigrants. Moreover, small businesses owned by female entrepreneurs have experienced the fastest growth rate in Australia in the 1990s (Roofey et al. 1996).

One of the keys factors in the apparent revival of self-employment is the important role immigrant entrepreneurs played in major capitalist societies in the post-war decades. This is evident in the Australian case, as the remainder of this chapter demonstrates.

Immigrant Entrepreneurship in Australia
Reviewing the US experience, Portes and Rumbaut (1990: 21) argue that 'entrepreneurial minorities are the exception in both turn-of-the-century and contemporary migrations'. If that is the case, ethnic business played a more significant role in the early years of Australian immigration than in other countries. Ethnic business has a long history in Australia. From the earliest days of the nineteenth

century, immigrants of non-English speaking background moved into entrepreneurship. This is particularly true of immigrants from China (Choi 1975; Wang 1988; Yuan 1988), Greece (Price 1963), Italy (Collins 1992; Pascoe 1988, 1990) and Lebanon (McKay and Batrouney 1988), and Jewish immigrants also exhibited high rates of entrepreneurship (Glezer 1988; Rubenstein 1988; Rutland 1988). These are the immigrant entrepreneurs who settled earlier in Australia. For example, it is estimated that a century ago, 85 per cent of the first-generation Greeks in Sydney owned or worked in cafés, milk bars, fish and chip shops and other small businesses (Wilton and Bosworth 1984: 102).

Immediately before the mass post-war immigration programme, these and other ethnic groups were more likely to be classified as entrepreneurs than as wage-labourers. By 1947 more than half the immigrants born in Greece, Poland and Italy, and more than a third of those born in Germany, Malta and the former Yugoslavia, were self-employed or employers, compared to only a fifth of the Australian-born (Collins 1991: 89–90).

In the post-war period, the rate of immigrant entrepreneurship fell, with most immigrants taking up wage-labour. But immigrant entrepreneurship remained very significant. Today about a quarter of Australia's small businesses are owned and operated by first-generation immigrant men and women. In 1991, 88,363 first-generation immigrant males were employers, comprising 25.3 per cent of all the male employers in Australia. In addition 141,257 first-generation immigrant males were self-employed, accounting for 27.8 per cent of the self-employed males (ABS 1996). Similarly, in 1991 38,662 first-generation immigrant women comprised a quarter (25 per cent) of the female employers in Australia and 65,673 were self-employed, 26.5 per cent of the Australian total (ibid.). These figures do not include second-generation immigrants in small business, so they underestimate the full extent of immigrant entrepreneurship in Australia.

The ethnic diversity of Australian society is reflected in the ethnic diversity of Australian entrepreneurship. Census data from 1996 (see Table 4.1) shows that some immigrant groups such as the Koreans, Taiwanese, Greeks, Italians, Dutch and Germans have at least a 50 per cent higher presence as entrepreneurs compared to that of the Australian-born. The Korean-born have the highest rate of entrepreneurship, with nearly double the Australian-born rate (Collins et al. 1995b: 84–90). A similar pattern emerges among female entrepreneurs in Australia. Immigrant women born in Korea, Greece, Italy, Germany, the Netherlands, Czechoslovakia, Hungary and Taiwan demonstrate the highest rate of female entrepreneurship in Australia. Korean-born women exhibit a presence among the female self-employed that is almost three times that of Australian-born women.

But other groups of immigrants – those born in China, Singapore, Malaysia, Egypt, Lebanon, Poland, Ukraine and the former Yugoslavia – have similar rates

Table 4.1 Rates of Entrepreneurship in Australia, Selected Birthplace Groups, Persons

Birthplace	Rate of entrepreneurship %
Over-represented	
Korea	12.5
Greece	11.5
Italy	11.2
Israel	10.7
Cyprus	10.3
Lebanon	9.1
Similar representation	
England	8.8
China	8.1
New Zealand	7.8
Australia	7.6
Canada	7.0
Pakistan	6.3
Under-represented	
Turkey	5.8
Singapore	5.7
Vietnam	5.3
Taiwan	5.0
Sri Lanka	3.6

Source: 1996 National Census.

of entrepreneurship compared to the Australian average. Moreover, immigrants from Japan, India, Sri Lanka, Vietnam, Indonesia and Turkey have lower than average rates of entrepreneurship. ESB immigrant groups, such as those born in the United Kingdom, New Zealand, Canada and the United States, also have rates of entrepreneurship very similar to those of the Australian-born. Ethnicity overrides gender in this respect, with similar rates of entrepreneurship for males and females from the same country.

Immigrant entrepreneurs in Australia are distributed across all the industries, with a particular presence in the retail industry where ethnic niches have emerged. These niche markets derive from specific culinary traditions, specialist trade skills, or by chance (Collins et al. 1995b: 44–6). Data for the largest Australian State, New South Wales, show that half the entrepreneurs in the 'fish shop, take away food', 'food stores, grocers' and 'fruit, vegetable' sections of the retail industry are first-generation immigrants. Other parts of the retail industry such as clothing and footwear shops, service stations, watchmakers and jewellers, and bread and cake shops also have a relatively high immigrant presence. Immigrant entrepreneurs are least represented in general stores, tyre and battery stores, milk and bread vendors, newsagents and booksellers and pharmacies (ibid.: 76–83).

The most prominent immigrant entrepreneurs in the retail industry are those born in Greece, Lebanon, Italy, the United Kingdom and Ireland, the Middle East, China and Hong Kong. Italian immigrants have an ethnic niche as owners of fruit and vegetable stores. While they comprise less than 2 per cent of the total population, the Italian-born comprise 22.2 per cent of the total employers and 18 per cent of the self-employed in fruit and vegetable shops in NSW. Greeks alone account for one in five of the entrepreneurs in the 'fish shops and take-away food and milk bars' industry. Immigrant entrepreneurs from Lebanon are prominent in the service-station industry, and entrepreneurs born in Vietnam, China and Hong Kong as well as Italy and the United Kingdom are prominent in the retail clothing industry. In the smash-repair industry many entrepreneurs were born in Italy, the United Kingdom and Ireland, the Middle East, Lebanon and New Zealand.

Finally, many immigrant entrepreneurs have restaurants in Australian cities and towns (Collins and Castillo 1998). By the mid-1980s, Chinese restaurants and cafés were a feature of the Australian suburban and country town landscape (Chin 1988) and most suburbs and towns had a Greek milk bar to sell sweets, drinks and meals (Collins et al. 1995b: 61–5). These ethnic entrepreneurs were the vanguard of cultural diversity in Australian suburbs and country towns. Today most Australian suburbs and country towns have 'ethnic' restaurants, the most visible feature of Australian cosmopolitanism. Most immigrant groups have a presence in the restaurant sector, with Italian, Chinese, Thai, Vietnamese, Japanese and French cuisines being very popular.

Importing Immigrant Entrepreneurs

The newest type of immigrant entrepreneur in Australia is the business migrant. The Australian business-migration scheme dates back to the early 1980s. Over the period from 1982 to 1990, the major source countries for new business migrants were Hong Kong (32 per cent), Taiwan (15 per cent), Malaysia (12 per cent), the United Kingdom (8 per cent), Indonesia (6 per cent) and Singapore (5 per cent) (The Parliament of the Commonwealth of Australia 1991: 30). By 1996/7, the business-skills intake increased to 5,600, or 8.4 per cent of the total for all the immigration categories (Castles et al. 1998: 11).

In August 1991 a report found that 45 per cent of the business migrants had established businesses within one year after their arrival and that 61 per cent had done so after two years, with less than a third of these businesses claiming to be export-oriented. The average employment generated was six persons per business, while half the businesses were in the services industry (DILGEA 1991a, b).

In one of the few Australian studies of Asian business migrants, Pe-Pua et al. (1996) studied the ethnic Chinese from Hong Kong. They are termed *astronauts* because they spend so much time in the air flying from Australia (and Canada) to Hong Kong and back (Chan 1990). Their children are called *parachute children* because they often spend time alone in Australia as their parents commute to Australia and Asia (Mak and Chan 1995). The study observes that these Hong Kong business migrants mainly operate businesses in the import-export trade. For example, one Hong Kong astronaut exports seafood to Hong Kong, and others import garments, textiles and toys made in China. Other Hong Kong astronauts run retail outlets, restaurants, manufacturing firms (textiles, clothing, leather, jewellery, toys, electronic parts, electrical appliances) and travel agencies. All of these business migrants continue to run their business activities in Hong Kong, China and Taiwan. Most return to Hong Kong to run their businesses (Pe-Pua et al. 1996: 43, 47).

Research into Ethnic Entrepreneurship in Australia

While Australian immigration has been subject to comprehensive research (Wooden et al. 1994), there was relatively little research on ethnic entrepreneurship in Australia (Strahan and Williams 1988) before the late 1980s. There have been a handful of major studies since then. Collins et al. (1995b) surveyed 280 immigrant entrepreneurs in Sydney in the late 1980s and early 1990s, and Collins et al. (1997) surveyed more than 1,500 ethnic entrepreneurs in Sydney, Melbourne and Perth in 1996. The immigrant entrepreneurs surveyed in both surveys were from Southern Europe, the Middle East, Asia, Latin America and the United Kingdom. In both cases, large numbers of female entrepreneurs and a large control group were included in the fieldwork. Lever-Tracy et al. (1991) surveyed 104 Chinese and 40 Indian entrepreneurs with retail businesses (including take-away food shops), restaurants, wholesale businesses, property and business services, and health in Brisbane and Sydney. Stromback and Malhotra (1994) surveyed 45 South Asians who were business-owners in the Western Australian capital city of Perth. Lampugnani and Holton (1989) surveyed 98 Italian entrepreneurs across a broad span of industry types in South Australia, and Kermond et al. (1991) investigated specific issues related to immigrant businesswomen in Australia, with an emphasis on finance and education.

The major international study of ethnic entrepreneurs (Waldinger et al. 1990a) emphasizes the need for a model of ethnic entrepreneurship that looks at the interaction of the *group characteristics* of immigrants and the *opportunity structures* that they face in their new country. While path-breaking, there are important shortcomings of this model or theory of ethnic entrepreneurship. First,

Waldinger et al. attempt to identify 'ethnic' business strategies or dynamics without comparing them to the activities of 'non-ethnic' entrepreneurs. Second, they do not devote enough attention to explaining different rates of ethnic entrepreneurship. Third, female ethnic entrepreneurship and the gender dimensions of immigrant entrepreneurship are not given sufficient emphasis. Fourth, they do not sufficiently recognize the diversity of paths and experiences of immigrant entrepreneurship. Fifth, they do not place sufficient weight on the influence of the state in shaping entrepreneurial outcomes. And finally, Waldinger et al. fail to sufficiently emphasize how complex and changing patterns of globalization and racialization shape immigrant entrepreneurship and the dynamics and characteristics of immigrant entrepreneurs (Collins et al. 1995b: 34–8).

One key fact that emerges from the Australian experience is the increasing diversity of the paths to immigrant entrepreneurship. Some immigrants arrive in Australia as successful business migrants with ample start-up capital. Immigrants with professional skills move into professional businesses, and others tread the 'traditional' path from low-wage jobs to entrepreneurship. Finally, some immigrants see entrepreneurship as an alternative to unemployment, with some unemployed immigrants taking part in the federal government's New Enterprise Incentive Scheme which encourages the unemployed to establish business enterprises (Department of Employment, Education and Training and Youth Affairs 1995). There is also a great diversity of education levels and class backgrounds among the immigrant entrepreneurs in Australia. Theories of immigrant entrepreneurship need to explain these diverse, uneven and changing patterns of immigrant entrepreneurship such as the ones that are evident in Australia.

Despite this diversity in class and ethnic resources (Light and Rosenstein 1995) exhibited by Australia's immigrant entrepreneurs, Australia's NESB immigrant entrepreneurs do have something in common: they are part of a racialized 'Other'. One of the main reasons for the relatively high rates of entrepreneurship among some NESB immigrant groups is not a cultural tendency of immigrants toward entrepreneurship but a response by many NESB immigrants to blocked-mobility. This explains the high entrepreneurship rate of immigrants born in countries such as Greece, Italy, Hungary, Taiwan or Korea. The low entrepreneurship rates of NESB immigrants from India, Malaysia or Singapore, also racialized immigrant minorities, is explained by the access of highly educated Asian immigrants to primary labour-market jobs. Other racialized immigrant minorities from Vietnam, Indonesia or Turkey have low entrepreneurship rates, but as these immigrants are generally unskilled they still experience blocked-mobility in the form of high unemployment rates as globalization eliminates or further marginalizes Australian manual and manufacturing jobs. As the opportunity structures for these NESB immigrants have deteriorated, they have found it much harder to earn sufficient start-up capital to move into entrepreneurship.

Lever-Tracy et al. (1991) also provide evidence to support the racialized blocked-mobility theory. They report that Chinese and Indian business-owners are faced with 'a residue of prejudice and discrimination and a battery of obstacles to the recognition of overseas qualifications' (ibid.: ix). Stromback and Malhotra (1994) also reinforce the 'blocked-mobility' hypothesis, with many entrepreneurs reporting difficulties in having their qualifications recognized in Australia and in gaining access to professional bodies, thus preventing them from fully utilizing their skills in Australia: 'As a result of such problems many South Asians start their own businesses' (ibid.: x–xi).

Ethnic Resources

Another theme in the international literature on ethnic entrepreneurship (Waldinger et al. 1990a) relates to the importance of the family and the co-ethnic community as a source of financing and employment and as a customer base and support for ethnic entrepreneurs, a phenomenon that Light and Rosenstein (1995) label *ethnic resources*. Australian research has supported this finding. Lever-Tracy et al. (1991) note that 80 per cent of the Brisbane entrepreneurs they surveyed use family labour, including spouses, children and other extended-family members. Family members are regarded as trustworthy and committed to the business. Stromback and Malhotra (1994: 13) also note the importance of 'a cooperative network of family and community', the importance of family labour, and the trustworthiness of family members for South Asian enterprises in Perth. Lampugnani and Holton (1989: 17) report that while most of the Italian entrepreneurs they surveyed rely on banks and not their families to finance their business, the family is described as 'the major cultural resource', providing partners and labour for the majority of the businesses surveyed.

Research in the late 1980s and early 1990s highlighted the importance of family labour in immigrant enterprises and noted that immigrant entrepreneurs in Sydney rely heavily on the family for financing, employment and general business support (Collins et al. 1995b). Similarly, a 1996 survey notes that just over a third of the businesses run by NESB immigrant men and half of the businesses run by NESB women report that between 75 and 100 per cent of their staff are family members: 80 per cent of the businesses run by South American women and 60 per cent of the businesses owned by Asian women report that family members fill between 75 and 100 per cent of all the jobs, as do those of half the South American male entrepreneurs (Collins et al. 1997). However, the importance of family is not confined to ethnic entrepreneurs: the control sample of third- or later-generation Australian (non-immigrant) entrepreneurs shows they also rely heavily on family resources, though to a lesser degree than immigrant entrepreneurs (ibid.). This demonstrates the importance of a control sample of non-immigrant entrepreneurs to help identify the extent to which these 'distinctive' traits of immigrant entrepreneurs are merely a generic characteristic of entrepreneurship per se irrespective of ethnic background.

Another dimension of ethnic resources relates to co-ethnic employment in immigrant enterprises. Williams (1992: 91) notes that in immigrant-owned firms over 85 per cent of the workers are immigrants, yet immigrant workers comprise just over 20 per cent of the workers in small businesses owned by Australian-born entrepreneurs. This finding is confirmed by other Australian research. Stromback and Malhotra (1994: 14) note that South Asian entrepreneurs in Perth create an average of just over four jobs per business. Of these, relatives fill half the jobs and 'co-ethnics' most of the rest. Similarly, Lever-Tracy et al. (1991) note that the family is a critical source of labour, with the Indian entrepreneurs in particular relying on tight-knit extended family solidarity and community networks as an important business resource. Collins et al. (1997) also observed a strong trend for immigrant entrepreneurs to employ co-ethnics with family and community networks accounting for half of the employment in enterprises owned by Middle Eastern, Asian and Latin American-born immigrants.

Another aspect of the ethnic resources of immigrant entrepreneurs in Australia relates to the nature of their customer base. Patterns of immigrant settlement are often linked to the growth of immigrant entrepreneurship. Urban ethnic ghettos and enclaves are strongly associated with the emergence of ethnic enterprise in North America, with the Cubans in Miami an often-cited example (Portes and Rumbaut 1990; Wilson and Martin 1982). In contrast, diversity and geographic mobility are key features of immigrant settlement patterns in Australian cities (Burnley 2000) with immigrant communities of diverse backgrounds sharing areas of high immigrant concentration, so that no one ethnic group dominates and no ethnic ghettos emerge (Jupp et al. 1991).

This is not to say that more than a century of ethnic entrepreneurship has not left its mark on Australian cities. Ethnic precincts, like Chinatown, Little Italy and Little Korea as well as multi-ethnic 'Asia towns' have emerged in downtown and suburban areas of Sydney (Collins and Castillo 1998) and Melbourne (Collins et al. 2001). These ethnic precincts developed their ethnic identity via the entrepreneurs who own the businesses in these suburbs rather than by immigrant settlement patterns.

While there are no ethnic enclaves in Australian cities, there certainly are ethnic market niches. Co-ethnic customers provide more than half the custom of one in three businesses in Sydney owned by immigrant entrepreneurs while for another one in three immigrant enterprises co-ethnics account for only a tenth of the custom. (Collins et al. 1995b: 153–4). Lever-Tracy et al. (1991) also observe that the extent of co-ethnic custom varies in Sydney and Brisbane and within groups of ethnic entrepreneurs in both cities. Lampugnani and Holton (1989) noted that while 'a certain enclave sector still exists', most Italian businesses in South Australia 'did not stay in the enclave or ghetto, but moved beyond it'. This suggests a diversity of experience among ethnic entrepreneurs in Australia in regard to the ethnic niche, with some entrepreneurs breaking out of captive markets while others are still highly dependent on them. In some instances, the experiences of entrepreneurs from the same immigrant groups demonstrate both breakout and ethnic-niche strategies. For example, many Chinese entrepreneurs in Sydney use Chinatown as their economic base, while others, particularly restaurant-owners, were based for decades in surrounding Sydney suburbs and rural towns.

Immigrant entrepreneurs also play a significant role in import and export trade. Lever-Tracy et al. (1991: 113) concluded that Chinese and Indian immigrant enterprises are 'successful, innovative and export oriented' while Collins et al. (1997) found that Asian entrepreneurs reported the highest rate of import and export trade of all those surveyed, including the control sample. Overseas networks of family and friends help develop the trading links of ethnic entrepreneurs, and represent another dimension of the ethnic resources of immigrant entrepreneurs in Australia.

Class Resources

Another theme in the international literature relates to the importance of factors related to social class and *class resources* (Light and Gold 2000; Light and Rosenstein 1995) in understanding the rates of immigrant entrepreneurship. One dimension is the class background of immigrant entrepreneurs, and another is the education or human capital of immigrant entrepreneurs, which is highly correlated to their class background. Australian studies have investigated this aspect.

Class resources play an important role in the path to entrepreneurship. Many Chinese and Indian entrepreneurs in Brisbane and Sydney had business experience prior to emigration and half of those surveyed arrived with substantial resources and had expected to set up a business once they arrived in Australia (Lever-Tracy et al. 1991). Stromback and Malhotra (1994: 13) also note that many immigrant entrepreneurs in Perth continued the business tradition they had in countries such as Fiji, Malaysia and Singapore where they had experience as minority traders before migrating to Australia. On the other hand, there is a great diversity in the class backgrounds of immigrant entrepreneurs in Australia. Just under half (47 per cent) of the immigrant entrepreneurs surveyed in Sydney in the late 1980s and early 1990s were from working-class families where the father was a blue-collar worker employed in the occupations of 'tradespersons', 'machine operator and driver' and 'labourer, unskilled' (Collins et al. 1995b). For these immigrant entrepreneurs, their move to entrepreneurship

represents upward class mobility from the working class to the petite bourgeoisie. Similarly, data from the 1996 survey of immigrant and non-immigrant
entrepreneurs in Sydney, Melbourne and Perth show that very few, generally
less than 10 per cent, of the immigrant entrepreneurs surveyed reported that
they had a family business background (Collins et al. 1997). This finding gives
some qualified support to the argument of Bechhofer and Elliot (1981) that the
petite bourgeoisie does not reproduce itself, though further research into
second-generation immigrant entrepreneurs is required before firm conclusions
can be made in this regard.

As Light and Rosenstein (1995) argue, education is one of the key markers of
social class and the human and cultural capital acquired through education is one
of the main class resources of immigrants. There has been some research into the
adequacy of the educational background of immigrant entrepreneurs in Australia
(Flatau and Hemmings 1991; Zinopoulos 1992). In one of the few Australian
studies on female immigrant entrepreneurs, Kermond et al. (1991) argue that
they do not have an adequate educational level to succeed as entrepreneurs.
However, findings from the 1996 national survey of ethnic entrepreneurs do not
support this conclusion. This study notes a great diversity of educational background: one in four had university degrees and another one in four did not finish
secondary school (Collins et al. 1997). This finding clouds the relationship
between the class resources of immigrants and their rates of entrepreneurship,
suggesting that not all immigrant entrepreneurs take the same route to entrepreneurship.

The lesson from the Australian immigrant entrepreneur experience is that
theories of ethnic entrepreneurship need to be able to account for diverse,
changing paths to immigrant entrepreneurship. They need to reflect on how
changing patterns of globalization and racialization are impacting the group
characteristics of new immigrants and the opportunity structures they face in
Australia. They need to investigate the complex and uneven patterns of class and
ethnic resources among different immigrant groups and within specific ones.
Theories of immigrant entrepreneurs also need to reflect on the growth of female
entrepreneurship and the critical role of gender and the family in understanding
the dynamics of immigrant entrepreneurship. They also need to consider how
state regulations, practices and policies impact on immigrants.

Immigrant Entrepreneurs Down Under

Immigrant entrepreneurs have a long history in Australia and play a significant
role in the contemporary Australian economy and society. Nevertheless
Australian immigration has been highly contested, with many critics' questioning
of the economic and social merits of Australian immigration (Blainey 1984;

Joske 1989; One Nation 1998; Rimmer 1991). Most attention has been placed on the economic, social and environmental impact of immigration, yet the contribution and impact of immigrant entrepreneurs has been generally ignored or downplayed in these debates. This partly stems from the dominance of neoclassical economics, which deals very inadequately with cultural diversity, and from the dominance of economic rationalist policy perspectives in the major Australian political parties. The Right opposes Asian immigration, while on the Left the Australian labour movement is also less than enthusiastic about immigration.

To date there has been little by way of policy development specifically for immigrant entrepreneurs in Australia (Holton 1988; Strahan and Luscombe 1991). No Australian federal or state government has developed policies specifically designed to address the needs of immigrant entrepreneurs. However, because of some of the research cited in this chapter – which has clearly pointed to the significance of the economic and social contribution of immigrant entrepreneurs – Australian federal and state governments are now attempting to develop a policy response. It is too early to tell how effective these policy developments will be in making the path to entrepreneurship in Australia easier for immigrants.

The Australian research highlights a number of issues relevant to the theory of immigrant or ethnic entrepreneurship. First, such theories must not only explain why some immigrant groups are over-represented as entrepreneurs, they must also allow for explanation of the under-representation of other immigrant groups. Claims about 'ethnic business strategies' can only be made when comparing immigrant to non-immigrant entrepreneurs. Theories of immigrant or ethnic entrepreneurship must investigate how the complex and changing dynamics of racialization and globalization shape the opportunity structures of immigrant minorities in Australia, blocking mobility into the mainstream labour market for some but allowing others to enter the primary labour market. The critical role of gender and the family in shaping the immigrant enterprise must also play a prominent role in such theories, particularly given the growth in female immigrant entrepreneurship and the key role of the family in enterprises owned by male immigrants. In addition, the diversity of paths to entrepreneurship – from the unemployed to millionaires to the many positions between – must be centrally addressed in theories of ethnic or immigrant entrepreneurship.

Finally, the role of the state is also a critical factor to be considered in theories of ethnic or immigrant entrepreneurship. As Kloosterman and Rath (2001b) point out, the interactive model of Waldinger and his colleagues does not give sufficient emphasis to the role of the state and the way in which formal and informal regimes of regulation from different levels of the state apparatus shape ethnic entrepreneurial outcomes. They call for a 'mixed embeddedness' approach to the study of ethnic entrepreneurship, and stress the importance of under-standing how direct and indirect regulations – as well as their level of enforce-ment – shape entrepreneurial behaviour in different ways in different countries. This 'mixed embeddedness' approach is obviously important for an under-standing of immigrant entrepreneurship in Australia, where the state – at the federal, state and local levels – develops a range of institutional structures, poli-cies, practices, procedures and by-laws that directly or indirectly shape the opportunities for entrepreneurs.

Note

1. In the United States and other countries, self-employment refers to sole oper-ators or own-account employees as well as enterprises with employees. In Australia the census uses the categories *self-employed* and *employers*. Self-employed are defined as those in independent or own-account employment without any workers, while small business is defined as all those non-agri-cultural employers with twenty or fewer workers except in the manufacturing industry, where firms with 100 or fewer employees are described as small.

–5–

South Africa: Creating New Spaces?

Sally Peberdy and Christian M. Rogerson

Introduction

South Africa has experienced unprecedented political, social and economic change over the past two decades.[1] The Afrikaner nationalist dream of 'separate development', the notion of South Africa as a community of 'nations' destined to live in separate and eventually 'independent' territories, collapsed under the weight of resistance and its own contradictions. By the end of 1986, although black, coloured and Indian South Africans were still excluded by the state from meaningful political and economic participation, apartheid legislation had undergone certain reforms. The apartheid project was all but over by 1990 and in 1994 South Africa's first democratic parliament was elected. For the first time since the formation of South Africa in 1910, all South African nationals have the right to vote and participate in the life and affairs of the state, and have access to its resources. The new government is publicly committed to nation building and developing a culture of diversity and human rights. These changes have had a dramatic impact on South Africa's urban entrepreneurial and residential land-scapes, on relationships with other countries, on patterns of migration and on responses to them.

The relaxing and lifting of racial restrictions on residence and entrepreneurial activity in South Africa's cities, which started in 1986, changed South Africa's urban landscape, particularly in its largest city, Johannesburg. At the same time, changes in the economy led to the white capital and residential flight from the city centre. These changes have opened up new spaces for the entrepreneur, whether citizen, migrant or immigrant, in the formal and informal economies of the city (Bremner 2000; Morris 1999; Rogerson 1995, 1996, 1997, 1999b; Rogerson and Rogerson 1997, 1999; Simone 1997; Tomlinson and Rogerson 1999).

In 1986, the state removed the racially exclusionary clauses of immigration legislation, thus opening new sources of migration. Around the same time, as a way of evading sanctions, the apartheid government established relationships with certain African countries whose nationals were allowed to enter as temporary residents (Bouillon 1996, 1998; Peberdy 1999a). Under the post-1994 government, migration has become highly contested and often mired in xenophobic and exclusionary attitudes and sustained dependence on apartheid legislation. After six years of debate a new Immigration Control Act was finally passed in June 2002. However, owing to challenges to Regulations promulgated under the Act (in November 2002 and February 2003) it has yet to come into force at the time of writing.

The apparent development since 1994 of increasingly xenophobic discourses among some officials is also reflected in a shift in the public discourse (Crush 1999; Crush and McDonald 2000; Danso and McDonald 2000; Gunter 2001; Human Rights Watch 1998; Mattes et al. 1999; Morris 1998; Peberdy 1999a, 2001). Immigration is often presented as a new, growing, illegal and negative phenomenon, and largely African. The 'influx' is linked to the 1990 political liberalization and the formation of the 'new' South Africa in 1994. This surge of xenophobia has manifested itself in intermittent but persistent and at times fatal attacks by South Africans on non-South Africans, including vendors selling on South Africa's streets and railways. In August 1997, protests on the streets of Johannesburg against non-South African street vendors, led by various South African hawkers' associations, erupted into violence and intimidation (*The Star*, 14 August 1997). Demonstrators physically assaulted vendors, stole their merchandise and forced them from their stands, sometimes at gunpoint. Many vendors lost their stock as well as the sites allocated to them by the City Council. The attacks were accompanied by angry and vitriolic anti-immigrant rhetoric. Official responses were muted. In September 1998, two non-South African vendors, selling their merchandise on a suburban train in Pretoria, were killed following a demonstration by one of the groups representing unemployed people in South Africa (*The Star*, 4 September 1998). Intermittent organized and individual assaults on non-South African street vendors continued into 2002.

Set within this context of transition and rising xenophobia, this chapter presents the findings of nascent contemporary research on immigrant and migrant entrepreneurs from sub-Saharan Africa in South Africa's 'small, medium-sized and micro-enterprise economy' (SMME). The SMME economy includes a spectrum of enterprises from formal small and medium-sized enterprises, emerging micro-enterprises and informal enterprises (see Rogerson 2000a). The analysis starts by placing the development of new discourses around migration and immigration, particularly African immigrant and migrant entrepreneurs, in a historical context, identifying the massive changes in South Africa's immigration and entrepreneurial regimes over the past two decades. The focus shifts to discuss some of the findings of current research on migrant and immigrant entrepreneurs from sub-Saharan Africa in South Africa. Before concluding, the chapter examines how new research in South Africa challenges the territorially bounded conceptions of the informal-sector as well as the immobile category of 'immigrants'. Certainly within the South African context, many African 'immigrant' entrepreneurs are 'migrants' and more often than not, entrepreneurs from the region are involved in informal and formal cross-border trade and transnational entrepreneurial networks (see Peberdy and Rogerson 2000).

Overall, this chapter represents a synthesis of contemporary research focused on the activities of migrant entrepreneurs from sub-Saharan Africa. It does not encompass the experiences of new immigrant entrepreneurs in South Africa from Asia, Eastern Europe and the Indian sub-continent. Indeed, the latter categories appear to represent a much smaller visible percentage of contemporary entre-preneurial migrants, and are largely ignored in South Africa's official and unof-ficial anti-immigrant discourses, and by researchers. Our focus is thus squarely upon the major actors in terms of immigrant entrepreneurship in post-apartheid South Africa.

Setting the Scene

Immigration to South Africa

From the introduction of the first Immigration Act (in 1913) after the formation of South Africa in 1910 until 1986, black, Indian and other 'non-white' potential immigrants were prohibited from immigrating to South Africa by statute. However, some Africans from the region could enter as contract workers (usually to the mining sector) under what has been called the 'two gates system' (Cooper 1997; Crush 1997).[2] Many more Africans, again mostly from southern Africa, entered as undocumented migrants (Peberdy 1998, 1999a). The presence of African undocumented migrants was often sanctioned by the South African state (ibid.).

While excluding black immigrants, the white South African state often went out of its way to encourage white immigration, introducing a generous assisted immigration scheme for whites in 1961, which lasted until 1991 (Peberdy 1999a). However, at particular moments specific groups of white immigrants were unwelcome, including those who were likely to become small entrepreneurs (ibid.). Despite attempts to exclude small entrepreneurs, the legacies of past immigration policies can be seen in South Africa's corner cafés (shops) and small artisanal industries, which are still often run by Portuguese, Greek and Italian immigrants who arrived in the 1960s, 1970s and 1980s. Some have been taken over by Eastern European and Russian immigrants who arrived in the late 1980s and early 1990s.

In 1986, the government lifted the racial prohibitions to entry although the state was highly selective when choosing black immigrants. This dramatic change was not motivated by a wish to de-racialize immigration policy. Instead, it was prompted by the state's plans for the 'independent' and non-independent 'homelands', as it sought new sources of professional labour for 'black' hospitals, universities and schools and foreign investors willing to establish businesses in and around the 'homelands' (Rogerson 1986). The change opened South Africa to new sources of immigrants, particularly Eastern Europe and Asia. Many Taiwanese immigrants were welcomed because they were willing to set up businesses in and around the apartheid 'homelands' (ibid.; Tseng 1991).

In 1991, in one of the 'dying acts of apartheid,' immigration legislation was consolidated into the Aliens Control Act (Act No. 96) (Peberdy 1997a; 1998; Peberdy and Crush 1998a). The post-1994 immigration regime is still based on the 1991 Act, although it was amended in 1995 and 1996 to bring it in line with the new 1996 Constitution.[3] Nevertheless, post-1994 immigration policy has been accompanied by a significant change in attitude as well as practice, which are increasingly exclusionary and xenophobic, particularly toward other Africans (Crush 1999; Peberdy 1999a).

South Africa's contemporary immigration framework is largely hostile toward the entry of small entrepreneurs, and routes of entry for this category of immigrants and migrants are limited. Requirements for permanent residence for the self-employed place significant barriers in the way of small entrepreneurs, as applicants have to bring substantial capital and employ at least three South Africans within one year of their arrival. The entry of self-employed professionals is limited, lawyers have to be trained in Romen-Dutch law and non-South African medical professionals are not allowed to enter private practice until they have taken South African medical examinations. Applicants for immigration permits also have to pay an administration fee.

Most African migrant entrepreneurs, particularly in the informal-sector, appear to enter on visitors' visas, since business visas are largely reserved for professional contract workers (Peberdy and Crush 1998b). They do so with the tacit acceptance of immigration officials, who know they are entering to trade, although the visitors' visa does not allow them to trade (ARPAC 1999; Peberdy 1999b, 2000a, b). Others enter as genuine or fraudulent asylum-seekers (approximately 50 per cent of the claims are false) and refugees. Under the new refugee legislation (effective from April 2000), refugees may be self-employed but asylum-seekers may not be self-employed (or employed). South Africa does not provide any state support for refugees or asylum-seekers (limited support is provided by non-governmental organizations). As a result, and given the poor employment prospects, many refugees and asylum-seekers use self-employment and entrepreneurship as a means of survival (Gema 2001; Geyevu 1997; Majodina and Peberdy 2000; Peberdy 2000b; Peberdy and Majodina 2000; Timngum 2001).

Official estimates (based on very dubious data) of the number of undocumented migrants in South Africa are usually somewhere between 2.5 and 4.5 million (Crush 1999; McDonald et al. 1998: 8; Peberdy 1999a). The 1995 census suggests that these figures overestimate the number of undocumented migrants (Peberdy 1999a; RSA 1998). However, fraudulent South African documents are readily available and may be used by some entrepreneurs as a means to stay and do business in South Africa (Peberdy 1999b; Reitzes et al. 1997). Although undocumented migrants are certainly involved in entrepreneurial activities in South Africa, it is still difficult to operate a successful public business without the proper papers (Peberdy 1998a, 1999b; Reitzes et al. 1997).

Patterns of immigration have changed, and the total number of immigrants has dropped significantly since 1993 (see Table 5.1). While this may be due in part to a reduction in the number of applications, the rise in the number of rejected applications (see Table 5.2[4]) and the fall in immigration from Africa do suggest that the new government is imposing a stricter immigration regime than its apartheid predecessor. Despite the decrease in permanent immigration, there has been an increase in the number of migrants (documented and undocumented) and asylum-seekers since 1990 (Crush 1999; Peberdy 1999a). The increase,

Table 5.1 Permanent Residents (Immigrants), 1990–1999

Year	*Legal immigrants*	*African immigrants*
1990	14,499	1,628
1991	12,379	2,065
1992	8,686	1,266
1993	9,824	1,701
1994	6,398	1,628
1995	5,064	1,343
1996	5,407	1,601
1997	4,102	1,281
1998	4,371	1,169
1999	3,669	980

Source: DHA annual reports.

Table 5.2 Rejected Applications for Permanent Residence, 1990–1997

1990	*1991*	*1992*	*1993*	*1994*	*1995*	*1996*	*1997**
282	194	229	1,703	556	596	680	129

*January to September only.
Source: Peberby 1999a: 290.

particularly in undocumented migration, does not, however, appear to be as great as the state sometimes suggests. In fact, black Africans have migrated to work and trade in South Africa since the late 1800s, to say nothing of the pre-colonial movements.

While South Africa continues to receive African migrants from its traditional source, Southern Africa, since 1994 migrants from West and Central Africa have become increasingly visible on South Africa's streets. Many of these 'new immigrants' come from countries which had established links with the apartheid regime: the Democratic Republic of Congo (DRC), the Ivory Coast, Mali and Senegal (Bouillon 1996; Peberdy 1998; Simone 1998a, b). These 'new immigrants' are supplemented by others from West and East Africa, particularly Ghana, Nigeria and Kenya. Overall, it is difficult to estimate the size of this highly mobile 'new immigrant' population, since many of them enter as asylum-seekers or on temporary residence permits.

Changing Urban Entrepreneurial Landscapes

The post-1986 changes to the apartheid framework wrought massive changes on South Africa's cities, particularly after 1991. The urban and economic policies of the apartheid state encouraged racially separated urban spaces and 'white' cities. The relaxing of some of the racially exclusionary legislation in 1986 led to 'grey' areas in certain cities, particularly in South Africa's largest city, Johannesburg (Crankshaw and White 1992; Simone 1997, 1998a, b).

The lifting of racially exclusionary residential and business restrictions in 1990 led to rapid changes in the complexion of Johannesburg's city centre. Although the change has been so rapid, it is difficult to monitor: over the past eleven years an estimated 250,000 black people have moved into the central city area (Simone 1997: 253). This movement has changed the complexion of the Johannesburg inner city from 80 per cent white to 70 per cent black (ibid.: 256) and to a multicultural and multiracial space (Simone 1997, 1998b). Areas of the city that were traditionally home to South Africa's white immigrants and then urban black migrants now house new international immigrants, mainly from Africa.

The post-1986 changes, particularly the post-1990 changes, led to the deregulation of the entrepreneurial urban space (Rogerson 1995; Rogerson and Rogerson 1997). Apartheid urban planning policies kept small black entrepreneurs from establishing businesses in the city centre and limited the activities of informal-sector entrepreneurs (Rogerson and Rogerson 1997). Terminating these restrictions has remoulded the face of inner-city streets, which are now lined by informal-sector street vendors. In an attempt to move traders off the streets the Johannesburg Metropolitan Council has created various 'designated' markets. The CBD is also now home to new black entrepreneurs, artisans running small and medium-sized enterprises, retail as well as manufacturing, in premises recently left by white entrepreneurs (Rogerson 2000b).

Policy changes were not solely responsible for the changing entrepreneurial environment of the city centre. The economic recession led to diminishing labour-market opportunities for South Africans and non-South Africans alike, pushing many into survivalist informal-sector activities (Rogerson 1996, 1997, 1999a, b, 2000b; Rogerson and Rogerson 1997). The 1996 census found that 34 per cent of the working-age population (and 42.5 per cent of black South Africans) were unemployed (RSA 1998: 46–7).

At the same time, new labour regulations and tightening economic conditions led to the demise of many small manufacturers and the outsourcing of production to informal-sector producers, particularly in the clothing sector. 'White flight' from central Johannesburg, involving businesses and residents alike, has opened office, retail and residential space for South African and non-national entrepreneurs (Bremner 2000; Rogerson and Rogerson 1997; Tomlinson and Rogerson 1999). 'White flight' has been precipitated by resistance to living and working in mixed areas and for economic reasons, but the high crime rates in the city centre have also contributed to the changes in the residential and entrepreneurial spaces of central Johannesburg (Bremner 2000).

Simultaneously, the post-1994 government, in contrast to its predecessors, has identified the support and upgrading of black-owned small enterprises as a priority policy issue (Rogerson and Rogerson 1997). The government's plan for social and economic transformation emphasizes its 'commitment to uplifting the role of small, medium-sized and micro-enterprises' and suggests they represent an 'important vehicle to address the challenges of job creation, economic growth and equity' (see Rogerson 2000a). This commitment to encouraging small and medium-sized enterprise was realized in 1995 in an official White Paper on strategies for supporting SMMEs and enabling legislation (ibid.). While the legislation and policy encourage South African-owned business, and their impact on SMME growth is unclear, it is apparent that the new government has a much stronger commitment to developing, particularly black-owned, SMMEs (ibid.).

Local and provincial government officials have shown a generally benign attitude toward the presence of documented non-South African SMME and informal-sector entrepreneurs in Johannesburg (Mushonga 2000; Peberdy and Crush 1998b; Rogerson 1997, 2000b). Following the attacks on street vendors, the former Premier of the Gauteng Province (where Johannesburg is located) said, '[t]hose who are in South Africa for business and other trade-related issues should not be viewed negatively, as long as they abide by the laws of the country' (cited in Rogerson 1997: 7). Similarly, Metropolitan Council officials do not seem to discriminate between nationals and non-nationals in the allocation of stalls and all vendors (regardless of nationality but with preference for nationals) are being moved into 'designated markets' (Mushonga 2000; Peberdy and Crush 1998b).

Non-national African Entrepreneurs

Research

Despite the attitudes of local and provincial government officials, post-1994 official and unofficial migration discourses are dominated by often hostile debates about migration and immigration from Africa. The new interest of the South African state in immigration and migration issues is reflected in a growth of research on contemporary immigration and migration policy.[5] Specific research on migrant and immigrant entrepreneurs is, however, extremely limited and focuses on small and medium-sized enterprises and informal-sector retail and cross-border trade (Gaoyu 1996; Mbaya 1999; Nethengwe 1999; Parsley 1998; Peberdy 1997b, 1999b, 2000a, b; Peberdy and Crush 1998b, 2001; Peberdy and Rogerson 2000; Peberdy et al. 2000a, b; Reitzes et al. 1997; Rogerson 1997, 1999a, b, c). Reflecting the state and public concern over migration from Africa, with the exception of Gaoyu (1996), these studies centre on migrant entrepreneurs from sub-Saharan Africa. This research focus on immigrant and migrant entrepreneurship is new to South Africa. Studies have focused on informing policy-makers and situating the research in local debates about the place of South Africa in globalization, transnationalism, and the move to a regional free-trade zone. Given the focus of the research and its still limited scope, it has not yet involved theoretical debates around immigrant entrepreneurship.

Beyond the research examined in this chapter, the entrepreneurial activities of immigrants, migrants and asylum-seekers who arrived in the post-apartheid years appear as peripheral issues in studies of the lives of (usually African) non-nationals in South Africa (Gema 2001; Geyevu 1997; Maharaj and Moodley 2000; Maharaj and Rajkumar 1997; Majodina and Peberdy 2000; Peberdy and Majodina 2000; Sungkekang 1998; Timngum 2001; Tseng 1991) and of changes in the country's urban entrepreneurial landscapes (Bremner 2000; Holness et al. 1999; Jennings et al. 1995a, b; Morris 1999; Mushonga 2000; Reitzes et al. 1997; J. Rogerson 1995; C. Rogerson 2000a, b; Rogerson and Rogerson 1997). Other contemporary non-national entrepreneurs appear in migration studies originating in their countries of origin (Frayne and Pendleton 1998; McDonald 2000; McDonald et al. 1998; Oucho et al. 2000). Little is known about the entrepreneurial activities of relatively recent non-African immigrants (but see Gaoyu 1996; Tseng 1991). Notwithstanding the limitations of this still small body of literature, it challenges generally held conceptions about African immigrants and migrants as well as conceptions of the informal sector.

Although limited, this nascent body of research represents a change. Despite the visible presence of migrant and immigrant entrepreneurs (and professionals) in national groups that arrived in the past (Eastern European Jews, Portuguese, Italians, Greeks and post-Communist Eastern European arrivals, and undocumented Africans), no specific studies have been conducted on their entrepreneurial activities (see however Boiskin 1993; Spanoudes 1982; Titlestad 1991). Entrepreneurs do, however, appear as sidebars in studies of specific white communities (Akenson 1990; Basson 1988; Bradlow 1994; Brownell 1985; Candy 1988; Dubb 1994; Kaplan 1986; Mantzaris 1978; Martin 1986, 1987; Saron and Hotz 1955; Stone 1973). Historical studies of South Africa's Indian and Chinese communities (most of whom arrived as indentured labourers) sometimes identify entrepreneurial activities (Arkin et al. 1989; Bhana and Brain 1990; Harris 1994; Human 1984; Yap and Man 1996), as do other urban histories (van Onselen 1982). Non-national African female entrepreneurs also appear in regional historiographies (Bonner 1990; Cockerton 1995; Miles 1991). Little is said in this literature about the activities of these migrant entrepreneurs – they appear but are not central to the literature.

This section of the chapter is based primarily on the findings of six recent studies on migrant and immigrant entrepreneurs from sub-Saharan Africa, including three studies of small and medium-sized entrepreneurs (Rogerson 1997, 1999b, c). They first interviewed seventy migrant entrepreneurs across a wide spectrum of activities (Rogerson 1997). The latter two interviewed sixty-two and thirty-six clothing manufacturers respectively (Rogerson 1999b, c). The three other studies focused on street vendors from southern Africa and informal-sector cross-border trade (ARPAC 1999; Peberdy 1999b; Peberdy and Crush 1998b; see also Peberdy 2000a, b, Peberdy et al. 2000a, b). The first study includes interviews with some 112 African migrant or immigrant street vendors in the handicraft and curio sectors in Johannesburg and Cape Town (Peberdy 1997b; Peberdy and Crush 1998b). Of these, some 70 per cent were directly involved in informal cross-border trade as an integral part of their business (ibid.). The last two were parallel studies conducted in Johannesburg and Maputo, exploring informal cross-border trade relationships between the two countries through in-depth interviews with a total of ninety-four Mozambican cross-border and street vendors (ARPAC 1999; Peberdy 1999b).[6]

The research used here challenges conceptions of participants in the informal-sector and informal-sector trade. The majority of participants are not at the extremes of economic margins; they hold valid permits to cross borders, and tend to hold valid trading permits where possible and required. They tend to employ non-family members rather than family members. Their activities cross the boundaries of the formal and informal-sectors as goods are sourced and sold in both and many traders only buy and sell in the formal sector. This suggests that their activities may be better classified as SMME cross-border trade.

Most of the research presented here also challenges commonly held perceptions of African migrants and immigrants in South Africa, which suggest that they are poorly educated, economically deprived (if not destitute), a drain on South Africa's social and economic resources and undocumented. In contrast, these studies suggest that African migrant entrepreneurs are relatively well-educated and capitalized, contribute to the South African economy, and make few demands on social services (ARPAC 1999; Peberdy 1999b; Peberdy and Crush 1998b; Peberdy and Rogerson 2000; Rogerson 1997, 1998). Furthermore, it indicates that most cross-border traders enter the country with passports and permits through border posts (although they may evade some if not all duties on the goods they carry). They represent a group of 'smart' entrepreneurs able to respond to the challenges of globalization (see Peberdy and Rogerson 2000).

Participation in Small and Medium-sized Enterprises

African immigrant and migrant entrepreneurs with small and medium-sized enterprises in South Africa participate in retail, service and production activities but appear to be centred in the retail and service sectors (Rogerson 1997, 1998, 1999b, c). Participants in the SMME sector include migrants from the Southern African Development Community (SADC) as well as non-SADC countries. Overall, participants in recent studies on migrant participation in SMMEs included foreign migrants from fifteen different African countries, highlighting the attraction of Johannesburg for migrant entrepreneurs from other parts of Africa (Rogerson 1997, 1999b).

The research suggests that African non-nationals in this sector are most likely to be involved in two specific areas of production: clothing manufacture and automobile repairs and maintenance (ibid.). These production activities were supplemented by miscellaneous groups of producers involved in belt-making, the production of wire goods, wooden curios and stone carving (ibid.).

Clothing manufacture offers particular opportunities for migrant entrepreneurs. Recent findings on the dynamics of industrial change in the Witwatersrand between 1980 and 1994 show that the local clothing economy has been in a state of decline, losing almost 40 per cent of its clothing employment base and 35 per cent of its factory establishments (Rogerson 1999c). Despite this decline, new opportunities have arisen for small-scale clothing enterprises in Johannesburg, particularly as many larger formal manufacturers appear to be outsourcing production activities to SMMEs (Rogerson 2000b).

Migrant entrepreneurs do not yet seem to be major participants in the outsourcing of clothing manufacture. Nevertheless, recent studies confirm that they are involved in a wide range of clothing-production activities including tailoring, dressmaking, specialized embroidery and the production of men's and women's garments, often with a 'traditional' West African motif (Rogerson 1999c). The makers of 'traditional' clothing produce clothing which was not previously widely available in South Africa but nonetheless seems to have a significant market. The fabric is often imported, and the skills involved, particularly embroidery, create a specialized niche in the clothing industry for these migrant entrepreneurs.

Distinct clusters have emerged in the kinds of SMME businesses operated by migrants from particular countries. In one study, over 50 per cent of the participants in clothing production were from West Africa and 36 per cent came from Malawi (Rogerson 1999b). West and Central Africans also gravitate toward clothes, music and food retailing as well as the operation of restaurants and clubs (Rogerson 1997). These entrepreneurs tend to specialize in supplying food, music and clothes from their home countries or regions. Those involved in automobiles repairs and maintenance tend to come from Zimbabwe and Mozambique, while those involved in producing wire products and curios come from Malawi and Zimbabwe (Rogerson 1997, 1999b).

Participation in Informal Sector Retailing and Cross-border Trade

Most migrant and immigrant entrepreneurs in the informal-sector appear to be involved in buying and selling, particularly on the street. Those in the retailing informal-sector fall into four sometimes overlapping categories: mobile street traders, street traders, street traders involved in cross-border trade, and cross-border traders (Peberdy 1997b, 2000a, b). Immigrants, migrants, refugees and asylum-seekers are found selling handicrafts and curios, wire goods, crocheted doilies and bedspreads, handbags, watches, shoes, 'traditional dresses', traditional cloth, cosmetics, fruits and vegetables and other food products on South Africa's city streets.

Despite their seemingly static poses behind their stands, many street traders (particularly those from the region) are involved in cross-border trade as an integral part of their businesses (Nethengwe 1999; Parsley 1998; Peberdy 1997b, 1998, 1999b; Peberdy et al. 2000a, b). Some are engaged in two-way trade, taking goods in both directions across the borders. Some are involved in more extensive networks of trade which extend to other countries in the region (Parsley 1998; Peberdy 1999b, 2000a; Peberdy and Crush 1998b; Peberdy and Rogerson 2000; Peberdy et al. 2000a, b).

Another relatively invisible cohort of entrepreneurs (or 'shoppers') travel to South Africa on regular short visits to buy goods to take back to their home countries in the region (ARPAC 1999; Peberdy 1997b, 1999b; Peberdy and Crush 1998b). There the goods are sold at street stalls or markets, and to individuals, other market traders, and formal-sector retail outlets. These traders are largely self-employed entrepreneurs, although a few, particularly from Mozambique, are employed to purchase and carry the goods (ARPAC 1999; Peberdy 1999b, 2000a, b; Peberdy et al. 2000a).

Migrant and immigrant participation in informal-sector retailing is dominated by African non-nationals. Non-African migrants in the informal-sector tend to be from Taiwan and China (Gaoyu 1996). As in the case of SMMEs, the range of African nationalities in informal retail activities is wide, and overlapping clusters emerge around the activities of people from different countries. West and Central Africans often sell sculpture, artworks and leather goods from their home countries, commercially made bags (Senegalese and Malians), watches (Congolese and Senegalese), shoes, and fruit (Ghanaians). Refugees from Somalia and Ethiopia also sell shoes, bags and watches (Majodina and Peberdy 2000; Peberdy and Majodina 2000). Southern and East African entrepreneurs, particularly Zimbabweans, Malawians and Kenyans, also sell handicrafts, curios and artworks. Southern Africans also sell fruit and vegetables from South Africa.

The goods imported to South Africa include handicrafts and artwork, wire products, 'traditional' dresses, crochet work, capulanas, and Mozambican fish, nuts and vegetables (Peberdy 1997b, 1999b, 2000a, b; Peberdy et al. 2000a, b). Goods exported include clothes, electronic equipment (TVs, videos, hi-fis), appliances (stoves, irons, refrigerators, washing machines), household goods (bedding, pots, cutlery), food (rice, mealie meal, sugar, eggs), cosmetics and 'lotions', car parts, cars, bicycles, jewellery, and wines and spirits (see also ARPAC 1999; Nethengwe 1999; Parsley 1998).

A Social Profile

The gender and age profiles of entrepreneurs from sub-Saharan Africa seem to be separated according to the type of economic activity. Studies suggest that African migrant entrepreneurs in the SMME sector tend to be young single men (Rogerson 1997, 1999b). One study of foreign-owned businesses notes that 84 per cent of the enterprises are male-run (Rogerson 1997: 10). The group of female-headed businesses is led by SADC (64 per cent) rather than non-SADC migrants. Similarly, studies of informal-sector street vendors suggest that young men predominate and women (over 60 per cent) come more from the SADC (Peberdy and Crush 1998b: 14; Peberdy 2000a, b; Peberdy et al. 2000a, b).

However, studies of visible entrepreneurship hide the participation of non-South African women from the SADC as they are more likely to be involved in mobile sectors of street and cross-border trade and entrepreneurship. Thus their participation is much greater than the figures suggest (ARPAC 1999; Nethengwe 1999; Parsley 1998; Peberdy 1997b, 1999b, 2000a, b; Peberdy et al. 2000b). In fact, research suggests that they are numerically dominant as cross-border traders comprising 80–90 per cent of mobile cross-border traders (ibid.). Studies of cross-border trade between South Africa and Mozambique note that over 70 per cent of the traders are women (ARPAC 1999; Peberdy 1999b; see also Nethengwe 1999).

The participation of women in entrepreneurial activities in SMMEs and mobile cross-border trade suggests that entrepreneurship provides a significant opportunity for economic empowerment for women. Female cross-border traders in these studies (ARPAC 1999; Nethengwe 1999; Parsley 1998; Peberdy 1997b, 1999b, 2000a, b; Peberdy et al. 2000b) are likely to be household heads (50 per cent were unmarried or widowed) and over 65 per cent of the women interviewed were the primary income earner in the household, whether in a long-term partnership or not. They used their income to support their families, pay school fees and household bills (ibid.). These women traders had less access to capital than their male counterparts, and, although more likely to be present at lowest levels of trade were also among those trading in the largest volumes (ibid.). Although, cross-border trade is demanding, female entrepreneurs expressed their satisfaction with the opportunities financial independence and entrepreneurship offered by cross-border trading. Their predominance suggests a need to reconfigure conceptualizations of who are key figures in regional migration, trade and integration.

Contrary to South African popular opinion, African migrant and immigrant entrepreneurs appear to be relatively well-educated as compared to their compatriots at home and South Africans in the same sector (Jennings et al. 1995a, b; Peberdy 1997b; Peberdy and Crush 1998b; Rogerson 1997). One study of foreign-owned SMMEs notes that almost half of the non-SADC entrepreneurs have university-equivalent or post-graduate qualifications (Rogerson 1997: 11). Some 47 per cent of the SADC participants in the same study are clustered at the South African equivalents of standards 8 or 9 or matric. One study of street vendors notes that over 90 per cent have some secondary school education; nearly 40 per cent have formal qualifications (including 9 with university experience) and over 66 per cent have had some form of higher education or training (Peberdy and Crush 1998b: 16). The latter category includes a wide range of activities relevant to their business.

Choosing Entrepreneurship

Self-employment seems to be an important income-earning option for non-South Africans living in South Africa whatever their immigration status. Some 25 per cent of a sample of non-South Africans in central Johannesburg were self-employed (Reitzes et al. 1997: 16). Specific communities may exhibit even higher rates of self-employment; indeed a study of Cameroonians in Johannesburg observes as many as 60 per cent involved in small businesses

(Sungkekang 1998: 15; see also Bouillon 1996; Mbaya 1999; Timngum 2001). Foreign traders also constitute a significant proportion of the street traders in the city centre. In 1995, some 14 per cent of the traders in Johannesburg's CBD were non-South Africans (Jennings et al. 1995a: 6). Studies in other South African cities confirm the growth of foreign street vendors from sub-Saharan Africa (Holness et al. 1999; Maharaj and Moodley 2000; Peberdy and Crush 1998b).

Although many traders entered the informal economy for reasons of survival, it seems that many are anxious to remain self-employed and see their future in terms of developing their businesses. Informal-sector street-trade interviewees were asked why they started street trading. Replicating some common perceptions about the informal-sector, some 42 per cent mentioned survival (Peberdy and Crush 1998b: 17). However, 29 per cent said it was because they 'enjoyed' trading and self-employment and a further 7 per cent categorized themselves as artists selling their own work.

Since it is identified with survival, the informal-sector is often perceived as a stopgap for the unemployed who, given the opportunity, would quickly abandon it for a regular paid job. However, fewer than 50 per cent of the street traders interviewed in one study were interested in finding formal employment and fewer than 5 per cent of these respondents were actually looking for a job (Peberdy 2000a). Interviewees actively seeking a job tended to have qualifications and experience they wanted to use.

Most street traders and 'shoppers' who did not want a formal job were content to work as entrepreneurs. They repeated their satisfaction with self-employment, 'independence' and 'selling and trading' (ibid.). Some were actively building their enterprises in an effort to establish businesses in the informal and formal sector in their home countries as well as South Africa (ARPAC 1999; Parsley 1998; Peberdy 1999b, 2000a; Peberdy and Crush 1998b).

Foreign SMME operators also seem to be committed to self-employment. Overall, they are optimistic and ambitious about their enterprises and their future as entrepreneurs, and are actively involved in efforts to improve their businesses (Rogerson 1997: 17). At least 50 per cent of the sample in one study of SMMEs reinvest their capital for further expansion and diversification (ibid.). The same study notes that despite difficulties establishing their businesses, only 6 per cent of respondents operate businesses that were not already profitable (ibid.).

Furthermore, immigrant and migrant informal-sector street traders and SMME operators, unlike their 'shopping' counterparts, are likely to have had previous entrepreneurship experience in their home countries (ARPAC 1999; Peberdy 1999b; Peberdy and Crush 1998b). Non-SADC traders are often part of international trading networks (Rogerson 1997; Simone 1998a, b). Productive SMME operators often had prior experience at a job in the field before moving into self-employment (60 per cent of SADC entrepreneurs) and non-SADC entrepreneurs also had previous experience in the sector (Rogerson 1997: 12–13). The findings show clear evidence of accumulated work experience among this group of immigrant entrepreneurs.

Employing Others

Non-national entrepreneurs and street traders are often accused of reducing the opportunities for South Africans. The research shows, however, that they frequently provide employment opportunities for nationals and non-nationals alike. One study of foreign-owned SMMEs in Johannesburg examines the generation of employment in detail (Rogerson 1997). Overall, the seventy SMMEs interviewed there provide a total of 227 job opportunities, or an average of 3.33 jobs per business (ibid.: 14; Table 5.3). The two largest enterprises (both West African-owned clothing producers), employ eleven workers alongside the entrepreneur.

Three points should be noted here. First, SADC migrant businesses draw the majority of workers from their home country (53 per cent); the percentage of workers from the home country is much lower (27 per cent) for non-SADC migrant businesses. Second, workers who are not from the home country of the entrepreneur constitute a sizeable segment of the workforce of businesses in the non-SADC sample. Third, and significantly, South African workers constitute over 45 per cent of the workforce of these enterprises. It seems that at start-up, most entrepreneurs employ relatives or fellow immigrants from the home country (Rogerson 1997). Only after a period of consolidation and business growth do they hire a growing percentage of South African workers. Although they are not as important as employers as the SMME entrepreneurs, a study of street traders from sub-Saharan Africa notes that they too are relatively significant employers as some 20 per cent of these respondents are also employers (Peberdy and Crush 1998b).

Table 5.3 Number of Employees and Origins of 70 SMMEs Owned by SADC and Non-SADC Nationals

Employees	SADC		Non-SADC	
Immigrants from home*	49	(53%)	36	(27%)
Immigrants not from home	7	(7.5%)	31	(23%)
South Africans	37	(40%)	67	(50%)
Total	93		134	

*This category includes family members.
Source: Rogerson 1997: 14.

Rules and Regulations

One of the defining features of the informal-sector is its unregulated nature. Nonetheless, participants in South Africa's informal-sector encounter a number of statutory bodies and regulations in the course of their activities. Migrant and immigrant informal-sector entrepreneurs, like their counterparts with SMMEs in the formal as well as informal-sectors, have to negotiate government regulations and officialdom at several levels.

As is noted above, under current and new South African immigration legislation there is no such thing as a 'trading permit'. Non-South African traders, particularly those from the SADC, usually hold a visitors' visa that allows them to enter the country, but not to trade. A much smaller group of SADC nationals may hold permanent residence permits. Others hold asylum-seekers and refugee permits (mainly non-SADC). Although some trade as undocumented migrants, cross-border traders and street traders are not, by and large, border jumpers. It is difficult to carry large quantities of goods through illegal entry points or trade in public places without a permit (Peberdy 1997b, 1999b; Peberdy and Crush 1998b; Reitzes et al. 1997).

Although visitors' visas allow entrepreneurs to enter South Africa, they do not officially permit them to trade, even if border officials are aware that the applicant will trade after settling in South Africa (Peberdy and Crush 1998b).

Although few problems are reported at the border itself, the difficulty over visas leaves entrepreneurs vulnerable to bribery and extortion from police and Home Affairs officials when in South Africa (Peberdy 1997b, 1999b, 2000a, b; Peberdy and Crush 2001; Peberdy et al. 2000a; Rogerson 1997). Furthermore, even entrepreneurs with permits allowing them to do business are vulnerable to harassment and venal demands (ARPAC 1999; Rogerson 1997: 16–17; see also Peberdy 1997b, 1999b, 2000a, b; Peberdy and Crush 1998b, 2001).

Cross-border traders also have to deal with Customs officials and pay tariff duties. Although fewer problems are reported with South African Customs and Excise officials, there are complaints that the 'duty isn't constant, it depends on the mood of the official', and that sometimes there is corruption (Peberdy and Crush 1998b: 33, 2001; see also ARPAC 1999; Peberdy 1997b, 1999b, 2000b; Peberdy et al. 2000a, b).

Non-South African entrepreneurs can also be confronted with local officials who require traders to hold permits to sell on the street and allocate trading sites on the street or at the new 'designated markets'. SMME operators also report encountering officials of the Department of Labour during disputes with workers (Rogerson 1997: 16). Thus, migrant and immigrant entrepreneurs have to negotiate their way through the state bureaucracy at a variety of levels and in legal as well as illegal ways.

Challenging Bounded Conceptions

Conceptualizing the Informal Sector

The studies discussed in this chapter challenge the conception of the informal-sector in four ways. First, informal-sector traders have to negotiate their way through national and local government regulations, which (when enforced) they have to obey. Second, it is difficult to disentangle the formal from the informal-sector, since these migrant and immigrant entrepreneurs have strong interactions with formal-sector retail and wholesale outlets which supply them with production inputs and goods for sale in South Africa (ARPAC 1999; Peberdy 1999b, 2000a, b; Peberdy and Crush 1998b, 2001; Peberdy et al. 2000b). Third, although the informal-sector is associated with survival and the respondents in these studies cite survival as a reason for entering the sector, a significant proportion do not want to enter or re-enter paid employment. Furthermore, few of them actively seek employment.

Finally, discussions of the informal-sector tend to suggest that participants are territorially bounded, trapped within the boundaries of specific nation states. Yet, research shows that African immigrant and migrant entrepreneurs in South Africa, whether cross-border traders, street vendors, or operators of SMMEs, are connected to strong informal and formal transnational networks of trade and entrepreneurship (Peberdy 1997b, 1999b; Peberdy and Crush 1998b; Peberdy and Rogerson 2000; Rogerson 1997; Simone 1998a, b). Some of them are direct, as in the case of informal cross-border traders and 'shoppers', and others are less direct, but still important to the sustainability of enterprises (Peberdy 2000a, b; Peberdy and Rogerson 2000).

Transnational Networks

Non-SADC immigrant entrepreneurs in the SMME sector are involved in complex transnational entrepreneurship networks which assist in the start-up and functioning of their enterprises in South Africa (Rogerson 1997, 1999b; see also Peberdy and Rogerson 2000; Simone 1998a, b). Some 61 per cent of the businesses in the study of SMMEs in Johannesburg financed their start-up with funds brought in from outside South Africa (Rogerson 1997: 12). In many cases, the capital came from other business interests either in their home country or elsewhere (Peberdy and Rogerson 2000). Several of the businesses were linked to similar businesses in other parts of Africa. For non-SADC entrepreneurs, these networks extend beyond continental boundaries to Europe, North America and the Far East and may involve the import of wholesale goods and inputs for businesses.

A significant proportion of non-SADC entrepreneurs with SMMEs have relatives living or working in other countries. The wide international linkages of the non-SADC entrepreneurs is exemplified by a Nigerian restaurant owner with older brothers in the United States and Britain and other siblings in South Africa, a Ghanaian curio retailer with two sisters in Canada, a Gambian traditional eye healer with brothers in Congo and Ghana, and a Malian clothes retailer with brothers in Gabon and Congo (Rogerson 1997: 13). In addition to these individual examples, there were many others with links to France, the United States and other non-SADC African countries (see Peberdy and Rogerson 2000). SADC nationals involved in SMMEs had much smaller networks and were unlikely to own businesses outside South Africa (Rogerson 1997). Start-up capital was obtained from jobs or relatives in the home country. Family members are most likely to work at home, in South Africa or in other SADC countries.

In contrast to their compatriots in the SMME sector, SADC nationals in informal-sector street trade appear to be highly mobile and directly involved in complex networks of transnational trade (Nethengwe 1999; Parsley 1998; Peberdy 1997b, 1999b; Peberdy and Rogerson 2000). Cross-border trade constitutes a significant part of the business of informal-sector street traders from the SADC, and to a lesser extent the rest of sub-Saharan Africa (Parsley 1998; Peberdy 1997b, 1999b; Peberdy and Crush 1998b). A study of the handicraft and curio sector notes that only 15 per cent do not import goods to South Africa while 56 per cent (and 78 per cent of SADC nationals) also export goods (Peberdy and Crush 1998b: 23). These networks of cross-border trade extend to other countries in the region besides the home country of the trader and South Africa (ARPAC 1999; Parsley 1998; Peberdy 1999b). Many have traded in other countries in the region and have broad international connections. For these traders, cross-border trader is intrinsic to their enterprises. Some street traders are also mobile within South Africa and travel around the country in search of customers (Peberdy and Crush 1998b).

'Shoppers' or informal-sector traders who source goods in South Africa as well as other countries are even more mobile and their enterprises actually straddle international boundaries (ARPAC 1999; Peberdy 1999b). They spend on average less than a week in South Africa and their home country respectively (Peberdy 2000b). Furthermore, they choose which country to go to, sometimes travelling to South Africa and sometimes to other countries in the region to source goods (ARPAC 1999; Peberdy 1999b, 2000a, b).

Immigrants or Migrants

Are these entrepreneurs migrants or immigrants? All too often it seems, non-South Africans are called immigrants as if they intend to stay in South Africa permanently. Yet, the use of the term 'immigrant' to describe SADC and non-SADC African non-national entrepreneurs obscures their mobility and transnational networks. Although the majority of entrepreneurs interviewed in these studies choose to stay in South Africa, their transnational connections suggest that mobility, not immobility, characterizes many African non-national entrepreneurs.

Informal-sector street and cross-border traders as well as SMME operators seem to see South Africa as a place to earn an income while their home countries remain their permanent home (ARPAC 1999; Nethengwe 1999; Peberdy 1997b, 1999b; Peberdy and Crush 1998b; Rogerson 1997). A study of street traders in South Africa notes that 71 per cent call their home country their 'permanent home' and only 4 per cent South Africa (Peberdy and Crush 1998b: 27), as do over 90 per cent of Zimbabwean and Mozambican cross-border traders in three separate studies (ARPAC 1999; Nethengwe 1999: 102–3; Peberdy 1999b).

Despite their allegiance to 'home', many of these entrepreneurs seem to want to have long-term access to South Africa to pursue their business interests. They see their immediate and sometimes their long-term future in South Africa, but remain a highly mobile group of entrepreneurs for whom the term immigrant is perhaps inappropriate, and who, even if they are asylum-seekers and refugees, would be better described as migrant entrepreneurs.

Conclusions

This chapter has sought to investigate the growth, features and operations of immigrant entrepreneurs in South Africa. It is evident that over the past two decades South Africa has undergone enormous political and economic changes which have had a significant impact on its immigration policies and patterns, as well as its entrepreneurial and urban landscapes. More specifically, since 1994, businesses owned by migrants from various parts of Africa have become a distinctive feature of the South African SMME economy (Peberdy and Rogerson 2000). These foreign-owned businesses have been an important component of the changing economic and social landscape of the Johannesburg inner city (cf. Bremner 2000; Rogerson and Rogerson 1997).

Overall, the enterprises run by non-South Africans from sub-Saharan Africa can be classified in different but sometimes overlapping categories. First, there are the SMME enterprises, often formal or semi-formal enterprises that employ more than one person besides the entrepreneur, which may engage in productive activity. The majority cluster in and around producing or retailing clothes and curios, automobile repairs and panelbeating, selling specialist foods and running restaurants, hairdressing salons, and import-export businesses.

Second, there are African migrants involved in street trade encompassing a wide range of merchandise such as art or handicraft products and curios, fruit and vegetables, and clothes, shoes, watches and other 'soft goods'. Street traders from SADC countries are also likely to be involved in informal-sector cross-border trade as an intrinsic part of their businesses. They may bring in goods to sell in South Africa (either directly or by having goods sent to them) and buy goods in South Africa to sell in their home country. Third there are 'shoppers' who spend their time travelling between their home country and South Africa, buying goods in South Africa to sell through the informal or formal sectors in the home country.

Recent research shows that these groups of immigrant entrepreneurs are relatively well-educated. Moreover, a significant proportion have chosen to become entrepreneurs and wish to remain self-employed. Often these 'smart' entrepreneurs have a record of trade or production experience gained outside and inside South Africa. This is particularly true for entrepreneurs from non-SADC origins. It also suggests that entrepreneurship, whether in SMMEs or cross-border trade, provides opportunities for women's economic empowerment for female migrants and immigrants.

SADC and non-SADC entrepreneurs both tap into important transnational trade networks which may extend beyond South Africa and their home country. It is also apparent that extensive informal-sector cross-border trade takes place between South Africa and the region and further afield. These trade and entrepreneurship networks suggest a need to reconfigure territorially bounded conceptions of the informal-sector. The mobility of these traders also suggests that they might perhaps be better called 'migrant' rather than immigrant entrepreneurs (see Peberdy and Rogerson 2000).

This chapter highlights some key features of African immigrant and migrant entrepreneurship in South Africa, presents an emerging area of research, and thus identifies new areas for investigation. More needs to be known about African migrant entrepreneurs and their activities. Little is known about the entrepreneurial activities of non-African immigrants and migrants or self-employed professionals (African and non-African). An examination of the trajectories of immigrant entrepreneurs who arrived in the apartheid years would also be useful. Further research will facilitate the integration of studies on immigrant and entrepreneurship in South and Southern Africa into the global literature on immigrant entrepreneurship and make it possible to conduct more theoretical and critical analyses of a changing but integral part of South Africa's post-apartheid entrepreneurial landscape.

As we write, the future of African migrants in South Africa is uncertain. It is unclear how the new Immigration Control Act and its regulations will accommodate small entrepreneurs and the movement of informal cross-border traders. But, initial indications are that it will be as hard, if not harder for migrant and immigrant entrepreneurs and cross-border traders to operate. Xenophobic public attitudes to foreigners in South Africa show little sign of abating, and official discourses around migration remain restrictionist if not hostile. Notwithstanding these difficulties, it does seem that migrant and immigrant African and other entrepreneurs will, in one way or another, sustain their place in South Africa's cities and provide fertile ground for anyone interested in investigating immigrant entrepreneurship.

Notes

1. A different, but related, paper has been previously published, see Peberdy and Rogerson 2000a, b.
2. The 'two gates' policy still exists. It allows contract workers from the region to enter for fixed periods, under agreements and treaties with neighbouring states, but excludes them from the formal migration and immigration process (see Cooper 1997; Crush 1997).
3. See Peberdy 1998 and Peberdy and Crush 1998a for critiques of the legacy of South Africa's immigration history in the post-1994 immigration framework. Crush (1998) provides a comprehensive analysis of contemporary immigration legislation and its constitutionality.
4. No explanation can be offered for the massive increase in the number of rejected applications in 1993.
5. This literature can be divided into three approaches to policy-making. For the 'fortress South Africa'/security approach see Hough 1995; Minaar and Hough 1995, 1996; Minaar et al. 1995; Solomon 1996a, b. For an open-border approach see Bernstein et al. 1997. For the managed migration approach see Crush 1997, 1998, 1999; McDonald et al. 1998; Peberdy 1998; Reitzes 1995a, b, 1996; Reitzes et al. 1997; Rogerson 1997, 1999b; de Villiers and Reitzes 1995).
6. Other recent studies of immigrant and migrant entrepreneurship in South Africa (which are also referred to here) include a PhD thesis examining the participation of Taiwanese and Chinese street vendors in Pretoria (Gaoyu 1996), an MA thesis on female non-South African handicraft and curio sellers (Parsley 1998), an MA thesis on informal-sector cross-border trade between South Africa and Zimbabwe (Nethengwe 1999).

–6–

United Kingdom:
Severely Constrained Entrepreneurialism

Giles A. Barrett, Trevor P. Jones and David McEvoy

Introduction

In certain fundamental respects the nature and development of immigrant-origin enterprise in Britain differs markedly from that in most other Western European nation states, with entrepreneurial self-employment generally playing a larger role than is usually the case for immigrant-origin groups in mainland Europe. Most strikingly, self-employment rates among South Asians and Chinese in Britain actually overtook that of the indigenous white population by the start of the 1980s (Campbell and Daly 1992) and went on to exceed it quite comfortably by the end of that decade (Ram and Jones 1998). This disproportionate involvement of ethnic minorities in business has a distinctly un-European and more American flavour, leading to the thought that ethnic-business proliferation in Britain is to be explained in terms of politico-institutional regime: the greater economic deregulation in Britain may have created a less restrictive opportunity structure than in most other European countries (Barrett et al. 2001; Kloosterman 1997, 2000; Kloosterman and Rath 2000). However, as Barrett et al. (2001) also note, ethnic-minority business ownership in Britain must also be viewed rather less benignly with reference to the massive de-industrialization of the 1980s, which created disproportionate job loss among many immigrant-origin groups and stimulated self-employment as a survival strategy (Jones et al. 1989, 1992, 2000; Ram 1992). One consequence has been acute entrepreneurial over-population with too many sellers chasing too few customers. There has also been an over-concentration of under-resourced ethnic-minority entrepreneurs in a narrow range of low-level often declining sectors such as corner-shop retailing (Jones et al. 2000). When we contemplate this lack of diversity, we begin to detect closer parallels between Britain and its European neighbours. Could it be that, for all the ostensible differences in economic policy and immigration regimes, the same broad structural forces are at play on both sides of the Calais-Dover divide?

The now extensive British literature in the field provides no ready answer to this question, since it is no understatement to say that empirical and theoretical understanding of minority-owned businesses in the United Kingdom is extremely uneven. With the exception of rare contributions such as that of Ward (1987), there is no European or global focus and, even at the domestic level, studies vary in their academic or policy focus and in their sectoral coverage; their geographical scale ranges from the local to the national; their disciplinary origins are diverse; and their definitions of ethnic groups differ. Comparison of findings is almost inevitably obscured by one or more of these differences.

Before proceeding further, a note on terminology is in order because, unlike many of the other contributors to this book, we use the term 'ethnic minorities', rather than 'immigrants'. In Britain, post-immigrant generations are becoming demographically dominant for many groups. To speak of immigrant businesses may be to mislabel the phenomenon. Thus when we say 'Indian' or 'Chinese', or name any other community, we are referring to both those born overseas and those born in the United Kingdom. Our conception of ethnic minorities follows common British usage, particularly that of government statistical services. Minorities are defined from a 'white' perspective. To be Spanish, French or even Scottish is not to be a member of an ethnic-minority. We are discussing people who would be labeled 'visible minorities' in Canada, that is, people of non-European ancestry.[1] This group's presence in Britain has developed mainly since 1945. We recognize that this definition may create inconsistencies with some of the other contributions to this book. (For an introduction to some of the white ethnic groups not covered in this chapter see Basu and Altinay 2002.)

Demographic and Economic Background

In 1991 the census of Great Britain recorded ethnicity for the first time.[2] Previously, ethnic identities had been inferred from the birthplace of household members and their parents. Such inferences became less reliable as second- and third-generation minorities grew. The new data allow us to identify the economic and social context of entrepreneurship in different ethnic groups. Table 6.1 provides general demographic information. It shows that ethnic minorities, considered collectively, still comprise only 5.5 per cent of the British population. South Asians make up 2.7 per cent, Blacks 1.6 per cent, and 1.2 per cent is Chinese and other. The largest individual group are the Indians (1.5 per cent), followed by Black-Caribbeans – popularly referred to as West Indians (0.9 per cent), and Pakistanis (0.9 per cent). Black-Africans constitute 0.4 per cent of the population, Bangladeshis 0.3 per cent, and the Chinese 0.3 per cent. The remaining three minorities, Black-Other, Other-Asian and Other-Other, represent aggregations of many smaller groups. The majority of the Black-Other group are of mixed descent: that is, their ancestry involves more than one specific ethnicity, including one or more of the Black categories. The Other-Asian group consists mainly of people from a large number of countries in South, South-East and East Asia, and partly of members of the Asian diaspora in other continents. The Other-Other group includes anybody not fitting into the other eight ethnic groups. This includes significant numbers from Middle Eastern countries, although others from these places are recorded as white. The group also contains people of very diverse ancestry, and some for whom the census data is inaccurate (Owen 1996).

Table 6.1 also gives median ages. All minorities are markedly younger than whites because immigration is recent; this is compounded by the birth and death rates associated with youthful groups. Mass migration to Britain accelerated in the 1950s but has been heavily restricted, especially since the Commonwealth Immigrants Act of 1968. The younger minority groups are the predominantly Muslim Bangladeshis and Pakistanis, who retain high birth rates, and the Black-Other group. Child dependency ratios indicate an

Table 6.1 Ethnic Groups in Great Britain, 1991

	Persons (000s)	Per cent of total population	Male median age (years)	Female median age (years)	Child dependency ratio *
White	51,873.8	94.5	35.8	38.9	31.7
Ethnic minority groups	**3,015.1**	**5.5**	**25.3**	**25.6**	**52.1**
Black	*890.7*	*1.6*	*26.6*	*26.8*	*44.2*
Black-Caribbean	500.0	0.9	30.2	30.3	30.8
Black-African	212.4	0.4	26.6	26.0	41.7
Black-Other	178.4	0.3	15.0	16.5	103.0
South Asian	*1,479.6*	*2.7*	*24.0*	*23.9*	*58.7*
Indian	840.3	1.5	28.2	27.9	45.1
Pakistani	476.6	0.9	19.6	19.7	76.7
Bangladeshi	162.8	0.4	17.1	16.9	91.2
Chinese and others	*644.7*	*1.2*	*25.7*	*26.5*	*49.2*
Chinese	156.9	0.3	27.9	29.6	31.9
Other-Asians	197.5	0.4	29.6	30.9	33.5
Other-Other	290.2	0.5	30.9	20.5	75.8
Entire population	**54,888.8**	**100.0**	**35.0**	**37.9**	**32.8**

*Child dependency ratio = population aged 0–15 as percentage of (men aged 16–64 plus women aged 16–59).
Source: Owen 1997: 30, 118.

economic challenge faced by many minorities. Table 6.2 demonstrates further minority economic disadvantage. Male economic activity is lower for every single minority than it is for whites. This is repeated for females, except for Black-Caribbeans. Whites also have lower unemployment levels than ethnic minorities, except for Chinese men. Some differences with whites are very marked. For example Black, Pakistani and Bangladeshi men have unemployment levels more than twice the white figure. Black female unemployment is also more than twice the white rate. Economic activity rates for females in the predominantly Muslim Bangladeshi and Pakistani populations are very low compared with those of any other group.

The British census does not report on incomes. Since 1992, however, the Labour Force Survey, a quarterly-sample survey of about 60,000 private households, has collected this information. Leslie et al. (1998) have analysed this data. For full-time male workers, the white hourly income was 9.5 per cent higher than the ethnic-minority figure. For part-time male workers, there was a 22.6 per cent white advantage. Within the ethnic minorities, those born overseas were particularly disadvantaged. Intriguingly, there is no significant ethnic wage gap for women. However, their average hourly rates are very close to the overseas-born ethnic-minority figures for males. It would seem that the British economy will disadvantage you for being either non-white or female, but will not further penalize you for being both!

Ethnic minorities are not distributed evenly across the country. They are concentrated disproportionately in the inner-urban areas of certain regions, including Greater London, the West Midlands, the North West of England, and West Yorkshire. These concentrations constitute the market for some ethnic-minority businesses. Only a small fraction of the minority population lives in Scotland (2.1 per cent) or Wales (1.4 per cent), in contrast to their shares of the white total for Great Britain (9.5 per cent and 5.4 per cent). Individual minorities have particular regional patterns, but for most groups the main area is Greater London. Pakistanis are an exception; only 18 per cent live in London. The Chinese also have a low relative presence in London and display the most even distribution across the country (Owen 1996: 91). This is related to their employment concentration in the catering trade, selling mainly to whites.

In business terms, all this is an ambiguous context. On the one hand ethnic minorities have less potential for accumulating capital in order to invest in business. On the other hand marginality in the economic mainstream may be a powerful incentive to self-employment. These factors need to be remembered when considering the figures for self-employment which follow.

Table 6.2 Economic Activity by Ethnic Group in Great Britain, 1991.

	Economic activity rate		Per cent in work		Per cent unemployed		Per cent inactive	
	Men	Women	Men	Women	Men	Women	Men	Women
White	87.0	68.3	77.5	63.8	9.4	4.5	13.0	31.7
Ethnic minority groups	**79.6**	**56.6**	**63.4**	**47.7**	**16.2**	**8.8**	**20.4**	**43.4**
Black	*81.9*	*69.2*	*61.2*	*57.6*	*20.7*	*11.6*	*18.1*	*30.8*
Black-Caribbean	86.4	73.3	65.7	63.2	20.7	10.1	13.6	26.7
Black-African	70.4	61.4	50.0	46.2	20.4	15.2	29.6	38.6
Black-Other	83.7	64.8	62.3	52.9	21.4	12.0	16.3	35.2
South Asian	*78.3*	*47.6*	*64.3*	*39.8*	*15.3*	*7.8*	*20.4*	*52.4*
Indian	82.3	60.4	71.2	52.8	11.0	7.6	17.7	39.6
Pakistani	75.7	28.3	54.1	19.9	21.6	8.3	24.3	71.7
Bangladeshi	74.3	22.2	51.4	14.5	22.9	7.7	25.7	77.8
Chinese and others	*76.7*	*57.0*	*64.8*	*50.1*	*11.9*	*6.9*	*23.4*	*43.0*
Chinese	72.4	56.7	64.8	52.1	7.6	4.7	27.6	43.3
Other-Asians	78.2	56.2	67.1	49.2	11.1	6.9	21.8	43.8
Other-Other	78.5	58.2	63.0	49.5	15.5	8.7	21.5	41.8
Entire population	**86.6**	**67.6**	**76.8**	**62.9**	**9.8**	**4.7**	**13.4**	**32.4**

Note: Per cent in work and per cent unemployed sum to economic activity rate. Economic activity rate and per cent inactive sum to 100 per cent of (males aged 16–64 plus females aged 16–59). Inactive population includes full-time students and full-time housewives.
Source: Owen 1997: 33.

The Scale and Scope of Ethnic Minority Business

Somewhat frustratingly for the researcher in this field, the census does not report directly on business ownership. Self-employment, the nearest reported equivalent, includes many workers who are not truly self-employed. Some employers, in areas including construction and computer software, reduce tax and other costs substantially by subcontracting to the nominally self-employed. The census does not distinguish between such subcontractors and true small-business activity. It does, however, separate the self-employed with employees from those without. Owen (1997) has suggested that most entrepreneurs are in the 'with employees' category, although he acknowledges that those with no employees include some running a genuinely independent business. They may include those who make informal use of family labour. They also include tradespeople such as plumbers, domestic electricians and gardeners.

This tenuous basis provides a national estimate of the number of ethnic-minority businesses with employees amounting to 65,300, with an unknown additional number of single-person enterprises. Table 6.3 shows that a higher proportion of ethnic minorities than whites have businesses with employees (6.3 per cent compared with 4.3 per cent). Black groups have a very low level of such business engagement (1.6 per cent), approximately one-fifth of the South Asian figure (9.1 per cent). Interestingly the Bangladeshis, who on grounds of unemployment, economic inactivity and wage levels appear to be the most disadvantaged group, have a higher involvement in businesses with employees (13.6 per cent) than do the less-disadvantaged Indians (8.7 per cent). Pakistanis (9.2 per cent), who seem to share the general disadvantage of Bangladeshis, resemble Indians more in business terms. The Chinese, strongly associated with the catering trade, display the highest levels of self-employment with employees (15.8 per cent). The picture painted by the total figures for self-employment appears broadly similar to that for those with employees, although Bangladeshis are now overtaken by both Pakistanis and Indians. Modood et al. (1997) suggest that subcontractors account for about 20 per cent of South Asian male self-employed persons. For white and Black-Caribbean males, the figure approximates 40 per cent; white and South Asian females have subcontracting proportions markedly lower than their male counterparts, but no figures are available for Caribbean females.

This mention of gender makes this a sensible point to note that the all-too-familiar story from other walks of life is also true of ethnic-minority entrepreneurship. Most ethnic groups have a much higher proportion of men in self-employment than for women. It is tempting to ascribe these gender differences to the traditions and religious values of intensely patriarchal minority communities. However, close examination of data provided by Modood et al. (1997)

suggests otherwise. For Whites the ratio between the percentage of men in self-employment and the percentage of women in self-employment is 2.6:1. Some ethnic minorities display greater inequality than this. The figure for the Caribbean population is 4.7:1, and for African-Asians 3.8:1. On the other hand the Chinese, with a ratio of 1.2:1 almost reach the ideal of gender equality. Moreover, both the predominantly Muslim Pakistanis (2.5:1) and Bangladeshis (1.5:1), along with Indians (2.2:1), do better than whites. One suspects nevertheless that these bald numbers conceal more than they reveal. It is possible that many family businesses in which husband and wife share nominal ownership are in fact somewhat unequal partnerships. (Note that Modood et al. use a different classification from the census.)

On the basis of the 1991 census data it certainly seems that Britain, with its relatively deregulated economy and absence of direct occupational restrictions on migrants, provides the commercial and legal space necessary for them to realize their entrepreneurial potential. We should remember, however, the limitations of census data, frozen in time and restricted in scope. Scrutiny of non-census sources suggests a need for qualification on at least two counts. First, South Asian business activity may have passed its peak and entered a phase of decline during the 1990s. Indian and Pakistani-Bangladeshi self-employment rates were recently recorded at 14.5 per cent and 18.4 per cent respectively (Table 6.4), little higher than their 1979–1983 level (Campbell and Daly 1992) and sharply down from their early 1990s summit. This is in line with a drop in the overall national rate of self-employment during a period of falling unemployment, hinting strongly that post-Fordist self-employment trends in Britain have been largely counter-cyclical, rising sharply in the early 1980s recession but falling (albeit gently) with the recent expansion of alternative employment opportunities. South Asian self-employment trends seem to amplify this overall tendency, which is essentially independent of both ethno-cultural and politico-institutional processes, and which gives the lie to any supposition that ethnic-minority business growth in Britain is somehow inevitable. On the contrary, all the evidence suggests that Asians are now being both pulled from self-employment by gradually improving prospects for alternative employment and pushed by severe competitive pressures in their traditional fields of enterprise. In the former case, we note that the Pakistani-Bangladeshi unemployment rate, while still appallingly high at 18 per cent, now stands at little over half its mid-1980s peak and that the Indian rate is now only three percentage points above the white level. With push effects, there are unmistakeable signs that many South Asian business specialities such as food retailing, retail pharmacy, and confectioners, tobacconists and newsagents (CTNs) are now lethally squeezed by the growing dominance of multiple retailers (Barrett et al. 2001). In the particular case of CTNs, a field numerically dominated by Asian family firms in many places

Table 6.3 Self-employment by Ethnic Group in Great Britain, 1991

	Self-employed		Self-employed with employees			
	000s	Per cent of all in work	000s	Per cent of all in work	Per cent of all self-employed	Per cent of all economically active
White	2922.9	12.8	978.7	4.3	33.5	3.8
Ethnic minority groups	**155.5**	**15.1**	**65.3**	**6.3**	**42.0**	**5.0**
Black	*22.6*	*6.7*	*5.5*	*1.6*	*24.2*	*1.2*
Black-Caribbean	13.4	6.0	3.0	1.3	22.2	1.0
Black-African	5.4	8.1	1.5	2.3	28.1	1.6
Black-Other	3.8	8.2	1.0	2.1	25.6	1.6
South Asian	*95.0*	*20.8*	*41.5*	*9.1*	*43.7*	*7.2*
Indian	67.3	20.0	29.2	8.7	43.3	7.4
Pakistani	22.6	23.9	8.7	9.2	38.5	6.3
Bangladeshi	5.1	18.6	3.7	13.6	72.7	8.8
Chinese and others	*37.8*	*16.2*	*18.3*	*7.8*	*48.4*	*6.5*
Chinese	17.9	27.2	10.4	15.8	58.1	14.1
Other-Asians	7.9	9.8	3.5	4.3	44.0	3.6
Other-Other	12.1	13.8	4.4	5.1	36.8	4.0
Entire population	**3078.4**	**12.9**	**1044.0**	**4.4**	**33.9**	**3.9**

Source: Owen 1997: 53.

Table 6.4 Ethnic Self-employment and Unemployment at the Turn of Two Decades

	1989–91 mean *per cent*	*Winter1999/2000* *per cent*	*Spring 1999* *per cent*
White self-employment	13.0	11.5	
White unemployment	7.2		5.6
Indian self-employment	20.2	14.5	
Indian unemployment	11.0		9.0
Pakistani-Bangladeshi self-employment	21.9	18.4	
Pakistani-Bangladeshi unemployment	21.0		18.0

Sources: *Campbell and Daly 1992, **National Statistics 2000, ***Sly et al. 1999.

(Jones et al. 1994), a recent market intelligence report laments that the future 'looks grim' for small independents (Mintel 2001).

Secondly, there is an urgent need to distinguish the quantitative and qualitative aspects of business development, since the impressive multiplication of ethnic-minority enterprise until the1990s masks serious structural weaknesses. While figures for self-employment may well provide a useful approximation of entre-preneurial numbers, they do not tell us how well or badly these businesses are performing. Expansion has mostly occurred in a narrow range of low-yielding labour-intensive sectors, where survival is dependent upon heavy work loads for both employees and owners and often the acceptance of non-economic rates of return (Jones et al. 1994, 2000). As Engelen (2001: 217) reminds us, the sheer accessibility of these sectors renders them 'synonymous with high levels of competition ... As a result profits tend to be low, failure rates high and the success (or often mere existence) of the firm increasingly depends on informal or illegal practices'. Hence it is no coincidence that, in the interview sample of Jones et al. (1992), the best performers tended to be located in higher-order sectors. It is difficult, however, to obtain systematic nationwide data on sectoral distribution.

Most evidence on the sectoral incidence of ethnic-minority businesses comes from studies of individual localities and/or industries. We attempted to remedy this in a study which set out, on a sample basis, to be a national survey of England (Barrett et al. 2001; Jones et al. 1992). The study was confined to Black-Caribbeans and South Asians. In order to avoid geographical bias, we studied four broad regions: London; the outer South East; the Midlands; and the North. Within each region we examined Black-Caribbean firms in an area of Black-Caribbean population concentration. We knew from earlier work that few Black-Caribbean firms would be found outside such localities. In the South Asian case however, while there were substantial clusters of business in South Asian residential quarters, there were also many firms in predominantly white areas. We therefore targeted three South Asian study areas in each region: one in an area with a large South Asian population; one in a mainly white area close to a South Asian area; and one in a white area distant from any South Asian concentration. Because London had no locality which is remote from South Asian populations, we were left with fifteen study areas, each with 10,000 to 20,000 or so residents.

Our figures (Table 6.5) indicate substantial numerical development of South Asian business. Retailing and associated consumer services are the main activities. Within retailing, there is a marked contrast between the range of activities present in strongly Asian areas, and a narrower range of activities elsewhere: small grocery stores, CTNs, and restaurants are to be found in most places, regardless of a substantial South Asian demographic presence. In the Asian areas, a number of sub-types, such as stores supplying traditional South Asian women's clothing, videotape vendors and jewellers, plainly cater to the specialist tastes of the South Asian community. Other firms in these areas, and almost all businesses elsewhere, supply a market for more general needs, such as groceries, tobacco and restaurant meals. Our study picked up only one place with a significant manufacturing and wholesaling presence, Coventry in the Midlands, but work by McGoldrick and Reeve (1989) in Kirklees, West Yorkshire and Fagg (1993) in Leicester, shows that, as in Coventry, there is a significant presence in clothing and textile manufacture in some localities.

South Asian firms are more numerous than Black-Caribbean firms, not only in areas of ethnic concentration, but also in nearby white areas. Black-Caribbean firms are also somewhat less evenly distributed across sectors than their South Asian counterparts. Moreover the Black-Caribbean concentration is greater than the categories in Table 6.5 reveal. Within the most common types of Black-Caribbean firm, particular specialities are prominent. Record stores are the most common sub-type of other retailer; cafés are characteristic within the catering trade; and hairdressers are the most numerous category of other consumer service. Each of these activities caters mainly to the demands of the Black-Caribbean population for particular hairstyles, music and foodstuffs. Entrepreneurs with other ethnicities are not usually credible purveyors of these specific needs. McGoldrick and Reeve (1989) and Wilson and Stanworth (1985) reveal similar patterns in Kirklees and the London Borough of Brent respectively. It would not be unfair to describe the development of business in this community as narrow and limited.

Unhappily, information on the entrepreneurial activities of other ethnic-minority groups in Britain is extremely fragmentary. Many studies of the Chinese refer to their concentration in the restaurant and take-away food sector. For example Watson (1975) states that the number of Chinese eating places in Britain increased from 100 in 1945 to 1,000 in 1970. Parker (1995) updates these suspiciously round numbers, citing a 1993 figure of 8,000 from a Chinese

Table 6.5 Sectoral Distribution of Ethnic-minority Business in England

	Black	South Asians			
		Percentage of minority businesses in named sector			
	Black	*All*	*South*	*Nearby*	*Distant*
Food Retailers	23.5	23.6	21.8	28.1	20.0
Confectioners, Tobacconists and Newsagents	2.9	11.3	4.9	25.2	13.3
Clothing Retailers	1.5	16.1	21.5	5.0	6.7
Other Retailers	16.2	18.2	21.1	13.7	0.0
Catering Trade	19.1	14.5	14.7	9.4	60.0
Other Consumer Services	23.5	11.1	11.7	10.8	0.0
Wholesaling and Manufacturing	2.9	3.5	1.6	7.9	0.0
Other	10.3	1.7	2.6	0.0	0.0
Total	**99.9**	**100.0**	**99.9**	**100.1**	**100.0**
Number of minority firms	65	461	307	139	15
Named minority share of all local businesses	11.2	23.0	41.5	20.1	2.6

Source: Jones et al. 1992

community newspaper. Comparison with the number of self-employed in Table 6.3 indicates that the vast majority of Chinese businesses are in this one niche.

It may now be evident that while Britain has a higher incidence of ethnic-minority-owned business than that in most other European countries, it nevertheless shares the lack of sectoral diversity found elsewhere. Most characteristic activities represent the classic form of ethnic-minority entrepreneurship, the *abandoned niche*, progressively deserted by indigenous incumbents, under the competitive pressure of corporate and global competition. The restaurant trade may be less susceptible to these rivals, but still suffers from potential market saturation as the rapidly expanding demand for 'exotic' cuisine is more than matched by the supply of would-be beneficiaries of this illusory goldmine (Beardsworth and Bryman 1999; Ram et al. 2002). Such sectoral imprisonment may appear as a constant theme throughout the continent, but although Britain may provide a business environment relatively free from the kinds of *direct* restrictions encountered elsewhere, there are sufficient indirect and covert barriers stemming from racism to create an essentially similar pattern of severely constrained entrepreneurialism.

Contrasts in Intellectual Approach

Despite the obvious salience of sectoral concentration for ethnic enterprise, many British writers ignore it or downplay it, a deficiency which largely results from the competing agendas of the main intellectual standpoints in the field – *social scientific* and *policy-orientated*. Although competition can make for constructive dialogue, it more often leads to intellectual fragmentation and an uneven coverage. Among the social scientists alone, there has been from the outset a fundamental tension between two dominant approaches, the *cultural* and the *political-economic*.

As Engelen (2001: 203) rightly notes, the literature in this field has come to be 'dominated by American approaches and assumptions' notably 'the emphasis on social capital and ethnic networks'. In Britain, especially in relation to South Asians, this cultural approach celebrates ethnic values, together with communal-familial solidarity as resources for enterprise, a form of social capital (Flap et al. 2000) which gives insider entrepreneurs a competitive edge over mainstream firms, assumed to lack such informal resources (Basu 1995; Srinivasan 1995; Werbner 1980, 1984, 1990). The salience of cultural values is perhaps the oldest approach to minority business in Britain. It was established in the 1970s by studies which addressed the establishment of minority communities in the country (Dahya 1974; Watson 1977). Given this internal focus, relationships with customers and markets tend to be overlooked, with sectoral distribution treated as given instead of as an active factor. Werbner, for example, tells us that

Pakistani entrepreneurialism in clothing and textiles is founded on networks of mutual loyalty and trust, presence in this sector being explained principally in voluntaristic terms, with the external context reduced to a secondary consideration. A nationwide study by Metcalf et al. (1996) has reinforced the cultural interpretation with a wealth of data suggesting that Indians in business prosper more than Pakistanis and Bangladeshis. There is no mention of sectoral distribution, but extensive consideration of the non-material benefits of being petty bourgeois, and how these articulate with the culture and attitudes of the self-employed.

Though it should now be self-evident that entrepreneurs 'do not operate in an institutional vacuum – not even in the US' (Engelen 2001: 204), the cultural approach refuses to die. Recently it has resurfaced in that part of human geography which has taken the 'cultural turn' (Crang et al. 2000; Hardill and Raghuram 1998; Pollard et al. 2000).

In its concern for ethnic specificity culturalism may, at times, risk inadvertently promoting a form of stereotyping by highlighting inter-group cultural difference as an explanation of entrepreneurial performance. In Britain, the principal divide is perceived to be that between high-performing Asians (itself an idealistic misconception) and underachieving African Caribbeans, whose business under-representation is often ascribed to an absence of the enterprise culture and ethnic support mechanisms which supposedly promote Asian entrepreneurialism (Ward 1987, 1991). This can only reinforce negative stereotypes widely attached to African-Caribbeans in Britain.

Our own work has consistently favoured a political-economy perspective which shifts attention from *internal* processes toward the *external* environment in which businesses operate (see especially Jones et al. 2000) and in this sense may be said to prefigure the current international focus on the economic and institutional embeddedness of ethnic-minority enterprise (Rath and Kloosterman 1999). While not denying ethnicity's value in countering racist and market barriers, this approach insists that tails do not wag dogs and stresses the often decisive and frequently negative influence of structural forces on ethnic business development. Economic restructuring, demographic pressure and a racialized job market have displaced uncomfortably large numbers of South Asians from employment into self-employment. There is a marked surplus of suppliers over potential customers, an imbalance reflected in distressingly low financial returns for abnormally long working hours, together with a high risk of failure (Jones et al. 1989).

Breakout

We have long argued that co-ethnic customer dependency is a serious restriction on development (Aldrich et al. 1981) and that real advancement hinges on breaking into mainstream unbounded markets in higher order sectors (Jones et al. 2000). We now maintain that similar considerations apply to traditional working practices, notably the reliance on family. Here we follow Monder Ram (1994), who focuses on working practices and industrial relations within the firm. While ethnicity functions as a positive resource endowment up to a certain level of scale, performance and ambition, beyond that it acts as a brake rather than an accelerator, for example when kinship or communal obligations dictate nepotistic rather than meritocratic hiring practices. At a certain point ethnic bonding becomes ethnic bondage and to break out into the mainstream, *gemein-schaftlicht* informality has to be replaced by standard business practices. Ethnic embeddedness, supposedly the Asian entrepreneur's trump card, is actually a losing lottery ticket, a major impediment to entrepreneurial advancement. Paternalism is no substitute for the more formal business assets of management skills, training and qualifications (ibid.; Ram and Jones 1998). It becomes clear that the two elements – market reorientation and working practice reorientation – are interlinked, the former depending on the latter. Successful performance in mainstream sectors where large-scale financial capital and specialized human capital are unavoidable prerequisites (Bruderl et al. 1992; Engelen 2001) cannot be sustained by practices appropriate to the local corner shop. The implication may be that 'ethnic' firms can best succeed by becoming 'non-ethnic'.

Breaking out of the low-level entrepreneurial trap is an acutely uneven process which leaves most individuals behind, through a combination of high entry costs, financial and otherwise, and a lack of ambition to go beyond making a satisfactory living under conditions of personal autonomy. In common with small entrepreneurs of all origins (Storey 1994) fast-track firms motivated by the classic goals of profit maximizing and growth are in a tiny minority among ethnic minorities (Jones et al. 1992). Most independent entrepreneurs, minority and majority alike, have non-materialistic business motives like independence and self-expression. For minorities, independence may be an attempted escape from racism as well as from the controls and frustrations which drive their white contemporaries. Nevertheless from the mid-1980s, British writers began to notice signs of diversification in the Asian enterprise economy, a detectable breakout from the ghettoized enclosure of labour-intensive low-order low-return activities dependent upon co-ethnic customers in the immediate neighbourhood (Ram and Hillin 1994). The spotlight has fallen on localities like Leicester (Clark and Rughani 1983; Fagg 1993; Soni et al. 1987) and Manchester (Werbner 1990), which appear fertile ground for Asian business networks to thrive in manufacturing and wholesaling, especially in the rag trade where there has been much ethnic vertical integration. Even in Bradford, the archetype of struggling marginal ethnic business, we have identified mould-breaking firms which have either relocated away from the inner city or switched away from low-order retailing (Jones et al. 1989). More recently, Dhaliwal and Amin (1995) have used case histories and Basu (1998) a sample survey to identify what it is that sets high-flying Asian firms apart from the general mass of survival-oriented strugglers. Perhaps most promising of all is the evidence of a new presence in emerging sectors, some of it at the high-technology cutting edge of the new economy, representing the ultimate in pushing back the frontiers of the ethnic economy (Deakins et al. 1997; Ram et al. in prep.). Unexpectedly in the light of the prevalent stereotypes, this move is not confined to South Asians. While the latter certainly are well-represented, Ram et al. have also identified a number of Caribbean and African entrepreneurs in such fields as health care, media, graphic design and information technology.

Clearly, then, some breakout is under way and various attempts have been made to generalize the process. For Ward (1991), expansion and diversification occur because the Asian enterprise economy has attained a critical mass, with an accumulation of capital and human resources sufficient to create increasingly large firms in previously closed sectors. This view is strongly supported by Ram et al. (in prep.), whose respondents are typically well-qualified academically and often strongly supported by family business backgrounds. For Jones and McEvoy (1992; see also Barrett et al. 1996; Jones et al. 2000), breakout is seen principally as a matter of market reorientation on two dimensions: first a shift away from co-ethnic customer dependence into mainstream markets, and secondly a move from localized to spatially unbounded markets. This implies a shift up the value-added chain from low-order to high-order activities, with potential for operating at a scale larger than the typical Asian family micro-business. This work contains a fourfold typology of market spaces intended for application by others working in the field. Although the authors demonstrate the superior performance of firms in less ethnically and spatially bounded markets, they warn that these richer pickings are denied to all but firms endowed with more than usual resources of capital, educational qualifications, training, technical expertise, information and perhaps above all motivation. It is important to stress however that this typology is not intended as a rigid formulation but simply as a coherent framework offering possibilities for cross-national comparisons of tendencies.[3]

A study of the Birmingham restaurant trade by Ram et al. (2002) cautions however against using the market-space typology as a prescriptive or predictive device since, although the majority of the Asian and African-Caribbean restaurants in the sample enjoy a non-ethnic non-local clientele, they do not necessarily profit from this. On the contrary they constitute an almost definitive example of the saturated market beset by hyper-competition – 'they are cutting each other's throats', according to one disillusioned respondent (Ram et al. 2002). Most of the firms interviewed are 'mainstream' in the sense that they address themselves primarily to a white clientele, and in some cases their reputation is powerful enough to pull in custom over a geographical radius extending as far as Wales and Manchester. This is not, however, a sufficient condition for breakout.

The pressures of over-competition have, however, inspired various members of the sample to take proactive measures to reposition themselves by product differentiation, by going upmarket, by developing portfolio businesses or by relocation. Product differentiation involves the provision of distinctive cuisine, as in the case of a Sikh restaurateur who sells authentic Punjabi food, as opposed to the somewhat bastardized 'curry' or 'balti' cuisine which now often prevails in this sector. Going upmarket involves appealing to status, prestige, glamour and sense of occasion as well as full stomachs. To deliver the required culinary-cum-theatrical experience (Beardsworth and Bryman 1999), such enterprises can hardly operate as traditional family businesses, even though they are compelled to retain a facade of ethnic authenticity. They generally operate on a scale greater than the Asian norm and their proprietors are genuine owner-managers rather than hands-on operators. This requires organization, delegation, planning, customer relations and all-round professionalism beyond the scope of the standard ethnic micro-business. It also requires capital on a scale beyond the capacity of traditional ethnic sources. Owners generally have a lengthy business track record enabling them to acquire all manner of mainstream *class resources* (Light and Bonacich 1988) such as credibility, contacts, self-confidence and creditworthiness. Labour requirements involve recruitment extending beyond the family and even the co-ethnic network. Portfolio businesses involve expansion through the multiplication of plants and outlets. In the Birmingham restaurant sample, there are several who own more than a single restaurant outlet and/or hold assets outside catering, such as property investment. Essentially these are people enjoying the same sort of class resources as those in the previous category. Both groups demonstrate the well-known principle of capital accumulation as a self-reinforcing process, and confirm that, beyond a certain threshold, class resources begin to take precedence over ethnic resources as the central business dynamic. There are also those who have relocated either to strategic city-centre locations, enjoying the customer potential created by the nightlife effect, or to affluent residential areas. This is a 'high entry fee' (Engelen 2001) strategy and according to several interviewees, the start-up capital required to launch a viable eating house in a high market-potential location is now well in excess of £100,000 (Ram et al. 2001).

Public and Private Arrangements Regarding Enterprise Support

From 1979 onward the governments of Margaret Thatcher, John Major and Tony Blair have advocated an enterprise economy. There has therefore been a whole series of public initiatives designed to support small- and medium-sized enterprises (SMEs). Many were aimed at SMEs in general, but some were focused on ethnic-minority businesses in particular. A critical post mortem might argue that some of the growth achieved in the number of small firms was happening anyway, independent of governmental intervention, albeit more slowly. Close inspection of the package of support highlights a deeply uneven geography of business-support provision, ineffective co-ordination between the measures implemented and a confusing array of support schemes.

In England and Wales, Ram and Jones (1998) identify four 'layers' of enterprise support: Enterprise Agencies, Training and Enterprise Councils (TECs), Business Links, and local government (different arrangements apply in Northern Ireland and Scotland). They conclude that, despite a potentially useful activity, there is a great deal of fragmentation, duplication and misapplication of resources. A more strategic approach is required to co-ordinate the essentially competitive activities which make up enterprise support. Within such a strategy, ethnic entrepreneurship needs to be explicitly identified. A coherent approach needs to be supported by the acquisition of accurate information on the level of ethnic-minority business activity. In most cases it is not possible to judge the efficacy of policy because such knowledge is deficient. One indicator of policy impacts is, however, to be found in survey results. Both our fifteen-locality research (Jones et al. 1992) and the Kirklees study (McGoldrick and Reeve 1989) found very few business owners who had made use of business-support organizations, and even fewer who could explain in any detail the role played by these bodies. Similar indications emerge from the work of Oc and Tiesdell (1998, 1999) on the parallel public policy field of urban regeneration in which policies are possibly even more numerous and confusing than their enterprise equivalents. They found that City Challenge, a 1991 initiative based on competitive bids co-ordinated by local government, was unknown to many ethnic-minority firms which might have benefited from it. Individual businesses, deeply involved in the day-to-day problems of survival, were unable to consider the longer-term issues with which City Challenge might have helped. Moreover, many businesses were antipathetic to receiving help from any outside source, particularly if it involved bureaucratic means of access and monitoring. In this regard, as in others, ethnic-minority entrepreneurs seem to echo the ideology of self-reliance characteristic of entrepreneurs the world over, whatever their ethnicity.

In addition to being potential beneficiaries of general public policies, ethnic minorities have also been a specific concern of government since the early 1980s. Government motivation seems to have been twofold. First, widespread civil disturbances in many of the inner-city areas where ethnic minorities lived drew attention to the economic disadvantages they endured (Cross and Waldinger 1992). Secondly, the large number of South Asian businesses was identified as a success story with the potential for eliminating these disadvantages. In the 1970s South Asian business colonization of decaying urban areas had already stimulated a vision of the minorities as potential urban regenerators (Forrester 1978; Hall 1977). Now the official report on riots in Brixton, South London, suggested that the promotion of self-employment among the Black population would be a useful step toward reducing its problems of unemployment, criminality and welfare dependency (Scarman 1986). As part of the package of extra incentives aimed at promoting ethnic-minority business, the Ethnic Minority Business Initiative (EMBI) was set up in 1985. The initiative established five core enterprise agencies in areas of significant ethnic-minority presence while also providing workers for other enterprise agencies and institutions such as banks, TECs and Chambers of Commerce. EMBI saw its role as raising awareness to the needs and diversity of ethnic-minority small firms (Oc and Tiesdell 1999).

Private-sector institutions have also responded to the perceived needs of minority business. In particular the British Bankers Association (BBA) has openly acknowledged the tepid relations between banks and minority-owned small businesses and has sought to introduce measures to tackle these problems. These include: training packages for staff in order to break down negative stereotyping; provision of dual-language information packages; and the establishment of local loan funds aimed at providing low-cost finance to viable businesses with past problems in raising bank finance (Home Office 1991). Although the banks would like to feel that business propositions from all clients are treated on an equal basis, they concede that cultural and language barriers can trigger an unfair assessment of a client's business proposal. The over-arching requirement is to provide bank managers with the opportunity to gain a vivid insight into the socio-cultural lifestyles of different racialized minority groups. Similarly, one of the guidelines produced by the EMBI pertains to the need for local enterprise-support services, such as enterprise agencies to collate information on the demography and history of local ethnic-minority communities. This portfolio of information could serve as a training pack for local providers and generate greater understanding of a locality's cultural distinctiveness and identities. Anecdotal evidence from enterprise-support agencies suggests, however, that the permanent importance of these proposals would have been no less had they been written in sand (Ram 1996).

Forces for Change

The characteristic business sectors in which Britain's ethnic minorities are involved are particularly sensitive to the impact of legislation and regulation. Specific measures include the abolition of the Wages Councils (which had set

minimum wages in many sectors), the relaxation of land-use planning regulations and the repeal of legislation restricting the opening hours of shops in
England and Wales. Such changes might be expected to assist enterprises known
to have been frequently in breach of the former rules. Conversely, the introduction of a minimum wage (by the 1997 Labour government of Tony Blair), and the
reimposition of some constraints on the location of retailing, might be seen as
restrictions on the activities of businesses with less-formal practices. The
phasing out of the Multi-Fibre Agreement, which restricts exports of textiles and
clothing from developing countries to developed countries (Dicken 1998: 302),
could be expected to expose Britain's ethnic-minority firms in this field, which
have been partly sustained by pay levels low by domestic standards, to the
bracing blast of competition from low-wage developing countries.

Because of the interaction of regulation and economic trends, it is difficult to
distinguish the impact of any particular change in regime on a particular sector.
It seems worth attempting, however, in the case of the 1994 repeal of the 1950
Shops Act. This banned Sunday retail trading, imposed an afternoon closure on
one other day a week, and required daily closure by 8.00 p.m. A series of sometimes bizarre exceptions was allowed. For example, fresh vegetables might be
bought on Sundays, but not canned vegetables; magazines, including porno-
graphic publications could be bought, but not the Bible (Auld Committee 1984:
5, 82–9). However, many small food stores and CTNs had, in defiance of the law,
opened on Sunday and 'after-hours' for many years; South Asians were particularly prominent (Aldrich et al. 1981).

Following the 1994 repeal of the Shops Act, many retail chains which had
previously obeyed the law began to extend their opening hours. Many supermarkets now stay open until 10.00 p.m. and some for twenty-four hours a day.
Moreover, limited-line food discounters originating in mainland Europe, such as
Aldi, Netto and Lidl, have begun to expand rapidly in inner city areas where
supermarkets were few and most existing food stores were minority-owned
(Wrigley 1996). Further competition has come from 168-hours-a-week convenience retail outlets attached to filling stations operated by major oil companies;
and Walmart, the world's largest retailer, now owns Asda, Britain's third largest
supermarket chain (Hallsworth 1999). Unsurprisingly, South Asian food stores
and CTNs have begun to suffer from this vigorous competition. Former competitive advantages of neighbourhood convenience and long opening hours no
longer ensure survival. Rivals have invaded both the geographical and the
temporal arenas where South Asians were predominant. Increasing, but as yet
uncounted, numbers of the most common types of ethnic-minority business are
closing (Arnot 1999).

Changing demographics are also influencing minority enterprise. Just under
half of Britain's ethnic-minority population was born in the United Kingdom. In

the Black Caribbean and Pakistani groups, the figure is over 50 per cent (Schuman 1999). Immigration restrictions ensure that these figures will increase. Among young people (aged 16–24), only one-third of whites are in full-time education compared with 51 per cent of ethnic minorities (Sly et al. 1998). The effects of a British upbringing and of high levels of post-school education are already apparent in the Chinese community. Young people are increasingly reluctant to assist in, or to take over, the traditional family restaurant or takeaway (Parker 1995; Song 1997a, b). Degree-level qualifications create an ambition for professional or corporate employment. The same trends are also developing in the South Asian communities (Cookson and Wolffe 1996). It has even been suggested that Indian restaurants in Britain are at risk because British-born Asians are reluctant to become waiters and chefs, and because potential immigrant replacements cannot gain admission to the country (Younge 1999).

Conclusions

Britain has been through a period in which South Asian enterprise has proliferated numerically. These businesses have, however, been concentrated overwhelmingly in a small number of economically difficult sectors for which there was relatively little indigenous competition. They are of course the same sectors which immigrant groups in the rest of Europe and in North America have also found accessible. South Asian involvement has been encouraged by the low capital and high labour requirements of these activities. As a poor minority, struggling with discrimination and disadvantage in the mainstream labour-market, South Asians found that self-employment in retailing, restaurants and low-technology manufacturing offered the beguiling prospect of autonomy and economic progress. For many, however, this vision has proved a mirage. These trades have proved, at best, a temporary refuge from the tempests of economic reality. The very factors which caused whites to disengage from these sectors – long hours, low rewards and grinding competition – have now begun to erode South Asian business numbers.

As the British-born and British-educated age groups grew larger in the minority population, willingness to accept the lot of the immigrant generation has waned. Well-qualified minority members, informed by a rounded understanding of British society, now seek employment commensurate with their certification. Their educationally less successful contemporaries take a more jaundiced view of the entrepreneurial 'opportunities' which ensnared their parents' generation in years of dubiously-rewarded toil. It may be that the multiplication of economically marginal businesses is mainly a feature of the immigrant generation. Our use of the term 'ethnic-minority' may have been unnecessary.

None of this means that South Asians have ceased to engage in entrepreneurship. It simply means that the gap between their business behaviour and that of the majority population has begun to reduce. The factors which prompt business formation among whites will also stimulate new enterprises among South Asians. These include lack of recognition and promotion in employment, acquisition of capital through inheritance, marriage or redundancy, and, of course, a healthy sprinkling of energy and ambition. Continuing racial discrimination and lack of rewarding jobs in the places where South Asians reside may also play their part. Works we have cited show that some at least of this continuing entrepreneurship will involve breakout into new industries and localities. Insofar, however, that breakout is successful, the reduced numbers of enterprises are likely to be of higher quality than their predecessors.

At least since the election in 1979 of Margaret Thatcher's first government, Britain has been a country which has favoured capitalism and encouraged small entrepreneurship. Four years of Tony Blair and 'New Labour' has done little or nothing to modify this ideology. Government therefore often takes the view that high levels of minority entrepreneurship are a favourable development.

Meanwhile, however, the academic community has been more sceptical. Many reservations have been entered about the wisdom of continued business proliferation and about the survival of existing firms. Analyses deriving from the newly promulgated concept of mixed embeddedness seem unlikely to change these differences of perspective. Indeed academics would be betraying their duty to offer a critical view of society if they simply sought to support public policy, whatever the legitimacy of the government promoting it. There seems nevertheless to be room for guarded collaboration in areas such as the identification of the most promising sectors in which to nurture firms with growth potential. Cultural distinctiveness may be one of the markers of such potential in areas linked to local identity, tourism and even heritage. For many younger entrepreneurs, however, the business-support needs deriving from ethnicity may be increasingly difficult to distinguish from the needs of entrepreneurship in general.

Notes

1. Note however that the Irish are recognized as an ethnic-minority in the 2001 census.
2. Note that Northern Ireland, though part of the United Kingdom, has a separate census from that of Great Britain.
3. Recently, the market-space typology has been questioned on the grounds that 'it is hard to imagine how the extent of the market could figure ... in the strategic deliberations of the entrepreneur' (Engelen 2001: 212) and we

would not for a moment contest Engelen's claim that our framework pays little or no direct attention to entrepreneurial decision-making; nor that a firm's location in a given market space may simply be an unconscious by-product of a conscious decision about some other variable such as choice of product line or change in purchasing arrangements. At the same time we are unapologetic about our framework because that is precisely what it is – a framework, a skeleton upon which we and indeed other researchers are invited to build flesh. Such flesh-building is already under way in the shape of Ram et al. (2002), a study of ethnic-minority-owned restaurants in Birmingham, which explicitly sets out to demonstrate the variety of forms taken by break-out strategy at the level of the individual firm.

–7–

The Netherlands: A Dutch Treat

Jan Rath and Robert Kloosterman

Introduction

Strolling down Ferdinand Bolstraat, a busy street in a nineteenth-century neigh-bourhood in Amsterdam, even the less-informed observer cannot help notice the presence of entrepreneurs from China, Surinam, Turkey, India or Pakistan (cf. Vink s.a.). Immigrant businesses abound and Amsterdam is anything but an exception. In the country's other cities and towns, immigrants have set up numerous businesses ranging from hairdressing salons, travel agencies, video rentals, clothing stores, driving schools and call shops to jewellery shops, brokers' offices, foreign-exchange dealers and insurance offices (Rath and Kloosterman 1998c). Immigrants have been especially active in the food sector with their restaurants, snack bars, falafel or kebab stands, ice cream parlours, coffee houses, tea rooms, and cafés as well as bakeries, butchers' and grocery stores, *tokos* (Indonesian grocers), fish shops, and food-production and wholesale companies. The *raison d'être* of their businesses originates in part from their capacity to create economies of scope. They sometimes specialize in specific ranges of prod-ucts, including 'ethnic' or religious products such as kosher or halal food. On the average, immigrant entrepreneurs are more willing to put in long hours at low wages (relative to the host society's norms). Today, first-generation immigrants own 6.1 per cent of the non-agricultural businesses in the Netherlands, but in the four largest Dutch cities Rotterdam, The Hague, Utrecht and especially Amsterdam, the percentage is much higher (van den Tillaart 2002).

One out of five immigrant businesses is located in the capital, Amsterdam. In the first instance the presence of immigrant enterprises would seem to be only logical: ever since the sixteenth century, multifarious artisans and merchants have been attracted by the relatively tolerant attitude of the Dutch, and by the economic opportunities (Bovenkerk and Ruland 1992; Lucassen and Penninx 1994; Miellet 1987; Rath 2000a; Schrover 2001). The arrival of Jews from the Iberian Peninsula in the sixteenth century and later from Eastern Europe, and of Romen Catholics from Westphalia throughout the nineteenth century, greatly influenced the Dutch economic landscape as their business acumen enhanced the nation's economic and cultural wealth (Israel 1989; Schama 1991). The current proliferation of immigrant enterprises continued this historical pattern and should not surprise any visitor to Ferdinand Bolstraat. The historical evidence notwithstanding, barely anyone foresaw the current proliferation of immigrant enterprises.

Until recently, the Netherlands was considered a country of *e*migration rather than *im*migration. In the post-war reconstruction period of scarcity and the Cold War, the Netherlands was viewed as overpopulated and the government launched programmes to support anyone willing to leave for the United States, Canada, Australia, New Zealand or South Africa.[1] The idea that people would *come* to the Netherlands and settle there was completely at odds with conventional wisdom at the time, let alone that they would make their mark on the Dutch economy. The Netherlands did experience immigration though, be it on a small scale in the period before and after the Second World War, and never exceeding the number of people leaving the country.

From the 1950s onward, the picture changed. Larger groups of immigrants arrived from what was once the Dutch East Indies, the former colony now known as Indonesia (Moluccans, Eurasians), the Dutch territories in the Caribbean (Surinamese, Dutch Antilleans and Arubans), and increasingly from Mediterranean countries (initially mostly Italy and Spain, later mainly Turkey and Morocco). The Dutch mindset, especially of Dutch politicians, was still not geared to becoming a country of immigration rather than emigration. The idea of the Netherlands as one big boarding house did not seem to necessitate any more comprehensive form of incorporation than employing the migrant workers in the secondary segment of the labour market. Only very recently did the government officially acknowledge the fact that the Netherlands is hosting a more or less continuous influx of immigrants seeking permanent residence (Kansen krijgen 1998). The Netherlands has become a country of immigration, but borrow a phrase from Cornelius et al. (1994) a reluctant one, and its for quite some time unwelcoming attitude made it hard to appreciate immigrant entrepreneurship.

Immigrants were not only viewed as people who would only be there temporarily, they were primarily seen as *workers* and this was indeed the case for quite some time, as most of the immigrants were economically active as wage labourers. This was particularly true of Turks, Moroccans and other Mediterraneans who were recruited to fill vacancies in the manufacturing sector. In 1998, 93 to 96 per cent of the *active* immigrant labour force in the Netherlands was employed as wage labourers (Martens and Veenman 1999: 136). The inactive immigrants, i.e. 10 to 20 per cent of the labour force, depending on the category (ibid.: 120), were commonly thought to be looking for a job. The evident significance of wage labour has led to a somewhat biased conception of the economic opportunities of immigrants. Policy-makers and social scientists usually view the economic incorporation of immigrants in terms of wage labour, and self-employed entrepreneurship has been systematically overlooked.

For years small firms were believed to be doomed. The prevalent economic theories of left-wing and mainstream economists alike predicted that only large firms would be able to survive in a modern capitalist economy. This, however, turned out to be only partially true. After 1970, a spectacular rise in the number of self-employed was registered, first in the United States and later also in Britain. For almost two decades, these developments seemed to bypass the Netherlands, but in the late 1980s the number of self-employed started growing here as well. Between 1986 and 2000, the number of immigrant entrepreneurs increased from 14,450 to 44,000, and the number of businesses operated by them increased from 11,500 to 36,461.[2]

The continuous immigration and the proliferation of immigrant entrepreneurs shed new light on the socio-economic incorporation of immigrants in Dutch society. What drives immigrants to set up shop on such a massive scale? How do they perform as entrepreneurs? What accounts for their success? How and to what extent is entrepreneurship a vehicle for upward social mobility? Additional questions pertain to the impact of immigrant entrepreneurship on socio-economic developments in the wider society. Even though most researchers in the Netherlands solely focus on the employment of immigrants for wages, some have also addressed aspects of immigrant entrepreneurship. In this chapter, we critically examine their studies and put this specific research into a wider perspective to generate a more general understanding of how immigrants and their entrepreneurial activities are studied in the Netherlands. Our meta-study examines how Dutch social sciences respond to the recent emergence of immigrant entrepreneurship.

In the next section, we start with a brief sketch of post-war immigration into the Netherlands, followed by an overview on immigrant entrepreneurship and a historical review of the studies on it, and then explore the kinds of research that have been conducted. We conclude by identifying certain research patterns.

Post-war Immigration into the Netherlands

From 1960 onward, the annual immigration to the Netherlands almost invariably exceeded the emigration figures (only 1967 exhibiting an emigration surplus). As noted above, the country did experience immigration in earlier years.[3] In the wake of the Second World War, and after the decolonization in Indonesia, a group of Moluccans arrived in 1951 as did cohorts of people of Dutch or mixed Dutch-Asian origin up till the early 1960s (van Amersfoort 1982). The Moluccan immigration mainly consisted of soldiers in the Royal Dutch East Indian Army

(KNIL) and their families, since the new Republic of Indonesia did not seem to be a very hospitable option for them. Initially, to the complete satisfaction of the trade unions, these ex-servicemen were barred from wage labour, and by the time the bar was lifted, they were out of touch with Dutch society. Contrary to the predictions of the blocked-mobility thesis, Moluccans have demonstrated a very modest inclination to become self-employed, since only an insignificant percentage started businesses.

The other immigrants from the Dutch East Indies, the 'repatriates' as they were curiously labelled, fared much better. Most of them quickly succeeded in finding a job notwithstanding the clear prejudices many Dutch had against them. Today, they are often portrayed as a group that successfully assimilated into Dutch society, and even serve as an as example for other newcomers.[4] It is interesting that their arrival in the Netherlands is linked to the proliferation of Chinese-Indonesian restaurants in the 1960s and 1970s. The 'repatriates' from Indonesia constituted a kind of collective launching customer. The restaurants were able to lure notoriously thrifty Dutch customers by offering cheap food. It should be noted, though, that it was mainly Chinese immigrants from Hong Kong or Mainland China rather than the 'repatriates' who opened these restaurants.

In the period from 1950 to 1973, following other European industries, Dutch manufacturing recruited 'guest-workers' from the Mediterranean region. Later, when the recession set in, many of the guest-workers were laid off, and their level of unemployment soon surpassed that of Dutch workers (Kloosterman 1994; Wolff and Penninx 1993). Meanwhile, some savvy guest-workers set up shop. Boarding houses, halal butchers, import/export businesses, travel agencies and coffee houses opened, targeting co-ethnics only. Immigrant unemployment had been high throughout the 1980s and most of the 1990s, but again contrary to the blocked-mobility thesis that the establishment of immigrant enterprises is counter-cyclical, it failed to generate many of them. Things changed in the 1990s when the economy flourished. The demand for labour rose rapidly and many immigrants got a job, and many others became self-employed.

The former colonies of Surinam and the Dutch Antilles were already in the habit of sending migrants to the 'mother country', usually from the higher social classes to attend the universities there. This pattern changed in the early 1970s when Surinam was about to become independent and many people left for the Netherlands in fear of political instability and ethnic strife. Compared to the Mediterranean guest-workers, the Surinamese were in a relatively favourable position: they had Dutch citizenship, knew the Dutch language and culture, were better educated, and came from a variety of social classes. Nowadays, especially in comparison to immigrants from Turkey and Morocco, the Surinamese do relatively well in terms of housing, education, labour-market performance and political clout. The first Surinamese enterprises were established back in the 1970s, and since then numerous others have followed suit (Boissevain et al. 1984).

Today, mass immigration continues. In addition to the family reunification of Mediterraneans and the immigration, mostly of students and professionals, from EU countries, Japan and the United States, Third World immigrants have been coming to the Netherlands from such countries as Vietnam, Nigeria, Ghana, Iraq, Somalia and Ethiopia/Eritrea. Insofar as they entered the country as asylum-seekers and have been accepted as refugees, besides family reunification the most important way of gaining access to the country, they have to overcome various barriers when they enter the Dutch labour market (van den Tillaart et al. 2000). Their level of education is often relatively high and in this respect they differ sharply from most of the guest-worker immigrants. A few categories like the Vietnamese and Ethiopians have nevertheless displayed a striking entrepreneurial drive.

Table 7.1 gives an overview of the immigrant population in the Netherlands. Germans and Indonesians constitute the largest category, but in everyday life (and contrary to earlier periods in history) they are rarely if ever regarded as immigrants.

In the first instance, official policy was not at all geared to the incorporation of immigrants. The only efforts that were made were focused on alleviating problems in the field of social work. But in 1980, the government shifted gears and embarked on a series of policies aimed at integrating immigrants in Dutch society. The people concerned, Surinamese, Dutch Antilleans and Arubans, Mediterraneans and refugees, people who generally occupied lower-class positions and were considered ethno-culturally different from the mainstream, were henceforth simply called 'ethnic minorities' and the programmes accordingly had a strong focus on their real or alleged ethno-cultural features (Rath 1993, 1999b). In the course of time, it has become increasingly clear that the government mainly paid lip-service to multiculturalism, and that assimilation is the track. Group-specific measures that were popular in the early 1980s and before then have gradually been abandoned. Since 1995, the government has also pursued a regionally organized urban policy that focuses specifically on urban-renewal projects. Education, housing, labour-market, and combating crime are all addressed. This policy is largely driven by a more general concern that socio-economic deprivation in poor neighbourhoods will pass the point of no return, creating a kind of Dutch ghetto. (For a critical overview, see Kloosterman and Rath 1996.)

The Development of Immigrant Entrepreneurship

Like many other countries in Europe and North America, the Netherlands has witnessed a strong decline in employment in manufacturing accompanied by an

Table 7.1 Population in the Netherlands by Country of Birth, 1 January 2000

		Country of birth	
	Total	*First generation*	*Second generation**
Italy	33,780	16,161	17,619
Portugal	14,281	9,509	4,772
Spain	30,013	17,282	12,731
Former Yugoslavia	66,947	50,416	16,531
Greece	11,232	6,495	4,737
Turkey	308,890	177,754	131,136
Morocco	262,221	152,540	109,681
Tunesia	6,596	3,614	2,982
Cape Verde	18,242	11,007	7,235
Dutch Antilles + Aruba	107,197	69,266	37,931
Surinam	302,514	183,249	119,265
China	29,759	20,054	9,705
Hong Kong	17,510	10,167	7,343
Others, of whom from ...	1,566,120	703,608	862,512
Indonesia	405,155	140,659	264,496
Germany	401,119	107,231	293,888
Somalia	28,780	21,418	7,362
Iraq	33,449	29,825	3,624
Egypt	14,398	9,056	5,342
Ghana	15,609	10,679	4,930
Pakistan	16,149	10,334	5,815
India	11,516	7,988	3,528
Vietnam	14,717	10,284	4,433
Total immigrant population	2,775,302	1,431,122	1,344,180
Dutch	13,088,648		
Total	15,863,950		

* One or both parent(s) born abroad.
Source: CBS 2000: 13; Muus 2000: 16–18.

even stronger rise in the number of jobs in services in the last few decades of the twentieth century (Kloosterman and Lambregts 2001). What is left of the manufacturing industries now increasingly consists of firms specialized in high-value-added, knowledge-intensive activities. The educational qualifications of many immigrants, especially from Turkey and Morocco, do not match the growing demand for highly-skilled workers in today's manufacturing or service industries. In addition their labour-market position is affected by discrimination on the grounds of their real or alleged ethnic or social features (Bovenkerk et al. 1995), or practices that funnel even highly-skilled immigrants to secondary tiers of the labour market (Bovenkerk et al. 1991; Buijs 1990; Lutz 1992). The Dutch government, which is not a typical model employer itself, employers' associations, trade unions and other institutions have made concerted efforts to turn the tide, and their interventions partly coincided with the restructuring of the welfare state. The results have been mixed at best. Kloosterman (1996) notes that it was mainly (Dutch) women who benefited from these measures, in Amsterdam especially in the SME sector and the hotel and catering industry, while immigrants remained at the bottom of the labour ladder. Only in the second half of the 1990s, when the economy boomed and immigrants' long-term unemployment decreased at last, did their self-employment gain momentum.

From 1991 to 1993, the total number of businesses outside the agricultural sector increased by a quarter to 550,000, with approximately 9 per cent of the active labour force self-employed (OECD 1995: 314–15). By 2001 the total number of firms even reached an all-time high of approximately 600,000.[5] In the four main cities, the number of businesses grew even more rapidly, particularly in Amsterdam (see Amsterdam in Cijfers 1990: 210; ibid. 1994: 198–9; ibid. 2000: 209). What is important is that immigrants contributed substantially to this growth (see Table 7.2). In 1987, 9,393 first-generation immigrants from the minority-policy target groups were self-employed, a mere 3.3 per cent of the corresponding labour force. Ten years later, this number has almost tripled to 27,380 immigrant entrepreneurs, or 7.4 per cent of the corresponding labour force. The percentage of self-employed Turks is even higher and now exceeds the national average, i.e. 12.2 per cent of the Turks and 10.2 per cent the entire population (van den Tillaart and Poutsma 1998: 39–40).[6] The latest figures show a continuation of this development. In 2000, 43,926 first-generation immigrant entrepreneurs of a total of approximately 730,000 entrepreneurs owned 36,461 of a total of 595,461 businesses (van den Tillaart 2001: 2). In addition to this category of first-generation immigrant entrepreneurs, there are an estimated 8,000 second-generation entrepreneurs (ibid.: 101). The precision of these figures may be debatable, but they do give a reasonable indication of the latest developments.[7]

A closer look reveals a marked pattern of entrepreneurship distribution among the groups of immigrants and in a spatial sense. Certain categories of immigrants, e.g. Chinese, Greeks, Italians and Turks, exhibit a marked tendency toward entrepreneurship. There are indications that Ghanaians, Egyptians and Pakistanis are also quite entrepreneurial, but these groups are still too small to be included in the 'large' surveys (cf. Choenni 1997). Other groups, such as Moroccans, Moluccans, Cape Verdeans, or Germans for that matter, demonstrate much less of a tendency toward entrepreneurship, although the Moroccans seem to be catching up. Some 22 per cent of the first-generation immigrant entrepreneurs are female, and the

Table 7.2 Development of First-generation Immigrant Entrepreneurs in the Netherlands by Country of Origin , 1986–2000

	Absolute numbers				Share of entrepreneurs in the labour force (%)				Percentage of total number of first generation	Development 1986–2000	Development 1998–2000
	1986	1992	1998	2000	1986	1992	1998	2000	2000	(1986=100)	(1998=100)
Italy	905	1,183	1,260	1,350					8.2	149	107
Portugal	84	174	196	228					2.1	271	116
Spain	221	334	385	442					2.4	200	115
(Former) Yugoslavia	338	706	839	1,038					1.9	307	124
Greece	448	655	709	760					12.0	170	107
Turkey	1,895	5,385	6,561	9,047	2.9	7.8	12.2		4.7	477	138
Morocco	886	1,912	2,572	3,424	3.3	5	5.9		2.0	395	133
Tunesia	78	179	186	192					unknown	246	103
Cape Verde	42	80	120	160					1.4	381	133
Dutch Antilles/Aruba	405	1,003	1,274	1,615	2.9	4.6	6.3		2.2	406	130
Surinam	1,725	4,148	5,209	6,439	2	4.5	5.4		3.3	373	124
China	1,332	1,852	3,003	3,450					16.7	259	115
Hong Kong	1,054	1,372	1,651	1,680					16.5	159	102
Others											119
Total		28,748	35,796	43,926	8	8.9	10.1				123
Dutch		512,339	512,339								
Total	450,649	541,087	632,843								

Source: van den Tillaart 2001: 117; van den Tillaart and Poutsma 1998: 39–40.

percentage of female entrepreneurs among second-generation immigrants is roughly 26 (van den Tillaart 2001: 2). There is a rise of immigrant businesses all over the country, but it is particularly evident in the larger towns and cities, especially in neighbourhoods with high concentrations of immigrants, such as the nineteenth-century neighbourhood De Pijp in which Ferdinand Bolstraat is located, and increasingly in the city centre and post-war high-rise neighbourhoods (Kloosterman and van der Leun 1999). Table 7.3 gives an overview of the numbers of firms and percentages of immigrant firms in Amsterdam, Rotterdam, The Hague and Utrecht.

Economically, immigrant entrepreneurship means providing jobs and incomes for entrepreneurs and their employees (e.g. Baetsen and Voskamp 1991: 49; BEA 1994: iv-v),[8] and indirectly providing jobs for others along the suppliers' chain and generally contributing to economic growth. In the 1990s, the numbers of

Table 7.3 Businesses by City, 1998

	Absolute numbers (=100%)	Amsterdam	Rotterdam	The Hague	Utrecht	Others
Italy	1,129	16	4	5	2	73
Portugal	186	20	10	14	3	53
Spain	361	16	9	3	2	71
(Former) Yugoslavia	753	16	13	4	1	66
Greece	545	7	10	2	8	72
Turkey	5,508	14	13	12	3	58
Morocco	2,233	24	13	7	7	50
Tunisia	172	25	2	12	1	60
Cape Verde	111	5	76	3	1	15
Aruba	53	40	2	6	0	53
Dutch Antilles	1,138	12	9	6	3	71
Surinam	4,640	25	17	15	3	40
China	2,010	6	7	4	2	81
Hong Kong	1,063	11	10	6	3	71
Others	27,706	17	4	6	1	72
Egypt	1,434	27	2	6	1	64
Ghana	311	65	4	7	1	23
Pakistan	886	40	16	16	1	28
India	864	41	10	13	2	34
Vietnam	604	3	2	0	0	95
Total	47,608	17	8	7	2	66

Source: van den Tillaart 2001: 157.

Table 7.4 Distribition of Immigrant and Native Dutch Businesses by Sector (Percentage)

	Immigrant businesses		Native Dutch businesses	
	1998	*2000*	*1998*	*2000*
Agriculture/forestry	1	2	Not included	Not included
Manufacturing	3	3	9	8
Construction	2	4	11	12
Car trade and repair	3	3	4	4
Wholesale trade	18	16	9	8
Retail trade	16	15	16	15
Catering	29	26	6	6
Transport	3	4	5	5
Business services	14	18	23	25
Personal services	10	9	18	18
Total number (=100%)	29,658	36,454	534,000	559,000

Source: van den Tillaart 2001: 38.

jobs in the Dutch cities grew considerably, partly thanks to the rise in small businesses (Verweij et al. 1999: 159).

Immigrant entrepreneurship, although increasingly diverse (see Table 7.4), is still strongly oriented toward specific segments of the opportunity structure. About 60 per cent of all the immigrant entrepreneurs work in sectors such as wholesale, retail and catering.[9] In relative terms, the percentage of immigrant enterprises in wholesale (especially food and clothing) is twice as high as the percentage of Dutch enterprises, and the percentage in catering is more than four times as high.

The Chinese and Greeks, but also the Egyptians, Vietnamese and Malayans, and to a lesser extent the Italians and Turks have carved out niches in catering. There are indications, however, that immigrants are gradually leaving this sector and venturing into other sectors, especially personal and business services. The niche of small Italian restaurants and pizza parlours is being increasing taken over by Turks (who own 24 per cent of the Italian restaurants) and Egyptians (21 per cent); in 2000, a mere 38 per cent of the Italian restaurants were still owned by the Italians. It is unlikely that Turks or Egyptians will continue to gravitate solely toward catering, as they already own employment agencies, janitorial services, driving schools, travel agencies and hairdressing and beauty salons. This diversification seems to be a general trend, though it is true that some groups follow this trend more closely than others. The penetration of Surinamese entrepreneurs in the business-service sector, consultancies, ICT companies, and advertising agencies in particular, is striking, as is the entrepreneurial drive of

Table 7.5 Distribition of Immigrant Businesses by Sector and by Country of Origin, Mid-2000

	Number of businesses (=100%)	Agriculture/forestry	Manufacturing	Construction	Car trade and repair	Wholesale trade	Retail trade	Catering	Transport	Financial services	Rental services	Other business services	Personal services
Italy	1,228	0	3	6	2	17	11	40	2	1	1	11	5
Portugal	218	0	4	7	5	12	11	14	6	0	1	30	10
Spain	427	1	4	11	2	18	10	14	2	1	2	23	14
(Former) Yugoslavia	949	0	5	13	4	24	9	13	2	1	1	20	7
Greece	592	0	2	2	4	12	6	54	1	1	2	7	6
Turkey	7,478	7	5	5	5	11	17	22	5	1	1	15	7
Morocco	2,883	2	2	5	4	9	26	23	7	0	1	11	10
Tunisia	182	0	3	6	2	18	14	25	3	2	0	17	10
Cape Verde	141	0	4	7	1	15	9	16	4	0	3	10	32
Aruba	23	4	4	9	4	4	4	4	0	9	4	39	13
Dutch Antilles	1,515	1	4	9	2	13	10	7	2	1	1	34	17
Surinam	5,690	0	3	5	3	14	14	10	5	2	3	22	17
China	2,297	0	0	0	0	10	4	79	0	0	1	4	1
Hong Kong	1,113	0	1	0	0	8	6	75	1	1	1	5	2
Others	11,809	1	2	2	2	24	17	24	4	1	0	16	8
Total	36,545	2	3	4	3	16	15	26	4	1	1	16	9

Source: van den Tillaart 2001: 38.

second-generation entrepreneurs. This said, some sectors are still strikingly Dutch. The construction industry has been short of staff for years and one would expect immigrant entrepreneurs to penetrate the sector without much trouble. But this has not happened for a variety of reasons, including the tendency to close off relevant networks to newcomers (Rath 2002f). Lastly, immigrants are not very prominent in agriculture and manufacturing. In the 1980s and early 1990s, there was a sharp rise in the number of immigrant contractors in the Amsterdam garment industry. Most of the entrepreneurs, who were mainly from Turkey, operated as contractors or subcontractors at the lower end of the industry and many resorted to multifarious informal practices, ranging from hiring undocumented workers and paying them off the books to evading VAT and so forth. Year after year, the government and its law-enforcement agencies turned a blind eye, but in the early 1990s, with the economic position of the contractors already under pressure from the new production facilities nearby and changing logistic procedures, the government started cracking down on unlawful practices. One garment factory after another was raided and forced to close down, sharply reducing the number of factories (Kumcu 2001; Raes 2000a, b; Raes et al. 2002; Rath 2002a, c).

Immigrants tend to gravitate to sectors with low entry barriers in terms of financial or human capital. Restaurants and shops can be small-scale operations and use simple technology. Business success there is mainly based on high labour input. Immigrant entrepreneurs are often able to increase their flexibility and reduce their costs by employing family members and people from their own social networks. Many enter these markets through mom-and-pop stores, partially replacing the businesses of local entrepreneurs via vacancy chains. They often cater to the 'captive market' of co-ethnics, although after a while many entrepreneurs start to cater to a wider clientele. Because of the low barriers of entry, the markets where immigrant entrepreneurs operate are generally highly competitive. The main competitors are often co-ethnics and competition is largely based on prices rather than on quality. Under these imperfect conditions, it is hard to survive and for a long time the mortality rate was much higher among immigrant businesses than elsewhere. However, the latest statistics show that this gap is gradually decreasing (van den Tillaart 2001).

The national and municipal governments, and various advisory bodies and sector associations have tried with varying degrees of involvement to promote small entrepreneurship in general and immigrant entrepreneurship in particular. The aim of special programmes is to make soft loans available (Wolff and Rath 2000), give advice to new entrepreneurs (help them design a business plan or find a location) or offer ready-to-use business or marketing concepts. The City of Amsterdam opened the Y-mart, a kind of 'tropical bazaar', in 1993 and witnessed its failure in the following year (Pool 2003), and the City of The Hague initiated the City Mondial walking tours along immigrant shopping strips in the downtown area.[10] However, group-specific measures on behalf of immigrants are no longer very popular among Dutch policy-makers. The Ministry of Economic Affairs and most business associations believe in a color-blind, liberalized economy. For some time now, they have assumed that immigrant or ethnic entrepreneurs are primarily *entrepreneurs* and that all entrepreneurs, whatever their ethnic origin, take equal advantage of all the opportunities. A general economic policy is pursued and deregularization is *de rigueur*.

The emergence of a new regulatory regime has far-reaching consequences. The establishment and daily operation of most businesses used to be subjected to a variety of rules and regulations, and entrepreneurs had to have certain qualifications and certificates, but many of these manifestations of corporatist governance have since been abolished. In combination with tax relief, this fundamental restructuring of the Dutch economy created an extremely favourable business climate. It is unlikely that the Amsterdam garment contractors would agree (Rath 2002c), but the fact is that the number of start-ups has risen dramatically. This is particularly evident in previously heavily regulated sectors such as temporary employment agencies or taxi drivers. The relaxation of the rules on opening temporary employment agencies resulted in a sharp rise in the number of immigrant employment agencies, especially in The Hague. Many of these agencies have their offices at home rather than in proper office buildings, and cater to the horticultural industry in the vicinity of the city. They claim to act as brokers between Dutch employers and undocumented immigrants. In the same vein, the liberalization of the taxi sector encouraged numerous immigrants to start driving a cab; within a year the number of cabs had tripled. It remains to be seen whether the newcomers can survive in such highly competitive economies. The odds are that many of them will not survive or at best will have a marginal existence. The point remains, though, that changes in how these markets are regulated have had a tremendous impact on the opportunities for new immigrant entrepreneurs. In some cases, aspiring immigrant entrepreneurs discover new openings, but in other cases deregulation only serves to increase their marginality. Repealing the legislation restricting shop opening hours was to the disadvantage of snack bars and take-away restaurants, and abolishing the legal minimum price of bread in the early 1990s only served to trigger off a bread war among immigrant bakers (Kloosterman et al. 1997b, 1999). Having said this, it is obvious that besides the numerous mere survivors, some immigrant entrepreneurs are doing extremely well (Lof 1997; van den Tillaart and Poutsma 1998; Tinnemans 1989).

The Development of Research

Studies on immigrants in the Netherlands are a rather recent phenomenon and this is particularly true of research on immigrant entrepreneurship.[11] In the 1970s, a number of social scientists took an interest in such topics as the international centre-periphery relations, migratory labour, and the class position of migrant workers. They followed the latest waves in social science and advanced an academic tendency based on Marxism, but overlooked the emerging bourgeois class. Other researchers, some of them closely connected to the government, also pondered the situation but none of them devoted much attention to self-employment (cf. van Amersfoort 1982; Penninx 1979; Verwey-Jonker 1973).[12] In its report on guestworkers, even the Society and Business Foundation (SMO), sponsored by employers' associations, made no mention of immigrant entrepreneurship (SMO 1972). The nascent business activities on the part of immigrants clearly stayed outside the view of researchers in the 'leftist' 1960s and 1970s. It was only toward the end of the 1970s and in the early 1980s, when the Dutch government began to acknowledge the permanence of immigration and design a comprehensive integration policy, that things changed (Rath 1993, 1999b). In close collaboration with leading researchers, the government endeavoured to establish a scientific base for its interventions and launched an extensive research programme on guest-workers, Moluccans, Surinamese, Antilleans and other newcomers. This fit the political routine, typical of the Dutch consociationalist welfare state, in which the struggle for resources historically manifested itself as competition between groups with different religions and philosophies of life, and sensitive issues were resolved by a technocratic compromise (Gastelaars 1985; Lijphart 1975).

The Advisory Committee for Research on Cultural Minorities (ACOM), a committee of academic researchers set up by the Minister of Culture, Recreation and Social Work to advise on the programmeming of research, mentioned in its first report to the government that some 'members of minority groups have established small enterprises or have plans to do so' (ACOM 1979: 43). In 1981, several cultural anthropologists called attention to the issue in a more sophisticated way. In a report for the European Centre for Work and Society, Boissevain (1981; see also 1997) stated that for the first time since the Second World War, the non-agricultural SME sector was on the rise, and this was partly due to the mass migration of people from Asia and the Mediterranean to Europe. These immigrants generated a new demand for specialized products and services, one that could not be met by local firms. In addition, the incorporation of these immigrants was not going well, so they were more or less forced to explore alternative routes of social mobility. Lastly, the immigrants were endowed with cultural attributes that made them suitable for a career as self-employed entrepreneurs. Boissevain concluded his report with a research programme and explicitly mentioned *ethnic enterprises* as a new and relevant area of research.

In the same year, two University of Amsterdam students supervised by cultural anthropologist Frank Bovenkerk wrote an article on the 'exceptional ways' in which Chinese restaurant entrepreneurs managed to earn a living (Blom and Romeijn 1981). In their introduction, they criticized the strong Dutch preoccupation with Chinese crime. They also criticized 'ethnic minorities researchers' who had no interest in the 'predicament' of the Chinese. A year later, Bovenkerk (1982a) himself took a firm stand against experts and social workers from the emerging and government-sponsored 'ethnic minorities industry'. In his view, they ignored the fact that a growing number of immigrants 'were able to find the key to success on their own, without the help of the welfare state'. This 'negligence' was all the more conspicuous since, in a typical immigration country like the United States, self-employment is customarily considered a classical route for upward social mobility.

Bovenkerk advanced five explanations for this ignorance. First, one of the largest categories of immigrants, Mediterranean guest-workers, was specifically recruited for temporary wage labour. Secondly, researchers (incorrectly) assumed that small businesses would inevitably have to make way for larger ones. Thirdly, they tended to associate immigrant entrepreneurship with 'a number of obviously illegal practices'. Fourthly, in marked contrast to immigrant workers, immigrant entrepreneurs had not done anything to draw the attention of policy-makers. Lastly the 'minorities industry' was more attuned to 'social needs' than 'independent initiatives of this sort'. Bovenkerk's criticism of the social sciences was on target, although he could have just as aptly noted the complete absence of economist and management scientists.

The papers, which are still worth reading today, initiated a series of studies on immigrant entrepreneurship that nicely fit the 'neo-liberal' tendency of the 1980s. The most important ones were Bovenkerk's own theoretical deliberations (Bovenkerk 1982b, 1983) and his empirical study on Italian icemakers, plasterers, chimneysweepers and terrazzo workers (Bovenkerk et al. 1983; Bovenkerk and Ruland 1984, 1992). In addition, Boissevain and Grotenbreg (1986, 1987b, 1988; see also Boissevain et al. 1984) conducted studies on self-employed Surinamese entrepreneurs, Vermeulen et al. (1985) published on self-employed Greeks, and Pieke (1987) on Chinese restaurants. Tap (1983) pioneered research on Turkish contractors in the garment industry, followed by the study he did with Bakker on Islamic butchers (Bakker and Tap 1985). Veraart (1987) explored Turkish coffee houses. Dijst et al. (1984; see also Cortie et al. 1986) took the Oude Pijp, a neighbourhood in Amsterdam as their starting point for research on immigrant businesses. Jeleniewski (1984, 1987), who compared the Oude Pijp with the Schilderswijk, a neighbourhood in The Hague, took the same approach. Van den Tillaart and Reubsaet (1988; see also van den Tillaart 1993) produced general national overviews on immigrant entrepreneurship. Several journals published special issues (e.g. Kroniek 1984), workshops were organized and discussion papers published (Gowricharn 1985).

In the second half of the 1980s, the euphoria ebbed as self-employment clearly was not a bed of roses for every immigrant. The research now seemed focus on the other side of the coin. Studies like the ones by Bloeme and van Geuns (1987a, b; see also van Geuns 1992) and Boissevain and Grotenbreg (1987a) were published on informal activities, like the efforts of Turkish contractors in the Amsterdam garment industry. Immigrants managed to penetrate this manufacturing sector more than any other economic sector, which had not gone unnoticed by self-proclaimed political spokesmen, interest groups and journalists. They published indignant articles about the inequality in the industry as a whole and the abuses at Turkish factories in particular (e.g. van Putten and Lucas 1985; Smit 1994; Smit and Jongejans 1989; Stichting Opstand 1993; Zeldenrust and van Eijk 1992).

Since the mid-1990s, in conjunction with the renaissance of entrepreneurship in general, there has been renewed interest in the subject:

1   There are mainly *quantitative overviews* and policy-oriented inventories. Renowned and less renowned commercial consultants funded by government agencies have conducted various studies.[13]

2   There are *descriptive studies* comparable to the ones of the early 1980s. Without much theoretical ambition, they examine particular aspects of immigrant entrepreneurship. Special attention is devoted to the specific ethnic character of the business activities of minority policy target groups and, in many cases, to the need for governmental support.[14]

3   There are an increasing number of *historical studies* of immigrant entrepreneurship by historians with an interest in the social sciences or social scientists with an interest in history. They have researched the activities of self-employed craftsmen, hawkers, tradesmen and manufacturers of various origins.[15]

4   A number of researchers have moved away from the focus on immigrant entrepreneurs' ethno-cultural or social features, and positioned their *work in a broader perspective* on immigration and socio-economic development. They engage in international theoretical debates and advance a view that encompasses political economic determinants. They also devote attention to dimensions of market relations and regulation.[16]

Patterns

In this overview of research of immigrant entrepreneurship, we discern the following patterns:

1   *Social scientists*, especially cultural anthropologists, sociologists and economic geographers, *dominate the research* on contemporary immigrant entrepreneurship, and there are barely any studies by economists. Incidentally, the absence of economists is not confined to the Netherlands nor to the study of immigrant entrepreneurship. According to Granovetter (1994: 453), contemporary economists have devoted so little attention to the study of entrepreneurship more in general precisely 'because of the bias to the assumption that profitable activities automatically take place'. Neoclassical economics has thus de-problematized entrepreneurship altogether by making it endogenous in its models: opportunities for entrepreneurs will be perceived and, subsequently, seized by rational economic actors (cf. Block 1990; Light and Rosenstein 1995). The fact that economists have taken so little trouble to examine entrepreneurship in general has hampered research into the primarily economic aspects of immigrant entrepreneurship in particular.

2   Many projects have been *commissioned by the national government*, particularly by the Ministries of Economic Affairs and Internal Affairs, local governments, especially in Amsterdam and Rotterdam, or governmental advisory bodies such as the Temporary Scientific Committee on Minority Policy (TWCM). Initially, business institutions such as sector/trade organizations, associated companies or Chambers of Commerce or Trades Councils kept fairly quiet, but they recently started to take a more active interest. In any case, a great deal of research has been strongly policy-driven and to a lesser extent theory-driven, and this even holds true for projects not initiated by government agencies. Consequently, research objectives and methods have mainly been based on policy definitions and policy priorities that only allow for limited theoretical reflection. Policy-makers with neo-liberal views on immigrant incorporation regard immigrant entrepreneurship as a form of socio-economic self-help. At the same time they doubt whether Third World immigrants from 'a different culture' are really able to accomplish this task. In the Dutch context, a typical report emphasizes the cultural distance, deficiencies and problems rather than the opportunities, and identifies areas for government intervention. Many social scientists, faced with poor employment prospects themselves, are only too eager to go along with the patronizing political agenda. Historians, also struggling on the labour market and even on the lookout for contract research assignments, could safely ignore the policy-makers' wishes. To put it bluntly, many immigrant-entrepreneurship researchers see it as their task to serve the community, advance a type of social science with strong political traits, and allow themselves, in the words of the criminologist Fijnaut (1990: 269), to be 'intellectually domesticated'.

3   Most immigrant entrepreneurship researchers have a great deal of interest in the *ethno-cultural* characteristics and processes of *ethno-cultural* incorporation. Completely in line with Dutch 'ethnic-minorities research' (Rath 1991, 1993), they regard entrepreneurship first and foremost in *ethnic* terms, as is illustrated by the indiscriminate use of the term '*ethnic* entrepreneurship'. Exactly what distinguishes *ethnic* entrepreneurship from entrepreneurship is rarely if ever made explicit. Does this adjective refer to the origins of the entrepreneurs, their management strategies, personnel, clientele, products, or a combination? Most researchers automatically assume *there are real differences*, just because they are dealing with immigrants. Explanations for every aspect of immigrant entrepreneurial behaviour are directly linked to ethno-cultural traditions, ethnic moral frameworks and ethnic behaviour patterns, ethnic loyalties or ethnic markets. They reduce immigrant entrepreneurship to an ethno-cultural phenomenon existing in an economic and institutional vacuum. Choenni (1997) makes an effort to do better than the term 'ethnic entrepreneur' and in a more general sense he uses the policy term 'allochtonous entrepreneurs'. His focus on entrepreneurship

as an incorporation route does not, however, rise above 'ethnic minorities knowledge'. Instead of affiliating with theoretical insights from economics or economic sociology, he turns to culturalist notions and van Amersfoort's thesis (1982) on the formation of ethnic-minority groups.

4   Many researchers are *out of sync with more recent theoretical developments* in international immigrant entrepreneurship research. The anthropologists Boissevain (1992; see also Boissevain and Grotenbreg 1987a, b, 1988), Bovenkerk (1982b; see also Bovenkerk et al. 1983), and Vermeulen (1991b) are among the few Dutch researchers to make any headway, insofar as they explored articulated theoretical viewpoints in international publications. The dearth of theoretical depth has a great deal to do with the policy-driven nature of most of the research so far. Most government agencies have very little time for theoretical reflections and contract research is strongly geared toward more pragmatic questions. More recently, we ourselves have initiated an ambitious research programme with an explicit international comparative dimension to advance this type of research in the Netherlands (see Kloosterman et al. 1998, 1999; Rath 2000c, 2002c; see also Engelen 2001).

5   In conjunction with the ethnic bias, most researchers have devoted very *little systematic attention to more structural political and economic dynamics*. With the exception of Boissevain and Grotenbreg (1986, 1987b) and Bloeme and van Geuns (1987b), many of them apparently found it perfectly sensible to assume that market conditions or regulation are of little importance. Only recently have researchers started to take an interest in political economics, partly in response to the one-sided nature of Dutch immigrant entrepreneurship research and partly in response to the exclusive focus on social capital. It is obvious that economic conditions and state and non-state rules and regulations vary from branch to branch, sector to sector, city to city and country to country. Structural determinants produce differential opportunity structures, demand different entrepreneurial skills and produce different results.

Conclusions

The immigrant population in the Netherlands is growing and rapidly becoming more diverse in terms of countries of origin, length of stay and socio-economic position. The recent rise in immigrant entrepreneurship contributes significantly to the growing diversity, which reflects the recent history of immigration to the Netherlands. In decades after the Second World War, the Netherlands was a country of emigration rather than a country of immigration. With a mental map still heavily dominated by agricultural concerns, the need for more space and the fear of the communist threat to peace stimulated people to leave the Netherlands for the vast and safe North America, South Africa, Australia and New Zealand.

It was only after 1960 that the yearly number of immigrants permanently exceeded the number of emigrants.

Apart from the immigration of Eurasians generated by de-colonization in the Dutch East Indies, immigrants were expected to be here on a temporary basis. It was not just the government that thought they would only stay in the Netherlands for a short while, many guest-workers also expected to return to their home countries. The government consequently refrained from any policies of incorporation, and the guest-workers themselves refrained from any social, cultural or economic investments in the Netherlands. Moreover, they were already employed, and many of them had even been hired in their country of origin. Immigrant entrepreneurship, which can be seen as a more long-term investment in one's future, was very marginal at first.

The long economic recession after 1973, which got even worse after 1980, fundamentally changed the situation. Notwithstanding a deteriorating position on the labour market, where they were over-represented in unskilled jobs in sunset industries, which made them extremely vulnerable for restructuring in general and closures in particular, most of the guest-workers not only decided to stay but also brought their families to the Netherlands. Meanwhile the official government policy on migration had become more restrictive, and there was no further recruiting of guest-workers. Immigration did however continue. First, the independence of Surinam triggered an exodus to the Netherlands. Secondly, especially after 1980 and continuing to this day, new groups of immigrants fleeing repression and war zones in Iraq, Iran or Somalia came to the Netherlands.

Only in the 1990s, when the Dutch economy exhibited an almost spectacular improvement, did immigrant entrepreneurship really take off. The economic boom reduced unemployment, but many immigrants found themselves at the end of the hiring queue and their rate of unemployment remained relatively high. In addition, product markets became fragmented, which eroded economies of scale and created more opportunities for small businesses. Moreover, family reunification and internal demographic trends had created critical masses of immigrant customers in urban neighbourhoods. Despite unemployment, the spending power of these immigrant customers was relatively high, buttressed as it was by social benefits. The economic environment had changed because of the neo-liberal deregulation favouring new and small businesses. At this juncture, push (supply side) and pull (demand side) factors came together and immigrant entrepreneurship started growing in an unprecedented way in the Netherlands. The combination of these factors was especially evident in the four largest Dutch cities. In Amsterdam, Rotterdam, The Hague and Utrecht, nowadays one firm in ten is an immigrant-owned business and this percentage is even considerably higher in specific sectors such as the retail trade and restaurants.

At first, immigrant entrepreneurship fell outside the scope of social scientists. There were not many immigrant entrepreneurs and since entrepreneurship was *bourgeois*, it was not considered very exciting in the days when Marxism reigned supreme in the social sciences, we ourselves being no exception, and research focused on working-class issues. In the 1980s, however, a different twist was given to entrepreneurship. Self-employment came to be seen and appreciated as a way for immigrants to pull themselves up by their bootstraps. This generated interest in immigrant entrepreneurship, especially on the part of social scientists rather than economists. Much of this research focused on the avowedly *ethnic* character of immigrant entrepreneurship, and ethnicity was the prism through which researchers examined immigrant entrepreneurship. This narrow view on immigrant entrepreneurship was often at the expense of other important aspects such as the political and economic environment in which the immigrant entrepreneurs operate. Although research in the Netherlands has revealed a number of interesting facts due to its empiricist and policy-driven nature, it has not contributed a great deal to a more thorough understanding of immigrant entrepreneurship.

The situation in the current phase that started in the mid-1990s is rather different than the one described above. The backdrop is different, with immigrant entrepreneurship exhibiting a clear and continuous rise in relative and in absolute terms. The drive toward the internationalization of social science has prompted researchers to look more intensively abroad for their inspiration and for the dissemination of their findings. This means a great deal of the research on immigrant entrepreneurship is now couched in vocabularies that make it possible for international comparisons to be made from the start. The first steps down this road have demonstrated once again that ethnicity is not a very good starting point, especially not for international comparisons. Looking at ethnicity will not suffice to account for the differences between countries, as is illustrated by comparing the success of a group of immigrant entrepreneurs in one city and the relative lack of success of their ethnic counterparts in another city. A more comprehensive explanation is needed, one that includes the broader political, socio-economical and institutional environment.

Notes

1. This was done in close collaboration with private and semi-private institutions based on religion or philosophy of life. For most of the twentieth century, the Netherlands was a consociational democracy based on 'pillars' (cf. Lijphart 1975). The pillars were organized along religious lines. In the Netherlands, there were three main pillars: Roman-Catholic, Protestant and Social-Democratic. Daily life took place largely within the framework of

these pillars and one could argue that in this polarized society, societal cleavages ran deeper than in contemporary multicultural societies. Many of these immigrants exhibited a striking proclivity toward entrepreneurship in their countries of destination (e.g. Peters 1999).

2. These figures refer to immigrants from non-Western countries and immigrants belonging to the target groups of the central government's minority policy (van den Tillaart 2001: 8–9). Surinamese, Dutch Antilleans and Arubans, Turks, Moroccans, immigrants from other Mediterranean countries, Chinese (including those from Hong Kong) constitute the majority of the target groups. The target groups include second- and third-generation immigrants from these areas, but exclude immigrants of other origins.

3. One example pertains to the Chinese sailors who were recruited as scabs in the 1910s and settled in 'colonies' close to the docks in Amsterdam and Rotterdam (van Heek 1936). In the early twentieth century, there were also groups from Germany, Poland and other Eastern European countries who fled from poverty and anti-Semitic persecution and came to work here, e.g. as domestic servants, entertainers or moviemakers (Dittrich and Würzner 1982; Henkes 1995). Another example is the Italian traders in subtropical fruits who arrived in the 1930s and spread all over the country to set up ice-cream parlours (Bovenkerk and Ruland 1992). In the southernmost part of the country, Italian, Slovenian and Polish immigrants worked in the mines (Brassé and van Schelven 1980).

4. As a consequence, the repatriates from the Dutch East Indies/Indonesia and their offspring are no longer a separate category in the population figures.

5. In 2000, there were approximately 100,000 businesses in the agricultural sector in the Netherlands.

6. Martens and Veenman (1999: 136) note on the basis of a survey that Turkish entrepreneurs represent 5 per cent of the corresponding active labour force, Moroccans, Surinamese and Antillean entrepreneurs 3 per cent, and the native Dutch 9 per cent.

7. These figures are based on the Chamber of Commerce company register. Companies have to be registered in the Netherlands and the company register should be an accurate measure of entrepreneurial dynamics. The registration includes the name and address of the company and its owner, his country of birth, what kind of legal body the company is, the starting date, the branch and so on and so forth. In practice, however, things are different, and not every company that registered is actually active and not every enterprise that is active is properly registered. Thus the company register only reflects a bureaucratic reality. Deviations vary from branch to branch and possibly also from one category of the population to the other. The registration of garment factories in Amsterdam was notoriously inaccurate (Raes et al. 2002).

8. This does not mean all immigrants necessarily want to work with their compatriots. Half the Turks interviewed by Veraart (1996: 87–8) definitely had no desire.
9. See also Choenni 1997; Kloosterman et al. 1997a, b; Rath 1995, 2000a; Rath and Kloosterman 1998a, b; van den Tillaart 2001; van den Tillaart and Poutsma 1998.
10. Go to http://www.citymondial.nl/. See Rath (2002d) for a discussion of the immigrant tourist industry.
11. Van Heek's study on Chinese immigrants in 1936 was an exception (see also Wubben 1986).
12. We could only find a short passage on Chinese cafeterias and restaurants in the chapter by Vellinga and Wolters in the book *Allochtonen in Nederland* (1973: 223–4).
13. Coopers & Lybrand (see Setzpfand et al. 1993), the Bureau for Economic Argumentation (BEA 1994), Regioplan (see Hulshof and Mevissen 1985) and Kybele Consultants (see Bayraktar and van der Weide 1996) conducted research projects. In 1996, the fully state-funded Social and Cultural Planning Bureau devoted attention to 'ethnic entrepreneurship' for the first time in their annual report (Tesser et al. 1996). Van den Tillaart (2000, 2002; see also van den Tillaart and Poutsma 1998) gave a few more general overviews on the number of immigrant entrepreneurs. Choenni and Choenni (1998) contributed to a handbook for the SME sector, and Jansen (1999) wrote a chapter in a handbook for the 'ethnic minorities industry'. Rath and Kloosterman (1998c) edited a collection of essays on qualitative aspects of immigrant entrepreneurship in the Netherlands, and wrote a critical overview of the research in this country (1998a, b, d, 2000b).
14. Becker and de Jong (1987), Choenni (1993, 1997), de Feijter et al. (2001), van der Meulen and Heilbron (1995), Hoffer (1998), Kumcu et al. (1998), Masurel et al. (2001), Minghuan (2000), Rijkschroeff (1998), Vogels et al. (1999), van der Torre (1998), van der Weerd (2001), Wermuth (1998) and Zhang (1999) touched upon the development of entrepreneurship among specific immigrant groups. A number of projects were commissioned by sector or trade organizations, associated companies or Chambers of Commerce, such as the Dutch Bakers' Foundation (see Swinkels 1991), the Board of Trade for the Clothing Industry, interested in arguments to settle once and for all with the Turkish (hence illegal) garment contracting industry (see BEA 1992), Atlas and Terp Onderzoeksbureau (1991), the Royal Association of Restaurants (see Bruin et al. 1997b; van Brussel and Veninckx 1997), the Hotel and Restaurant Trade Association (see de Wit 1999) about the market dynamics for Chinese restaurants, the Trades Council about neighbourhood retail shops (see Benner 1988; Suyver and

Lie A Kwie 1998a, b), the Turkish business support agency Annifer about immigrant entrepreneurship in the Utrecht neighbourhood Lombok (see Canak and Haanstra 1998), and the Rotterdam Chamber of Commerce about Moroccan entrepreneurship in Rotterdam and Gouda (see Kamer van Koophandel Rotterdam 2001). Others were commissioned by the government, such as Bronsveld and van der Giessen (2000) about the employment of immigrant youngsters by immigrant employers in Rotterdam, Choenni (1998, 2000, 2001) about the role of location and business accommodations in the Amsterdam retail trade, Cuperus (1999) about Turkish entrepreneurship in the town of Almelo, van Delft et al. (1988) about business-support programmes in Southeast Amsterdam, van Dijk et al. (1993) about a soft-loans programme, Piard et al. (1988), Martina (1999) and Steenkamp (2000) about immigrant entrepreneurship in the Province of Gelderland, Nienhuis et al. (2001) about the activities of the Amsterdam business support agency STEW, de Jong (1988) and Wolff and Rath (2000) about financing immigrant entrepreneurship (in Amsterdam), and SER (1998) about immigrant entrepreneurship in general.

15. Immigrants from Belgium and Portugal, Eastern European Jews, French Huguenots, Romen Catholic Westphalians and gypsies have been the subjects of studies (see Berg et al. 1994; Doortmont 1998; Knotter 1995; Lucassen 1998; Lucassen and Vermeulen 1999; Merens 1996; Miellet 1987; Rath 1998, 2000a; Schrover 1996, 1998, 2001).

16. Flap et al. (2000) and Kumcu (2001) examined the role of social networks, Rekers (1993) and Kloosterman and van der Leun (1999) explored the role of the urban economic structure immigrant entrepreneurs operate in. Raes (1996; see also Raes et al. 2002) and Kumcu (2001) examined the impact of local and international market developments on immigrant entrepreneurs in the Amsterdam garment industry. Reil and Korver (2001) and Zorlu (1998; see also Hartog and Zorlu 1999) analyzed labour market dimensions of the same sector. Bruin et al. (1997a), Burgers et al. (1996), Kloosterman (2000), Kloosterman et al. (1997a, b, 1998, 1999), and Rath (1995, 1999a, b, 2000a, c, 2002a, b) discussed various other matters related to regulation and processes of informalization. Kehla et al. (1997) wrote a report on immigrant entrepreneurs at a weekly market in Rotterdam, Bovenkerk and Fijnaut (1996) reported on criminal entrepreneurs, Pool (2003) focused on the role of the City of Amsterdam at the establishment of an 'exotic' covered market, Rath (1997, 1998, 2002e) assessed the game of ethnic musical chairs in Amsterdam, and explored the construction industry (2001, 2002f). Engelen (2001), Kloosterman (2000) and Rath (2000c, 2002a, d) conducted more general theoretical research, addressing an international readership. Rath (2002c) did an international comparative study on the garment industry.

Italy: Between Legal Barriers
and Informal Arrangements

Mauro Magatti and Fabio Quassoli

The General Characteristics of Migrant Flows

In the last twenty years, Spain, Italy and Greece have been experiencing migration processes which are rather different from what happened in Central-Northern European countries and America during the whole twentieth century and before (King 1999). After being among the main labour-exporting areas, since the end of the 1970s Southern Europe has become an increasingly popular goal for migrations coming from Africa, Latin America, Asia and Eastern Europe. This change has coincided with the progressive border closing carried out by the main labour-importing European countries and has happened in a general framework of progressive restriction and increasing regulation of access possibilities to the European territory (Sciortino 2000). The most considerable results of the new control tools, which were concomitant with the closing of borders in traditional immigration countries, have been the growth of illegal immigration flows and the increasing precarious character of documented immigrants' legal status. In all the countries on the Northern Mediterranean coast, there is now a considerable and diversified segment of illegal immigration, which has become officially visible during the 'legalization campaigns' that have repeatedly taken place in Spain, Italy and Greece (Fakiolas 1999; Reyneri 1998a).

The peculiarities vis-à-vis previous experiences are not confined to a strictly legal ground and to immigration control policies, which are now co-ordinated at a European level. They also concern the socio-economic conditions where recent immigration has taken place, the characteristics of migration projects, the settling modes and the political and cultural climate that migrants find upon their arrival in Southern European countries.

As far as the Italian case is concerned, statistical evidence clearly reveals that immigration into Italy has been on a smaller scale than into other northern and central European countries (Bonifazi 1998). The immigrant inflow accelerated in the second half of the 1980s, then gradually decreased in the first half of the 1990s (Caritas di Rome 1997). Even today, the number of immigrants does not exceed 2.5 per cent of the total population (Caritas di Rome 2001).

The 'timing' of immigration flows has produced some important consequences. The social system with which immigrants are confronted in Italy exhibits a significant reduction in some of the features that granted stability and integration in the Fordist societies. First, immigrants could not 'benefit' from a developing industrial economy requiring a large amount of cheap unqualified labour. Instead, they were faced with a much more complex society and labour market, and could not rely on sizeable, strongly rooted communities and networks of fellow citizens to serve as a first reference point for job opportunities, as in the past migratory processes. Second, some of the socialization agencies (trade unions, mass parties and social movements) that played a crucial role in industrial society are no longer available to mediate the process of integration. Third, they could no longer benefit from an expanding welfare state and universalistic welfare provisions: on the contrary, nowadays their citizenship status and rights to access welfare provisions are being debated all across Europe (Baldwin-Edwards and Schain 1994; Cesarani and Fulbrook 1997).

We can summarize the main characteristics of immigration into Italy as follows.

1 *Gender differentiation.* There is a clear 'gender gap' among the new immigrants. First-comers are usually males, particularly from southern Mediterranean and some West African countries, who are joined by their families. However, in some instances females migrate first, e.g. from Central and South America, the Philippines, Eritrea, Cape Verde and Nigeria, and then start networks that subsequently include male migrants. Some migrant groups consist of both males and females from the start (Caritas di Rome 1997).

2 *Multiple socio-geographical backgrounds.* Immigrants come from urban and rural settings alike. Rural immigrants are generally older and less educated and tend to emigrate according to the 'traditional' pattern: a temporary economically motivated stay (Piore 1983). They maintain strong ties with their country of origin, particularly via their relatives and fellow nationals, and develop an 'instrumental' approach to the job market; they are more ready to accept bad jobs while minimizing non-survival spending, thus reproducing a well-known model of first-generation migrants. Migrants from urban settings are on average better educated, younger (though this is truer for some groups than for others, for example Moroccans as opposed to Senegalese), and less embedded in networks linked with the country of origin (remittances can be used as an indicator). In many cases, they are much more oriented toward exploratory migration projects and consider Italy a temporary step to other European countries, as is typical of

immigrants from Somalia or the former Yugoslavia. At the same time, they are more open to interaction with Italian culture and society (IReR 1994). With the exception of Somalians, Eritreans and in part Albanians, immigrants come from countries with no historical relationships or contacts with Italy. This fact has had numerous consequences. As regards immigrants' skills, for instance, a basic problem is their poor mastery and control of the Italian language; they generally lack the linguistic competence as a strategic resource in a society where control over information is increasingly important (Quassoli and Venzo 1997).

3 *Relevance of circular migratory patterns.* Immigration projects reveal a new characteristic: a great geographical mobility, which has been encouraged by the possibilities offered by much cheaper and more efficient communication and transport tools than those available in the past and which seems to follow at least three different patterns. First, a sizeable part of immigrants (the same is true also for Spain and Greece) coming from the Mediterranean basin (which in all the three countries, especially in Greece and Spain, represent the vast majority of foreigners) is characterized by circular migration projects. Many Moroccans who have migrated to Italy and Spain spend a few months every year in Morocco, where they have temporary jobs or try to start a business with the money they have earned (IReR 1994). Albanians who have come to Italy and to Greece since 1991 exhibit similar circular patterns (Barjaba et al. 1996). Another typical phenomenon is *trabendo*, or informal trade between northern and southern Mediterranean cities. For some young people from North Africa it is an important part of their migration trajectory (Colombo 1998). Immigration laws, which are highly rigid and have not yet acknowledged many of the basic traits of migration to Italy, are the main obstacle to the further spread of this kind of migratory project. Secondly, immigrants show a high territorial mobility within the countries of immigration, which must be linked both to the rather unstructured pathways of incorporation into the labour market (mainly, as we show below, in the underground economy) and to an increasing flexibility of the labour market. Thirdly, a growing mobility within the European territory and to other immigration countries (Canada and United States) has been noticed for different immigrant groups: people from Somalia, Philippines, ex-Yugoslavia, for instance, seem to consider Italy as just a step toward a better destination, such as the United Kingdom, Canada and the United States.

4 *Complexity of migrants' social networks.* Immigrants are embedded in social and communicative networks usually described with the terms of 'community', 'clan', 'family links', 'solidarity', 'enforceable trust', 'ethnic enclave' and the like. However, the concept of network has a much broader meaning and should not be associated with certain ethnic or cultural characteristics of migrant groups. Migrants' social networks are extensive and heterogeneous (Barbesino and Quassoli 1997). They mainly consist of compatriots, but often involve

migrants from other countries and Italians (friends, colleagues, acquaintances and people working for agencies or public services). Within these networks, different criteria apply to the organization of social relations and the flow of information. The country of provenance is one of the criteria, but not always the most relevant. Religion, socio-economic status, age, and language all play a role in defining the network boundaries.

5   *Patterns of socio-economic integration and geographical distribution.* A long-term common characteristic of the Italian economy is a big and widespread underground economy, where immigrants have been incorporating massively over the last two decades (Reyneri 2000). Either in possession of residence permits or not, immigrants in Italy have been working massively in the under-ground economy where absence of any kinds of protection, high exploitation and work mobility seem to be widespread. At the same time, an increasing number of immigrants find regular and stable employment in small industries and some public services (Ambrosini 1999).

Migrants in Italy are not evenly distributed over the country. Initially concen-trated in Rome and the south, in the past few years their presence in the northern regions has grown. Since 1994, at least half of the immigrants have settled in the north, where job opportunities are greater and more diversified. There are various jobs in the tertiary sector (restaurants, trade, street-selling, domestic services), and in small and medium-sized firms in the prosperous regions of Piedmont, Lombardy, Veneto and Emilia Romegna, and temporary and seasonal work in construction and agriculture (Ambrosini 1999; Palidda and Reyneri 1995). The geographical shift to the north also reveals a new trend toward immi-grant location stabilization, though mobility within the country remains high.

A comparison between the conditions in the south and the north of Italy reveals marked differences. In the south, in the 1980s and early 1990s, conditions for integration into local society were more favourable,[1] while economic oppor-tunities were less attractive. Labour relations are generally very one-sided, which is not to the advantage of immigrants. All the sectors are characterized by a high degree of exploitation. The fact that it is difficult or even impossible to obtain a residence permit makes the decision to move to the north of Italy to benefit from better job opportunities a problematic one. Immigrants usually associate the north with more bureaucracy and police control and fewer opportunities in the informal sector. Opinions about the north are, however, now rapidly changing, as more and more immigrants are discovering that there are job opportunities in the formal and informal sectors too. This change has been reinforced by the increasing presence of social networks that support newcomers in their first contact with local society. At the same time, social life is harder in the metro-politan areas of the north and problems of maladjustment and social isolation are more common.

6 *A difficult political and cultural climate.* Since the first half of the 1990s, immigrants in their pathways toward integration in the Italian society have had to face rather unfavourable conditions. These were characterized by revivals of xenophobia; a rising criminalization by the political system (Palidda 2001), accompanied by the increasing precariousness of their legal status; highly stigmatizing social representations circulated by local and national media (Dal Lago 1999) and, more generally, a difficult social integration and universalistic access to citizenship rights (Zincone 1999).

Immigrants on the Labour Market

Some General Remarks

To explain the position of immigrant workers on the Italian labour-market, we need to describe the history of the normative framework and its recent transformations (Nascimbene 1995, 1997; Pastore 1995; Quassoli 1999). The basic distinction is between foreign workers who live in Italy (with an official permit) and those who want to but still live abroad. As for their rights on the labour-market, the first group is assimilated in the native population, but the second is subjected to a number of restrictions, the main one being the priority given to resident workers for jobs in Italy. But when they are officially admitted to the Italian territory and authorized to hold a job, immigrants are formally equal to Italian workers in the private-sector, though they cannot be employed by the state or by two large ex-state companies, FS (State Railways) and Poste (National Post Service).

Having said that, the whole picture can be reconstructed using two main data sources. The first is the INPS archives on dependent employment in non-agricultural firms; the second the Ministry of Labour registration of job entering.[2] INPS data for the 1992–1998 period confirm a stable and relevant increase in the number of immigrant employees regularly employed by Italian firms (see Table 8.1). The absolute number is rather low, as is the percentage in Italian employment as a whole (less than 1 per cent); nevertheless, in the last six years, immigrant employment has doubled, growing at a much faster pace than native employment. A second point concerns the regional distribution. As Table 8.1 demonstrates, most of the immigrants are employed in the north, which absorbs almost 80 per cent of the total foreign workforce, especially in manufacturing. Foreign workers are mainly employed in the richest and most dynamics areas, especially the ones with a strong industrial orientation, such as the northeast (Veneto and Emilia Romegna). As far as the economic sectors are concerned, trade and the metal industry and manufacturing absorb the largest share of employees, with respectively 48,000 and 41,000 immigrant workers in 1998. Together they employ more than 50 per cent of the total foreign workforce (see Table 8.2), followed by construction (20,000 workers), chemicals (16,000 workers) and textiles (10,000 workers).

Table 8.1 Immigrant Workers Employed in Non-agricultural Firms by Region, 1992–1996

Regions	1992	1993	1994	1995	1996	1996	1992–96 a.v.	1992–96 %
Abruzzo	692	996	1,159	1,217	1,506	1.1	814	117.6
Basilicata	76	82	53	66	94	0.1	18	23.7
Calabria	138	135	168	179	428	0.3	290	210.1
Campania	441	521	538	667	1,889	1.3	1,448	328.3
Emilia Romagna	16,828	14,268	15,154	18,041	20,993	14.7	4,165	24.8
Friuli-Venezia Giulia	3,619	3,961	4,477	5,052	5,543	3.9	1,924	53.2
Latium	6,091	6,120	5,861	5,871	7,583	5.3	1,492	24.5
Liguria	1,487	1,411	1,371	1,477	2,198	1.5	711	47.8
Lombardy	25,319	25,896	26,899	31,059	37,357	26.2	12,038	47.5
Marche	2,275	2,524	3,148	3,996	4,662	3.3	2,387	104.9
Molise	66	42	31	30	47	0.0	-19	-28.8
Piemonte	7,342	6,882	7,387	8,791	12,355	8.7	5,013	68.3
Puglia	752	670	685	668	1,268	0.9	516	68.6
Sardinia	168	147	117	111	217	0.2	49	29.2
Sicily	1,294	1,174	1,074	1,001	1,304	0.9	10	0.8
Tuscany	4,314	4,770	5,438	6,343	10,458	7.3	6,144	142.4
Trentino Alto-Adige	3,848	4,367	4,797	5,871	6,808	4.8	2,960	76.9
Umbria	1,130	1,076	1,269	1,412	1,961	1.4	831	73.5
Val d'Aosta	404	364	303	318	367	0.3	-37	-9.2
Veneto	13,041	13,093	15,757	20,154	25,307	17.8	12,266	94.1
Total	89,325	88,499	95,686	112,324	142,345	100.0	53,020	59.4

Source: Data from INPS, processed by ISMU.

Table 8.2 Immigrant Workers by Economic Sector and by Region, 1998

Regions	Agriculture	Mining	Furniture	Food industry	Metal and steel industry	Textile and garment	Chemical sector	Paper sector	Construction	Transport	Private and public administration	Credit and insurance sectors	Trade	Rest	Total
Valle d'Aosta	2	12	3	22	31	0	3	1	104	10	0	0	190	16	394
Piemonte	15	436	463	499	4,105	789	668	172	2,520	735	39	5	3,362	323	14,131
Lombardy	22	1,026	1,048	1,184	12,918	3,005	3,893	548	4,141	2,457	98	100	13,634	1166	45,240
Trentino Alto-Adige	17	387	245	238	788	131	225	40	919	488	38	2	4,106	161	7,785
Veneto	20	1,776	2,345	674	9,206	1,988	6,232	321	3,541	1,666	21	7	4,698	526	33,021
Friuli-Venezia Giulia	2	228	1,161	91	137	151	158	29	904	459	13	2	1,633	130	6,331
Liguria	3	46	35	59	222	14	28	9	651	104	24	0	1,167	86	2,448
Emilia Romagna	24	1,501	659	1,268	8,164	1,076	1,368	233	3,033	1,426	27	5	6,362	576	25,722
Tuscany	41	330	275	245	1,215	2,542	1,445	105	1,648	290	16	1	3,531	215	11,899
Umbria	48	128	76	82	383	114	46	24	731	115	18	0	453	45	2,263
Marche	16	205	616	128	1,529	225	1,870	62	746	224	6	1	1,040	218	6,886
Latium	9	181	106	278	493	105	91	58	1,076	257	32	21	5,890	233	8,830
Abruzzo	4	42	53	80	212	112	66	7	328	118	0	1	544	157	1,724
Molise	0	3	1	4	10	3	2	0	6	1	0	0	20	3	53
Campania	4	42	33	88	115	203	70	13	95	41	0	4	605	24	1,337
Basilicata	0	1	4	3	35	4	0	0	16	3	1	0	25	2	94
Puglia	1	37	65	76	136	78	160	13	87	38	0	0	459	33	1,184
Calabria	0	12	10	25	25	10	4	0	33	30	0	1	119	7	276
Sicily	1	27	25	73	117	13	33	14	69	17	7	5	826	49	1,276
Sardinia	0	15	7	10	25	1	4	2	22	8	0	0	131	4	229
Italy	229	6,435	7,230	5,127	41,099	10,564	16,366	1,651	20,670	8,487	341	155	48,795	3,974	171,123

Source: INPS

A very different piece of information emerges from Table 8.3 on housekeepers regularly employed in families since 1995. There are 104,000 of them, which is 38 per cent of the total. The rate of increase is even higher than in the previous case, since they more than doubled in just three years from 45,000 to 104,000. A major difference is that most of these employees are female: 75 per cent, while women are just 10 per cent of firms' dependents. This means there is a strong job specialization by gender among immigrants in Italy: men usually work in factories and firms, while women are housekeepers and generally work for families. The territorial distribution is rather different too: as for personal services, the main region is now Latium (mainly Rome) followed by Lombardy (mainly Milan): Latium and Lombardy together employ about 55 per cent of the total foreign workforce in the service sector.

The second source of data pertains to the new jobs registered by the Ministry of Labour. This source is more exhaustive than the INPS data, since it covers the whole private-sector, but it is also less reliable since it registers the entrances, which, in a labour-market becoming more flexible, do not necessarily involve full time and long-term jobs. Therefore, sectors such as agriculture or tourism – characterized by high levels of variability in the course of a year – may be over-estimated. However, these data offer further information that may help to complete the picture.

As Table 8.4 suggests, the distribution of immigrant work is territorially less concentrated here than in the INPS data. Though still the region with the highest share of new jobs, Lombardy is reducing its gap with other regions. An explanation is that in the central and southern parts of Italy, the job supply for immigrants is less stable than that in the north. A second observation concerns employment in agriculture, where a very low number of job entrances is only registered in Sicily, while regions characterized by the massive presence of Mediterranean agriculture, and where some studies showed a widespread presence of immigrants, appear to have very low percentages of new jobs for immigrants (Zanfrini 1998). This suggests that in these regions, informal work is rather widespread (Calvanese and Pugliese 1990; Mingione and Quassoli 1999).

Immigrants are mainly employed as unskilled (75 per cent) or semi-skilled workers (less than 20 per cent) at the most (see Table 8.5). It is extremely unlikely that they can get white-collar jobs or even become specialized workers (technicians). As a matter of fact, some studies shown that they often do work with a higher profile than is implied by their formal status. These studies also show that immigrant job positions have slowly but constantly improved in the last few years (Zanfrini 1999). However, the process is rather slow and problematic: for a foreign worker, job mobility to a higher position has to be negotiated with the internal workforce to avoid objections.

Table 8.3 Immigrant Housekeepers by Gender, 1995–1997 (Absolute Numbers)

Regions	1995			1996			1997		
	Male	*Female*	*Total*	*Male*	*Female*	*Total*	*Male*	*Female*	*Total*
Valle d'Aosta	6	64	70	11	65	76	10	84	94
Piedmont	644	2,564	3,208	1,343	4,917	6,260	1,120	5,091	6,211
Lombardy	3,151	10,139	13,290	7,136	19,394	26,530	6,342	19,673	26,015
Trentino Alto-Adige	40	507	547	72	628	700	59	620	679
Veneto	698	2,412	3,110	1	3,287	4,287	912	3,543	4,455
Friuli-Venezia Giulia	98	1,013	1,111	130	1,156	1,286	119	1,150	1,269
Liguria	511	1,632	2,143	745	2,516	3,261	605	2,352	2,957
Emilia Romagna	690	2,945	3,635	1,277	4,400	5,677	1,107	4,665	5,772
Tuscany	1,175	3,857	5,032	2,639	6,188	8,827	2,185	6,315	8,500
Umbria	246	654	900	385	1,147	1,532	305	1,224	1,529
Marche	173	857	1,030	293	1,307	1,600	261	1,292	1,553
Latium	4,231	12,632	16,863	7,300	21,021	28,321	7,975	23,951	31,926
Abruzzo	48	345	393	108	558	666	98	574	672
Molise	15	80	95	18	110	128	14	92	106
Campania	782	1,791	2,573	2,236	2,925	5,161	1,711	3,300	5,011
Basilicata	23	50	73	35	59	94	11	46	57
Puglia	529	914	1,443	1,184	1,540	2,724	781	1,373	2,154
Calabria	157	495	652	460	877	1,337	370	914	1,284
Sicily	2,478	2,350	4,828	5,138	3,690	8,828	1,937	1,972	3,909
Sardinia	107	273	380	288	430	718	99	447	546
Italy	15,802	45,574	61,376	31,798	76,215	108,013	26,021	78,678	104,699

Source: INPS.

Mauro Magatti and Fabio Quassoli

Table 8.4 Immigrant Workers Placed by Employment Agencies by Sector and Sex, 1997

Regions	Agriculture			Manufacturing		
	Male	Female	Total	Male	Female	Total
Valle d'Aosta	198	4	202	102	2	104
Piedmont	1,713	230	1,943	5,281	395	5,676
Lombardy	2,955	242	3,197	14,267	1,264	15,531
Trentino Alto-Adige	2,278	303	2,581	1,326	118	1,444
Veneto	5,565	823	6,388	14,943	1,998	16,941
Friuli-Venezia Giulia	333	148	481	2,374	293	2,667
Liguria	499	27	526	815	71	886
Emilia Romagna	4,133	756	4,889	10,714	986	11,700
Tuscany	3,150	292	3,442	4,508	744	5,252
Umbria	1,601	243	1,844	1,247	84	1,331
Marche	453	115	568	2,479	342	2,821
Latium	2,072	185	2,257	1,414	109	1,523
Abruzzo	1,712	146	1,858	1,161	95	1,256
Molise	172	14	186	14	0	14
Campania	688	126	814	824	213	1,037
Basilicata	1,699	140	1,839	1,064	99	1,163
Puglia	655	45	700	165	13	178
Calabria	708	119	827	272	22	294
Sicily	5,821	454	6,275	970	279	1,249
Sardinia	187	7	194	143	4	147
Italy	36,592	4,419	41,011	64,083	7,131	71,214

Source: Ministry of Labour.

Table 8.5 Immigrant Workers Placed by Employment Agencies by Level of Skills, 1997

	Unqualified workers		Qualified workers		Specialized workers		Employees		Total
	a.v.	%	a.v.	%	a.v.	%	a.v.	%	a.v.
Valle d'Aosta	201	33.8	46	7.7	347	58.4	0	0.0	594
Piedmont	8,249	79.7	1,713	16.6	234	2.3	153	1.5	10,349
Lombardy	22,131	69.5	5,868	18.4	3,206	10.1	629	2.0	31,834
Trentino Alto-Adige	5,782	76.3	1,616	21.3	127	1.7	52	0.7	7,577
Veneto	22,039	74.5	6,409	21.7	740	2.5	382	1.3	29,570
Friuli-Venezia Giulia	3,302	58.0	1,692	29.7	505	8.9	193	3.4	5,692
Liguria	1,957	67.3	882	30.3	42	1.4	27	0.9	2,908
Emilia Romagna	17,562	74.1	5,344	22.6	379	1.6	411	1.7	23,696
Tuscany	9,398	72.5	3,078	23.7	280	2.2	212	1.6	12,968
Umbria	3,372	87.8	449	11.7	0	0.0	20	0.5	3,841
Marche	4,040	79.2	894	17.5	100	2.0	69	1.4	5,103
Latium	4,571	64.3	2,495	35.1	24	0.3	20	0.3	7,110
Abruzzo	3,484	82.9	641	15.3	25	0.6	52	1.2	4,202
Molise	164	91.1	15	8.3	0	0.0	1	0.6	180
Campania	2,455	92.9	102	3.9	72	2.7	14	0.5	2,643
Basilicata	731	92.6	57	7.2	0	0.0	1	0.1	789
Puglia	3,740	87.1	443	10.3	45	1.0	65	1.5	4,293
Calabria	1,439	96.1	28	1.9	2	0.1	28	1.9	1,497
Sicily	9,879	96.3	318	3.1	29	0.3	32	0.3	10,258
Sardinia	710	80.0	134	15.1	22	2.5	21	2.4	887
Italy	125,206	75.4	32,224	19.4	6,179	3.7	2,382	1.4	165,991

Source: Istat, Annuario statistico italiano, 1998.

From a formal point of view, there are no signs of clear discrimination against immigrants in manufacturing: labour conditions and the contractual relations are basically the same for immigrants and Italians (Mottura and Pinto 1996). In fact, empirical findings show that what is important for explaining the significant presence of immigrants is the nature of the work involved: strenuous and unskilled jobs, dangerous and unhealthy work environments, longer working hours and low wages (Reyneri 1998b). The most important difference between foreign and Italian workers is that the former are 'willing' to accept bad jobs for longer periods of time. In addition to the assumption that immigrants are willing to accept temporary jobs as one of the most important requirements of the new labour-markets and a condition that explains their greater suitability, in Italy we also see the opposite: in many cases, employers actively seek immigrant workers because they are available for long-term unskilled jobs.

Immigrants are faced with sizeable job-search difficulties. As Table 8.6 indicates, the unemployment rates among immigrants are extremely high and in 1997 they were higher than the employment rates according to INPS data (179,696). Many of the immigrants (34 per cent) were long-term unemployed, which is an indicator of the difficulties foreign workers still have in the Italian formal labour-market. Most of the unemployed immigrants make ends meet by working in the informal economy.

As is well known, the Italian informal economy is rather large, especially in the south where, according to some scholars, a quarter of the total employment is irregular. According to official estimates (ISTAT), the number of immigrants working outside the formal sector is about 700,000, i.e. 14 per cent of the total irregular employment. Not everyone agrees with these estimates. Some consider them too high. According to the inspections effectively carried out by the Ministry of Labour, the percentage of irregular immigrant workers is 31 per cent, which is twice the percentage of the Italian ones (Reyneri and Baganha 1998). However, the inspected sectors have been those with a high propensity for informality.

On the whole, immigrants are largely present in sectors that are at risk in terms of informal work: home and personal services, construction and agriculture. The issue is certainly important in agriculture, especially in the south, where the work is conducive to the widespread use of informal employees and a huge exploitation of the immigrants. According to some scholars, one out of ten employees is informally employed in this sector in the southern regions of Italy. This helps to create a sort of typical path followed by numerous immigrants – especially the illegal ones – who reached Italy in the last few years: after having entered the country illegally, they find a survival job in the southern agriculture in the informal sector; which allows them to earn some money and survive. As soon as there is there is a chance for an official residence permit (thanks to the *sanatorie*), the immigrant tries to move to the central or northern regions to find a

Table 8.6 Unemployed Immigrants Registered at the Employment Agencies by Registration Period, 1997

Regions	Up to 3 months		From 3 to 12 months		More than 12 months		Total
	a.v.	%	a.v.	%	a.v.	%	a.v.
Valle d'Aosta	86	27.3	173	54.9	56	17.8	315
Piedmont	3,233	22.9	5,076	35.9	5,828	41.2	14,137
Lombardy	15,588	51.6	8,579	28.4	6,043	20.0	30,210
Trentino Alto-Adige	1,631	62.6	721	27.7	255	9.8	2,607
Veneto	4,975	38.5	5,319	41.1	2,642	20.4	12,936
Friuli-Venezia Giulia	793	27.8	981	34.3	1,082	37.9	2,856
Liguria	1,342	26.7	1,420	28.2	2,271	45.1	5,033
Emilia Romagna	3,370	22.7	5,345	36.0	6,135	41.3	14,850
Tuscany	4,163	33.0	5,166	40.9	3,287	26.1	12,616
Umbria	745	21.6	1,120	32.5	1,585	45.9	3,450
Marche	957	27.0	1,338	37.8	1,244	35.2	3,539
Latium	5,884	17.6	15,252	45.7	12,269	36.7	33,405
Abruzzo	849	21.5	1,067	27.1	2,028	51.4	3,944
Molise	68	35.6	94	49.2	29	15.2	191
Campania	2,142	15.9	5,579	41.3	5,776	42.8	13,497
Basilicata	86	15.9	215	39.8	239	44.3	540
Puglia	1,266	25.0	2,251	44.5	1,543	30.5	5,060
Calabria	724	21.8	1,243	37.4	1,357	40.8	3,324
Sicily	3,237	22.2	4,986	34.1	6,388	43.7	14,611
Sardinia	592	23.0	919	35.7	1,064	41.3	2,575
Italy	51,731	28.8	66,844	37.2	61,121	34.0	179,696

Source: data from Ministry of Labour, processed by ISMU.

better-paid, regular though often hard job. A flow from the south to the north is what happened after every *sanatoria*. However, as Table 8.7 shows, this problem is still very large and more than 50 per cent of the employees – according to Reyneri (1998b) – are off the books (see Table 8.7).

Table 8.7 Estimates for Irregular Immigrant Workers by Sector and Region, 1994

	North	Centre	South	Total
Agriculture	27.8	44.4	79.2	49.3
Industry	39.8	52.0	55.9	41.8
Handicraft	57.4	69.0	63.9	61.2
Retail Trade	49.7	49.6	68.5	51.4
Turism	34.7	80.0	44.7	41.6
Entertainment Ind.	37.6	36.0	96.9	38.1
Food Sector	61.8	84.1	57.5	73.2
Cleaning firms	92.9	76.7	60.0	92.6
Housekeeping	48.2	57.0	34.5	48.3
Total	52.9	58.6	70.8	56.8

Source: Reyneri 1998b.

Generally speaking, irregular jobs do not diminish with the increase of the regular ones. Rather than a preference of the immigrants to stay in the informal sector, their continued presence there should be explained in terms of the prefer-ence of the employers to have a highly flexible, low-paid, unstable workforce (Zanfrini 1999: 44–5). The permanence in the informal sector is usually due to the immigrants' inability to get formal work. Moreover, some studies show that, beyond those trapped in the informal (or even illegal) sector, there are those who are borderline, since they are compelled to stay part in the formal and part in the informal economy. We have already mentioned part-timers or immigrants working outside the firms as an external supplier (mainly a co-operative), but this may be also true for housekeepers and construction workers.

Three Models of Integration

The picture sketched above makes it possible to distinguish three models of immigrant integration in the Italian labour market in recent years. These models basically vary according to four variables: economic sector, geographical area, gender and level of informalization. On the whole, they describe how the Italian economy and society are trying to absorb the immigrant workforce.

The first model, which can be called *subaltern*, mainly involves young male immigrants working at small and medium-sized firms in the most industrialized areas of northern Italy, above all Lombardy and the north-east. Firms regularly employ a large percentage of subaltern workers, who receive a fair treatment, basically similar to that of Italian workers. However, a striking percentage work at least partly irregularly, and in many cases firms try to exploit the weakness of this population by creating poor working conditions. Whenever possible, firms employ immigrants indirectly by externalizing some functions.

Why has there been such a diffusion of immigrant work in these regions? Scholars agree that the main reason is that in a labour market not too far from full employment the hardest jobs are left unfilled by natives so that immigrants may fill up a segment of the labour market that is not very satisfying. In many cases, especially in small and medium-sized highly industrialized towns, the employers themselves – through their local associations – organize the search for immigrant workers to fill these jobs. Usually, they are industrial firms, and immigrants are mainly employed as unskilled workers at the lowest ranks of the internal hierarchy. It should be noted that – mainly in the first wave of immigrants – quite a large percentage of them had a high level of formal education.

The large number of formally employed immigrants in these regions and in these sectors confirms that the shortage of native workers is often the reason, which can explain the search for immigrant workers. But it is clear that many firms in these areas, especially the ones in sectors where price competition is still strong, try to exploit the immigrant workforce by reintroducing labour conditions and social protection levels that are no longer suitable for the local population. From that point of view, immigrants guarantee the availability of a flexible, structurally weak workforce, an essential condition for reducing costs and coping with fierce competition.

The second integrative model, the *servile* one, is mainly diffused in the large cities (Rome, and then Milan) and pertains to the whole area of personal services (especially housekeeping) and more generally the unskilled jobs in the tertiary sector (such as cleaning firms). The workforce here is largely female and Philippine women tend to 'monopolize' this market. The labour conditions are very different from what we have said about industrial employment: many workers work on an irregular basis (at least partly); the work relationship is not with a company, except for the cleaning firms, but directly with an individual or a family and this creates a strong sense of dependence.

The main reason for the expansion of this sector is probably the weakness of the Italian welfare state, which is not able to satisfy the demand for personal services. Most of the women employed as housekeepers come from countries with a Romen Catholic background, as the migratory chains have often been triggered by Romen Catholic associations operating as intermediaries between the demand and supply: it is the case for women from the Philippines, El Salvador,

Eritrea and Somalia. Then, the migratory chains are sustained through family and ethnic connections, which play a crucial role in organizing the arrival of new immigrants. This favours the development and strengthening of ethnic communities within the main cities and the creation of close-knit links among their members. It is usually very hard for an immigrant to change or improve his or her job situation, as this sector cannot offer any career prospect or links with the surrounding context.

The third integrative model, the *exploitative* one, is mainly diffused in the south, especially in agriculture, though it is not absent in other regions, especially in the north and east, where it is not uncommon in the construction and service sectors. The main feature of this model is its irregularity and informality: many of the employees work in the underground economy without any formal contract or regulation.

The absence of any legal protection makes for a fierce exploitation of the immigrant workforce, which is compelled to accept any conditions. In order to survive, immigrants have to work, but they cannot modify the labour irregularity since they do not have a stable job: they are trapped in a situation it is very hard to get out of.

There is no detailed data on how these people are recruited in the labour market, but it is clear that there is a market, which is able to guarantee the supply of new workers. This is particularly true in the south, where a real organization is irregularly bringing immigrants to Italy. Once they are in the country, immigrants are easily recruited as a flexible and informal workforce in agriculture, where poorly paid farmhands are sorely needed, in street selling (for years the streets in the richest cities or most popular beaches have been teeming with street vendors illegally selling all kinds of goods) or in low-level service activities. The informal employment of immigrants is also largely diffused in the restaurant and construction industries, in the north and south. Poor labour conditions, low wages and instability are the usual features of these activities, whose exploitative effects are extremely high.

Immigrant Self-employment and Micro-firms in the Italian Model

The Italian model is unique with respect to other Western countries as far as self-employment and micro-firms are concerned.[3] According to ISTAT, in 1996 about 28.8 per cent of jobs in Italy were filled by self-employed workers, i.e. about 5,770,000 individuals. Men are more frequently involved than women in this kind of activity, which often is organized on a family basis. This category not only includes self-employed workers, but also employers and professionals. Another 1,000,000 people are 'atypical' workers, who offer their services to a few firms regularly or to many firms occasionally.

Self-employment is more diffused in trading, restaurants and hotels, where the numbers are as much as 55 per cent; then the private service (to firms and families, where it is about 40 per cent) and construction industry (30 per cent) follow; in manufacturing and other sectors (such as communication and transport) the proportion is only between 15 and 20 per cent. In addition to self-employment (involving an activity where there are no employees involved), a major component of the Italian economy consists of millions of micro-firms, spread all over the country. They constitute an essential component of the Italian economy as well as of Italian society. Their presence is stronger in the north and centre of Italy than in the south.

There are so many explanations for this aspect of the Italian economy that it is difficult to even offer a synthetic summary here. There are economic, cultural and institutional reasons for the strength of self-employment and small firms. The artisan tradition so strong in many Italian regions, the role of the family as an economic unit, the tacit pact between the *ceti medi* (middle classes) and the political power since 1945, the weakness of large Italian corporations, the deep-seated inclination toward autonomous initiative and the existence of a cooperative climate in many localities, the possibility of social mobility made available by autonomous activities, the high level of unemployment and the rapid industrial reorganization which encouraged redundant workers to find alternative employment, and strategies followed by many firms towards externalization. These important factors all served to reinforce this sector in Italy.

It should also be stressed that self-employment is mainly prevalent in the most advanced and dynamic Italian regions (Emilia Romegna, Veneto, Lombardy, etc.), and that in the Italian social hierarchy, self-employment offers good opportunities for social mobility, which can be taken even by people without a formal education. As far as immigrant businesses are concerned, they have remained under-developed in Italy,[4] compared to those in Britain, France, the Netherlands, etc. (see other chapters in this book). There are some basic factors to be taken into consideration in explaining this situation.

Mass immigration has occurred over a short time-span. Italy has historically been an exporter of labour, and it was only in the 1980s, and even more so in the 1990s, that a significant flow into Italy began. This means that with rare exceptions,[5] the vast majority of the immigrant population is first-generation, and has not yet had time to put down social and economic roots. Add to this temporal aspect the national fragmentation of the new arriving immigrants, who continue to come from a wide range of countries. In 1998 and again in 1999, even the most significant country of origin of the immigrant arrivals did not account for 10 per cent of the total (Caritas di Rome 1999). This means a large number of relatively small 'ethnic' communities distributed over a wide territory, largely consisting of adult males. All this has numerous important implications for the projects immigrants pursue once they have landed in Italy. Many newcomers have a short-term plan, and consider a stable presence in Italy only one of the possible developments for their future. The weakness or absence of strong and tight 'ethnic' communities, which in many cases represent an enabling condition for the development of immigrant business (Waldinger et al. 1990a), has favoured the diffusion of semi-dependent activities rather than entrepreneurship, and these activities are carried out in an informal manner, often bordering on illegality, which lacks any element of autonomy or long-term prospects.[6]

Immigrants have found various ways to insert themselves into the Italian labour-market, but have always occupied a subordinate position. Particularly in the manufacturing sector in the northern regions, where, in certain sectors especially, local labour is scarce, most immigrants formally enter the workforce as workers, which makes it impossible to develop other strategies (Reyneri 1998a). The alternative to this route is illegal entry or informal labour, as generally occurs if there is no ethnic community to welcome the immigrants and insert them into internal labour networks. This means most immigrants find themselves doing the individualistic types of informal semi-entrepreneurial work outside of any social group to use as a point of reference.

We should consider the importance of self-employment in Italian society, especially in the northern and central areas. Italy not only has a much higher percentage of self-employed workers and small companies than other developed countries, for many decades and in many regions, certainly in the richest ones, it has been a strategy of the middle and lower-middle classes to go it alone, to gain access to otherwise unattainable income and status levels. In a country where the lack of large structures reduces the opportunities for reasonably or well educated people to make professional progress, having one's own business is socially and economically a very attractive proposition. From the immigrants' perspective, this has principally meant two things: first, to some extent the deep-rooted and widespread phenomenon of self-employment and small businesses within the native population has filled many of the spaces in the market, making it more difficult for an immigrant to start his own business (except, in the case of Milan, in certain niche activities). Secondly, relatively high prestige accorded to this entrepreneurship in many regions of the centre and north, can explain the widespread concept of the immigrant as an employee rather than a self-employed person. Immigration may be considered a source of labour where there would otherwise be a shortage, but it is far more difficult to accept the notion of immigrants starting their own businesses in the way that Italians do. The idea of immigrant subordination in Italy is principally expressed in the concept of the immigrant as an employee.

Entrepreneurial activities are subject to strict social and institutional rules. Trade-related activities are an interesting example. They are highly regulated by multifarious state and local laws and rules. Furthermore, trade associations

(*Confesercenti* and *Confcommercio*) have been very powerful from an economic as well as a political point of view. For many years, they have successfully used their power and influence to prevent large retail-trade chains from spreading across the country. Licences for new retail outlets, which are issued by local councils, were under the tight control of the two trade associations. Accordingly, access to the market was highly regulated. It is not yet possible to estimate the importance of the introduction of residence permits for the self-employed in the new law (no. 40/98): regular residence permits, or permits issued under the amnesty which accompanied the passing of law no. 40, have only been issued over the last two years. It should be noted that although in some respects the new law (*legge* 40/98) has modified the institutional framework governing the economic incorporation of immigrants, many of the formal restrictions regarding residence permits for the self-employed continue to apply. Permit applicants must show (Bernasconi 1999):

1 that they have sufficient resources to carry out the activity
2 that they have complied with the requirements for enrolment in professional associations or registers
3 that they have satisfactory living accommodation and an annual income above the minimum required to exempt them from having to contribute to medical expenses
4 that they have an unspecified document from the competent authorities to the effect that there are no reasons why they should not be granted the authorizations or licences necessary to carry out the activity.

These are all requirements that are not made of Italian citizens who want to engage in the same type of activity. Italy differs in this respect from other countries such as the Netherlands, where policies have been introduced to support immigrant entrepreneurs (e.g. the EMPORIUM project) and where there has been a general reduction of restrictions and the formal and socio-economic obstacles which immigrants meet on their path toward becoming businessmen.

All these factors explain why the immigrant entrepreneur has remained rather under-developed in Italy all over the 1990s, and why so little attention has been devoted to this phenomenon in recent years. Except for some local research no detailed studies have been conducted. Academic literature on immigrant businesses in Italy is very limited. The only cases which have been studied quite carefully are Egyptian entrepreneurs in Milan (Ambrosini and Schellenbaum 1994; Baptiste and Zucchetti 1994; Zucchetti 1995) and Chinese entrepreneurs in Milan (Farina et al. 1997) and Tuscany (Campani et al. 1994; Failla and Lombardi 1993). A recent research which has been done in Milan (Colombo et al. 2000) provides also basic descriptive information on African businesses (especially on trade activities and different kinds of service for the migrant population). Comparison between Chinese and Egyptian businesses basically shows us that concepts such as 'ethnic business' and 'ethnic economy' can be usefully employed to describe the economic organization of the Chinese community, but are largely irrelevant with regard to Egyptian entrepreneurship and self-employment. On the one hand, Chinese entrepreneurial activities, especially in the last two decades, have largely benefited from different kinds of resource coming from the Chinese community (loans, skills, low-paid workers, family support, niche markets, etc.). On the other hand, Egyptian businesses have developed in the absence of any community-based support: Egyptian entrepreneurs, who are mostly present in the food sector, first acquire professional basic skills working for Italian restaurants, then usually start their own business with Italian associates. In general, these people follow individual patterns of social mobility which are supported by the family but they do not insert themselves in the Italian economy by applying some kind of community-based model of economic success. The only and not completely satisfactory attempt to define a typology of immigrant businesses in Italy can be found in a book by Ambrosini (1999). The author identified five types of immigrant business in the Italian context:

1 'ethnic business' (*impresa etnica*) which is typically represented by some types of Chinese entrepreneur
2 'intermediary business' (*impresa intermediaria*) which provides basic services to the immigrant communities (travel agencies, lawyers, doctors etc.)
3 'exotic business' (*impresa esotica*) such as ethnic restaurants, foods and music performances
4 'open business' (*impresa aperta*) which are managed by foreign entrepreneurs but do not differ from any other similar businesses owned by Italians
5 'shelter business' (*impresa rifugio*) which is typically represented by precarious and totally informal street-selling activities.

Starting from the literature mentioned above, we can find some sectors where migrants' businesses are visible, increasingly important and largely characterized by various sorts of informal arrangement.

First, there is street selling (which involves immigrants from northern Mediterranean countries, Senegal, Sri Lanka and China), as well as more 'normalized' but less diffused forms of the retail trade, often benefiting from market niches created by the very existence of immigrant communities. Street selling is almost completely irregular and from the very beginning it has been associated with the presence of immigrants in Italy. It exhibits high territorial mobility and turnover, requires low entry and exit costs, and can be done on a temporary basis even by immigrants who are permanently employed in other sectors. Immigrants usually sell 'ethnic goods', merchandise with counterfeit brands, or products whose sale is controlled by a state monopoly (audiocassettes, videotapes and cigarettes). As far as this kind of economic activity is concerned, it is difficult to identify the boundaries between what is informal and what is criminal. The profitability, in any case, is highly dependent on the strength of law enforcement (Quassoli 1999).

Second, ethnic restaurants represent a special case and only involve a few ethnic groups. In Milan the main national groups in the restaurant business are the Chinese and the Egyptians (Ambrosini 1999; Baptiste and Zucchetti 1994; Colombo et al. 2000; Failla and Lombardi 1993; Zucchetti 1995). Even a superficial comparison between Chinese and Egyptian restaurants demonstrates the role played by the institutional framework in shaping ethnic businesses in Italy. Chinese and Egyptian restaurants are managed by Chinese or Egyptian people who employ fellow countrymen as cooks or waiters. They are usually in the metropolitan areas and provide an exotic and cheap cuisine for Italian customers. The former Chinese restaurants are formally owned and actually managed by Chinese people, while the Egyptian ones are often owned by Italians. The reason for this has to do with one of the characteristics of the institutional framework: the reciprocity rule. The reciprocity rule, which was partially abandoned in the last migration law, states that a foreigner (an Egyptian, for instance) can open his own business in Italy, and get a permit to stay as a self-employed worker, only if Italian citizens are granted the same right in the foreigners' country of origin (Egypt). In the Chinese case, a bilateral agreement signed in 1987 allowed Chinese people to escape the reciprocity rule's constraints and get a permit to stay and regularize their legal position as self-employed. They are one of the few cases of non-EU citizens living in Italy who are legally allowed to start businesses in the industrial and service sector. This enabled many of the informal Chinese businesses to emerge from the shadow economy where they had been for many years (Farina et al. 1997). Chinese self-employment and entrepreneurship suddenly had favourable institutional grounds to spread and develop outside the restrictive boundaries.

Third, there are some crafts and industrial activities in the clothing and leather-production and -preparation industries, which only involve Chinese entrepreneurs. These small firms are located in parts of the country characterized by a traditional diffusion of informal arrangements – Chinese 'communities' that work in Tuscany (Campani et al. 1994; Colombo et al. 1995; Failla and Lombardi 1993) – as well as some metropolitan areas (especially in Milan). These activities can be viewed as an embryonic form of ethnic entrepreneurship, which is perfectly coherent with the tradition of domestic micro-firms. Immigrant self-employment in small workshops and firms has not yet introduced any relevant innovation into the social organization of these economic activities. On the contrary, there is exactly the same organization as in the small firms and work-shops managed by Italian entrepreneurs: undocumented workers, exploitation of familial and parental resources, child labour, total tax evasion and high depend-ency on the purchaser. The only unique characteristic of the Chinese workshop is the use of undocumented Chinese workers deeply indebted to their employer. The employers often pay part of the travel expenses, binding the newcomers to years of hard and invisible work to pay the debt. Still more interesting are the changes that have taken place over the last few decades. Some businesses – e.g. retail trade and leather firms – were entrenched in the surrounding (Italian) economic environment at the start. They relied upon Italian people and firms for financial resources to start the business for straw men workers (in the 1950s and 1960s the informal Chinese leather firms in Milan used to employ Italian female workers) and customers. In the last few decades, these activities have developed toward a self-sufficient ethnic business model, which relies upon the local Chinese community and increasingly tight trade relationships with the country of origin (Farina et al. 1997).

Immigrant self-employment and entrepreneurship tend to produce forms of social integration outside the supporting networks of the immigrant community and require the creation of a complex set of interactions with the local society. Despite the importance of informal arrangements in the Italian context (Mingione and Magatti 1994; Mingione and Quassoli 1999), the largely informal economic incorporation of immigrants has not yet acquired a connotation of ethnic economies and subcultures. The Chinese are the single exception. Small Chinese communities settled in large Italian cities – Milan and Turin – in the first decades of the twentieth century and stayed there during the fascist regime. Long-term migration and settlement, a community life characterized by cohesion and cultural attitudes favourable to entrepreneurial activities, along with a unique normative arrangement, have made the Chinese the only example of the successful formal/informal economic organization of immigrants in Italy. They are a very special case as a result of their ability to create and/or exploit some economic niches (handicraft activities, restoration, street selling and import of goods from China), which enabled them to survive and prosper until the post-Fordist changes.

Conclusions

In the last ten years, immigration into Italy has grown rapidly, becoming one of the main issues on the political agenda. Although the percentage of immigrants in the total population has remained rather low, public opinion has been very sensitive to the topic and a diffused sense of invasion has become widespread (Dal Lago 1999).

The relative newness of the phenomenon (which started in the 1980s) is a factor in how immigrants have settled in the country in recent years. Immigrant communities have not had time to organize or to establish any relevant internal web. There is also the fact that the Italian institutions were largely unprepared to cope with the newcomers. For ten years now, immigration has created an emergency situation in Italy, without any clear and coherent policy and without any success in controlling the inflow. As a matter of fact, most immigrants worked outside the system at the beginning of their stay or after their first permit expired. This promoted the confusion between the regular and the irregular immigrant, which in turn fostered distrust and suspicion toward foreign people. The integration of immigrants in the labour market has not been that bad. Despite the social alarm in public opinion, the economic actors soon understood the usefulness of this new workforce. The immigrants proved to be functional in the maintenance and transformation of some crucial components of Italian capitalism.

The use of immigrants as employees has been very relevant and has enhanced the capacity of the Italian economy to employ these resources to satisfy its own needs: they were employed as factory workers or in the service sector, mainly in medium-sized or large cities, and many of them were trapped in the informal/illegal economy (mainly in the south).

On the whole, the detachment between the public-opinion perception of the immigration issue and the use made by economic interests of this workforce was a marked feature of the Italian context in the 1990s. While attention was devoted to the 'invasion' of immigrants and the consequent fears on the labour-market economic interests went on using the foreign workforce. As a result of a more successful policy in controlling the inflow, a few years ago the positive role played by immigrants in economic terms began to be recognized in public debates. It is hard to predict what this will mean for the future.

In the 'ethnic business' sector, immigrants have been marginally involved in self-employment and entrepreneurial activities. If we exclude the Chinese case, the phenomenon of ethnic entrepreneurship in Italy has only developed in the last few years, alongside the mitigation of various emergency situations linked to immigration. The first signs of immigrant entrepreneurship were connected with the roots immigrants have begun to put down, at least from an economic standpoint. Furthermore, three new forms of immigrant businesses have begun developing recently. In the first place, some new kinds of trading activities have been spreading for the last five years, especially in the urban areas. Immigrant entrepreneurs usually sell exotic goods mainly acquired by immigrants themselves or provide specific services, such as the intercontinental mail or phone services, to the foreign population. In the second place, the 'model' of Chinese business communities, which characterized cities like Milan, Turin and Rome, has been 'exported' to some traditional or new industrial districts (e.g. Prato, the provinces of Vicenza and Treviso, the hinterland of Naples). In the third place, there is the growing importance of a special type of immigrant self-employment, which is stimulated and driven by the needs of Italian entrepreneurs operating, for instance, in the garment and construction sectors (Confartigianato della Marca Trevigiana 2000). It is an interesting and in certain respects worrisome case of immigrant self-employment created by a system of small and medium-sized local businesses with the purpose of improving their performance: local businesses are increasingly shifting from hiring foreign workers to 'helping' immigrants create their small businesses to which part of the work is entrusted (Zanfrini 1999). In the coming years it will be interesting to examine the extent to which these new immigrant businesses are able to increase their autonomy and create their own market.

In conclusion, we would like to add that Italy is a country of small businesses and, as many studies have shown, for many people owning a business has been the channel that made access feasible to a higher income and true upward mobility. We are interested in understanding the extent to which this model will repeat itself in the case of immigrants in the coming years, and whether the socio-economic context and its interest groups will raise barriers (formal and otherwise) to keep the immigrant population structurally weak, and reproduce situations of ethnic exploitation within the labour market.

Notes

1. Being irregular or clandestine in a less regulated socio-economic context characterized by the marked presence of informal practices and arrangements was perceived as less problematic by immigrants: a destiny shared with the local population. Everyday life in the metropolitan areas of the south is described as being warmer and richer in terms of social relations and solidarity; nevertheless, the relationships between Italians and immigrants are not truly multi-ethnic. There are closed and well-integrated immigrant communities within the local societies (Perrone 1991; Scidà and Pollini 1993).

2. Only partial statistics on the number of migrants and their occupations are available, and are of a very problematic nature. The available data for immigrant employment are incomplete, heterogeneous and very unreliable. The way immigrants obtain residence permits gives rise to distortions in official statistics. As we anticipated above, regular housekeeping is greatly overestimated as for many years it represented the only ploy for entering Italy legally. On the other hand, the actual number of housekeeping jobs may also be underestimated since many migrants, as well as many Italians, are housekeepers on an informal basis. Data on unemployment are similarly

problematic because in 1986 and in 1990 to declare oneself unemployed was the usual way to obtain a residence permit during the first two regularization campaigns. As far as the informal sector is concerned, quantitative information can be obtained from surveys, the inspections carried out by the local agencies of the Ministry of Labour, and official data collected by ISTAT. It follows from what we have said so far that the data available should be approached with great caution. Although the Government is now claiming to have been successful at regulating the admission, as far as the past is concerned the large number of illegal arrivals makes all the statistics (at least partly) unreliable.

3. Greece represents a partial exception, with a large diffusion of micro-firms mainly concentrated in agriculture.
4. This is true until the year 2000, when the effects of the Immigration Law no. 40, passed in 1998, started to show themselves. On this aspect see Magatti and Quassoli forthcoming.
5. The most significant exception is the Chinese community.
6. A typical example of this is street selling, which is often done on a seasonal basis (Catanzaro et al. 1997).

–9–

France: The Narrow Path

Emmanuel Ma Mung and Thomas Lacroix

Migratory Policy and Immigration

Unlike most other European countries, France has a long history of attracting immigrants.[1] Until the 1920s, France had always welcomed foreigners and often encouraged families to settle there to alleviate population shortages. Migratory policies developed in the late nineteenth century were designed to attract immigrant settlers as well as labourers. Until the Great Depression of 1929, a laissez-faire policy of benign non-intervention prevailed. The 1930s witnessed the dawn of a period of immigration restriction, which became increasingly discriminatory and stringent until 1945. After the Second World War, the government passed a law which has acted as the legislative basis for immigration policy ever since. However, this policy has undergone many revisions: thus, labour was imported during the 1950s and 1960s, until the borders were closed in 1974. The 1945 law encouraged immigration as a means of accomplishing two goals: relieving France's population deficit by stimulating 'settlement'-type immigration, and obtaining the work force needed to rebuild the country and its industrial infrastructure after the war. This process has been underpinned by a relatively easy naturalization procedure.

In 1974, however, the government officially puts an end to labour immigration. The immigration of family members, though, was still authorized and comprised the major part of post-1974 entry flows. The number of immigrants increased until 1975, and then stabilized.[3] Italian immigration, which had begun before the Second World War, continued though it declined steadily. Immigration of Spanish labourers started in the 1950s and the flow stabilized in 1960, at which time Portuguese immigration became significant, continuing until 1974.

The decolonization process, begun in the mid-1950s, stimulated African immigration. From the 1950s until the mid-1970s, North African immigrants would come to dominate the numbers of immigrant workers entering France. Algerian immigration hit a peak during the Algerian War and following independence. Tunisian and Moroccan immigration presented a similar pattern.

Migrant flows from French-speaking sub-Saharan Africa also emerged. In 1990, Africans comprised 45.4 per cent of the immigrant population (Algerians 17.1 per cent, Moroccans 15.9 per cent, Tunisians 5.7 per cent, sub-Saharan Africans 6.7 per cent). New data from the 1999 census (INSEE Première 2000) show that immigrants born in the Maghreb number 1.3 million, i.e. 6 per cent more than in 1990, while immigrants from European Union member nations number 1.6 million, i.e. 9.3 per cent fewer than in 1990. The latter decrease is chiefly attributable to people from older migratory flows: in 1999, there were 210,000 fewer immigrants from Italy, Spain and Portugal than in 1990.

Localization of the Foreign Population and Immigrant Entrepreneurs

The foreign population is quite clearly localized in the major urban and industrial centres. Over a third of France's foreign population lives in and around Paris (in the Île de France region). Nearly 60 per cent are concentrated in only three of France's twenty-two regions: Île de France, Rhône-Alpes (Lyons, Grenoble), and Provence-Alpes-Côte d'Azur (Marseilles, Toulon, Nice). The percentage of foreigners in the total population thus varies greatly: 12.9 per cent in the greater Paris area and 1 per cent in Brittany. This has a direct impact on the settlement of immigrant businesses. On a national level they tend to be located where the immigrant communities are (Ma Mung and Simon 1990).

On a micro-level, however, the localization of immigrant businesses does not follow the same pattern. In Paris, for example, one can find two different kinds of localization of businesses. Some are concentrated in immigrant neighbourhoods and sell goods oriented toward the needs of ethnic local populations (North African, African, Chinese). Garment production shops (especially Chinese) avail themselves of the proximity of a co-ethnic workforce. But even if concentration seems to have a high profile – viz. such districts as the North African 'Goutte d'Or' or the Chinese 'Triangle de Choisy' – concentration affects less than 20 per cent of North African or Chinese businesses (Ma Mung and Simon 1990). The other type of localization, less visible, is dispersion all over the city to distribute goods and services to native-born communities. Dispersion is the case of the immense majority of immigrant businesses.

French Policies and Immigrant Businesses

French state policy toward self-employed immigrants is to regulate (and restrict) access to the trades: immigrants are not entitled to open independent businesses. Nevertheless, restriction and regulation have varied in degree depending on the era. Although the overall philosophy of the legislation has not evolved since the 1930s, it has been more or less strictly enforced in the intervening decades.

In the 1930s, a long moratorium on licensing immigrant businessmen began (see p. 181–2). Restrictive legislation was drafted. It was not slackened until the 1980s, at which time access to self-employment was granted chiefly to nationals from European Union countries. For immigrants from non-EU member nations, the laws are essentially the same as in the 1930s, and many sectors of economic activity are closed to them. Of course, these restrictions have an impact on the types of self-employment immigrants adopt, because it is still illegal for them to engage in certain trades.

The only measure which could be construed as encouraging immigrant businesses is the July 1984 law waiving the requirement that foreigners carry 'foreign merchant' licences.[3] The liberalization can be explained by the government's interest at the time in reducing unemployment in the foreign population. However, this intention is not explicitly stated in the official text of the law.

Discrimination within the Professions

To this day, many sectors of economic activity remain closed to immigrants, but nationals from EU member countries are in a privileged position, because they are entitled to practise the profession of their choice on the territory of any member state. This legislation applies mainly to nationals from non-EU countries: in France, that means African and Asian immigrants.

People who do not hold French citizenship are barred most explicitly from the health-care professions and cannot work as physicians, dental surgeons, midwives, pharmacists or veterinarians (CERC 1999). Licensed architects are subject to the same requirements, as are surveyors and certified public accountants. The same is true of the legal professions. As a result, not only do notary publics, bailiffs and licensed auctioneers have to have French nationality, so do court-appointed administrators, estate brokers and attorneys. Foreign lawyers cannot practise in France unless they come from a country signatory to a reciprocity convention. The severity of this rule is attenuated by the existence of a fairly large number of such agreements, enabling immigrants from former colonies to practise (ibid.). Due to the legislative barriers, it is understandable why the number of foreigners engaging in professional practice is so low: just over 3,000, representing about 1 per cent of the total number of licensed professionals in France (ibid.).

Immigrants from non-EU countries are banned by law from a large number of other independent pursuits. This ranges from owning a periodical, a television or radio broadcast agency or a co-operative newspaper-and-magazine distribution business to selling tobacco or alcoholic beverages or engaging in self-employment in the insurance sector as a broker, general agent, etc. Overall, the list of self-employment opportunities that excludes the medical and legal professions covers at least 200,000 jobs subject to nationality restrictions (ibid.).

Immigrant business has developed within the confines of this discriminatory legislation. Obviously, foreigners gravitate to the sectors subject to the least regulation on the basis of nationality: the grocery trades, other retail and wholesale trades, the restaurant sector, construction, the garment trade, etc.

One way of getting around these discriminatory restrictions is to acquire French citizenship. As a result, a large number of 'naturalized French citizens' engage in business activities (see Table 9.1 on page 183); 11.7 per cent of naturalized French citizens were contractors or merchants in 1990, as opposed to 8.9 per cent of native French citizens. Another strategy is to marry a French spouse who holds the nominal title of head of the business. It is impossible to quantify the immigrant businessmen and -women who resort to this strategy, but field studies indicate that it is common practice. Likewise, a non-spouse who is a French national may hold the title of head of the business. Here again, the number of these businessmen and -women is difficult to evaluate.

The Evolution of the Foreign Job Market and Small Business

While the French working-age, employed population increased overall by 1.3 million (+6.3 per cent) between 1975 and 1990,[4] 200,000 jobs (−13.7 per cent) were lost within the foreign working population. Two main trends explain this decrease. The first is related to such parameters as unemployment, feminization and ageing; the second reflects an increasing differentiation in the immigrant working population.

Unemployment, Feminization and Ageing
The decrease in the number of jobs held by foreigners and naturalized citizens does not correspond to a reduction in this work force. On the contrary, this population has undergone a significant increase (+330,000, +10.4 per cent). However, it is true that it has risen at a slower rate than that of French-born citizens (+3.3 million, +16.8 per cent).

Prior to the recession, the unemployment rate among foreigners and naturalized French citizens was already greater than that of French-born citizens. However, the gap has become more pronounced. If we consider a scale of 100 for the French unemployment rate, we see that the jobless rate among aliens and naturalized French citizens combined reached 124 in 1975; 155 in census-year 1982; and 158 in census-year 1990.

For fifteen years, the feminization of the working population was not affected by the increase in unemployment and its subsequent crisis. As Marie (1992: 30) points out:

One major feature of the change in the foreign working population is feminization. Even though the phenomenon currently seems stagnant as far as the employed are concerned, it is still a new trend in the change of foreign immigration which, on the whole, fits in with overall developments of the entire working population in France, albeit on a smaller scale.[5]

Nevertheless, the foreign working population, despite this feminization, remains more masculine than the French-born working population: the gap has diminished but has not disappeared.

Of all the groups, women are more affected by unemployment than men: French-born women 13.9 per cent (men 9.2 per cent) and foreign women 26.8 per cent (men 16.3 per cent). In this area, gender and foreign origins appear to be a double handicap.

Men and women continue to be employed in different fields, to perform different jobs, and to hold different positions in professional hierarchies. Feminization of the working population brings about changes in the structure of its activities and in its social make-up. Between 1975 and 1990, as a direct result of the restrictive immigration laws of 1974, the foreign working population aged. Globally speaking, the number of workers between the ages of 20 and 34 decreased, while the number aged 35–64 increased.

Increasing Differentiation of the Foreign Working Population

In 1990, *workers* dominated the socio-professional structure of the foreign working population. However, major changes have occurred which are quite significant with regard to the evolution of the socio-professional groups. Thus, Marie (1992: 30) states that

> only a paradox in appearance, the deterioration of foreign employment since 1973 has certainly enhanced the progression of the hierarchy for the qualifications of those who were employed. The result was, first of all, a decline in the number of workers (12 per cent points in twelve years) to the advantage of the number of employees.

Nonetheless, these new employees did not find better conditions in those working sectors than their counterparts who remained in manufacturing and the construction and *civil* industry. Yet it is in the other socio-professional groups that the evolution is the most striking.

The socio-professional groups can be divided into three main echelons: middle-level personnel, executives and upper-echelon professionals, as well as contractors, tradesmen, shopkeepers, heads of companies with ten or more employees. The work force of foreigners and naturalized French citizens has evolved at a surprisingly rapid rate.

1   The number of naturalized or foreign men and women in middle-level occupations has significantly increased (men 40.7 per cent, women 107.3 per cent).
2   The number of foreign contractors, tradesmen, shopkeepers and heads of companies with ten or more employees is also growing at a much more rapid rate than among naturalized French citizens.

It is among executives and upper-echelon intellectual professionals that the evolution is the strongest since the number of foreigners in these groups increased by 65.2 per cent for men and by 179.8 per cent for women. The number of foreigners in these groups was small to begin with, representing only 3 per cent of the foreign working population in 1982. However, the social consequences of the increase in this group are certainly significant in the structure of foreign populations.

These trends have affected the structure of socio-professional groups of foreign and naturalized populations. In short, it is necessary to bear in mind that the foreign socio-professional group was strongly composed of *workers*, which still represented more than two-thirds of the foreign working population in 1990. Even though rates of employment in other occupations are still quite low compared to those among the working-age population as a whole, they have increased significantly compared to those of 1982. Therefore, the socio-professional structure of the foreign population tends to reflect that of the entire population in France. The growing number of women has greatly changed the socio-professional make-up of the foreign working population. The socio-professional structure of naturalized French citizens, on the other hand, resembles that of the entire working-age population to an even greater degree than that of foreigners.

These modifications allow us to assume a social mobility whose effects are less quantitative (foreigners remain mainly workers) than qualitative, as a result of the creation of an economically, intellectually and technically trained class. However, we must moderate the consideration of social mobility by taking into account the heterogeneous origins of the immigrants. Depending on whether they are from North Africa, Southern Europe or Africa, their status in France will differ. Foreigners from European Union nations are entitled to a different status than the others. Other significant factors are culture and prior know-how. The constraint on the hypothesis of social mobility is also due to the technical difficulty involved in analysing the flow of a large amount of people whose sector-based, professional and national origins are unknown because of the lack of a specific survey.

Evolution of Small Business

We can attempt to trace this evolution in four sectors of business in which immigrants are likely to engage: the retail trade, catering, the textile industry and construction contracting.

Retail Trade and *Catering* In 1995, in the retail sector as a whole, large chains accounted for 25 per cent, average-sized chains for 14.5 per cent, and small businesses for 60.5 per cent; 75,000 grocery shops were registered that year (INSEE 1995b). That figure has since been declining at a steady rate. One reason for this is the increasing specialization of goods according to the socio-demographic features of local consumers.

Foreigners filter into this sector, filling the vacancies left open by the French-born (Ma Mung and Simon 1990). The grocery store is one of the main features of the retail trade business. In Paris, it corresponds to 25.7 per cent of the shop-keepers and half the foreign shopkeepers (annual statistics of the town of Paris, 1990, cited by Pairault 1995).

As far as the catering industry[6] is concerned, the presence of foreigners is not a new phenomenon. However, this sector has undergone unprecedented growth from the quantitative as well as qualitative standpoint. Generally speaking, this sector is growing steadily: between 1991 and 1995, the number of catering establishments grew by more than 2,000 a year from 48,000 to 56,000 (INSEE 1995a).

Construction and Textile Because of their comparable evolution, these two sectors are considered together here. Their production systems broke up considerably during the 1980s. Peak periods alternated with off-peak periods within the business calendar. The case was the same with the women's ready-to-wear garment industry. A new means of production, quick and flexible enough to adapt to a fluctuating demand, was required. The 'Sentier system' (named after the Paris garment district) is an example of this means of production (Morokvasic 1987). The textile industry was seriously affected by the recession. The job market dropped by 33 per cent between 1977 and 1987 (ibid.). At the same time, the number of businesses doubled between 1979 and 1984. In 1995, this field included 2,500 official businesses (INSEE 1995b). The textile industry experienced strong fluctuations, during which many businesses were forced into bankruptcy. The same process of segmentation is noticeable in the construction sector, but with different modalities. Businesses increased their number of subcontractors to externalize their production costs. Businesses must adapt to the strong variations of the demand (Morokvasic 1987).

In the construction industry, the distribution of contractors reflects to a greater degree the profile of the foreign population in France. The percentage of foreigners, as of naturalized French citizens, has greatly increased. In Alsace, for example, Italians and Algerians have been replaced by Turks. The latter represent more than a third (36 per cent) of the foreign entrepreneurs in this sector, most of whom are former construction and civil-engineering employees. Unemployment and the incentives of their former employers stimulated them to apply for contractor's licences of their own. However, production is often subordinate to their former employers and to businesses that subcontract.

Development of Immigrant Entrepreneurship in France

An Old Phenomenon

The entrepreneurial activities immigrants engage in were long considered a marginal phenomenon, peripheral to international migrations, and received very little scholarly attention until fairly recently. The first study explicitly devoted to the subject was published in the 1980s and concerned shopkeepers.[7] Following this, other studies were published.[8] Previously, the subject was only alluded to in passing in publications on immigration. Today, the number of studies has increased but overall, the output on the subject is still modest.[9] Research has been chiefly confined to North Africans and Asians, usually as shopkeepers, and Italians and Portuguese, usually as craftsmen. The circumstances of other groups, such as Turks,[10] Indo-Pakistanis or Haitians are still unexplored. From a strictly quantitative standpoint, immigrant activity has in fact been marginal since 1945, but the number of foreign shopkeepers and craftsmen was higher before the First World War than in 1990. The 1911 census counted 121,000 foreign business owners (as compared to 98,394 in 1991), and

> the percentage of self-employed workers in the immigrant working population was much higher than it is today: 20.4 per cent in 1911 as compared to 6.1 per cent in 1988. Before World War One, the great majority of immigrant craftsmen (67,000) and shopkeepers (43,000) was made up of Europeans from countries bordering France (1/3 were Belgian, especially in the hotel and restaurant trades, 1/3 were Italians in the construction trades, and the remaining third consisted of Swiss (hotels, clockmaking, cabinetmaking), Germans, and Central European Jews). (Simon 1993: 118)

The high percentage of self-employed workers in the immigrant population can be explained by the fragmented nature of the commercial and industrial structure at the time, when small businesses and shops were a far more important part of the overall economy.

In the period between the two wars, the geographic origin of the immigrants engaging in business and trade changed. Chinese immigrants opened shops in the 1920s (Archaimbault 1952; Live 1991), and North African communities sprang up in Paris and its suburbs (Chevalier 1947; Kerrou 1987; Rager 1950):

the Moroccan Soussi in Gennevilliers being an example (Ray 1937). They accompanied the early North African labourer immigration, and usually opened businesses – as shopkeepers, boarding-house owners, or café-restaurantkeepers – in the neighbourhoods where the community had settled (central Paris and its northwestern suburbs). The national origin of the other immigrants remained more or less the same as before the First World War, although the percentage of immigrants from bordering countries may have begun to taper off. Georges Mauco (1932: 302–3) pointed out that in Paris, in 1926,

> of 20,000 immigrant business owners, a great many came from Eastern and Central Europe, including many Russian and Polish Jews, Greeks, and Armenians. These nationalities made up 7,500 of them; i.e. nearly 30 per cent of the total number. Likewise, a high proportion of Eastern European and Balkan elements was noted among the 22,800 from miscellaneous backgrounds, especially small craftsmen … Immigrant business owners and those from miscellaneous backgrounds tended to cluster in sectors like the garment trade (both manufacture and retail) and the fur and leather trade … In shopkeeping [chiefly grocery stores, bars, hotels, and restaurants], elements from the earlier immigration of Italians, Belgians, and Swiss remained at the top, with the Slavic and Balkan elements just behind them … Garment manufacture and retail, including the fur and leather trade, was dominated by immigrant business owners and craftsmen from Russia, Poland, Romenia, Greece and Armenia.

The Depression of the 1930s and the rise of xenophobic sentiments resulted for immigrants in a series of discriminatory measures aimed at salaried labour (such as the law of 10 August 1932). But the economic crunch also affected tradesmen, craftsmen and professionals; seeing their clientele dwindle, they accused immigrants of unfair competition.[11] 'In France, anyone from anywhere is permitted to trade in anything', cried a conservative deputy in 1935 (quoted by Schor 1985: 611). Immigrants who faced unemployment or lost their work permit were accused of setting up shop as tradesmen or craftsmen, activities for which a work permit was not (yet) mandatory. The influx of refugees in 1933 aroused intensified criticism, especially of Jews who opened retail stores or garment shops.

Suspected of taking advantage of loopholes in the labour regulations, immigrants were accused of unfair competition. Trade organizations initiated lobbying against immigrant competition, evidence of deep-seated unity founded on a commitment to monitor immigrants closely. They called for other ways to restrict the number of immigrants in independent businesses, such as legislation similar to the law of 10 August 1932 regulating salaried labour, to set quotas for the number of immigrants in each business sector or region (Schor 1985: 599). The decree of 8 August 1935 subjected immigrant business owners to the same obligations that had been mandated in 1932 for immigrant salaried workers. It required the possession of a special identity card, a mechanism that made it possible to regulate the number of immigrants. This legislation was only weakly enforced, however. Lobbied with increasing vigour by angry French businessmen, tradesmen and craftsmen, the Daladier government decided by the decree of 2 May 1938 to tighten regulations by expediting the issuance of tradesmen's permits which, from then on, would serve as residence permits as well as licences to engage in business. The decrees of 12 November 1938 and 2 February 1939 required immigrant shopkeepers to apply for and obtain a business licence (ibid.: 600). These restrictions were not lifted until 1984 by the law of 17 July, exempting immigrants with a residence permit from applying for a special immigrant business licence; until then, holders of residence permits had been subject to the law of 1938. Foreigners in the legal or medical professions were also targeted: they were banned from practising in French courts (law of 19 July 1934), and from practising medicine or dentistry (law of 26 July 1935).

These discriminatory measures and the overtly xenophobic and racist policies of the French government during the Second World War were factors in the sharp drop in the number of immigrants among businessmen. Anti-Semitic persecution put an end to the numerous small Jewish businesses, often run by immigrant tradesmen. Moreover, anti-immigrant discrimination served as an incentive to some members of the community to apply for French citizenship so they could set up or continue their business or trade activities: this explains the large percentage of naturalized French citizens among business owners until the 1980's. Others hid behind native French figureheads. Still others married French women. It was only in the 1970s that the presence of immigrants in independent business regained measurable significance as a result of the migratory flows developing in the three decades after 1960.

Developments from 1982 to 1990

Between 1982 and 1990, the number of craftsmen, tradesmen, and business owners employing at least ten wage-earners (a category the INSEE national economic statistics bureau calls 'ACE') of native French origin dwindled by nearly 55,000 (see Table 9.1). This drop was largely compensated for by the increase in the number of naturalized French ACEs (+7,300) and immigrant ACEs (+35,800) at a time when the total number of independent business owners (French and immigrant) stagnated at around 1,800,000. If we add the immigrants to the number of naturalized French, there are a total of 173,970 non-French business owners, who account for 9.5 per cent of the total number of business owners (as opposed to 7.1 per cent in 1982). That percentage is quite comparable to the number of immigrant wage-earners in the total working population (9.7 per cent).

Table 9.1 Foreign ACE in France in 1982 and 1990

	Shopkeepers		Craftsmen		Company heads with at least 10 employees on the payroll		Total	
	1982	1990	1982	1990	1982	1990	1982	1990
Total	797,100	795,706	903,600	850,464	133,924	176,686	1,834,624	1,822,856
French-born citizens	740,748	721,734	838,144	763,730	124,868	163,422	1,703,760	1,648,886
Naturalised French citizens	28,812	33,208	34,296	35,692	5,176	6,676	68,284	75,576
Aliens	27,540	40,764	31,160	51,042	3,880	6,588	62,580	98,394
Naturalized + Aliens	56,352	73,972	65,456	86,734	9,056	13,264	130,864	173,970
Detailed nationalities								
Total, Aliens	27,540	40,764	31,160	51,042	3,880	6,588	62,580	98,394
Algerians	8,328	10,292	3,212	5,292	168	408	11,708	15,992
Moroccans	2,456	4,660	1,000	2,640	88	180	3,544	7,480
Tunisians	1,888	2,708	984	2,748	172	244	3,044	5,700
Total North Africans	12,672	17,660	5,196	10,680	428	832	18,296	29,172
Italians	3,366	3,744	11,026	8,444	876	1,100	15,268	13,288
Spaniards	1,420	1,736	4,864	4,104	324	364	6,608	6,204
Portuguese	744	2,804	4,540	15,008	172	716	5,456	18,528
Total South Europeans	5,530	8,284	20,430	27,556	1,372	2,180	27,332	38,020
South-east Asians*	912	2,088	280	1,120	44	140	1,236	3,348
Africa french speak.	1,740	2,012	208	848	80	112	2,028	2,972
Turks	172	968	328	3,464	36	144	536	4,576
Other nationalities	6,514	9,752	4,718	7,374	1,920	3,180	13,152	20,306

* Vietnam, Laos, Cambodia.
Source: INSEE: Census 1982 and 1990.

Moreover, the percentage of business owners in the total immigrant working population, which did not exceed 3.9 per cent in 1982 (whereas for the native French working population it was 8.1 per cent), is 6.1 per cent today. If naturalized French business owners are also taken into consideration, this percentage of the corresponding working population is 7.1 per cent, a percentage equivalent to the percentage of the native-born French working population in 1990 (7.2 per cent).

As to business owners,[12] the structure of the immigrant working population tends to mirror that of the native French working population. We are thus observing the emergence and identification of a class of business owners arising from immigration. The question is whether this is a result of 'true' entrepreneurship or merely an administrative formality, a means of cutting payroll costs.

During the last period between two censuses, the number of immigrant ACEs increased by 36,000. This trend was due to the reinforcement of groups which had traditionally been present, like North Africans (+11,000) and Southern Europeans (+11,000). However, major modifications within the latter group could be observed: a decrease in the number of Spanish (–400) and Italians (–2,000 or –23 per cent) within the context of a sharp drop in the Italian immigrant working population as a whole (–30 per cent). Conversely, the number of Portuguese increased sharply (+13,000). However, the percentage of Portuguese ACEs is still low (4.7 per cent).

Two groups which were fairly insignificant in 1982 underwent a boom: the Asians (+2,100 or +171 per cent),[13] and, to an even greater degree, the Turks (+4,000, or +754 per cent). Although their immigration is fairly recent, these two groups contained a higher percentage of businessmen than the average for all the nationalities combined: respectively 6.7 and 6.3 per cent of the working population, as compared to 6.1 per cent. The percentage of Africans rose only slightly (+4.7 per cent).

It is important to combine this group with the immigrant entrepreneurs. Indeed, businessmen who are naturalized French citizens are perceived, especially by their clientele, as immigrants and associated with their ethnic origin.

If we take the percentage of ACEs among naturalized French citizens as an index (see Table 9.2), we see that they are overrepresented in every business category in comparison to the non-naturalized immigrant population and even in comparison to native-born French citizens. Although the number of native-born French businessmen exceeded the number of immigrant ones in 1982 (68,284 as opposed to 62,580), they are now greatly outnumbered by the immigrants (75,575 as opposed to 98,394).

In addition to the fact that naturalization as French citizens is related to the applicants' permanent residence in France, a prerequisite for engaging in entrepreneurial activity, one of the reasons for the overrepresentation of this group is

Table 9.2 Percentage of ACEs in Various Working Populations

	Naturalized French cit.	*French born cit.*	*Aliens*
Craftsmen	4.32	3.34	3.15
Shopkeepers	4.02	3.16	2.52
Company heads > 10 employees	0.81	0.72	0.41
Total	9.15	7.22	6.08

Sources: INSEE résultats, démographie-société, n°21, novembre 1992.

undoubtedly the restrictive legislation which prevailed until 1984 concerning immigrants wishing to set up shop as tradesmen or craftsmen. Naturalization was a way to bypass this legislation, and was often a necessary step toward entrepreneurial activity. This hypothesis can be confirmed in part by the slowdown in the number of naturalized citizens, since the deregulation of 1984 made naturalization unnecessary. Nevertheless, it would be unwise to overestimate this factor, if only because before 1984 it was still possible to set up shop, and after 1984, the number of naturalized French business owners continued to rise.

The category that increased most quickly was the one of owners of businesses with at least ten employees (+70 per cent). The rate of increase was greater than that of craftsmen or shopkeepers but also that of native-born French business owners (+31 per cent) or naturalized French business owners (+29 per cent). An observation which could have been made in 1982 (cf. Guillon and Ma Mung 1986) was still valid, namely that in general, North Africans tend to be shopkeepers (60.5 per cent) and Southern Europeans are usually craftsmen (72.5 per cent), but this distinction was beginning to fade (having been 69.2 per cent and 74.7 per cent in the previous census). Newcomers also tended to cluster in certain sectors, with 62.4 per cent of the Asians and 67.7 per cent of the Africans self-employed as shopkeepers while 75.7 per cent of the Turks preferred craft industry.

Although the percentage of native-born French shopkeepers is dwindling (−3 per cent), the percentage of naturalized French shopkeepers increased by 15 per cent, and that of immigrant shopkeepers by nearly 50 per cent. North Africans strengthened their position (+39 per cent), and remained the majority of foreign shopkeepers (43 per cent). Within the North African immigrant population as a whole, the increase was largely due to Moroccans (+2,200), whose numbers are increasing more quickly than those of Algerians. The latter make up the largest group of immigrant shopkeepers (25.2 per cent of the total). Moroccans currently make up the second-largest group of immigrant shopkeepers, replacing Italian shopkeepers, who only exhibited a small rise (+11 per cent). In this sector as well, new groups appeared; percentages insignificant in the 1982 census

showed a sharp rise: Turks (+463 per cent, but from a very small initial population), Portuguese (+277 per cent), and Asians (+129 per cent).

The category that changed the most and exhibited the most contrasting trends
was that of craftsmen. Indeed, the percentage of immigrant craftsmen increased
sharply while the percentage of native-born French craftsmen plummeted by
nearly 10 per cent, and the percentage of naturalized French craftsmen stagnated.
It was mainly, however, the percentage of craftsmen of certain traditional nationalities that dropped: the Spanish by 16 per cent and the Italians by a staggering 23
per cent. Italian craftsmen, who used to account for a third of the immigrant
craftsmen, are currently only 16.5 per cent. Nevertheless, Southern European
immigrants still dominate the contracting market (54 per cent of the total), with
Portuguese immigrants (+10,500) accounting for the bulk of the increase in the
total number of immigrant craftsmen (+19,900). Certain nationalities burst upon
the scene, like the Turks, whose numbers increased tenfold, the Africans and the
Asians, although the presence of the latter two groups is still small. North
Africans, whose presence had little impact up to now, have doubled their numbers.

As was noted above, owners of businesses with at least ten employees constitute the category that increased the most (+70 per cent). Nevertheless, immigrant
business owners remained underrepresented, constituting only 3.7 per cent of the
population in this category and 0.41 per cent of the total immigrant working
population. The nationality that contributed the most to this trend was the
Portuguese,[14] who rose to second place behind the Italians. However, nearly half
the business owners were still of 'other nationalities' which, in this socio-professional category, would seem to indicate other industrialized countries (Germany,
the Netherlands, the United Kingdom, the United States, etc.).

Various Interpretations

In French studies on ethnic entrepreneurship, various interpretations sometimes
oppose each other, depending on whether they explain the phenomenon by
external or internal factors. The first interpretation adopts a theory of '*de facto*
employment practices designed to externalize labour costs', and one of 'discrimination' (people become shopkeepers because they are excluded from the job
market). The second interpretation relies on the presence of specialized groups
within the immigrant groups (supporting the thesis of intermediary minorities)
and 'ethnic resources'

Craftsmen, the Job-market Crunch, and Subcontracting
Efforts to explain the development of immigrant entrepreneurship often indicate
a scarcity of jobs combined with the increased segmentation of industrial activities and the development of subcontracting, an associated trend, as its causes.

The hypothesis is fairly simple: immigrant workers, especially vulnerable to unemployment, are forced to set up their own businesses in order to survive, especially in economic sectors where subcontracting is developing.

This explanation – usually cited as being self-evident – is generally valid for craftsmen, many of whom are former employees who faced unemployment (Auvolat and Benattig 1988) and now work in the same trade as their former employers. The transition to self-employment occurred within the context of increased subcontracting. In the case of the construction trades – the main sector where immigrant tradesmen set up shop (two-thirds of them obtain this type of contractor's licence (ibid.) – subcontracting is a widespread means of cutting payroll costs (Garson and Mouhoud 1989) and encourages undeclared labour. As a result, 'many of the immigrant tradesmen licensed as independent by the Registre du Commerce are in reality under an informal obligation to work for their last employers' (ibid.: 23). This would explain the great increase in the number of Portuguese craftsmen, since they nearly always work in the construction sector.

In the garment trade, although subcontracting has developed in a different way, it also evokes to the creation of businesses (Montagné-Villette 1991). However, it is not a case of disguising a payroll cut as a formality, since the new contractor is rarely encouraged by his former employer to set up shop, although he is often a former employee in the garment trade. Instead, this is due to an adaptation to the structure specific to the garment trade, the best example being the 'Sentier system' (see Marie 1992; Montagné-Villette 1991). It would explain in part the increase in the number of Turkish and Asian tradesmen often operating in the garment trade.

The job shortage also has an influence at a different level: workers are likely to seek jobs working for these craftsmen, who usually hire their employees from within their own ethnic group. This labour pool, all the more vulnerable to unemployment because they are immigrants and may not have a legal work permit, is quite likely to work for extremely low wages and without employee benefits like state health insurance, thus cutting labour costs and facilitating the smooth running of the contracting business. In addition to these structural market factors, a political measure, the 1984 deregulation of the legislation on contractor's licences,[15] accelerated the creation of small contracting businesses, not without eliciting protests from certain trade associations (Marie 1992).

The first argument for immigrant entrepreneurship, which applies chiefly to craftsmen, is outlined above. It assigns a significant role to external constraints and restrictions, as though the craftsmen were merely pawns in interplay of economic forces beyond their control. This theory of push and pull factors portrayed them as helpless victims, the flotsam on the surface of vast economic waves. However, this approach, which emphasizes the power of the economic structure and adopts such factors as the job shortage and the segmentation of industrial activities as explanations, omits any mention of how group strategies and individual desire for social mobility fit into the structure. Yet, from the point of view of the immigrants, the entrepreneurial approach, regardless of the modesty of its effective results, is part of a strategy for social mobility which originated with the migratory process. The creation of a business is the means to an end. Michel Poinard (1992: 18), the authority on Portuguese migration, which is by far the most significant group among immigrant craftsmen, points out: 'If immigrants are joining the ranks of the self-employed in great masses, it is not only because the recession has exacerbated the economic fragility of the "labourer for hire" – it is also because the migratory logic spontaneously adheres to the credo of the free-market economy.' The congruence between the migratory project and the creation of businesses is also enlightened by Salvatore Palidda (1992: 88): 'The accession of certain immigrants to self-employment is a product of the combination of their dynamism and the impetus of the host society they have decided to join.'

Retail Shopkeepers: Adaptation and Resources

Conversely, for retail shopkeepers, this set of explanatory factors seems less relevant. Although the loosening of the legislation on immigrant access to commerce[16] benefited retail shopkeepers, the shortage of salaried jobs did not have such an immediate and direct impact on the creation of businesses. To take North African retail shopkeepers as an example, it is true that many of them are former employees of French companies, but all of them had solid plans to open retail shops. Only a very few were unemployed. Their motivation to become shopkeepers was more the result of their fear of losing their jobs than of a real unemployment situation. If we take the case of Asians, the explanation is irrelevant, since very few of them work for French companies and the ethnic job market is not in a recession.

As regards general trends in the economy, unlike the industrial sector where immigrant craftsmen have found a niche, the market is not evolving toward a proliferation of small businesses dependent on larger ones. Instead, there are two main trends that are not organically related. Mass-market products are retailed from huge sales outlets, and small sales outlets tend to specialize in products and services aimed with increasing precision at socio-demographic features like the spending capacity of the potential customers. This has resulted in immigrants taking over small neighbourhood shops, but providing different services. More shops specialize in exotic wares; others stock only the more expensive groceries and choice produce.

At the same time, consumer trends and tastes in the host population are evolving toward dining out more and enjoying exotic food. As a result, many restaurants with a 'daily special' menu have opened in neighbourhoods where offices or small factories predominate, as have exotic restaurants of every nationality and in every price range. Moreover, the increased consumption of convenience food, requiring less time spent cooking, has led to a proliferation of take-out restaurants of every sort.

In addition to these factors, which are external to the immigrant groups and entrepreneurs – external in that the latter have little control over them – certain internal factors are common to the Asian and North African retail shopkeepers. In a very general way, they are the following:

1   Most of the shopkeepers are from groups with a migratory or merchant tradition in their home countries, which certainly does not necessarily mean all the members of these groups were entrepreneurs in their home countries or in France.

2   The integrity of the community and the prevalence of cooperative structures is manifest in the strong capacity to finance an enterprise from within the community. Most of the shops were financed by internal credit systems, which differed according to the group. Also, workers are hired from within a community structure which begins with the family circle and successively broadens until it includes the regional group, and so on. In addition, their suppliers are often willing to extend credit.

3   The presence of the immigrant population is reinforced, with two results: an increase in the number of potential candidates for entrepreneurship, and a growth in the demand for specific products and services on the intra-community market. This demand is reinforced by the ethnicization of the consumption of immigrant populations, especially as concerns food. As a result, an ever-increasing range of specific products is supplied. Although this tends to produce a spectacular effect (because shops of the community type – that is, oriented toward clientele from the home country – are usually geographically concentrated), it should not mask the fact that most of the shops are designed to attract customers from the host country, and are usually geographically dispersed. The combination of external factors (an economic recession and unemployment, new trends in the retail distribution apparatus and consumption patterns, etc.) and internal factors (a migratory, merchant tradition, cooperative structures, the development of an 'immigrant demand', etc.) explain the development of retail shops run by immigrants.

In the field of theoretical arguments, there are several analyses that develop hypotheses to support a 'theory of identity-related mediation', i.e. ethnic entrepreneurs represent immigrant presence and thus immigrant identity (Ma Mung 1998b), and in favour of a 'theory of reputation', i.e. the smooth flow of intra-ethnic and inter-ethnic transactions between economic partners is guaranteed by 'mutual trust', a trust which is itself guaranteed by 'reputation' (Ma Mung 1996).

Cosmopolitan Crossroads, the Force of Place

Another interesting approach has been described by Tarrius (1995) and Péraldi (1999), particularly through the study they conducted in Marseilles. From 1980 to 1988, some 400 shops in the vicinity of Belzunce produced a turnover of 3.5 billion francs, thanks to a stream of 40,000 regular customers arriving from North Africa during the weekends supplemented by local and regional consumers.[17] This economic arrangement not only brings together produce and other food products impossible to find in European shops, particularly hàlal meat, spices, and other North African products, but also various manufactured products difficult to access in the countries of origin: cloth, car parts, household appliances, new or used cars, etc. As Péraldi (1999: 57–8) states,

> the commercial arrangement of Belzunce is the concretizing of an intercultural ordering of commercial functions, where, more than the ethnic relations, it is the flow of the migrants themselves and of their differentialities that serve as economically mobilizable resources ... The Marseilles arrangement is therefore not a commercial niche as it is usually used in urban anthropology. The whole puzzle of this commercial activity is rooted in its singularly urban capacity it has shown to diffuse, at a local and at a global level, without losing the constitutive features of the social forms and the ways of doing business that organize it: the importance of oral agreements, trust, the fluidness of roles, or what can be called, overall, a face-to-face economy ... As it extends itself, from one market square to another, commerce leaves an entrepreneurial opening for others, Tunisians, Moroccans, Lebanese, Syrians, Africans. And each one of these newly arrived migrants, at the same time successors and competitors of those who are already established, is one piece of another economic arrangement of smaller or greater amplitude that, each in turn and each in its own way, has a hold in a market of local exchanges and global commercial arrangements: the Algerian arrangement crosses the Russian arrangement in Istanbul, Aleppo or Dubai, the Tuniso-Libyan, Moroccan or African one in Marseilles or Dubai.

Conclusion

Immigrant entrepreneurship is not new in France. It dates back to the 1920s and 1930s at least, when it was targeted by the discriminatory measures in pre-fascist France that impeded it for several decades. In the 1970s, it cropped up again as statistically significant and mainly visible in urban settings. The stereotypical Arab grocery and Chinese restaurant are only the most obvious signs of this phenomenon. Transformations in the French trade system evident in the development of retail chain stores at the expense of small independent retailers, the rise of the restaurant sector, and mutations in the construction or textiles and fashion sector have played a key role by creating the niches immigrant entrepreneurs were able to occupy. But the development of immigrant entrepreneurship goes well beyond seizing the opportunities not taken by the native French. It also attests to considerable abilities to adapt and innovate. Studies have shown that by the 1980s, immigrant entrepreneurs were creating new opportunities, since they were doomed to fail in the long run in the sectors that were dying out. They were able to revive and renew neighbourhood retail stores by transforming them or specializing in the distribution of products (exotic imports, for example) and services that the old system was unable to provide. These new products and services correspond to new demands from society. In the construction or textile industries, they have succeeded in positioning themselves to provide new services. Today, immigrant entrepreneurship has diversified in terms of the entrepreneurs' origins: currently, Indo-Pakistanis, Turks and Africans are also working as contractors. Likewise, the products and services they offer have expanded to include computer electronics, business services and travel.

France has never adopted a policy encouraging immigrant entrepreneurship. Indeed, it has done quite the opposite. Until the mid-1980s, foreign businessmen were subject to discriminatory legislation in effect since the late 1930s. The 1984 law did not give them any special advantages: it simply abolished the legislation that had kept them from plying their trade under the same conditions as French contractors. Nevertheless, immigrants are still banned by law from many economic sectors. If immigrant entrepreneurship has played a role in incorporating immigrants into society, it is not thanks to government policy. Instead, it is because it generates a social dynamic related to identity by acting as the vector for symbolic identity-related transactions between the host society and foreign communities (Ma Mung 1994, 1998a). Admittedly, this mediatory position relies upon the specificity of the French assimilationist model, which recognizes no other political allegiance than a national one on the basis of a single and indivisible nation. But we can surmise that immigrant entrepreneurs play this role as symbolic mediators in other countries less inclined to grant supremacy to national representation. The role of immigrant entrepreneurs as mediators for identity would be a good topic for further study, and could be explored within a comparative framework.

Notes

1. For example, we might recall Colbert's advice to King Louis XIV to import labourers from Coblenz to work in French industries.
2. 1946: 1,744,000; 1962: 2,170,000; 1968: 2,621,000; 1975: 3,442,000; 1982:

3,680,000; 1990: 3,600,000; 1999: 3,260,000. The decline between the last two dates can be explained by the high number of naturalizations and the fact that many South Europeans returned to their country of origin.

3. From 1935 to 1984, foreigners who wished to engage in trade had to apply for a special licence as 'foreign merchants'. These licences were only granted in very limited numbers by local administrations.

4. The source of this detailed representation of the foreign job-market evolution in France is census data. Data on the foreign population from census year 1999 was not available at time of writing, so we refer to data from the previous census (1990).

5. This quotation is translated into English from the French; this also counts for other quotations from French sources.

6. Catering includes restaurants, cafés and hotels.

7. Except for a pioneer article in 1976 by Gildas Simon on Tunisian shopkeepers.

8. See Ait Ouaziz 1989; Boubakri 1985; Dahan 1985; Guillon and Ma Mung 1986; Ma Mung and Simon 1990; Raulin 1986, 1988; Salem 1981. On craftsmen: Auvolat and Benattig 1988; Garson and Mouhoud 1989; Moulier-Boutang et al. 1986; Palidda 1992; Wisniewski 1982.

9. For a bibliographical presentation of research on retail shopkeepers, see Battegay (1990). In addition to this catalogue, only two publications have been devoted to the theme: Ma Mung and Simon (1990) and a special issue of *La Revue Européenne des Migrations Internationales* (Body-Gendrot and Ma Mung 1992).

10. Very little research on the creation of businesses by immigrants in Alsace contains information about Turks, who are the main immigrant group in this region (Idiri 1997). See also Barthon 1992.

11. To our knowledge, there are no historical works available on the subject. Only Ralph Schor, in his thesis on French opinion and immigrants, devotes one chapter to shopkeepers and professionals (Schor 1985: 597–611). Much of what follows was borrowed from him.

12. Nevertheless, this tendency may be deceiving because the majority (55.2 per cent) of immigrant adults (but only 31.7 per cent of naturalized French adults) have working-class jobs, as opposed to 27.1 per cent of native-born French adults. As Michelle Guillon (1992: 161) notes concerning the Île de France region: 'Though we may accentuate the social diversification of the immigrant population, we must not forget that its basic characteristics change slowly. In 1990, half of the immigrant working population [in Île-de-France] was still unskilled labourers. Mainly, the gap between immigrants and French remained wide: social diversification affected both populations. Thus, the spread of immigrants through every stratum of society had not

eradicated their overrepresentation in the lower-income classes and, inversely, their underrepresentation in the highest-income categories.'

13. In regard to this group in particular, the lack of information as to the number of entrepreneurs who had been naturalized as French citizens results in a severe underestimation of the size of the entire group (immigrants and naturalized French), whose coherence is based on the fact that the majority of its members are of Chinese origin and have developed business relationships independent of their nationality (Ma Mung 1992). Concerning Asian immigrants who have been naturalized as French citizens, it should be noted that in 1982, the number of ACEs was higher than of immigrant Asian ACEs. Secondly, during the period 1982–1990, the number of naturalized French Asians increased by 380 per cent although the number of immigrant Asians increased by only 8.4 per cent. The group of Asian ACEs is thus probably much more significant than what we can infer from the average percentage of naturalized French to immigrants in the total of ACEs.

14. The fact that the findings came from a 1/4 random sample does not warrant any comments on the small numbers, since the uncertainty about the real numbers rises in proportion to the small size of the sample. In a 1/4 random sample, the real population is approximately located between $e \pm 4\ e^{1/2}$, where e is numbers.

15. See above: 'French policies and immigrant businesses'.

16. See above: 'French policies and immigrant businesses'.

17. All the statistics cited here and further on are taken from the pioneer study by Alain Tarrius (1995) on this commercial arrangement. See particularly Tarrius and Missaoui 1995.

–10–

Belgium: From Proletarians to Proteans

Ching Lin Pang

Introduction

Research on immigrant entrepreneurs in Belgium is not abundant. Many questions and blind spots arise whenever efforts are made to approach this issue. How does the Belgian case fit in with the renaissance of immigrant businesses throughout Western advanced economies in recent years? What do we know about the impact of governmental policies, both restrictive and supportive, on immigrant entrepreneurs? Do social networks play a pivotal role in setting up and sustaining immigrant enterprises? Does it pay off to examine immigrant entrepreneurship from the gender perspective? The existing studies underline the precarious position of immigrants. The potential of immigrant entrepreneurship as an avenue to social mobility has apparently been overlooked. Despite the numerous problems and barriers facing immigrant entrepreneurs, their situation is not hopeless. In the emerging hypercapitalistic urban economy, new opportunities are open to some immigrant entrepreneurs.

This chapter aspires to address some of these issues, albeit largely handicapped by a general shortage of data. First, the general context is outlined in a discussion of the main migration trends and the general labour market. There is also a focus on the social position of immigrants in mainstream society. In a second part, the development of immigrant entrepreneurship is discussed and some figures and other empirical findings are presented on immigrant entrepreneurship. The third part assesses the available literature. There is also discussion of the role of governments and other institutional organizations, whose policies and actions impact immigrant entrepreneurship. The immigration policy of the past two decades clearly targets immigrants as 'working-class' or at best as 'wage earners' but never as 'self-employed'. This explains the relative lack of attention devoted by researchers to immigrant entrepreneurs. Most studies on immigrant entrepreneurship quite rightly – but one-sidedly – contest discriminatory practices and other obstacles facing immigrants, including the need for a labour card. In the following section, I plunge into the blurred waters of policies and research paradigms. I argue from a meta-analysis perspective that immigration policy has set the tone for the general discourse and research on 'immigrants' from a 'disadvantage' stance. This 'victim-driven' approach has become the all-encompassing frame of reference for any discussion on migration and immigrants. The players in this 'discourse' game involve a wide range of opinion makers with multifarious agendas. To name a few: academics, journalists, policy-makers, politicians of various persuasions and social workers. This meta-analysis makes an effort to reveal the ever-precarious relationship between policy-making and academic output. Finally, I ruminate on the potential role of immigrant entrepreneurs in the new urban economy.

General Setting: Migration, General Labour-market Trends and Position of Immigrants

Labour migration, mostly from Eastern Europe and Italy, started in the 1920s. After a temporary halt right before and during the Second World War, a new wave took off in the mid-1950s and 1960s, during the rapid economic recovery and expansion in the aftermath of the war. It culminated in the 'Golden Sixties', characterized by wage increases, the expansion of employment and income security. In 1944 the economic revival had already been reinforced by the social pact between the employers and the trade unions, which was fostered by the government. The social pact established the general social-security system and the principle of regular wage increases in conjunction with productivity gains. The social-security system covers unemployment and sickness benefits, pensions and children allowances. By 1974 this system was perfected with the introduction of a guaranteed minimum income for all Belgian citizens. Labour migration began in this period when so many Belgians ascended to middle-class status as a result of the expansion of the tertiary sector and their higher educational levels. This explains why the white majority embraces employeeship and shuns insecurity-ridden entrepreneurship. The relatively small percentage of entrepreneurs, either native Belgian or immigrant, and the generally decreasing rate in the three decades after the Second World War are intricately linked with the elaborate welfare system, offering job security and supporting the jobless.

Given the general social mobility of the majority group, the 3-D (dangerous, dirty and difficult) jobs were abandoned, and then filled by cheap foreign labour. 'Guest workers' from such countries as Italy, Spain, Greece, Turkey and Morocco entered the Belgian labour market. The first generation of Moroccans arrived in the 1960s, during which period recruitment offices were set up in numerous cities in Morocco. At the same time, migration agreements were ratified between the two countries (Attar 1992). Similarly, the first bilateral agreements between Belgium and Turkey were signed in 1964, regulating 'the export of Turkish labor forces' (Atalik and Beeley 1992: 164). Family migration was encouraged from the outset for demographic reasons and because of policy priorities. The Belgian government reckoned that immigrants would have fewer adaptation problems if immigrant men could live with their families in the host society. Second, the inflow of immigrants could counterbalance the ageing population in Wallonia (Kesteloot and Cortie 1998; Vermeulen 1997).

The percentage of foreigners in the total population increased from 4.3 in 1947 to 8.9 in 1981. In 1999 the total population of Belgium was 10,213,752. Of this total 9,321,772 were Belgians and the remaining 891,980 foreigners, or 8.7 per cent of the total population. The largest group of foreign nationals, constituting 63 per cent of the total foreign population, consists of EU citizens. The two largest non-EU migrant groups are the Moroccans and the Turks, respectively 125,082 or 14 per cent and 70,701 or 8 per cent of the total foreign population (NIS 1999). Here the term 'foreigner' is used in a strictly legal sense to mean someone who does not hold Belgian citizenship. It seems safe to assume that in reality there are more immigrants than the official figures indicate. Since the national statistics register according to nationality, many 'new' Belgians who became citizens through naturalization are not included in the figures. Moreover, there are the 'illegal' workers, who do not have the appropriate residence or work permits. Evidently they do not figure in the statistics. Still others, the 'twice' migrants, are citizens of a third country which is neither the sending nor the receiving country.

The two largest groups are in a highly vulnerable position on the housing, education and job markets. Given their poor socio-economic position and the alleged threat they pose to the homogeneity of mainstream society, they are categorized as 'problematic'. They tend to live in the nineteenth-century inner-city neighbourhoods long abandoned by the native Belgians who prefer new homes in the suburbs. The favourable credit system and the Christian Democrat ideology explain the lack of gentrification in the inner-city areas and the success of suburbanization among the native Belgian middle-class. This ideology prioritizes home ownership in the suburbs to avoid the concentration in the urban areas, which would reinforce the growth of the working class and the concomitant threat of a workers' movement in the city (Goossens 1988). As a result, there was a sharp fall in the rent and real-estate prices in these abandoned and dilapidated inner-city areas. This is where the new labour migrants sought housing (Kesteloot and Cortie 1998). The strategy of curbing the growth of the working class did not apply to them, given their status as 'guest-worker'. However, suburbanization did not lead to 'ghettos' with an exclusive immigrant population since some 'residual' whites remained in the city. These people, mostly poor and elderly whites, could not join this movement for lack of financial means. At school migrant youngsters are not doing as well as their Belgian counterparts

(Verlot 2001; Verlot and Sierens 1997). In the 1995/6 school year, there were only 852 foreign first-year students at the college level or 2 per cent of the total. Of this 2 per cent, 1.36 per cent consisted of European students and the remaining 0.81 per cent were non-Europeans (van de Velde 1997). The ethnostratification of immigrants in the Belgian labour-market is striking in terms of labour-market entry, the position of wage earners and of the unemployed (Verhoeven 2000). In Brussels, 74 per cent of the Moroccans work as manual labourers, 76 per cent of the Turks, as compared to 24 per cent of the entire working population (Kesteloot and Cortie 1998: 1839). In the two Flemish cities Antwerp and Ghent, a clear ethnostratification can be discerned in the labour-market. Immigrants are overrepresented in certain sectors including construction, retailing and restaurants. On the whole, they earn less and work more on a part-time basis than their Belgian counterparts (Rosvelds et al. 1993). Last but not least, the unemployment rate is higher among the Moroccan and Turkish immigrant groups (Stoop and Neels 1998). After a long recession resulting from the oil crisis in the mid-1970s and its effect on the high rate of unemployment, a slight change can only be noted in recent years. In 1997 the rate of unemployment was 9.4 per cent of the total labour force. The rate in the following years were respectively 9.5 per cent in 1998, 9 per cent in 1999 and 7 per cent in 2000.[1] The share of the non-EU immigrants in the total unemployed population accounted for about 10 per cent in 2000.[2]

Recent findings show that they are being discriminated against in the recruitment process. According to the country case study of the larger ILO study on discrimination in recruitment procedures (Centre for Equal Opportunities and Opposition to Racism 1997) preferential treatment is given to Belgian rather than to migrant candidates in the recruitment of male semi-skilled workers.

Empirical Development and Potentialities of Immigrant Entrepreneurship

For a number of reasons, figures and quantitative data on immigrant entrepreneurship are hard to find (Feld and Biren 1994; Hubeau 1997; Janssens 1999). First, the topic has not been thoroughly studied. Second, the national statistics (NIS) only provide very general data such as the total number of self-employed foreigners with no further indication of their nationalities, their distribution in the different sectors or their geographical ditribution. Fortunately the data provided by the National Institute for Social Insurances of Self-Employed Workers (RSVZ) are very useful, at least for documented self-employed people. Every self-employed person is required by law to register at this Institute. Spouses of the self-employed, generally females, have been able to register since 1990 in order to benefit from labour insurance and maternity leave. However, this is not mandatory. This explains the invisibility of the role of women in self-employment (Pang 1998).

In terms of the empirical development of self-employed workers in general, the post-Second World War period is marked by a general decrease in the self-employed percentage of the total labour force (Feld and Biren 1994). As explained above, this has to do with the comprehensive social benefit system. However, from the 1980s onward, the number has been rising, but at a slower pace than in other European countries. Depending on the sources, there has been an increase of self-employed workers from 5 to 10 per cent from 1983 to 1992 (ibid.: 58).

Figure 10.1 shows that in the 1990s there was a slight growth of self-employment in the general category of self-employed workers as well as in the category of foreign self-employed workers. In 1990, immigrant entrepreneurs represented 5.2 per cent of the total number of self-employed people. This percentage increased to 6.7 per cent in 1996 and remained constant until 1999, when it dropped slightly to 6.1 per cent.

EU migrants constitute the majority of the foreign self-employed workers. In 1991, according to Feld and Biren (1994: 61), the largest groups of self-employed migrants were the Italians (13,746 or 2.9 per cent of the total of foreign self-employed workers), the French (11,152 or 2.3 per cent) and the Dutch (9,464 or 2 per cent). These three countries collectively account for 59 per cent of the foreign self-employed people in Belgium. Among the non-EU migrants, in descending order the following nationalities demonstrate a tendency toward entrepreneurship: Moroccans (3.3 per cent of the total non-EU self-employed), Turks (1.7 per cent), and to a lesser degree Algerians (0.5 per cent), Chinese (0.5 per cent) and Tunisians (0.6 per cent). According to the 1996 RSVZ data, once again the Italians (1.7 per cent), Dutch (1.3 per cent) and French (1 per cent) headed the EU self-employed immigrants. Among the non-EU self-employed migrants, the leading nationalities are Moroccans (2,051 or 0.2 per cent), Turks (1,798 or 0.2 per cent) and to a much smaller extent Americans (0.075 per cent), Chinese (0.05 per cent) and Japanese (0.04 per cent). In 1999, EU immigrant entrepreneurs accounted for 5 per cent of the total self-employed, and non-EU immigrant entrepreneurs for 1.4 per cent. Within the group of the non-EU immigrant entrepreneurs there was a slight fall in the number of Moroccans (1,938) and a slight rise in the number of Turks (1,848) but not percentage-wise (0.2 per cent and 0.2 per cent respectively).

As to the geographical distribution of foreign self-employed people, in 1996 they were located in the provinces of Hainaut (11.13 per cent), Liège (8.67 per cent), Antwerp (7.95 per cent), Brabant-Wallon (7.16 per cent), Limburg (5.52 per cent), Namur (4.47 per cent) and Flemish-Brabant (4.19 per cent). The provinces Luxembourg (3.5 per cent), East Flanders (2.08 per cent) and West

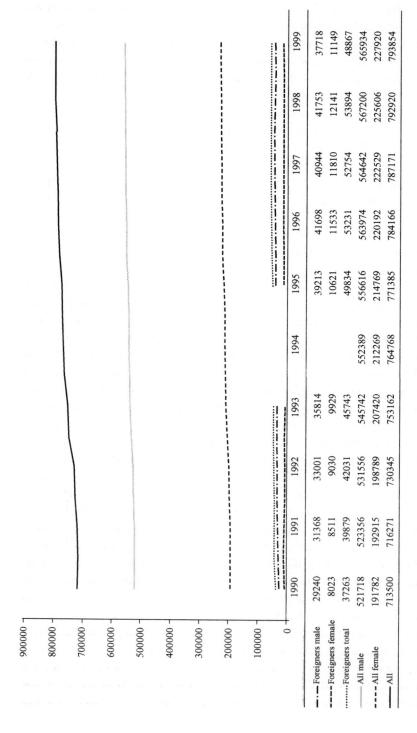

	1990	1991	1992	1993	1994	1995	1996	1997	1998	1999
Foreigners male	29240	31368	33001	35814		39213	41698	40944	41753	37718
Foreigners female	8023	8511	9030	9929		10621	11533	11810	12141	11149
Foreigners total	37263	39879	42031	45743		49834	53231	52754	53894	48867
All male	521718	523356	531556	545742	552389	556616	563974	564642	567200	565934
All female	191782	192915	198789	207420	212269	214769	220192	222529	225606	227920
All	713500	716271	730345	753162	764768	771385	784166	787171	792920	793854

Figure 10.1 Development of Native and Foreign Self-employed Male and Female Workers According to the RSVZ.

Flanders (1.17 per cent) clearly attract fewer migrant entrepreneurs (RSVZ 1996). This pattern has been relatively constant since 1990. The rural character of West Flanders can explain the low percentage there, since this is usually not the most ideal breeding ground for immigrant entrepreneurship. Immigrant entrepreneurs tend to flourish in metropolitan areas with a wide range of nationalities, ethnicities, subcultures and other forms of subdivided groups.

As amply documented in the international literature on immigrant entrepreneurs, they incline to cluster in the SME sector of commerce, including restaurants and retail shops. The reason is plain and simple. This sector generally requires relatively limited amounts of capital and low professional skills, although investment in some immigrant restaurants has risen significantly. Indeed in the sectoral distribution of the foreign self-employed, this sector including commerce, restaurants and retail shops scores very high. In 1991, two out of three immigrant entrepreneurs were in this sector. Percentage-wise, 65.4 per cent of the foreign self-employed are active in these small businesses. Throughout the 1990s, the overrepresentation of immigrants in this sector remained more or less stable. A number of studies indicate, at times indirectly, that some immigrant entrepreneurs do relatively well. In the study by de Witte (1997), some Turkish caterers consider themselves rather successful, and are unwilling to change their status of entrepreneurs into that of wage earners in the formal labour market. Turkish restaurant owners in Ghent serve their co-ethnics and Belgians alike. The more successful ones are in predominantly white areas, whereas the less successful ones are in ethnic neighbourhoods. Similar accounts are given by Greek restaurant owners and Turkish shopkeepers in Liège (Feld et al. 1993).

In my study on the Chinese food sector (Pang 1999, forthcoming) I discern an assimilation as well as a creolization process. The assimilation of immigrant food, be it Chinese, Greek or Turkish, means they have become part and parcel of the daily diet of members of majority as well as minority groups. Chinese and other Asian food are readily available at major supermarkets. On the other hand, some immigrant entrepreneurs sell 'non-ethnic, mainstream' products to Belgians as well as immigrants. Leonidas & Co., owned by a Greek immigrant family, has always produced a typically 'Belgian' product, namely chocolate. Second-generation Turks in Brussels have shops selling French fries to co-ethnics and Belgians living in the neighbourhood (Kesteloot and Mistiaen 1995).

Creolization refers to the current renovation trend, mixing 'ethnic' food and ingredients and leading to new types of 'fusion food' or 'world food'. So far it is mostly majority-group members who are shaping this process, with a minimal contribution by immigrants. However, if immigrant entrepreneurs succeed in responding to the demands of the current eating culture, with novelty, 'exoticism', freshness, health and texture as key ingredients, they have a good chance of transforming their simple ethnic restaurant or grocery shop into a cosmopolitan eating temple. Within the paradigm of creolization and the celebration of cultural mixing, one might pose the rhetorical question: who else but the immigrants has the street credibility to bring 'the taste of distant lands and cultures' to the city centres of the West? The potential role immigrant entrepreneurs can play in the new urban context is discussed later.

Research on Immigrant Entrepreneurship

Searching for academic studies on immigrant entrepreneurship in Belgium can be quite disconcerting. The fact is that there just is not much out there. Given the applied nature of most research findings and reports, most of the energy was devoted to the formulation of policy recommendations rather than the development of new or complementary theoretical models.

The first publication on immigrant entrepreneurship (Vanhaverbeke and Leman 1988) was conducted by Foyer, a minorities centre in Molenbeek, Brussels. With the resource and labour-market disadvantage theory as its point of departure, this study underlines the precarious position of migrant entrepreneurs. Many immigrants are driven into entrepreneurship because they cannot find a job on the regular job market. They do not have the required qualifications (labour-market disadvantage) and they are not embedded in the social network of mainstream society (resource disadvantage) (for commentary, see Drijkoningen 1998; Vanhaverbeke and Leman 1988). Foyer was the first organization to show an interest in immigrant entrepreneurship as a viable but modest way to include immigrants in mainstream society.

The most widely cited publication with the self-explanatory title *Ethnic Entrepreneurship in the Brussels Capital Region* by Vanhoren and Bracke dates from 1992. Its main objective is to map the socio-economic profile of immigrant entrepreneurs in Brussels and to assess the viability of immigrant entrepreneurship as a vehicle for the creation of employment, social mobility and integration (ibid.: 10). Another equally important reason for commissioning this project is the negative image of immigrant entrepreneurs as tax-evaders, non-law-abiding and rule-breaking business people, operating within their own social and cultural network and shunning contact with native organizations and firms. In contrast to other publications, the authors did make an effort to consult the theoretical models available at the time. Concerning the emergence of immigrant entrepreneurship, they refer to the Dutch cultural anthropologist Bovenkerk (1982a) who discerns three models to explain why immigrants seek their fortune in self-employment. These models are (1) the cultural model of immigrants who have entrepreneurial skills prior to migration, (2) the theory of the ethnic infrastructure or economic opportunities model and (3) the 'reactive' or disadvantage model. Examining the 'determinants of successful entrepreneurship', Vanhoren and Bracke (1992) subscribe to the interactive model of Waldinger et al. (1990a) emphasizing the market opportunity structures and business resources of immigrant entrepreneurs, go on to map immigrant entrepreneurs in the Brussels Capital Region by minutely describing the rules and regulations for immigrant entrepreneurs and providing sets of figures, and discuss the relationship between immigrant entrepreneurs and third actors, including native associations of the SME sector (*middenstand*), the local authorities, clients and suppliers. Finally, immigrant entrepreneurs in one commune voice their needs and aspirations toward their professional activity and future plan or vision. So far, this remains the most comprehensive work on immigrant entrepreneurship despite its geographical limitation to the Brussels Capital Region.

Other publications are more 'neighbourhood-oriented' (Cassiers 1999; Kesteloot and Mistiaen 1995; Willems 1996; de Witte 1997) or 'ad hoc' (Drijkoningen 1998). These neighbourhood-oriented studies provide rich and dense information and insights in specific areas such as the study on the Turkish restaurants on the Chaussée de Haecht, Brussels (Kesteloot and Mistiaen 1995). However, the scope of such studies tends to be limited. Still others are the works of convinced adepts of the 'disadvantage model' (van den Bulck 1992; Caestecker 1995a, b; Hubeau 1997). Other common aspects in most of the literature are the target groups and local focuses. Whereas the academic output in Flanders is deplorable, the situation in French-speaking Belgium is even more alarming. One exception to the rule is the research group of Feld, Biren and Manço. Feld and Biren (1994) have extensively published on foreign workers including entrepreneurs of foreign origin. A qualitative study has been conducted on twenty-four Moroccan cab drivers in Brussels, thirty-three Greek restaurant owners in Liège, twenty-four Turkish (foodstuffs) shop owners (including bakeries) in Liège and twenty-eight Portuguese entrepreneurs in the cleaning business in Brussels (Feld et al. 1993). This study testifies once again to the success of immigrants, in this case Greeks and Turks, in the food and catering sector. Their experience is in sharp contrast to the survival strategies of Moroccan cab drivers or Portuguese cleaning people. The success of the former two groups might be attributed to the firm position that ethnic food has attained in the food ways and lifestyle of consumers in advanced Western economies.

Studies on the Chinese as a diasporic community (Pang 1993, 1994, 2000) and on Chinese food (Pang forthcoming) do not fit in the well-entrenched 'disadvantage' paradigm. In most of Europe, the Chinese are clustered in the catering business. A textbook example of an ethnic-minority in small business, they have not yet been subject to analysis on immigrant entrepreneurship in Belgium.

As a result of the renewed interest in immigrant business on the part of certain policy-makers and professional associations such as UNIZO (the Small Business

Association), some projects are now in the pipeline. These projects should provide more accurate figures and insight into individual immigrant entrepreneurs and their trajectory. Other research focuses on female entrepreneurs and helping spouses. A large survey is being conducted on immigrant entrepreneurs in Flanders by Martens and Verhoeven, with more than 300 immigrant entrepreneurs being surveyed, mostly former labour immigrants including Moroccans, Turks and Italians.

For sure, the innovative and exciting research on immigrant entrepreneurship should be warmly welcomed. Yet it is still too early to grasp the significance of these research projects on immigrant entrepreneurs and the scholarship on immigrant entrepreneurship.

Role of Governments and Organizations vis-à-vis Immigrant Entrepreneurship

During the guest-worker migration regime from 1936 to 1975, the labour immigrant was seen as a mere economic entity. Migrant policy was limited to their integration at the workplace and in the labour-union structures. In the 1980s immigrant policy was formally introduced (Martens and Caestecker 2001). In 1981 the Roman Catholic-blue coalition, led by Wilfried Martens, officially acknowledged that Belgium was a receiving country. The return programme for first-generation immigrants was not successful in the second half of the 1970s. It was clear that immigrants and their children were in Belgium to stay. The need for a specific immigrant policy became all the more urgent given the emergence of the extreme right wing and its successive electoral gains from the mid-1980s onward. The extreme rightist party Vlaams Blok, with its hostile and racist stance to immigration and immigrants, has fuelled the issue of immigration and the integration of immigrants from a negative perspective. Thus, it has become an important topic on the agenda of political parties and policy-makers at various administrative levels. As a demonstration of its success, it got 28 per cent of the votes in the local elections in Antwerp in 1994. In June 1999, 15.5 per cent of the Flemish voters voted for this party in the regional, federal and European elections (ibid.). In some cities and municipalities, it got 30 per cent of the votes. The Belgian migrant policy aimed to combat the deprivation, subordination and discrimination (Vermeulen 1997) of the former guest-workers and their offspring. The restrictive immigration policy toward newcomers was compensated by more stringent anti-discrimination legislation and liberalized naturalization procedures as regards ethnic minorities. Another ingredient of the migration policy was the idea of dispersal, particularly in schools and housing. It was argued that dispersal would facilitate the smooth incorporation into mainstream society.

In 1989 the Royal Commission on Migration Policy (KCM/CRPRI) was set up by royal decree for a period of four years. It was in charge of conducting research and making policy proposals related to the disadvantaged position of migrants in housing, education and the labour market. The Commission formulated a definition of 'integration' as a third mode of incorporation balancing between assimilation and segregation. Its notion of integration implies that immigrants need to conform to the same rules and laws at the public level. They have to respect the basic principles of the modern Western state including modernity and emancipation. However, they have the right to maintain and develop their culture, language and customs at the private level. Pluralism and respect for cultural diversity are not only tolerated in mainstream society, they are viewed as mutual enrichment. In 1993 the Centre for Equal Opportunities and Opposition to Racism replaced the Commission. Its main tasks are to promote equal chances and combat discrimination of all kinds, experienced by immigrants and Belgians alike. The two functions of this centre, equal opportunity and anti-racism, reflect the two incorporation models in Flanders and Wallonia. Whereas a targeted or 'category-oriented' (*categoriaal*) policy was pursued in Flanders, in Wallonia there has always been a clear-cut preference for a more general policy combating deprivation of the poor and the disadvantaged, including immigrants and native Belgians. In the mid-1990s, there was a shift from a more targeted to a more general or 'inclusive' (*inclusief*) policy in Flanders.

Immigrant entrepreneurship was and still is a marginal issue in immigration policies. After all, the target group of migrant policy is working-class labour migrants, at least the first generation, who were 'invited' to come and work in the mines and the steel factories. Aside from the lack of interest on the part of policy-makers, candidate entrepreneurs from non-EU countries are facing more administrative barriers in entering self-employment than Belgian and other EU citizens. As foreigners, they have to apply for a 'professional card', based on the law of February 1965 on foreigners conducting self-employed activities. (As of 4 March 2003 this rather discriminatory practice of foreign entrepreneurs to dispose of a professional card has been abolished.) It was based on a law, now repealed, of 16 November 1939, when the Belgian economy was in a recession. Due to resentment against successful immigrant entrepreneurs, local business people urged the government to protect them from 'foreigners' (Caestecker 1995a, b). Aside from being discriminatory, it is a time-consuming and locality-restrictive procedure. Recently, negotiations have been launched to discard this unnecessary and discriminatory obstacle to immigrants who wish to start small businesses.

After two decades of official migrant policy, some institutional organizations started to 'discover' immigrant entrepreneurship. As mentioned above, the Foyer, an integration centre in Brussels, was the first organization concerned with these migrants. In addition to qualitative research, it set up consultancy offices for immigrant entrepreneurs in Schaarbeek and Molenbeek. The objective is to assist potential and actual immigrant entrepreneurs with legal and administrative facets of self-employment. A second objective is to encourage more cooperation on the part of the immigrant self-employed with native self-employed workers. These offices also cooperate with the VIZO (Flemish Institute for Entreprises), a professional organization that formulates recommendations. These offices have mainly attracted potential immigrant entrepreneurs or those with problems.

A second organization, UNIZO (Union of Self-employed Entrepreneurs) has recently been active in championing the cause of immigrant entrepreneurs. A special unit has been set up in the Research and Training Department to deal specifically with immigrant entrepreneurs. They organize information sessions for native Belgian and immigrant entrepreneurs and prospective entrepreneurs and assist individual immigrant trajectories. The aim is to improve the image of immigrant entrepreneurship and 'integrate' immigrant business people into their organization in particular and into mainstream society in general.

In Antwerp the 'Ethnic Entrepreneurship' (*Allochtoon Ondernemen*) project was set up in 1997. It is part of the European forum Local Integration Action (LIA). Its aims are to promote immigrant entrepreneurship and improve their image in the various neighbourhoods of Antwerp. It was reasoned that if small businesses were left alone, there was a risk of ghettoization, which would fuel the 'fear' on the part of native Belgians and the ever-increasing popularity of the extreme-rightist party, the Vlaams Blok.

At present the Platform of 'Ethnic Entrepreneurship' functions in conjunction with the UNIZO and the Centre for Equal Opportunities and Opposition to Racism to promote immigrant entrepreneurship and assist immigrant entrepreneurs in their efforts to become self-employed. A similar project has been set up in Ghent in the nineteenth-century inner-city areas and in Genk (Limburg), a former mining area. Other projects include the Brabant neighbourhood in Brussels, an area close to the North station with a high concentration of mostly Turkish shopkeepers, with the neighbouring street, the Chaussée de Haecht, consisting almost exclusively of Turkish restaurants.

Research Paradigm and Policies: An Ancillary Relationship?

The federal integration policy striving to combat labour-migrant deprivation in housing and education and on the job market has had a great impact on immigration and immigrant research. This research focuses on the disadvantaged position (*achterstand*) and/or discrimination (*achterstelling*) (Billiet and de Witte 1991) of labour migrants in education (Byram and Leman 1990), housing, the job market, health-related issues (Peeters and de Muynck 1997), identity

(Roosens 1989, 1998) and political rights and participation (Martiniello 1994, 1995). In gender studies, attention has been exclusively devoted to the disadvantaged position of mostly Muslim women (Alsulaiman 1997). In recent years the integration policy has targeted not only migrants but also the native underprivileged (*kansarmen*; for a detailed discussion, see Kruyt and Niessen 1997). New actors including asylum-seekers (Ramakers 1997) and undocumented foreigners (Leman 1995) have joined migrants as a specific social category. In the general discourse, these newcomers constitute a separate category besides the labour migrants or 'migrants'.

The dominant research paradigm emphasizes the disadvantaged and generally poor position of immigrants in the fields of housing, the labour-market and education for cultural and structural reasons. This 'minorization' paradigm needs to be embedded in the policy-making basis of most studies on immigrants. In the welfare-system regime, policy-makers strive to generate equal chances for all the members of society and thus the disadvantages facing immigrants should be discarded. This one-sided representation of 'needy' immigrants is also evident in neighbouring countries like the Netherlands (Penninx 1988). This explains the ample output of studies on their precarious position in mainstream society and their divergent cultural-ethnic-religious background, keeping them from a smooth incorporation into the host society. Moreover, almost all the studies deal with the two numerically large groups of Muslim immigrants, Moroccans and Turks. Yet starting from the 1990s this paradigm has been subject to incisive critique in the Netherlands (Rath 1991) and Belgium (Blommaert and Verschueren 1998; Pang 1998; Ramakers 1996). Notwithstanding this critique and lip-service paid to more diversity in the literature on immigrants, the minorization paradigm is still dominant. As a result, very little is known about other groups, the newcomers including asylum-seekers and undocumented foreigners. Furthermore, a comprehensive theoretical reorientation of the literature on migration and immigrants is still called for. This is admittedly no easy task.

Also to immigrant entrepreneurship, there is not much data on 'immigrant entrepreneurship' at either the practical or the theoretical level. The reason for the minimal output of academic work on this subject and its limitation to Moroccans and Turks (and to a lesser degree Italians, Greeks and Portuguese) have to do with the above-mentioned paradigm of 'minorization', with immigrants seen as lacking agency and unable to achieve upward social mobility on their own. To put it bluntly, immigrant entrepreneurship, its potentialities for social mobility and more generally the representation of migrants as actors capable of assessing and improving their position in the host society (Demirçi 1995; Leman 1997; Peeters et al. 1996) blatantly contradict the major premise of the 'minorization' paradigm and are therefore not fit for research unless its aim is to demonstrate the immigrant's lack of capacities. In addition, the government commissioned most of the research, and most research findings on immigrant entrepreneurship are policy-preparing studies at the local or regional level. Given the policy-driven nature of these studies, the area of research is generally confined to the local level. The target groups of most studies are the two 'majority minorities', Turks and Moroccans, and oddly enough not the immigrants who display a preponderance for entrepreneurship, such as the Chinese, Jews, Indians, Pakistani or Vietnamese. The main argument in these studies is that immigrant entrepreneurs are driven into self-employment because they are excluded from the formal labour market. Given the small-scale nature of most research and the relatively short investigation period, researchers uncritically adopt existing theoretical frameworks for immigrant entrepreneurship. For instance, the study by Vanhoren and Bracke (1992) refers to the model developed by Bovenkerk (1982a) and the interaction model of Waldinger et al. (1990a). In the past year or so, an interest in immigrant entrepreneurship has emerged in Flanders following the trend in the Netherlands and to a lesser degree in Great Britain. It has resulted in many small-scale projects at the local level. The academic community has responded to this trend in rather slow motion. For example, the term 'ethnic' in 'ethnic entrepreneurship' has been deconstructed since it excessively and one-sidedly favours the 'ethnic' dimension of immigrant entrepreneurs and overlooks market and institutional changes (Rath 2000c). Yet in Flanders and Wallonia, the term 'ethnic entrepreneurship' is still widely used in a blissfully unproblematic way. Recently, there seems to be a tendency to replace 'ethnic' with 'non-native' or 'allochthonous' in the expression *allochtoon ondernemerschap* (immigrant entrepreneurship), following the trend started by civil servants in the Netherlands, where immigrants are called *allochtonen.*

Conclusion and Ruminations on Potentialities of Immigrant Entrepreneurship and Future Research Topics

In most European welfare states, entrepreneurship only gained momentum in the second half of the 1970s. This is also the case of Belgium, where there was a decrease in self-employment in the post-war period from 1947 to 1980. This might be explained by the new welfare state with its safety net and economic expansion, which guaranteed nearly full employment until the early 1970s. With the recession it is argued that households, mainstream and immigrant alike, were driven into self-employment as a survival strategy. During the 1980s the strategies of informalization were sustained in terms of the flexibilization of formal work and the use of dependent and semi-independent informal labour. The absence of trade unions and the avoidance of indirect wage costs such as taxation and social-security led to lower labour costs. The movement of natives and immigrants into self-employment did not really attract much attention on the part of policy-makers, academic researchers, the media and the general public except for some fragmentary studies. In these few studies, however, immigrant entrepreneurship was viewed as a viable, albeit humble, avenue for immigrants who had few skills and limited financial capital (Vanhaverbeke and Leman 1988; Vanhoren and Bracke 1992). Yet the general image of the pitiful immigrant entrepreneur has very little in common with the 'heroic self-made man' type of entrepreneur. The social mobility of immigrants, i.e. Moroccans and Turks, means an improvement above an unemployed status in the formal labour-market. No studies have been conducted on the Jewish or Indian communities in Antwerp in the diamond trade, or on the Vietnamese refugees who arrived in the 1970s and soon engaged in self-employment. Despite their differences from the majority group, they succeeded in becoming invisible in the discourse on migration and immigrants as a result of their smooth incorporation into the labour-market as self-employed small-scale entrepreneurs. Another good illustration is the case of the Chinese, who are concentrated in the catering sector (Pang 1998). Of course to varying degrees these 'success stories' negate many underlying problems and conflict areas situated within the group or originating outside such as discrimination and exclusion by the majority group. Indeed, more studies need to be done on topics such as the relation between social mobility and social costs.

In general, the literature is too scarce, too neighbourhood-oriented, too ad hoc, unsatisfactory and unrepresentative of the swift development of immigrant entrepreneurship in the larger society. Only very recently, as a result of changing research trends in other European countries, has immigrant entrepreneurship become an increasingly important research item. Moreover, as the minorities themselves, especially the second generation that is coming of age, and the current coalition government aim to project a positive image of the multicultural society, there is room for more open and multiple approaches to migration and settled immigrants. The 'minorization' paradigm has been all too easily manipulated by the Vlaams Blok, the extreme-right party in Flanders. It has gained considerable power by consciously misrepresenting the immigrant issue as one of the core threats to mainstream society. This altered context, along with the generally bright economic environment in Belgium and throughout the EU and the new opportunities provided by the 'new' economy will induce more people, including immigrants, to engage in entrepreneurship.

Finally, I would like to present a possible scenario, which is a far cry from what has been written so far about immigrant entrepreneurship from the 'disadvantage' point of view. It is more a vision than a reality. It is argued that in the process of glocalization, Western cities function as nodal points in transnational movements of money, commodities, ideas and people. Sectoral changes in the urban post-industrial economy have led to a wide variety of services. At one end of the spectrum there are the high-tech services provided by the 'dotcom' industry and at the other end the highly personalized services befitting the lifestyle of the new urbanites, 'la nouvelle urbanité' (Bourdet and Dams 2000; Mort Subite 1990). The cosmopolitan cultural economy seems to have fine options to offer to immigrant entrepreneurs. Physical capital has been replaced by intellectual capital, which is the driving, coveted force of the new era (Rifkin 2000). Concepts, ideas and images and not material things are at the core of this hypercapitalistic system (Jensen 1999; Rifkin 2000). As a result of the shift from industrial production to cultural production, cutting-edge commerce will increasingly shape the marketing of a vast array of cultural experiences. They include 'global travel and tourism, theme cities and parks, destination entertainment centers, wellness, fashion and cuisine; professional sports and games, gambling, music, film, television, the virtual worlds of cyberspace ...' (Rifkin 2000: 7). What are the potential and actual roles of immigrant entrepreneurs in the urban cosmopolitan cultural economy? The catering sector no longer revolves exclusively around food but also or even more so around entertainment. Immigrant entrepreneurs can capitalize and elaborate on 'the ethnic' or 'cosmopolitan' experience of eating at their restaurants. In fact, the current success of 'ethnic' food might be explained by the changing taste and lifestyle of the new 'protean' generation, which maximizes access to experiences rather than to the accumulation of goods. From a spatial perspective, tourism to cities has led to the thematization of public spaces (Sorkin 1994; Swyngedouw 1998). Within the same context, the city is increasingly seen as a collection of images and experiences to be consumed by tourists as well as city dwellers. Once immigrant or other entrepreneurs consciously and successfully reshape and rewrap cultural products such as cuisine and fashion and turn them into an appealing experience for the new urbanites, we can speak of 'ethnic' or 'cosmopolitan' entrepreneurship, depending on the specific mono-ethnic or multi-ethnic presentation of the product.

As regards future research topics on immigrant businesses, a wide range of research needs to be done. First, more data is needed on different immigrant entrepreneurs, males and females, and their business activities from a mixed embeddedness perspective. In doing so, a body of data and analysis on immigrant entrepreneurship will be generated. Second, the term 'ethnicity' and its role in immigrant business needs to be critically assessed. This is particularly important since 'ethnicity' has proven to be highly optional and malleable, as in the case of the United States. It seems that cultural anthropologists no longer have a monopoly on 'ethnicity'. Only by problematizing 'ethnicity' can we understand some of the processes, such as the creolization of postmodern lifestyles that are now taking place in advanced urban economies. In a lucid way, Marilyn Halter informs us in her recent book *Shopping for Identity: The Marketing of Ethnicity*

(2000) that immigrants need to be approached as clients by main businesses. They increasingly constitute unserved constituencies that are barely known to traditional marketing experts.

To conclude, given the recent setback in the ICT sector, leaving many 'dotcommers' jobless, critical voices will challenge the new economy of connectivity and networks. Yet there are reasons to believe that culture has been commodified and largely appropriated by the economy and that in the emergence of the cosmopolitan cultural economy, immigrants can play a pivotal role. Aside from tackling the barriers for enterprising immigrants, researchers also need to look at this issue. In support programmes, they should not be forgotten and condemned to the status of 'proletarians', since they have all the potentialities to join the new 'protean' generation of urbanites in the new economy.

Notes

1. See www.meta.fgov.be/pe/peb/nleb04.htm, the website of the Federal Ministry of Labour.
2. See www.wav.be, the website of the Centre for Employment, Labour and Education (WAV).

–11–

Austria: Still a Highly Regulated Economy

Regina Haberfellner

Introduction

Austria's Chamber of Commerce holds that in much the same way as for employees, for business people from Central and Eastern Europe a quota regulation should be introduced to limit their number for a period of seven years (*Der Standard*, 4 April 2001). This gives an impression of the spirit in which foreign business people are welcomed in Austria and the barriers they face. It is in the long Austrian tradition of exclusionary mechanisms for newcomers in general and foreigners in particular.

Despite the not very inviting formulation, there was a considerable rise in the number of self-employed immigrants in the 1980s till the mid-1990s, with Austrian self-employment declining in the same period. Since both these trends reversed in the past few years, we might wonder which factors affect the business start-up decision. Conditions have apparently changed in such a way that their impact on the tendency toward self-employment among these two groups has differed noticeably.

Two aspects that greatly influence the potential developments of immigrant businesses are of interest to us in the Austrian context: the nature of the welfare state and its business and immigration regimes. According to Esping-Andersen (1990), Austria's welfare state belongs to the group of 'continental-corporatistic' states. However, its immigration policy has been highly influenced by the 'guest-worker' approach, which implies a perception of immigrants as employees. This chapter gives an overview of the development of immigrant entrepreneurship against the backdrop of special features of the Austrian system of social partnership and its restrictive labour and business regimes in the 1980s and 1990s. It reflects upon the complexity of intertwining regulations concerning business start-ups, residence and labour-market access, and its effects on the dynamics of business start-ups by immigrants.

Regina Haberfellner

Austria's Political Pillars: Consensus and Corporatism

The roots of Austria's political and institutional framework go back to the first two decades after the Second World War. The most important one is the extensive system of social partnership (*Sozialpartnerschaft*), with some unique characteristics. Another one is the long and, until recently, lasting predominant position of the two main parties that got about 90–95 per cent of the votes for decades. These are not only highly interlinked developments that reinforce each other, they have also influenced the institutional frame of immigration policy in Austria.

From a Two-party System toward Moderate Political Pluralism

Two parties dominated the political landscape until the mid-1980s, the Austrian People's Party (ÖVP, Österreichische Volkspartei) and the Austrian Social Democratic Party (SPÖ, Sozialdemokratische Partei Österreichs). For twenty-nine years (1970–1999), the Austrian chancellor was a member of the Social Democratic Party, which governed from 1986 to 1999 in coalition with the ÖVP. The dominance of these two parties and the prevailing position of the social partnership led to a strategy of proportional allocation of the parties' members (sometimes political friends) in all the important state-influenced sectors such as health care, education, the state-owned industries, and banking, often from top management positions down to the lower end of the job hierarchy (*Proporzsystem*). It is even assumed that qualifications are the main reason for getting jobs in the large state-influenced sector.

The 'two-party system' ended in the mid-1980s, when the Green Party (die Grünen), which supports the interests of immigrants, entered parliament and became a stable part of the political landscape. Since the mid-1980s, the Freedom Party (Freiheitliche Partei Österreichs, generally associated with Jörg Haider) has become increasingly important. For about thirty years, it only got 4–5 per cent of the votes and was a marginal group in the political landscape. The upward trend of the Freedom Party started in 1986 and peaked in the elections of 1999, when it got 27 per cent of the votes throughout Austria. The Freedom Party, which often opposes the Green Party on immigration issues, has been heading the Austrian government together with the People's Party since February 2000.

The System of Social Partnership

The political system in Austria is dominated by an elaborate system of social partnership, the main pillar of Austria's corporate political system. It is reinforced by the two main parties and the relevant organizations are heavily interconnected with them. The Chamber of Commerce and Chamber of Agriculture have always been well connected to the People's Party, and the Chamber of Labour and the Trade Unions Congress (ÖGB) have close connections to the Social Democratic Party.[1] Neither the Green Party nor the Freedom Party participate in the proportional division of power and influence in the social partnership.

The social partners have a far-reaching influence on the political system. In policy decisions concerning the economy and the labour market and in central questions of social policy, they have decisive influence based on a network of personal, formal and informal linkages with decision-makers in the government, the administration, the parliament, and the political parties (Tálos et al. 1993). The establishment of a forum for institutionalized cooperation involving the interest groups of employers and employees had been a main concern of the Chamber of Labour and the trade unions since the end of the 1940s, but the employers' interest groups reacted reluctantly (Wollner 1996). The institutionalization of the *Sozialpartnerschaft* started, however, in the early 1960s and expanded in the following decades, but was never anchored in a legal frame and always remained on a voluntary level. Numerous committees, commissions and meetings of representatives were established, interlinking politics and interest groups horizontally as well as vertically. The parliament only passed a series of laws after extensive co-ordinating activities among the social partners. The main pillars to keeping the system working were the high degree of centralization in the four organizations, the power of the national umbrella organizations, and the lack of competition based on the system of compulsory membership in one interest group for all businesses, one for all workers, and one for all farmers (Tálos 1997).

Although they have often been criticized as a 'shadow government', the social partners have been able to maintain their influence. There is, however, some evidence that the current government is trying to reduce the influence of the social partners by no longer involving them in decision-making processes. Although the Freedom Party has extensively addressed immigration issues in the election campaigns, no reliable assessment of the effects on immigration policy as a result of the changed mode of cooperation and the new division of power has been feasible so far.

Immigration Policy, Labour-market Access, and the Role of Social Partners

Immigration policy, particularly the issue of immigrant access to the labour market, has always been controversial among the social partners. This dispute was already evident in the late 1950s when the labour-market shortage became more and more pronounced, resulting in a conflict between the Chamber of

Labour and the ÖGB on the one hand and the Chamber of Commerce on the other hand. While the former obstinately refused to open the labour market for foreigners, the latter increased the pressure to open the labour market. The petrified front lines made it impossible to find the consensus necessary for a law to regulate the employment of foreigners. This conflict ended with the 'Raab-Olah' agreement in 1961, which became crucial for the stabilization of the social partnership. In addition to measures to bring inflation under control, the unions agreed to open the labour market and the borders for the first temporary immigration wave of 47,000 'guest-workers' in 1961 under the condition of equal payment, one-year contracts, and the dismissal of immigrants in the event of job losses. The main reason for this was an agreement on the increased influence of the interest groups representing the employees in the 'parity price and wage commission', which became a main pillar of *Sozialpartnerschaft*.

While the unions controlled the employment of immigrants inland, the Chamber of Commerce tried to stimulate 'guest-worker' immigration via special agencies in the potential sending countries. In spite of these endeavours, the percentage of foreign workers did not increase noticeably until the end of the 1960s, with the most important immigrant groups coming from the former Yugoslavia and Turkey. For the first time, more than 100,000 work permits were issued in 1970. Although the basic idea of the 'guest-worker' system was the rotation principle, in the economic boom neither the unions nor the employment office saw a need to restrict the number of work permits issued. In 1973 the first peak was reached with 226,800 foreigners working in Austria (see Figure 11.1). After a slump, the number of employed foreigners started increasing again at the end of the 1980s and reached a peak with 319,400 foreign employees in the year 2000.

The spirit of the 'Raab-Olah' agreement remained the framework that shaped regulations concerning immigrant labour-market access in the following decades. As the Chamber of Commerce continuously postulated an additional need of foreign workers, the unions and the Chamber of Labour were able to strengthen their positions within the social partnership until 1975 by using the annual negotiations concerning the quota of foreign workers as lever (Bauböck 1997; Wimmer 1986; Wollner 1996). The first Foreigners' Employment Act (*Ausländerbeschäftigungsgesetz*) was enacted in 1975, and reaffirmed the influence of the social partners by establishing a parity commission which had extensive influence on all the regulations on the access of foreigners to the labour market.[2] According to the law, only after eight years of continuous employment could a foreigner obtain a *Befreiungsschein* – limited to two years, but renewable – allowing the employee to change employer (Bauböck 1997). That regulation brought about an ethnic segmentation of the labour market and a high degree of dependence for the immigrant employees on their employers (Gächter 1995).

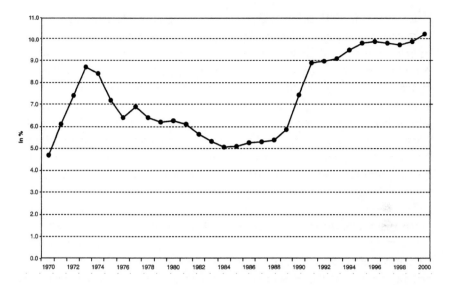

Figure 11.1 Non-Austrian Female Entrepreneurs, 1970–2000 (percentage)

The trade unions had two options in this period: either support the immigrant workers' interests and co-ordinate their interests with those of the Austrian native workers, or use their influence on immigrant employment issues as leverage in negotiations within the framework of *Sozialpartnerschaft* and force the prioritized employment of native workers. There is some evidence that the unions adhered to the latter strategy (Bauböck 1997: 683).

Mainly because of the unions' concern about losing influence, no great reform of the legal framework that regulated residence and labour-market access for non-Austrians was feasible at the end of the 1980s. Consequently, only minor changes of the regulations were made and – still in accordance with the 'guest-worker' concept – a national quota system was introduced for work permits. The yearly fixed quotas vary from 8–10 per cent of the total workforce and show that even people with a legal residence permit can be in the situation of not having access to the labour market. Particularly young people, women, and self-employed immigrants are affected (ibid.: 684; Haberfellner and Böse 1999).

The opening of the Eastern European borders, an additional need for immigrant labour because of the economic upswing, and a rising number of asylum-seekers led to more than a doubling of the foreign population from 326,000 to 713,000 between 1987 and 1994. The high influx of immigrants and the rising unemployment rates caused concerned and excited discussions in the media as well as the political arena in the early 1990s about immigration into Austria. Since the enactment of the new Asylum Law and the institution of a yearly quota for new residence permits in 1992, net immigration to Austria has been dramatically reduced.[3]

Although the severity of some of the regulations was reduced in the late 1990s, having a job and sufficient income is still an important requirement for non-Austrians who do not want to lose their residence permit. In a situation of unemployment, it is thus much more important for immigrants than it is for Austrians to find a new job quickly. The pressure to accept even low-paid or low-quality jobs is therefore high and tends to lead to a segmentation of the labour market, where immigrants are found in the lower, more unattractive outsider positions. The high pressure on immigrants to make a living also makes it clear why the average unemployment rate of immigrants in Austria is normally only about 1–2 per cent above the overall unemployment rate.

Entrepreneurship in General and of Immigrants in Particular

Although Austria experienced a long period of economic growth starting at the end of the 1950s, the environment for private business has not been very favourable (OECD 1999). As the importance of the private-sector decreased, the Austrian state became a very important employer because, for historical reasons, there were numerous state-owned industries. The number of civil servants and other public-sector employees is still quite high. Compared with other OECD countries, Austria is in the top third.

The political programmes of the governments consequently ignored the needs of the SME-sector till the mid-1990s. While no demand for more companies or business start-ups was ever mentioned, the aim of increasing the number of employed persons was highlighted in each programme. Thus, the rate of employment has been rising steadily for decades and a total of more than 3.1 million (average 2000) is the highest number of employees since the foundation of the second republic; in the same time there was a sharp fall in the rate of self-employment in Austria.

The main reason for this reduction is the decreasing importance of the agricultural sector (see Table 11.1). Other reasons for the diminishing self-employment rate are the long-lasting positive labour-market development, the extensive social-welfare system from which employees profit much more than the self-employed, and the high access barriers to self-employment (Biffl et al. 1997: 44). In addition, if they fail, business people in Austria are not only stigmatized, they can be prosecuted (and imprisoned in the event of proved negligent conduct) and called to account for bankruptcy within a period of seven years. Organizations counselling over-indebted persons record two main reasons for over-indebtedness in Austria: one is (former) self-employment. For many Austrians, avoiding these high risks has therefore been a main reason for not carrying out the idea of starting up a business (IfGH 1996).

Table 11.1 Self-employed and Helping Family Members

	1980	1981	1982	1983	1984	1985	1986	1987	1988	1989	1990	1991	1992	1993	1994	1995	1996	1997	1998	1999
Self-employed and helping family members including agriculture and forestry	16.98	16.39	15.51	15.49	14.86	14.55	14.48	14.43	14.44	14.32	14.12	13.67	13.10	12.78	12.50	13.02	12.78	12.57	12.67	12.50
Self-employed including agriculture and forestry	12.34	11.94	11.16	11.28	10.48	10.28	10.12	10.04	10.20	10.30	10.28	10.03	9.95	9.79	9.84	10.24	10.10	10.14	10.33	10.27
Self-employed and helping family members without agriculture and forestry	8.73	8.40	7.68	7.78	7.66	7.62	7.83	7.75	8.14	8.18	8.01	7.98	7.70	7.57	7.66	8.08	7.83	7.91	8.25	8.30
Self-employed without agriculture and forestry	7.44	7.17	6.48	6.62	6.05	5.85	5.96	5.98	6.22	6.45	6.47	6.38	6.23	6.18	6.37	6.75	6.52	6.69	7.04	7.16

In order to curb the dwindling self-employment rate, the Austrian government has been trying to actively increase the number of business start-ups since the mid-1990s. Supportive measures like additional guidance, reduced barriers and new subsidy programmes were introduced, accompanied by a media campaign which seems to be successful. Until the beginning of the 1990s the Austrians highly trusted the state's ability to provide jobs and only a third believed in the importance of additional private businesses as a means of job creation, but nearly 50 per cent were convinced of the need to increase the number of private businesses in 1998.[4] In fact the number of self-employed people increased by about 50,000 (without agriculture) in the 1990s, i.e. a growth of 25 per cent. However, it still did not equal the decrease in the agriculture sector and, due to the rise in the total workforce of about 400,000 in the same time-span, only led to small changes in the rate of self-employment.

Table 11.2 New Businesses in Austria

1990*	13,100
1991*	13,400
1992*	14,500
1993	14,631
1994	14,306
1995	14,161
1996	19,843
1997	21,706
1998	19,722
1999	21,954

Source: WK Österreich.

The rising number of self-employed people in the second half of the 1990s was additionally influenced by a change in the law. Self-employed people earning above a certain income have been bound by the insurance requirement in the same way as employed workers since 1996. This new regulation has made it more difficult to work in the shadow economy and obliged people who had been self-employed before to register their activities. Table 11.2 shows a significant increase in business start-ups since 1996. This is why much of the augmentation is assumed to be imputed to the new regulations and indicates a shift rather than a new impetus (Wanzenböck 1998). In addition, the trend toward outsourcing and the fact that unemployment reached its peak in 1998, also affecting native workers to an unprecedented extent, reinforced the rise even more.

The Emergence of Immigrant Entrepreneurship in Austria

As in many other countries, data on immigrant self-employment and particularly on immigrant business start-ups is very limited. We rely on data from the complete national census carried out last in 1991, and the micro-census. Table 11.3 is based on the complete census and gives an overview of the largest groups of foreign self-employed people in Austria in relation to the situation in Vienna between 1971 and 1991. The data indicate that self-employment is a relatively recent trend among the largest immigrant groups, which are from Turkey and former Yugoslavia. Although the data from the complete census of 1991 might only be viewed as a trend, there are interesting variations in the distribution of the various groups. Germans were the largest group of self-employed foreigners in Austria, but immigrants from Turkey and former Yugoslavia were already far more important self-employed groups in Vienna. The data correspond to the distribution of foreign residents in Austria: nearly 40 per cent of the immigrants from non-EU countries in Austria lived in Vienna in 1999, whereas the corresponding percentage of EU citizens was about 26 per cent.[5]

Table 11.3 Self-employed by Citizenship in Austria and Vienna in 1971, 1981 and 1991

Citizenship	Austria			Vienna		
	1971	*1981*	*1991*	*1971*	*1981*	*1991*
Germany	2,504	2,111	3,791	–*	304	632
Yugoslavia	753	2,078	2,047	–*	1,453	1,220
Turkey	156	537	986	–*	283	549
Other	2,972	2,867	5,686	–*	1,467	2,947
Total	6,385	7,593	12,510	2,178	3,507	5,348

* No figures available.
Source: Statistics Austria, complete national census 1971–1991.

The foreign population includes a smaller percentage of self-employed people than the native Austrian population. But we have to take into consideration the fact that so many of the Austrian self-employed people are engaged in agriculture. If we focus on the self-employed people outside agriculture, the difference is smaller: according to the 1991 national census, about 7 per cent of the Austrian citizens were self-employed, as were only 4.2 per cent of the immigrant working population. In comparison with many other European countries, these are fairly small percentages. At the same time, the percentage of failed business start-ups is very low in Austria, since nearly 70 per cent of the businesses run for more than five years (OECD 1999).

Table 11.4 Self-employed by Citizenship – in Austria and Vienna 1984–1999

Region	Native self-employed[1] 1984	Native self-employed[1] 1993	Native self-employed[1] 1999	Foreign self-employed[2] 1984	Foreign self-employed[2] 1993	Foreign self-employed[2] 1999
Vienna	45,200	42,100	54,106	2,000	6,400	6,035
Austria total	344,200	343,100	373,020	4,800	14,900	14,285

[1] Self-employed persons with Austrian citizenship.
[2] Self-employed persons with non-Austrian citizenship.
Source: Statistics Austria (microcensus), own calculation.

The complete census figures indicate the same trends for the 1980s as the micro-census data, which provide insight into the developments in the 1990s. The micro-census data show a more pronounced movement of business start-ups among immigrants between 1984 and 1993 than during the decade 1981/91. For several reasons, these figures still do not represent the real scale of immigrant self-employment. In Austria, all labour-market participants (employers and employees) are statistically registered according to their citizenship, not their ethnic-origin. The ethnic origin category does not exist in the Austrian statistical system, so the figures tend to underrate the involvement of immigrants by only referring to their citizenship.[6] Additionally, the micro-census survey tends to underestimate the involvement of marginal groups. The data should be interpreted with caution, but can be useful indicators of trends.

Table 11.4 clearly shows however that between 1984 and 1993, the number of self-employed persons rose much more among non-Austrians. In Vienna, with the largest number of self-employed immigrants, their number more than tripled in these ten years. Without the start-up activities of immigrants, Vienna would have lost 3,100 business people, and to a lesser extent so would the country as a whole. Immigrant start-up activities thus bear witness to an unexpected development for that period, since the general trend showed a small decrease in the number of self-employed Austrians. The period between 1993 and 1999 again exhibits contrary trends, but this time in the opposite direction. While the number of self-employed Austrians increased until 1999, immigrant self-employment remained at nearly the same level.

Immigrant Business as a Research Agenda

Neither policy-makers nor social scientists have devoted much attention to self-employment and business start-ups in general. The low self-employment rate did not incite any attention of social scientists for decades, but this has changed since the government aims at increasing the number of business start-ups. Researchers focused on such issues as qualifications, information, vocational background and other aspects influencing the decision to start a business (Arbeitsmarktservice Österreich 1998; Wanzenböck 1998).

As immigrants in Austria tend to be viewed by the academic community as well as policy-makers as dependent employees rather than as self-employed, very little research has been undertaken so far. Due to the 'guest-worker' history and the manifold exclusionary mechanisms immigrants face on the labour market, that is where the research mainly focused (Biffl et al. 1997; Faßmann 1993; Gächter 1998; Matuschek 1985; Parnreiter 1994). The limited opportunities for political participation and the civil rights of immigrants did attract the attention of the academic community (Bauböck and Wimmer 1988; Cinar et al. 1995), as did the disadvantaged position of immigrants on the housing market (Giffinger and Reeger 1997).

Research on immigrant business commenced in the 1970s and 1980s in many other countries, but the first studies about self-employed immigrants in Austria were only carried out in the early 1990s when the crucial case of newspaper vendors was investigated. These exclusively male migrants were mostly from Arab countries and the Indian subcontinent. Though they are self-employed in a legal sense, in reality these 'entrepreneurs' depend on the large media companies as much as employed people do. The focus was thus on the circumvention of labour law by the companies and the vulnerable situation these immigrants are in as regards various conditions of their lives (Fuchs 1992; Hummel 1996; Rechberger 1992). Further research was carried out about immigrants as market traders in Vienna by the geographer Hatz (1997), and an ethnological study was conducted about South Asian entrepreneurship (Fuchs 1997).

This chapter is mainly based on research conducted in the late 1990s on businesses run by immigrants from Turkey and former Yugoslavia (Haberfellner 2000b; Haberfellner and Betz 1999; Haberfellner and Böse 1999). Since the characteristics of immigrant business people have not yet been studied on a national level, the only available quantitative data have been generated by a special analysis of Vienna's 1991 census data. It can be assumed however, that the situation in other parts of Austria does not differ considerably from the one in Vienna, particularly concerning the groups of main 'guest workers'. Although immigrant business people in Vienna have been selected as a central theme, these are the most comprehensive studies available in Austria so far and allow first conclusions about the predominant influence of the regulatory frame.

Self-employed Immigrants: What Can They Expect?
One might wonder why immigrant self-employment has remained steady while that of Austrians increased until 1999. These developments and their underlying causes require further detailed analysis.

Welfare states tend to create 'insider-outsider' cleavages (Esping-Andersen 1990) and Austria is no exception. The Austrian system of self-employment is characterized by restricted access, pushing immigrants into an outsider role. In general, a complex legal framework regulates the conditions to be fulfilled before a business can be started. Non-Austrian citizens, however, face additional barriers. They have to obtain a *Gleichstellung*, which puts them in the same position as Austrians who want to set up their own business. According to the law, the *Gleichstellung* can only be obtained from the local authority if the applicant shows that the proposed business will support the Austrian national economy and not interfere with Austria's public interests.[7] In practice, this means the business is not in a sector that is overrepresented in the local economy, the applicant has no criminal record, and no other law is violated by the permission for that particular business start-up.

In the process of applying for the *Gleichstellung,* the Chamber of Commerce plays a crucial role. The Chamber is asked by the local authority for an expert opinion on whether the planned business meets the criteria of supporting the national economy, and its response is usually negative. Since the Chamber sees supporting its members as its main task, it tends to obstruct competition and protect the existing businesses. Although in some sectors immigrants already represent a sizeable number of members, they are still underrepresented in two ways. First, very few immigrants are employed at the Chamber, e.g. as advisers. Secondly, only Austrian citizens[8] may be elected as representatives of the Chamber. So far only a few immigrants have been elected as representatives of the Chamber of Commerce, and the same holds true for the unions.

While the *Gleichstellung* is only a barrier for immigrants, the requirements that also hold for Austrians include the specific proof of individual qualifications, which are fairly high in some fields, and this too is a particularly high barrier for many immigrants. Since very few immigrants have higher educational qualifications, and only very few can have had experience as top-management employees, they often fail to fulfill the application requirements for a business licence. Against the backdrop of Austria's legal framework regulating access to the business sector, the low level of their apprenticeships and technical schools and the high percentage of people who only completed compulsory school among the traditional 'guest-worker' groups constitute the main barriers.

Its lower income levels in relation to those of other countries is one reason why Austria has not been a preferred immigration country. Compared with Germany, this is why Austria attracted fewer qualified people, and mostly people with a rural background. A situation which was not recognized as problematic for a long time, as companies hired immigrants according to their age and health rather than their qualifications during the 'guest-worker' period. During my collection of empirical data, I was surprised about the lack of information on the

Table 11.5 Highest Educational Degree Acquired by Self-employed Persons in Vienna (Percentage)

Education	Citizenship			
	Yugoslavia	*Turkey*	*Other foreigners*	*All self-employed*
University-level	13.3	13.7	29.2	8.60
A-level	14.2	13.3	27.5	7.90
Apprenticeship/ technical school	28.3	13.5	16.2	55.80
Compulsory school	44.2	59.5	27.1	27.70

Source: Complete National Census 1991, own calculations.

immigrant self-employed, mostly due to their poor mastery of the German language and low qualifications. Both barriers, the *Gleichstellung* and the requirement of giving formal evidence of qualifications, are often overcome by setting up some form of corporation (e.g. limited company) and hiring an Austrian executive manager. While most Austrians establish businesses as sole proprietors, setting up a corporation is the most common type of business owner-ship among immigrants (Haberfellner and Böse 1999; Hatz 1997).

As a legacy of Austria's 'guest-worker' history, labour-market issues have so far dominated the discussions on immigration policy. Immigrants are still expected to act as the workforce cushion, but not to depart from their ascribed role as standby employees and become employers in their own right. In addition to the legal barriers, there is also the fact that the supportive structures for immi-grant business people have still only been developed on a rudimentary level. Guidance and counselling for starting up a business is primarily provided by the Chamber of Commerce and several organizations associated with it, and no guid-ance is given in the languages of the main immigrant groups. Although there are opportunities for financial support for business start-ups, they are at scattered locations. Immigrants are often not familiar with this complex system and have problems gaining access to these opportunities. Against this background, it would be extremely useful to adjust the supportive structures to the needs of immigrant business people. The existing situation now leads to a strategy in which immigrant entrepreneurs seek the help and advice of other immigrants or start up their businesses without any advice at all. Immigrant entrepreneurs are frequently misinformed and make decisions that often reduce their chances for success before they have even passed the start-up phase (Haberfellner and Betz 1999; Haberfellner and Böse 1999).

Immigrants not only face additional barriers in starting up a business, it is now nearly impossible for them to leave the self-employment segment again. This has been an effect of the regulations concerning labour-market access for immigrants that were altered at the beginning of the 1990s. If they want to return to dependent employment, foreigners normally have to apply again for a *Beschäftigungsbewilligung*, which means starting again at the lowest level like new entrants, regardless of the status they had before the business start-up. In the past few years, due to the quota regulation, it has been nearly impossible to obtain a *Beschäftigungsbewilligung*. This leads to a situation where non-preferred self-employed immigrants *cannot fail* and have to go on with their businesses, since they have no other way to earn a living.[9]

Due to the disadvantages immigrants face on the labour market, self-employment has been an increasingly favourable alternative for them. At the end of the 1990s, most of them traded a marginal labour-market position for a fringe position with high risks in the business sector. The obstructive regulatory framework together with their unfavourable resources concentrate immigrants in disadvantaged economic sectors with low entry-barriers but little prospects for a prosperous future. They not only work under unfavourable conditions with little earnings, if they are not Austrian citizens they are often in a dead-end street and returning to the labour-market is nearly impossible. In addition, running a business can get in the way of naturalization: the complex legal framework makes it very easy to violate some law in the course of running a business. This is also true for Austrian business people, but there are additional consequences for immigrants as it can lead to a rejection when applying for citizenship.

Policy Strategies and Their Impact on Immigrant Business Activities: Latest Developments

After describing the framework for immigrant labour-market access and business start-ups, let me go back to the somewhat surprising figures and two-fold contrary developments indicated by Table 11.4. Two phases can be distinguished: the first phase covers the 1980s and the early 1990s and shows a rising number of self-employed immigrants, and the second phase going from 1994 to 1999 is characterized by a steady number of immigrant businesses.

The Rise of Immigrant Businesses

The rise of business start-ups by immigrants in the first phase was unexpected for two reasons: self-employment had not been perceived as a desirable career path in Austria for decades, and immigrants were still mainly seen as competitors on the labour market and not as employers. Immigration movements accompanied by disadvantageous labour-market developments presumably favoured the formation of an immigrant business sector. The labour-market situation had significantly worsened for immigrants since the beginning of the 1980s, when the immigrant unemployment rate increased noticeably for the first time. Since, due to the regulations concerning residence and labour-market access, the unemployment rate of immigrants will never greatly exceed that of native Austrians, a more meaningful indicator of labour immigrant market opportunities seems to be the low percentage of foreign employees in the total workforce in the course of the 1980s as in Figure 11.1. Interviews with immigrant business people also suggest that most of them did not start their business in a situation of current unemployment. Instead, their perception of blocked chances for upward mobility (glass ceiling) and of increasing unemployment in general often stimulated them to look for other ways to make a living. While most natives found starting up a business too risky, some of the immigrant business people said that reducing risk was an important reason for becoming self-employed (Haberfellner and Böse 1999).

An immigration movement to Austria started in the late 1980s and more than doubled the immigrant population by 1994. With an average yearly net immigration of 80,500 people without taking naturalization and birth figures into account, from 1990 to 1993 a peak was reached with an annual 1 per cent growth of the total population. Although it was often argued that opening the borders to Eastern Europe caused that influx, it is more likely that traditional migration chains were reactivated (Bauböck 1997: 658). Thus the ethnic consumer market, an important basis for the start-up phase of many immigrant businesses, was noticeably expanded.

Restricted Labour-market Regulations and Saturated Ethnic Consumer Markets: Immigrants' Business Sunset?

Since disadvantaged conditions on the labour-market and the expansion of the ethnic consumer market were cited as factors that influenced the rise in the first phase, let us have a closer look at labour-market and immigration-policy developments between 1993/4 and 1999. As additional framing conditions, I would like to consider the general economic developments and express some thoughts about the modes of data collection in order to qualify the statistical information.

The tremendous reduction in net immigration since the mid-1990s had a twofold impact: the immigrant consumer market, which had been a substantial growth factor until 1993, was no longer expandable. The preferred ethnic market niches became saturated and it was difficult for many immigrant business people to bridge the gap to the mainstream consumer market. In addition, the decreased net immigration reduced the pressure on the secondary labour market and made it easier for immigrants to stay employed or become re-employed.

The altered labour-market regulations made it riskier for immigrants to start up a business because it was now virtually impossible to obtain a work permit again after having been self-employed. Starting up a business became a 'dead-end street' with limited options for escaping, even for those who started their business before the new regulations came into force. Thus, the rational choice for an immigrant with access to the labour market is to stay there.[10] Due to the increasing percentage of foreign employees in the total workforce and the low level of new immigration this strategy became possibly easier to follow than in the 1980s and early 1990s. As the legislators and policy-makers were not aware of the restrictive effects of the altered Foreigners' Employment Act on the self-employed, information on the blocked chance of returning to the labour market was never part of an official information strategy, but started circulating through networks of immigrants with a considerable time lag.

The reasons for the currently rising self-employment rate of native Austrians were already cited: new supportive measures, changes in the law, and increased unemployment rates. Whereas the upward trend of self-employment among native Austrians was anticipated, the slow-down of business start-ups among immigrants comes more as a surprise, since the improved supporting measures and first steps towards deregulation were expected to increase the number of self-employed immigrants. As a matter of fact, immigrants were never viewed as the target group for the promotion campaign to increase the number of start-ups nor for the other supportive measures such as several new subsidy programmes. It is quite probable that this was merely a result of the one-sided perception of immigrants as employees. Although immigrants are not formally excluded from the supportive measures or subsidy programmes, they find it difficult to sort them out and fulfil the criteria for supporting grants. Guidance and advice is still only available in German and the advisers, who are usually linked to the Chamber of Commerce, are often not sensitive to the needs of immigrants.[11] The recommendations that are made are highly specialized and until now no organization has bundled the information on all relevant aspects, such as business law, Foreigners' Employment Act, regulations concerning residence or subsidy programmes. Another push-factor for the increased self-employment rate among native Austrians was a change in the law on mandatory inclusion in the social-insurance system. Immigrants were probably only marginally influenced by the new law because they have always had to register their activities to prove their income to keep their residence permit.

Austria's economy in general and sectors with a high percentage of self-employed immigrants in particular were faced with unfavourable dynamics in the 1990s. Immigrants' businesses are largely concentrated in risky sectors. As is evident in Vienna and all across Austria, large-scale concentration processes took place in the food retail sector, the construction sector came under high pressure, and a wave of bankruptcies dominated the catering sector.[12] Furthermore, the high regional and sectoral concentration of immigrants' businesses led to intensified competition in some niches, which made it hard for new entrants to succeed. Due to their low qualifications, it was difficult for many immigrants to leave the saturated niches and enter new sectors.

Lastly, I would like to examine the statistics, since the modes of data collection are assumed to have led to a more pronounced bias of the picture from immigrants than from business people in the 1990s. In the 1980s the number of naturalizations remained between 7,000 and 10,000 a year, but increased noticeably in the 1990s. In the interesting period between 1994 and 1999, all over Austria 103,524 foreigners became Austrian citizens; 54,131 (52.3 per cent) of them stayed in Vienna. A rising rate of naturalization combined with diminishing net immigration tends to reduce the percentage of the foreign self-employed in the statistics. Due to regional variations, this effect could even be additionally biased since Vienna exhibits the highest rate of immigrant business people and of naturalizations during this same period. The fact that Austrian citizenship can normally only be obtained after at least ten years in the country could have influenced the statistics. Interviews carried out in Vienna with immigrants from Turkey and former Yugoslavia in 1997/8 show that they had already spent an average of twelve years in Austria before they started up their business. Furthermore, half of the interviewees were Austrian citizens and some others had already applied for citizenship (Haberfellner and Böse 1999).[13] Although the figures of the 1999 micro-census can be assumed to be more biased and to underrepresent the immigrant self-employment percentage to a larger extent than those of 1984 and 1993, it is not even possible to estimate these effects. Only examination of the national 2001 census will allow for a reliable assessment of the data.

Conclusions

The case of Austria as a corporatistic country with specific pronounced features such as the elaborate system of social partnership and the 'guest-worker' history makes it possible to review the impact of the regulatory framework on immigrant business activities. The exclusionary mechanisms of Austria's business regime, still defended by the Chamber of Commerce as an important player in the system of social partnership, tends to prevent competition and exclude potential new entrants. Somewhat surprisingly, except for the *Gleichstellung*, most of the barriers immigrant business people face can be assumed to be effects of the one-sided perception of immigrants as employees designed to advance Austria's economic prosperity via a flexible standby workforce. The findings show that in a highly regulated economy like Austria's, the restrictive labour and business regimes are extremely relevant to the dynamics of immigrant business activities.

Due to the one-sided perception of immigrants as employees, up to now the academic discourse on immigrant entrepreneurship has been rather limited in Austria (Haberfellner 2000a). However, the findings contribute to the critique on the interactive approach developed by Waldinger et al. (1990b) which significantly influenced immigrant business research in the 1990s. Rath (2000b) has criticized the unsatisfactory discussion on the politico-institutional framework of the interactive approach, and against the backdrop of the Austrian case, the short-comings can be corroborated once again. The experience of the 1980s shows that in spite of rigorous business laws, immigrants became increasingly self-employed and found ways to overcome the barriers. These dynamics were obviously obstructed by changes in immigration policy and restrictive labour-market access regulations, although measures were simultaneously taken to increase the number of business start-ups. These developments emphasize the role of immigration and labour-market policy in highly regulated economies. In the case of Austria, so far they have mainly been influenced by the social partners.

Notes

1. The Chambers representing various occupational groups were never involved in the system of social partnership. They have always acted on the level of representing specific interests.
2. Until 1975, the negotiations of foreign-worker quota were still based on the first 'Raab-Olah' agreement from 1961.
3. Reformed in 1995 and 1997.
4. Representative survey on 'Entrepreneurship' carried out by Fessel-GfK, Vienna 1998.
5. In absolute figures: 258,233 non-EU citizens and 26,458 EU citizens lived in Vienna. A total of 756,505 foreigners (654,075 non-EU citizens and 102,430 EU citizens) lived in Austria, i.e. 9 per cent of the whole population. Vienna with 18 per cent had the highest percentage of foreign residents among the nine Austrian provinces.
6. A total of forty-five immigrant business people were interviewed on a qualitative basis. The group included twenty-three Austrian citizens; some others had already applied for Austrian citizenship (Haberfellner and Böse 1999).
7. EU citizens and citizens of countries that have signed a bilateral treaty with Austria do not need a *Gleichstellung*. The groups that interest us most, immigrants from Turkey and former Yugoslavia, do need it.
8. … and citizens of countries that signed a bilateral agreement. There are no agreements with the important sending countries of migrants to Austria.
9. After eight years of continuous residence in Austria, permission to stay has not been automatically linked to proof of income since 1998.
10. This new package of regulations, also called the 'integration package', aimed to reduce labour-market fluctuation.
11. The initial steps were taken in Vienna by the Centre for Social Innovation within a pilot project in 1999–2000. A series of information brochures was issued in four languages (English, Serbian-cyrillic, Croatian, Turkish) and a

multilingual information website was designed (www.zsi.at/business). The project was part of the URBAN Gürtel Plus programme funded by the Federal Ministry of Labour, Health, and Social Affairs, and by the European Social Fund, the Vienna Integration Fund and Vienna's Employees Promotion Fund.

12. The reduced trend of immigrants running a business in Austria and Vienna goes along with the findings of Barrett et al. (2000) and Hillmann (2000). In cities in the UK and in Berlin, they found that in periods of economic contraction, the number of immigrant businesses declined. This can be explained by the marginalized position of many immigrant businesses which have problems withstanding economic fluctuations.

13. Since forty-five interviews were conducted with a qualitative approach, the figures need to be handled with care because no representative survey has been carried out yet.

Germany: From Workers to Entrepreneurs

Czarina Wilpert

Introduction

Insights gained from research on immigrant businesses could be useful for reaching a better understanding of processes of business creation, successes and failures.[1] In the classic countries of immigration, ethnic minorities have tended to be more entrepreneurial than members of the dominant majority group. Research has focused on the patterns of group solidarity as social capital that has given certain minorities an advantage over others in becoming entrepreneurs. Particular forms of group solidarity are considered to enable business strategies based on trust and limited liability (Granovetter 1995: 156). Couldn't it be that immigrants and ethnic minorities make the essentials of the business and social processes more visible? Do we need to explain an 'against the tide' rise of ethnic business' (Jones et al. 2000)?

Immigrants bring new energy, cultural resources in terms of new products, greater service orientation, greater flexibility, motivation to work hard and take risks in order to become successful for the future of their children or the security of family investments in their countries of origin. In Germany immigrants have been known as 'foreigners' and they are rather visible. The small shops of former guest workers revitalized and added colour to neglected areas of cities (Gitmez and Wilpert 1987). Businesses initiated by persons of the main guest-worker 'communities', Greek, Italian and Turkish origins, have contributed to a greater variety of new culinary tastes and consumer demands in the four decades since the guest-worker labour recruitment era.[2] They have created their niche in the sector of foods-grocery stores and restaurants.

By 1992 foreigners owned almost one-third of all restaurants in the country (von Loeffelholz et al. 1994). In 1998 the most recent year for which we have data, the self-employment rate averaged 10.1 per cent for Germans and 8.8 per cent for all foreigners (cf. Table 12.5). In 1999 there were over 263,000 self-employed foreigners in Germany who were estimated to be responsible for the creation of some 780,000 jobs (Bericht der unabhängige Kommission

'Zuwanderung' 2001). It is often assumed that this development is directly related to the impact of the settlement of guest-worker communities in the country and the upward mobility from one-time industrial workers to the ranks of the self-employed.

Experts in Germany tend to differ from those in classical countries of immigration in terms of their interpretations about the value of self-employment for the individuals involved and especially about the long-term chances for success in terms of the social mobility. Does the increase in self-employment rates result from the growth of unemployment (Bögenhold and Staber 1990: 288–9; von Loeffelholz et al. 1994)?[3] And are these self-employed entering those areas of the economy marked by marginal returns and difficult working conditions: restaurants, grocers, cleaning, construction, transportation, hairdressers and tailors and clothing repairs? Do they, as Sassen (1991) and others suggest, make an ideal contribution not only to the 'global city', but in general to the process of economic restructuring? Or are there (also) other forces that encourage foreigners to become self-employed?

Germany differs from other EU countries with respect to relatively modest self-employment rates among the Turkish population. While German citizenship could be expected to be an advantage for entry into self-employment, the high self-employment rates of Greeks and Italians over citizens from Turkey would suggest that among non-Germans other factors play a role. How can we explain the relatively low self-employment rate among persons with Turkish citizenship?[4] Which factors can help explain this specific development in Germany? Do persons of Turkish origins prove, contrary to the expectations of much of the literature, to have less social capital than Greeks and Italians? After thirty-five years of migration can this be sufficiently explained by the fact that the Turks started to arrive in large numbers slightly later than these nationalities? Can the self-employment rates of the two EU nationalities be interpreted as a case of upward mobility out of the guest-worker proletariat into entrepreneurship? Or, is a better explanation to be found in the qualitative study of the nature of self-employment among Greeks and Italians that has permitted business immigration?

Could it be that restrictive policies toward the non-EU nationalities – i.e., the differential treatment of the former guest workers – results in exclusionary processes toward certain groups of residents which also has an impact on their economic integration? This chapter pursues that issue based on existing research and outlines some of the institutional factors that contribute to the different patterns of self-employment among immigrants in Germany.

Important for understanding the issue of immigrant self-employment is the specific immigration history of Germany. The Federal Republic recruited temporary foreign workers for manual labour in industry during the post-Second World

War reconstruction period. Since this was a policy of temporary worker migration, the recruited guest-worker nationalities were placed under stricter legal conditions than workers from the European Economic Community. This applied as well to permission to set up a business (Gitmez and Wilpert 1987; Kontos 1997).[5] Certain labour recruitment countries eventually achieved free movement as full members of the European community, such as Spain, Greece and Portugal. The policy toward others, such as Turkey and the former Yugoslavia, with larger numbers of recruited workers remained in this sense restrictive.

The present analysis views the most important non-German entrepreneurs. In the German tradition the term 'ethnic minorities' is reserved for regional minorities, such as the Danes and the Sorbs, who have certain legal rights. In this chapter I apply the term immigrant business, on the assumption that we are addressing the issue of the self-employment of the one-time guest workers. In Germany, the concept of immigration, understood as a policy to offer integration and citizenship to foreign workers, has to date not been politically acceptable. De facto immigration, in the sense of settlement without a policy, has been regulated by labour-market policy. Foreign residents in this logic could not be immigrants. A plethora of terms have been employed (e.g. guest workers, foreign workers from the recruitment countries, *ausländische Mitbürger*) constructing social categories which de-legitimize rights to active citizenship. Missing in the debate untill now have been the terms immigrants and ethnic minorities.[6] Only recently has there been a move toward recognition of Germany as a country of immigration.[7] The original exclusionary guest-worker policy has, thus, continued to have an impact despite de facto settlement.

To better understand the situation facing immigrant business it is helpful to look at business and the tradition of self-employment in a wider context. Between 1950 and 1980, the self-employment rate in Germany dropped from 16.0 per cent to 9.0 per cent (Bögenhold 1989). Since the mid-1980s, however, it has begun to rise parallel to economic re-structuring. In 1998, the self-employment rate averaged 9.5 per cent (cf. Table 12.4). These self-employment rates conceal, especially with respect to the size of firms, quite different meanings (Duchenaut 1997). The category of self-employed can include anyone from an owner of an enterprise with no other employees to an employer with a workforce of 500 or even larger. Self-employment also covers a range of categories from persons earning a marginal existence to persons belonging to highest income brackets (Bögenhold and Staber 1990: 267–9).

History of Migration and Foreign Workers in Germany

The main migratory patterns we observe in the new migration into Germany from East and Central Europe must be seen in the context of German history.

Germany has traditionally had a demand for migratory labour from its surrounding neighbours, especially the Poles (Bade 1992; Dohse 1981).[8] The recruitment of foreign workers occurred not only during the German Reich, but also during the period of National Socialism when *Fremdarbeiter* and *Zwangsarbeiter* were imported from Poland, Italy and elsewhere (Dohse 1981). The post-war Federal Republic has had tremendous migratory inflows. Migrants were primarily *Aussiedler*, ethnic Germans, many of whom were forced to move due to the political reorganization of territories in Eastern and Central Europe. In absolute numbers there have been greater numbers of migrants entering Germany in this period than entering any of the classical immigration countries. Between 1950 and 1988 West Germany gained some 7.7 million residents through migration: about 62 per cent of these were *Aussiedler*, ethnic Germans or *Übersiedler*, from the GDR (over three million) and Poland (almost a million).

The next most important migratory process resulted from the guest-worker recruitment policy of the late 1950s and 1960s. The guest-worker period began in 1955 with the first labour recruitment treaty with Italy. In the early 1960s this policy was extended when a series of treaties were established with Spain, Greece, Turkey, Portugal, Morocco and Yugoslavia. The recruitment stop and the absolute ban on the further entry of workers into the country came in 1973. This abrupt stop at the high point of migration from Turkey without the possibility of re-entering Germany once returned home led to a surge in family reunion in Germany.

Policies established during the post-war era had dramatic consequences in the wake of the fall of the Iron Curtain. Changes can be observed at a number of levels. The most significant of these are in the demographic, legal and economic spheres due to the demise of the Soviet control and the transformation of the communist regimes within Eastern Europe and in East Germany. In the period of *c.* fifteen years between the recruitment stop and the fall of the Iron Curtain, Germany's foreign population increased by 13.2 per cent although the share of EU foreigners dropped by one-quarter (27 per cent). In 1989, the former Federal Republic of Germany had about five million documented foreign residents; five years later in 1994, the number had increased by over two million persons.[9]

Barriers Facing Immigrant Business

All citizens of the European Union have the same right as German citizens to set up a business in Germany. This right has been secured since 1970. The right to self-employment for foreigners from outside of the EU depends on the nature of their residence permit. Persons who have a *Aufenthaltsberechtigung* (right to stay residence permit), which can usually be obtained after eight years' legal residency, face no legal restrictions to self-employment. All other resident permits contain a clause stating that the foreign resident may not become self-

Table 12.1 Foreigners in the Federal Republic of Germany According to the Most Important Nationalities, 31 December 1999

Country of citizenship		Foreigners in Germany			
		Total	*Male*	*Female*	*%*
1.	Turkey	2,053,564	1,113,629	939,935	28
2.	Yugoslav Rep.				
	(Serbia/Montenegro)	737,204	414,292	322,912	10
3.	Italy	615,900	367,373	248,527	8.4
4.	Greece	364,354	200,289	164,065	5
5.	Poland	291,673	151,392	140,281	4
6.	Croatia	213,954	109,941	104,013	2.9
7.	Austria	186,090	102,133	83,957	2.5
8.	Bosnia und Herzegovia	167,690	86,446	81,244	2.3
9.	Portugal	132,623	76,115	56,508	1.8
10.	Spain	129,893	68,319	61,574	1.8
11.	Iran	116,446	69,160	47,286	1.6
12.	Great Britain and	113,487	67,764	45,723	1.6
	North Ireland				
13.	USA	111,982	64,219	47,763	1.5
14.	Netherlands	110,519	59,732	50,787	1.5
15.	France	107,191	49,607	57,584	1.5
16.	Romania	87,504	48,800	38,704	1.2
17.	Vietnam	85,362	47,257	38,105	1.2
18.	Morocco	81,450	49,391	32,059	1.1
19.	Afghanistan	71,955	39,874	32,081	1
20.	Lebanon	54,063	31,787	22,276	0.7
21.	Hungary	53,152	33,678	19,474	0.7
	Total – all Foreigners	7,343,591	4,011,890	3,331,701	100

employed.[10] In some cases it is possible, however, to maintain permission to set up a business in Germany, if one applies before arriving in the country. In this case the decision on the type of residence permit and the possible right to self-employment will depend on a number of other factors: nationality of the applicant, marriage to a German citizen. If exceptions cannot be made on one of these cases, there is still a possibility that, 'eine übergeordnetes wirtschaftliches Interesse' (a significant economic interest) or 'besonderes örtlichen Bedürfnis' (special local needs) can be met, which the new firm would fulfil.

If the applicant has met the eight-year residency requirement, then access to a permit to set up business will depend primarily on whether or not his proposed venture is considered harmful or not to the overall economy. In this case the police who regulate the legal status of foreigners consult the Chamber of

Industry and Commerce: if they find no fault with the proposed business, the police will remove the restrictions (see below for the unique exception of the former Vietnamese contract workers).

Self-employment in most crafts requires registration in the *Handwerksrolle* (Crafts Listing), which in most cases stipulates that the candidate brings proof, i.e. certification of his professional competence (*Meisterprüfung*). Exceptions are possible if one can prove that one has earned enough experience and skills, which are comparable to a certification, and that it would be an extreme hardship to complete the certification process. There are a few occupations within this list, such as clothing repairs, which are not as exacting as others. The recognition of certification of professional competence, however, still remains a barrier.

Government programmes to assist self-employment do not reach a major target group. Foreigners have the highest rate of unemployment, but the lowest likelihood to have had access funds made available for self-employment. Nor were the immigrant unemployed significantly represented in the special EU-wide educational programmes (NOW; INTEGRA) designed to encourage self-employment in Germany (Kontos 1997).

Participation of the Foreign Population in the Economy

Post-war West Germany needed to recruit labour in the wake of an economic boom. During that period Germany, particularly Berlin, filled their labour demand with workers from the German Democratic Republic. After the wall built in 1961 eliminated that source of labour the guest-worker system established the systematic recruitment of foreign workers. Foreign labour were 10 per cent of the overall workforce in the 1970s and averaged about one-quarter of the manual labour. Foreigners softened the blows of economic restructuring. Between the early 1970s and 1980s the absolute number of persons economically active in manufacturing and construction were reduced at the expense of foreigners. Foreigners accounted for about 45 per cent of the redundancies between 1974 and 1977 and over 50 per cent between 1980 and 1982. Due to their legal status, permits to stay were often dependent on employment, and so numerous workers were forced or motivated to return to their countries of origin (Wilpert 1988). Today the share of the socially insured foreign workers is 9 per cent of the total registered employment and foreign workers are still more often than Germans manual workers (60 per cent) (Beauftragte der Bundesregierung für Ausländerfragen 2000: 260).[11]

Economic restructuring transformed the labour market, reducing jobs in manufacturing and adding to jobs in the services. This was accompanied by a growth in irregular, informal and precarious jobs as well as self-employment (Wilpert 1998b). According to official data from the micro-census there were

250,000 self-employed foreigners in Germany in 1998 (Beauftragte der Bundesregierung für Ausländerfragen 2000: 260), a figure which had more than doubled in the decade since 1987.[12] The self-employment rate for foreigners reached 9.5 per cent in 1997, closely approaching that of Germans (10 per cent) (European Observatory 1999: 21).[13]

Research on Immigrant Business in Germany

The extensive list of references on immigrant business in Germany might give the impression that there has been a great deal of research. But, on the contrary, there has been only a very limited amount of original empirical studies. In the early phase, research was primarily descriptive, studying the background characteristics and motivations of immigrant entrepreneurs from Turkey (Blaschke and Ersöz 1987) or giving a qualitative historical overview of the beginnings of the ethnic economy in Berlin (Gitmez and Wilpert 1987). These focused on migrants from Turkey in Berlin-Kreuzberg. The Zentrum für Türkeistudien (1989, 1991) conducted two large surveys among Turkish entrepreneurs in North Rhine Westphalia. In Berlin additional historical research has studied businesses established by entrepreneurs of other national origins, such as immigrants from Greece (Stavrinoudi 1992) and Italy (Pichler 1997). In a preliminary study a small number of firms initiated by Jewish 'contingent refugees' from Russia have been studied by Kapphan (1997).

Another focus has been on motivations leading to self-employment. A second issue, especially with respect to those entrepreneurs of Turkish origins, asks whether these businesses are primarily restricted to an ethnic market, or whether they attract a wider clientele, such as is the case for the Italians. Rudolph and Hillmann (1997), raise questions about the role of the Turkish economy in the food sector for the integration of the population of Turkish origins, especially the opportunities for the descendants of immigrants in Berlin to use this as a vehicle of social mobility. A few studies have focused on gender and the self-employment of immigrant women (Hillman 1998; Kontos 1997; Morokvasic 1988; Wilpert 1999a).

Many groups of foreigners remain unstudied. Little research has been done, for instance, with respect to the businesses of the one-time Vietnamese contract workers, 50 per cent of whom claimed to be self-employed in 1996 (Mehrländer et al. 1996). Only recently have economists (von Loeffelholz et al. 1994) begun to study this issue. Little is known about informal businesses, for example, as run by craftsmen from Poland, who organize the interior renovations of houses and flats with teams of fellow countrymen or undocumented migrants from other countries (Wilpert 1999b).

Table 12.2 Economically Active Foreigners According to Occupational Status*

Year	Economically active		Self-employed		Family employees		White collar[1]		Manual workers[2]	
	in 1000's	in %	in 1000's	in %	in 1000's	in %	in 1000's	in %	in 1000's	in %
1987[3]	1,844	100	121	6.5	13	0.7	352	19.2	1,358	73.7
1989	2,132	100	138	6.4	13	0.6	451	21.1	1,531	71.8
1991	2,539	100	169	6.7	14	0.5	590	23.2	1,767	69.6
1993	2,884	100	213	7.4	18	0.6	729	25.3	1,925	66.7
1994	2,982	100	246	8.2	24	0.8	809	27.1	1,902	63.7
1995	2,997	100	239	7.9	25	0.8	797	26.5	1,935	64.5
1996	2,934	100	251	8.5	26	0.9	749	25.5	1,898	64.7
1997	2,868	100	248	8.7	22	0.8	812	28.3	1,775	61.9
1998	2,837	100	250	8.8	29	1.0	822	29.0	1,725	60.8

[1] Includes apprentices.
[2] Includes apprentices.
[3] Revised estimate (Census 1987).

The Development of Immigrant Business

Italians were among the first immigrants to establish enterprises in Germany. They began importing and selling Italian goods and specialties such as wine at the end of the last century. The restaurant trade also became significant directly following the end of the Second World War. Pichler (1997) especially focuses on Berlin, where businesses were often initiated by the families of the Italian one-time forced labourers or interned soldiers who decided to settle in the city. These persons set up the classic Italian ice-cream parlours and the first restaurants, calling for family members from the home country to help out. Berlin was never a main centre of the Italian labour migration although the numbers of Italians grew from some 1,380 in the 1960s to almost 12,000 in the city in 1996. Due to the atypical structure of the Italian migration to Berlin, the restaurant trade assumed an important role in the economic life of Italian migrants in the city. In 1996 there existed about 1,000 Italian restaurants in the city (Pichler 1997).[14]

Immigrants from Greece and Turkey began creating small firms and business activities as early as in the 1960s. The first restaurants in Berlin were set up often by academics who had studied in Berlin but saw other potential opportunities. Greeks took advantages of the taste for exotic foods developed by Germans during island vacations. And, Turkish entrepreneurs saw the market among the newly arriving workers from Turkey (Gitmez and Wilpert 1987). They sensed a demand for familiar cultural products, such as halal meat, lamb and the wide range of vegetables and fruits commonly found in Turkey. At the end of 1968 the first Turkish butcher shop was set up in Berlin. By 1970, five grocery stores were owned by immigrants from Turkey in Berlin (ibid.). Fourteen years later in 1984, there were some 3,000 firms owned by persons from Turkey in Berlin, which was about one-half of the officially registered foreign-owned establishments. At the end of the 1990s almost double as many firms owned by persons with Turkish nationality have been estimated to be doing business in Berlin.

Although Italians are not the largest immigrant group in Germany, they have long been the most important nationality with respect to numbers self-employed on a national level. Until 1994 the absolute number of self-employed Italians surpassed the more numerous population originating from Turkey. This has changed since. In 1998, the greatest numbers of foreign-owned businesses were held by nationals of Turkey (39,000), Italy (31,000) and Greece (20,000) (Statistisches Bundesamt 1998), also the major countries of labour recruitment.

Entrepreneurs of Greek nationality continue to have the highest self-employment rate, which rose from 13.3 per cent in 1994 to 16.0 per cent of the economically active in 1998. Italians have dropped from a self-employment rate of 13.3

per cent to 11.5 per cent. Compared to the other two groups the more numerous self-employed from Turkey have a relatively low self-employment rate (5 per cent). This has often been explained as being because of the fact that migrants from Turkey were the last to arrive. However, it could also be interpreted as being due to the heavier restrictions placed on the non-EU Turks. Indicators from the studies of Italians and Greeks suggest that a certain number of the self-employed came expressly for the purpose of business creation, which they were free to do as citizens of EU member states.

Nonetheless, self-employment rates among Turks[15] continue to grow steadily (Goldberg and Şen 1999: 29). On a national level we observe high share of self-employed achieved among Greeks (11.9) and Italians (11.3) between 1974 and 1992. The self-employment rate for Turks in 1992 looks in comparison quite minor, 3.6 per cent (cf. Table 12.3a). A major jump in the yearly rate[16] was in 1986 for the Italians and Turks, for the Greeks already in 1980.

The self-employment rates (SE) of the different nationalities vary from year to year. The biggest jump in rates of self-employment among Turks took place between 1980 and 1986. Only in 1988 did they, along with the Greeks, suffer a slight reduction in growth (see Table 12.3a). Nonetheless, there has been a steady and continuous growth among Turkish self-employed since the advent of the 1990s, as there has been for Germans. The self-employed among German males grew from an 11.7 per cent rate in 1994 to 12.9 per cent in 1998. For Turkish males the SE rate grew from 4.5 per cent in 1994 to 6.2 per cent in 1998.[17] Between 1996 and 1998 it is the Germans (5 per cent) who have the highest SE growth rate, whereas Turks had a 19 per cent increase between 1994 and 1996 but slowed down between 1996 and 1998. Italians and Greeks have negative rates during this period and the average for all foreigners is as low as 1 per cent (see Table 12.4a).

Unfortunately the micro-census does not permit a comparison of women according to nationality. The average self-employment rates do not differ greatly between those for German women and those for foreign women. Foreign women had a 6.2 per cent rate in 1996 and German women 5.9 per cent. In 1998, the direction changes and we find that German women (6.5 per cent) are only about 0.5 per cent more likely to be self-employed than foreign women (5.9).

Self-employment rates have been the highest for the Turks in the 1990s. This and the demographic structure of the population might suggest that this will be the case in the future as well. Not only is the German population in the younger age groups in decline, but the population with Turkish citizenship has a much larger share of the respective younger age groups.

Table 12.3 Self-employment Rate of Foreigners According to Selected Nationalities and the Absolute Number of Self-employed Per Thousand between 1974–1992

	Self-employed	1974	1977	1980	1983	1986	1988	1990	1992
Italians	Absolute number	12	16	17	17	30	30	27	37
	In %	3.3	5.2	4.8	5.7	9.5	9.8	8.5	11.1
Turks	Absolute number	6	6	7	10	16	15	18	30
	In %	1	1.1	1.1	1.6	2.6	2.6	2.6	3.6
Greeks	Absolute number	6	7	11	17	15	14	16	23
	In %	2.1	3.2	6.4	10.8	10.3	10.4	9.3	11.6
Austrians	Absolute number	8	9	9	11	13	12	15	16
	In %	8.4	11.4	11	11.7	12.6	12.4	14.7	13.7
Yugoslavs	Absolute number	–	–	9	7	12	10	12	15
	In %	–	–	2.3	2	3.7	3.4	3.4	3.4
EC total	Absolute number	19	28	30	50	65	60	69	94
	In %	6.7	6.2	8.6	8.7	10.2	8.6	7.3	10.3
Non-EC total	Absolute number	42	43	56	46	66	64	76	114
	In %	2.7	3.3	3.1	5.1	4.7	5.1	7.5	7.8
Sum total	Absolute number	61	71	86	96	131	124	144	208
	In %	2.5	3.5	4	4.6	6.4	6.3	6.2	7.2

% refers to the self-employment rate: the share of the economically active population.
Source: von Loeffelholz et al. 1994: 46.

Table 12.3a Self-employment Per Thousand, Growth Rates between Intervals and Index of Relative Growth Rate (Index – 1974 =100)

Nationality		Year							
		1974	1977	1980	1983	1986	1988	1990	1992
Italians	Absolute number	12	16	17	17	30	30	27	37
	Interval growth rate (%)	(= 100)	25	6	0	44	0	-10	28
	Index	(= 100)	133	106	106	250	250	225	308
Turks	Absolute number	6	6	7	10	16	15	18	30
	Interval growth rate (%)	(=100)	0	15	30	58	-6	17	40
	Index	(=100)	100	116	166	266	250	300	500
Greeks	Absolute number	6	7	11	17	15	14	16	23
	Interval growth rate (%)	(=100)	15	37	36	22	-7	13	31
	Index	(=100)	116	180	183	250	233	266	383

Table 12.4 Self-employed* According to Selected Nationality, Gender, and SE Rate as Percentage of the Respective Economically Active Population

	Males						Females**						Total / both sexes					
	1994		1996		1998		1994		1996		1998		1994		1996		1998	
Nationality	In 1000s	In %	In 1000s	In %	In 1000s	In %	In 1000s	In %	In 1000s	In %	In 1000s	In %	In 1000s	In %	In 1000s	In %	Absolute number	In %
Italians	37	14.8	30	13.5	31	13.5	–		–		–		27	3.1	39	4.9	39	5.0
Greeks	18	15.7	21	18.8	20	18.8	–		–		–							
Turks	27	4.5	33	5.	34	6.2	–		6	2.4	5	2.1						
All foreigners	188	9.5	187	9.8	189	10.8	58	5.6	64	6.2	61	5.9	246	8.2	251	8.5	250	8.8
Germans	2,239	11.7	2,306	12.2	2,419	12.9	804	5.7	852	5.9	925	6.4	3,043	9.1	3,158	9.5	3,344	10.1

* Self-employed without family workers.
** The micro-census does not include the absolute number of self-employed foreign women for all nationalities.
The number is too small to be accurate.
Source: Statistisches Bundesamt: Data from the Micro Census of each year. Own calculations.

Table 12.4a Growth Rates for Self-employed Males for Selected Nationalities between 1974–1998

Nationality		Year		
		1994	*1996*	*1998*
Italians	Absolute number	37	30	31
	Interval growth rate[1]		−19	-4
	Index	(=100)	77	83
Turks	Absolute number	27	33	34
	Interval growth rate		19	3
	Index	(=100)	122	125
Greeks	Absolute number	18	21	20
	Interval growth rate		15	−5
	Index	(=100)	116	111
All foreigners	Absolute number	188	187	189
	Interval growth rate		-1	1
	Index	(=100)	99	105
Germans	Absolute number	2,239,000	2,306,000	2,419,000
	Interval growth rate		3	5
	Index	(=100)	102	108

Yearly growth rates are calculated on % of difference between current year and previous year.
[1] Changes in per cent over two years.
Source: Statistisches Bundesamt for each year (Micro Census).

The Sectoral Distribution of Immigrant Entrepreneurs

The sectoral distribution of foreign entrepreneurs differs from that of the German self-employed. Traditionally they have been highly represented in the restaurant trade: 26 per cent of all foreign entrepreneurs own restaurants compared to 6 per cent of Germans. In fact 28 per cent of all restaurant owners (55,000) registered in Germany in 1992 were foreigners (von Loeffelholz et al. 1994). The high share of foreign ownership indicates that restaurants are serving a German clientele. In the food sector we also find the Döner Kebab and pizza fast-food stands which have usurped nearly all of Germany. The Turkish specialty, Döner Kebab, invented in Berlin, has been shown to have a greater financial turn-over than the major competitor McDonalds, or Burger King (Seidel-Pielen 1996). The second most important economic activity of immigrants is in retail: foods, grocery stores, vegetable stands, etc. Almost 20 per cent of all self-employed foreigners operate such retail stores (43,000). Grocery shops were originally set up to serve the needs of ethnic clients, but they go beyond this today. These branches are considered to be especially attractive since they do not require high skills or a high investment (von Loeffelholz et al. 1994).

Foreign business owners are also present in manufacturing (7.5 per cent) and construction (5.5 per cent). These were in 1994 primarily in trades (5,500) and related areas (19,500) where trained craftsmen are required. Foreign ownership is often difficult in these trades, which require a certain level of professional certification (*Meisterbrief*) before being granted the right to set up business. Vocational training or certification gained outside of Germany often does not meet the local requirements. This has been especially significant for the butcher trade. Gains are also being made in the share of foreigners involved in business ventures in the more lucrative trades and crafts, which require a German professional certification (von Loeffelholz et al. 1994). Goldberg and Şen (1997) explain this by the transition between generations, pointing out that young foreigners educated in Germany are beginning to enter the trades.

The Background of the Immigrant Entrepreneurs

Early studies in Berlin-Kreuzberg found businessmen from Turkey to originate primarily from a rural and peasant background with little (elementary) education in Turkey. Only a minority (*c.* 20 per cent) had any kind of further education (Blaschke and Ersöz 1987). They all came, however, from families which had a tradition of self-employment: farmers, tradesmen, small shopkeepers, street vendors. These neighbourhood businesses included a variety of activities from a general store to restaurants, hairdressers, grocery stores, repair shops, transport, bakery, gambling hall, coffee shops, fast food stand, video shop, TV repair shop, a book store and a travel agent. Almost two-thirds of the sample were found to have had little preparation or skills to run a business.[18] A more recent survey of 1,187 firms (Zentrum für Türkeistudien 1998), however, found higher qualifications among the entrepreneurs.[19]

Although assumptions are made about motives and strategies of the foreign self-employed, there have been few qualitative studies, which can differentiate nationalities or reach systematic comparisons. Rather, economists such as von Loeffelholz et al. (1994) characterize foreign entrepreneurs from the immigrant worker nationalities as potentially seeking self-employment out of a crisis situation (economy of desperation). This observation conflicts with a great deal of the research on first-generation migrants from Turkey. The desire to be one's own boss has been one of the most striking observations in research with first-generation migrants. The migratory project has been seen by many of the first generation as an opportunity for social mobility (Wilpert 1980). Early research reports that one of the major motivations of immigrant workers has been to earn enough money to invest in small business in the country of origin. Factory work and

Table 12.5 Self-employed According to Nationality and Economic Sector, 1992

	Number in 1000s		Percent in economic sector		Self-employment rate		% Foreign
	German	Foreign	German	Foreign	German	Foreign	
Agriculture /Forestry	6	1	15	3	38	15	2
Manufacturing	7	5	16	15	5	2	8
Construction	4	7	8	6	11	5	5
Commerce	8	7	18	21	13	16	9
Including:							
Retail trade	6	5	14	15	14	17	8
Transport/Communication	2	2	4	5	6	8	10
Banking/Insurance	2	0	4	0	8	0	0
Other Services	14	17	35	50	13	14	10
Including:							
Restaurants	2	9	6	26	25	25	28
Education/Culture/Science	2	3	5	8	8	14	12
Health and Veterinary	3	1	6	4	10	6	5
Commercial Services	5	2	11	7	25	21	5
Total	42	34	100	100	9	7	8
Including:							
Percent in Production	16	8	39	25	9	3	5
Percent in Services	26	26	61	75	12	14	9

Source: von Loeffelholz et al. 1994: 52.

other forms of manual work in firms was viewed as a transitional phase to help collect capital to set up a business (Kontos 1997; Wilpert 1988). Migration is also seen, at least initially, as an entrepreneurial venture. This suggests that migrants may be especially prepared for risk-taking. It is also found that immigrants who set up their own businesses seek greater autonomy, social mobility and self-fulfilment (Kontos 1997; Pichler 1997). Other studies suggest how this desire became more urgent with the growth of unemployment, where increasingly self-employment appeared to be the best alternative (Goldberg and Şen 1997).

According to Pichler (1997), rising self-employment among Italians is viewed as evidence of a new type of migrant, who differs in his 'career' planning and is prepared to work in less regulated jobs. Pichler explains this by the origins of these migrants who stem from peasant, agricultural, trades and commercial backgrounds. As non-proletarians, they are acculturated to the tradition of the autonomous family economy, which in Italy has been found to be significant for self-employment. Stavrinoudi (1992: 15) suggests that 'self-employment is the dream of all Greeks'. Thus, a socio-cultural factor might also be considered to explain the high rates of self-employment among the Greeks. Some of the first businesses in Berlin were set up by former students who perceived a market for Greek cuisine (Stavrinoudi 1991). Initially self-employment was often undertaken to supplement other activities and income. Unique professional qualifications of the Greeks contributed as well to business opportunities. In the late 1960s the high expertise of Greek furriers led to the establishment of a niche and a small business trade for Greek immigrants.[20]

Goldberg and Şen (1997) hold the view that multiple motivational factors best explain venturing into business, such as: hopes for a higher income, the independence of being self-employed and the desire to gain social recognition via the achievement of a higher social status. Indications are that there is good reason that higher income could also play a role. Von Loeffelholz et al. (1994: 354) find that the average monthly income of foreigners is about DM1,100 less than Germans (DM3,400) earn. Self-employed foreigners, however, claim to earn about DM1,000 more than they did as dependent workers.

There have been few studies of other groups. Jews from states of the former Soviet Union have come to Germany as contingent refugees (Kapphan 1997), and Vietnamese former contract workers to the GDR (Liepe 1997). These two groups both emanate from socialist systems, but with very different socio-economic backgrounds. Both have faced conditions which, however, have made self-employment frequently the only possibility for earning their livelihood. The legal conditions facing the Vietnamese originating from the GDR contract-worker system have been harsher than for Jewish contingent refugees, who are granted a secure legal status upon admission to the country.

After much political mobilization against sending Vietnamese en masse back, a special exception was made for the former GDR contract workers. Within the states of the former GDR they would be permitted to set up their own businesses without the eight-year residency requirement. In the mid-1990s it was found that as much as 50 per cent of the former contract workers were 'self-employed' (Mehrländer et al. 1996). The majority of these persons were involved in retail trade, in restaurants or in clothing. In addition to these sectors a few were in the travel-agent business or import-export. A number of the 'self-employed' had set up stands at the daily and weekly outdoor markets (Liepe 1997).[21] Many of these economic activities are extremely marginal and insufficient to guarantee survival and many are also engaged in some form of unregistered work (Wilpert 1999b).

The situation of Jewish contingent refugees differs because of their better acceptance and legal status as well as their much higher average education levels. However, they face barriers to finding employment in their trained professions (Kapphan 1997). Medical doctors have difficulty in gaining recognition of their training and experience. Engineers find competition difficult. And often persons between forty-five and fifty are considered too old, or they have difficulties mastering the language. Thus, self-employment appears for some to offer a possibility to free themselves from dependency on social welfare and offer integration into the economy.[22]

Advantages of the Ethnic Business

A number of assumptions exist, based on research abroad, about the uniqueness and particular advantages and disadvantages of ethnic business. A primary issue is the assumption of the access of immigrants of certain ethnic groups to social capital, which gives them access to investment capital. Another is the particular advantage of the ethnic market for immigrant entrepreneurs.

Social capital has become one of the most important concepts used to explain the likelihood that immigrants will become entrepreneurs and be successful. Portes (1995) views social capital as the command one has over scarce resources by virtue of membership in social networks and social structures. Granovetter (1995) formulates the question which leads to his interest in immigrant families this way: 'How is it possible for entrepreneurs to assemble the capital and labour required to sustain the cooperative venture … the firm?' Classic research (Light 1972; Light and Bonacich 1988; Werbner 1984) finds that among certain ethnic groups the immigrant family more often (than the settled majority) acts as an economic unit. Family structures and cultural traditions are considered to play an important role in the ability and tendency for immigrants to enter self-employment.

In Germany, there has been a very limited attempt to investigate the sources of investment capital and less about how this works in practice for immigrant families. Studies have found that the sources of the investment capital were primarily from personal savings, often combined with the support of family members in arranging bank loans or with loans from family and friends (Blaschke and Ersöz 1987). Findings from the research of the Zentrum für Türkeistudien (Goldberg and Şen 1997) supports the above interpretation. About 60 per cent of all businesses were initiated with investment capital that the owners borrowed from their families and friends. In fact almost 72 per cent of the wholesale firms were set up in this manner. Bank loans were less frequent, but more common in the area of restaurants (41 per cent) and crafts (28.7 per cent). The research on Greek entrepreneurs finds, to the contrary, few signs of the role of ethnic solidarity for this immigrant group in Germany. In fact it has been suggested that Greeks in Berlin would tend first to trust a German before trusting a fellow countryman (Stavrinoudi 1992).[23]

Ethnic Clientele, Ethnic Niches

Business development especially among Turks in Germany profited greatly from the size and density of ethnic concentration in urban areas. Clearly, the first business initiatives relied on the use of their ethnic and cultural capital to provide services and products which the German market could not provide for their fellow countrymen (Gitmez and Wilpert 1987). Alone the fact that the meat sellers were Muslims gave their meat a competitive advantage over the German shops, since in the beginning the meat was bought from ordinary slaughterhouses and only the distributors were Turkish.

Doubtlessly, the original impetus for ethnic business was stimulated by the demands perceived for certain cultural products as well as special services for newcomers to German society. Among the first businesses initiated in 1966 was a grocery shop on wheels with door-to-door sales, the delivery of packaged foods to workers' dormitories. Turkish women also sold linen, crockery and pots through informal networks of relatives and friends. From 1970 onward business began to expand from foods to other areas. Multi-purpose businesses were set up starting out as travel agencies and providing a number of other services, translation and help with the completion of bureaucratic papers. Import-export shops sprouted up to import music and video cassettes from Turkey. Travel agencies extended into the development of charter services. Some of these managed to extend their businesses to the tourist trade with Germans (Gitmez and Wilpert 1987). However, with over two million persons of Turkish citizenship in Germany and a significant continuation of networks and ties between settled families and the country of origin there remains a large market with demands from fellow countrymen.

'Breaking Out' – Beyond the Ethnic Enclave!

Entrepreneurs from Turkey have created a new fast-food product (Döner Kebab) in immigration which competes with McDonalds and pizzas within the market for street-corner foodstalls throughout Germany and in other parts of Europe. Businesses initiated by Turkish migrants have moved from retail to wholesale, from serving an ethnic clientele to meeting vacancy chain needs in the wider market of mending and clothing repairs or local grocery stores in the inner city (Gitmez and Wilpert 1987). Immigrants from Turkey have also initiated other new products, such as sausages produced in Germany by Turks in Cologne and sold in Turkey. And, major new markets have resulted from Turkish migration with respect to tourism for Germans in Turkey and elsewhere (Goldberg and Şen 1999).

There is no doubt that with respect to foods, groceries and restaurants, many businesses established by persons of Turkish origins reaches beyond an ethnic clientele. This has been true for Greek and Italian entrepreneurs from their very first initiatives (Pichler 1997; Stavrinoudi 1992). This would be the case for the much smaller groups of Vietnamese and former-Soviet 'Russian' Jews. While the former participate in the Asian food niche for the general population, they also provide a wholesale structure for Vietnamese and others (Liepe 1997). The Jewish contingent refugees serve the dominant clientele via vacancy chains in local neighbourhood services providing shoe repairs, clothing repairs, grocery stores. They also serve an ethnic Russian clientele with video shops, bookstores, Russian speciality shops, etc. Russian restaurants serve both an ethnic and a wider clientele (Kapphan 1997).

A diversification of sectors and the desire of entrepreneurs of Turkish origin to reach out and serve a broader clientele is documented in other research (Golderg and Şen 1999). About one-fourth of all firms in this study stated that half or more of their clients were German. Especially firms established in construction and the foods sector were more likely than others to have German clients.

However, when immigrant businesses 'break out', extending beyond an ethnic clientele, such as is the case with the *Änderungsschneiderien* (clothing repair shops), Döner Kebab, fast-food stands or in the restaurant trade, the specific advantages of the ethnic self-employed lies in the exploitation of family resources. In these areas of marginal profits it is assumed that survival is not possible without the resources of cheap or unpaid family labour (von Loeffelholz et al. 1994).

It has long been thought that local corner grocery stores and other forms of small family businesses are dying out. Observers have upheld the argument that these traditional sectors of the economy cannot pay for themselves, since they cannot compete with the development of shopping malls and mega-stores in the suburbs and outside the city centres. There seems however, to be contradictory interpretations about the demand for inner-city local shops and services and the ability for these enterprises to survive or at least be profitable. The issue is one of how viable these businesses can be in this country when to make a profit they must rely on some form of informal activities (Kloosterman 2000; Sassen 1991; Wilpert et al. 1999).

Business Practices

In addition to ethnic clients, it is also assumed that the ethnic economy uses the resources of poorly paid family labour and creates as well jobs for fellow nationals. Micro-census data demonstrates that 10.7 per cent of Germans and 11.6 per cent of foreigners claim to employ family members in their businesses. Thus, the foreigners on an average have about 1 per cent higher likelihood to report employing family workers than Germans. At face value this is not very significant. There is no evidence to whether immigrants are more likely than others to under-report invisible or unregistered workers.

Employing fellow countrymen also appears to be common for immigrants from a number of different national origins at least in the early phases of migration. This is, however, particularly noticeable for the majority of business established by immigrants from Turkey. Goldberg and Şen (1999) report from their survey in North Rhine Westphalia that on an average only 3.5 per cent of the businesses studied employed German workers. But 93 per cent employed on average five persons of Turkish origins. Stavrinoudi's (1992) study of the Greek community indicates more clearly than any other research that ongoing entrepreneurs have often used the opportunity of working in, for instance, Greek restaurants, or other firms owned by fellow ethnics, as a preparation for later self-employment.

The wholesale trade set up by immigrant employers in Germany has received little attention. A case study in Berlin traces the first wholesale developments among Turkish owners in Berlin to 1971 when one businessman took the initiative to provide supplies for a number of other grocers (Gitmez and Wilpert 1987). Turkish wholesalers established a number of dependent retail shops in German names and delegated these to Turkish shopkeepers, providing as well all of the supplies for their stores. In 1972 each wholesaler had set up a number of retail stores, with between twenty and forty retail stores obligated to them. This practice developed between the early 1970s and the 1980s into a larger Islamic business, which suffered over the years from competition and numerous ups and downs (Gitmez and Wilpert 1987).

Research directed at the informal aspects of immigrant business is practically non-existent. Nonetheless, it is generally the case that those sectors of the economy where immigrants are more likely to set up business are also those sectors of the economy where informal practices are known to exist, such as restaurants, construction, transport, cleaning services, interior decoration and repairs (Cyrus 1999; Pichler 1997; Rudolph and Hillmann 1997; Wilpert 1999b).

Gender and Immigrant Self-employment

The share of immigrant women self-employed is very close to that of the German population (27.6 per cent). Women were about one-quarter of the immigrant self-employed in 1998. Accordingly, the self-employment rate among immigrant women (5.9 per cent) is also very close to that of German women (6.4 per cent). Research on gender and self-employment is relatively limited,[24] and the role of women in family businesses has been overlooked.

The findings on immigrant women suggest that they may employ different strategies in becoming self-employed than that which is generally considered the case for ethnic business, seen primarily as 'ethnic' and male. Self-employed immigrant women may desire, or may be forced, to be more independent or isolated from the ethnic network system than what is considered typical for their male counterparts. Some indications of this are found in the small surveys that have been conducted with women. If one takes the likelihood of having support from family and ethnic networks as an indicator of integration into the ethnic community, there are some indications that immigrant women are less likely than men to rely primarily on resources of the ethnic economy.

In a Berlin study in the early 1990s of immigrant women from diverse nationalities who started up their own business, it was found that that more than one-quarter of the women managed through their own savings and another one-fourth from the financial support of family and friends. About 17 per cent relied on a bank loan, and the rest some combination of all factors (Wilpert 1999b). Studies that focus on women of Turkish origins in Berlin find a lower share, about one-fifth, who had opened their own business without the aid of family members or friends (Goldberg and Şen 1999; Hillmann 1998). Hillmann concludes from the attitudes of women entrepreneurs of Turkish origins, however, that the ethnic community plays less of a role than is assumed for males.

Conclusions

Has immigrant business 'arisen against the tide' in Germany? The latest self-employment rates for Germans suggest that the tide has changed course. Economic demands and very likely structural changes and informalization of the economy of the kind Pichler (1997) and Wilpert (1998b) have pointed out have created a more favourable climate for small business and self-employment in general. The unification processes required a change of mentality, which has meant a steady increase of self-employed among Germans. Moreover, despite the visibility of persons originating from Turkey as immigrant entrepreneurs, they have the lowest rate of self-employment among the most important migrant worker groups. This can be interpreted to be a result of the restrictions that were placed on non-EU immigrants.[25]

The German economy is undergoing tremendous changes. As a result attitudes have changed as well. Attitudes toward the informalization of working conditions have also been softened (Wilpert 1998a, 1999b). Unclear is how these will be resolved with the German model of responsibility of the state for the welfare of all citizens, especially the protection which unions demand for labour agreements, social benefits and minimum wages. International economic competition is motivating a change in mentality toward attracting an international elite.

Attempts are being made to make Germany more attractive for the most highly skilled experts especially in the field of information technology, but also to win investments and business start-ups to create jobs (cf. Bericht der unabhängige Kommission 'Zuwanderung' 2001). Moreover, for the first time in twenty years the government is initiating a policy to encourage foreign students to study in German universities and not to hinder as in the past, but to motivate those who are excellent to stay.

From the perspective of the size of the immigrant communities, trends indicate that the resident foreign population with the greatest potential for self-employment in the future are of Turkish origins. In terms of absolute number of self-employed they have recently surpassed the Italians. The 5 per cent self-employment rate among citizens from Turkey remains, however, substantially behind the smaller communities of Greeks (18.8 per cent) and Italians (13.5 per cent). However, persons of Italian origins could enter as Pichler (1997) notes, profiting from EU membership to enter Germany and start up their own businesses. It is very likely that the different treatment of the non-EU foreigners with respect to access to self-employment has caused the delay in the development of self-employment among Turks. Nonetheless, in 1998 it is the Turks and Germans who continue to have a positive rate of increase in 'self-employed', in contrast to the other foreigners.

On the basis of the data and findings available one could be tempted as some consultants have done to extrapolate the self-employment rate to 9 per cent for the year 2010 for immigrants from Turkey (ATIAD 1996). On the other hand, the recent drop in the self-employment rates for Italians suggests caution. Has a saturation point in the restaurant trade been achieved? Immigrants from Turkey demonstrate, however, a broader sectoral participation than Greeks and Italians. Moreover, both the size of the potential clientele among Turks in Germany, and possibly in Turkey, would support the view that the share of entrepreneurs among persons of Turkish origins will continue to move steadily ahead. Immigrants can and do have an innovative potential with respect to new products and the quality of services they offer. This has not been sufficiently studied.

There is a need for more systematic research. Research is needed on the small business economy, as is comparative work to grasp how Germans and immigrants cope with the challenges of small business. There is a need for more qualitative research which investigates the use of social capital and other resources among immigrant entrepreneurs. Along with the potential for immigrant business, studies of local market demands and the feasibility of meeting these demands by small businesses need more attention. Studies of demands should also be linked to the development of the informal. New forms of migration most likely play this role for certain sectors of the economy today. Research on informal, undocumented migration illustrates the significance of migration from Poland and Eastern and Central Europe for interior remodelling. New markets evidently exist not simply for cheap labour, although this plays a role, but for new tasks which can be considered new kinds of enterprise which may serve the needs of the local population. The future of immigrant businesses must be put into the context of the overall economy and specifically to issues challenging small business.

Notes

1. The term immigrant is being used here to identify those persons registered as foreigners who belong to the former guest-worker recruitment nationalities. The term immigrant is not officially used in the German context. The available statistics cannot distinguish between immigrants in this sense and other foreigners who may have come from abroad to set up business in Germany. Since statistics refer either to non-Germans or foreigners, it is difficult to use the term ethnic, since this term should include as well persons of foreign origins with German citizenship. No term is precise enough.
2. Guest workers originated from Italy, Greece, Morocco, Portugal, Spain, Turkey and the former Yugoslavia. The greatest number originated from the later two countries.
3. This relationship between self-employment and unemployment is often referred to as a consequence of an 'economy of desperation'. The most recent data from the micro-census from the state of Hessen in Germany indicates very clearly that in the last fifteen years self-employment has grown the most significantly exactly among those foreign nationalities most hit by unemployment (Apitzsch 2000a).

4. One explanation of the low rates might be explained by naturalization, i.e. that the self-employed of Turkish origins are more likely than the EU nationalities to become citizens. This could be plausible, but generally the citizens of Turkey have had low rates of naturalization, and existing surveys do not provide data to support this argument.

5. A 'right to stay residence permit' (*Aufenthaltsberechtigung*) was required which meant at least eight years of residency. According to one study (Schuleri 1982) until 1980 more than half of the applications from foreigners to establish a business were denied. Moreover, this permit was not given automatically, and in 1981 less than 5 per cent of the residents from Turkey had this permit; in 1984 it was 18 per cent. For this reason the first shops initiated by residents from Turkey in Berlin opened with German trade names. Often a German citizen would be paid for the use of his name (Gitmez and Wilpert 1987).

6. In German the term *Zuwanderer* is used for all categories of new entrants. Immigration in German would be *Einwanderung*. In addition to this there has existed a category of migrants who were never officially referred to as such. These are the *Aussiedler* from colonies of Germans living for centuries in the states of Central and Eastern Europe whose rights to entry and access to citizenship are based in the German constitution and derived from their position vis-à-vis Nazi Germany during the Second World War.

7. With the appointment of the independent Commission for 'Zuwanderung' new signals were set and it was expected that the German parliament would recognize itself by the end of 2001 as a country of immigration. At this writing it remains doubtful if this can be achieved in the current legislature period.

8. Poland is a special case due to the long-standing territorial unity of Germans and Poles in Silesia and other areas of pre-war Poland, areas that controversially were ruled by either the Polish or the German state at different periods in history. As a result of the agreements reached after the war, some of these territories became again Polish since parts of East Poland were taken over by the Soviet Union. In the *Kaiserreich* in the last decades of the nineteenth century the political debate in Germany already centred on the Polonization of the East (Max Weber), *Überfremdung* (over-foreignization) and the displacement of German workers by the Slavs (Bade 1994: 322). But also, Italian construction workers were viewed by labour unionists as strike breakers, slave labourers, or wage suppressers (*Lohndrücker*).

9. Part of this increase was due to the natural increase of the foreign population, births to foreigners who did not have citizenship rights, marriage to partners in the country of origin and family unification. Another share entered as asylum-seekers, obtaining temporary permits to stay and a prob-

lematic refugee status subject to periods of toleration (Wilpert 1999b).

10. According to Schuleri (1982) until 1980 more than half of the applications from foreigners to establish a business were denied. Moreover, this permit was not given automatically, and in 1981 less than 5 per cent of the residents from Turkey had this permit; in 1984 it was 18 per cent. For this reason the first shops initiated by residents from Turkey in Berlin opened with German trade names, and a German citizen would be paid for the use of his name (Gitmez and Wilpert 1987).

11. Foreigners are overrepresented in blue-collar jobs in manufacturing and the service sector. Over a fifth to a third of all the registered workers in the mineral, glass, ceramic, chemical, metal, food-production industries, cleaning personnel, and employers in restaurants/hotels are foreign.

12. This figure includes the numbers of family members employed. Moreover, it does not distinguish between immigrant residents and those foreign owners who have entered from abroad to set up business in Germany.

13. Unfortunately the data categorizations for self-employment are inconsistent. The above includes registered family workers among the self-employed. I quote this source here because of its longitudinal significance.

14. With a much smaller presence in the city, the Chinese have about 700 restaurants (Hong 1996). Unfortunately research is non-existent on the Chinese restaurant trade in Berlin, or other parts of Germany.

15. Here the expression 'Turks' refers to all persons who are interviewed for the micro-census as having the citizenship of Turkey. This should not include persons who were Turkish citizens but who became naturalized Germans.

16. The interval growth rate refers to the growth between the years reported. This is obviously more significant than the relative growth, since the Turks had the smallest number of self-employed to begin with. Relative refers to the current number with respect to the number per thousand in 1974.

17. Unfortunately, the self-employment data from the micro-census for the period 1994–1998 differ from those used by von Loeffelholz et al. in 1994. The latest data made available by the Statistisches Bundesamt are broken down according to gender, but the data on women cannot be accurately averaged, due to the size of the sample. For this reason I have focused on the males to show the rates of growth which are comparable to those for Greeks and Italians as well as for Germans and Turks.

18. Only a minority appeared to be successful despite their lack of specific skills. Success and skills were measured by self-perception and participant observation.

19. More than half of the self-employed had attended school in Germany and 8 per cent had finished university. Among the older businessmen the majority had finished middle school in Turkey. About 60 per cent of these self-

employed were workers before setting up their own businesses. With respect to generations this research finds that younger entrepreneurs, eighteen to twenty-nine years old (20 per cent), were more likely than older ones to have been unemployed beforehand.

20. This sector has been greatly reduced with the success of animal-protection movements.

21. Immigrants from Vietnam began their business ventures informally, by setting up market stands for Asian products, which then were forced to become institutionalized with the support of the local district administrators in Berlin.

22. Statistical studies of this issue are practically non-existent. Once German citizens, they do not appear as immigrants. Jews are not differentiated separately from other citizens of their states of origin.

23. The same study, however, also demonstrates how the networks of Greeks has played a role in on-the-job training and experience for future entrepreneurs.

24. Compare Table 12.4 for data on gender and nationality, and Hodenius (1997) for research on German women.

25. It is more difficult to refer to statistics about the Yugoslavs who could have been an important unit before the civil wars.

Bibliography

A

ABS (Australian Bureau of Statistics) (1996), *Small Business in Australia*, Canberra: Australian Government Publishing Service.

Ackland, R. and L. Williams (1992), *Immigrants and the Australian Labour Market: The Experience of Three Recessions*, Canberra: Bureau of Immigration Research, Australian Government Publishing Service.

ACOM (Adviescommissie Onderzoek Minderheden) (1979), *Advies onderzoek minderheden*, The Hague: Staatsuitgeverij.

Ait Ouaziz, R. (1989), 'Les commerçants soussi dans l'agglomération parisienne: Insertion spatiale et relations avec le pays d'origine, Maroc', MA thesis, Université de Poitiers.

Akenson, D. (1990), *The Irish in South Africa*, Occasional Paper no. 32, Institute of Social and Economic Research, Rhodes University, Grahamstown.

Aldrich, H. and A. Reiss (1976), 'Continuities in the Study of Ecological Succession: Changes in the Race Composition of Neighborhoods and Their Businessmen', *American Journal of Sociology*, 81: 846–66.

Aldrich, H.E., J.C. Cater, T.P. Jones and D. McEvoy (1981), 'Business Development and Self-segregation: Asian Enterprise in Three British Cities', in C. Peach, V. Robinson and S. Smith (eds), *Ethnic Segregation in Cities*, London: Croom Helm.

Aldrich, H., T. Jones and D. McEvoy (1984), 'Ethnic Advantage and Minority Business Development', in R. Ward and R. Jenkins (eds), *Ethnic Communities in Business: Strategies for Economic Survival*, Cambridge: Cambridge University Press.

Allen, S. and C. Trueman (eds) (1993), *Women in Business: Perspectives on Women Entrepreneurs*, London: Routledge.

Alsulaiman, A. (1997), 'De positie van de vrouw in de Islam en van de islamitische vrouwen in België', in M.C. Foblets, B. Hubeau and A. de Muynck (eds), *Migrantenonderzoek voor de toekomst*, Leuven and Amersfoort: Acco.

Ambrosini, M. (1999), *Utili invasori: L'inserimento degli immigrati nel mercato del lavoro italiano*, Milan: Franco Angeli.

— and P. Schellenbaum (eds) (1994), *La comunità sommersa: Indagine sull'immigrazione egiziana a Milano*, Quaderni ISMu no. 3, Milan: Franco Angeli.

Amersfoort, H. van (1982), *Immigration and the Formation of Minority Groups: The Dutch Experience 1945–1975*, Cambridge: Cambridge University Press.

Amsterdam in Cijfers (1990), *Amsterdam in Cijfers: Jaarboek 1990, deel 1*, Amsterdam: Bureau O+S.

— (1994), *Amsterdam in Cijfers: Jaarboek 1994*, Amsterdam: Bureau O+S.

— (2000), *Amsterdam in Cijfers: Jaarboek 2000*, Amsterdam: Bureau O+S.

Apitzsch, U. (2000a), 'Beratungs- und Bildungsangebot für Selbständigkeitsprojekte in Europa', *Hessiche Blätter für Volksbildung*, 1: 1–13.

— (ed.) (2000b), 'Selbständigkeitsprojekte', special issue *Hessische Blätter für Volksbildung*, 1.

Arbeitsmarktservice Österreich (Employment Service Austria) (ed.) (1998), 'Selbständigenkarrieren: Erwerbsbiographien und Qualifikationsprofile von Selbständigen', study carried out by BIG, ibw and IBE on behalf of the Austrian Employment Service, Vienna/Linz.

Archaimbault, C. (1952), 'En marge du quartier chinois de Paris', *Bulletin de la Société des Etudes Indochinoises*, 28: 275–94.

Arkin, A., K. Magyar and G. Pillay (eds) (1989), *The Indian South Africans: A Contemporary Profile*, Durban: Owen Burgess.

Arnot, C. (1999), 'Battles in the Balti Belt', *The Guardian*, 11 August.

ARPAC (Archivo do Patrimonio Cultural) (1999), 'Preliminary Findings of a Survey on Informal Sector Cross-border Trade between Mozambique and South Africa', unpublished paper for the Southern African Migration Project.

Arthur Anderson Enterprise Group and National Small Business United (1994), *Survey of Small and Medium-sized Businesses: Trends for 1994*, New York: Arthur Anderson.

Atalik, G. and B. Beeley (1992), 'What Mass Migration Has Meant for Turkey', in R. King (ed.), *Mass Migrations in Europe: The Legacy of the Future*, London: Belhaven.

ATIAD (Verband türkischer Unternehmer und Industrieller in Europa e.V.) (ed.) (1996), *Türkisches Unternehmertum in Deutschland. Die unsichtbare Kraft: Bestandsaufnahme 1996 und Perspektiven für das Jahr 2010*, Düsseldorf: ATIAD.

Atlas and Terp Onderzoeksbureau (1991), *Buitenlandse restaurants en allochtone ondernemers*, The Hague: Ministerie van Economische Zaken.

Attar, R. (1992), 'Histoire de l'immigration maghrébine en Belgique', in A. Morelli (ed.), *Histoire des étrangers et de l'immigration en Belgique, de la préhistoire à nos jours*, Brussels: Editions Vie Ouvrière.

Auld Committee (1984), 'The Shops Act: Late Night and Sunday Opening', report of the Committee of Inquiry into Proposals to Amend the Shops Act (Cmnd 9376), London: HMSO.

Auster, A. and H. Aldrich (1984), 'Small Business Vulnerability, Ethnic

Bibliography

Enclaves, and Ethnic Enterprise', in R. Ward and R. Jenkins (eds), *Ethnic Communities in Business: Strategies for Economic Survival*, Cambridge: Cambridge University Press.

Australian Bureau of Statistics (1996), *Small Business in Australia*, Canberra: Australian Government Publishing Service.

Australian Institute of Political Science (1953), *Australia and the Migrant*, Sydney: Angus and Robertson.

Auvolat, M. and R. Benattig (1988), 'Les artisans étrangers en France', *Revue Européenne des Migrations Internationales*, 4: 37–54.

B

Bade, K. (1992), *Ausländer, Aussiedler, Asyl: Ein Bestandsaufnahme*, Munich: Beck.

Baetsen, P. and J. Voskamp (1991), *Kopen en verkopen op Zuid: Een onderzoek naar de omgang, betekenis en ontwikkeling van het etnische ondernemerschap in Rotterdam Oud-Zuid*, Amersfoort: Stichting Werkgroep '2duizend.

Bailey, T. (1987), *Immigrant and Native Workers: Contrast and Competition*, Boulder, CO: Westview.

— and R. Waldinger (1991), 'Primary, Secondary and Enclave Labor Markets: A Training Systems Approach', *American Sociological Review*, 56: 432–45.

Bakker, E.S.J. and L.J. Tap (Onderzoekers Kollektief Utrecht) (1985), *Islamitische slagerijen in Nederland*, Mededelingenreeks no. 40, The Hague: Hoofdbedrijfschap Ambachten.

Baldwin-Edwards, M. and M.A. Schain (eds) (1994), *The Politics of Immigration in Western Europe*, Newbury Park: Frank Cass.

Baptiste, F. and E. Zucchetti (1994), *L'imprenditorialità degli immigrati nell'area milanese: Una ricerca pilota*, Quaderni ISMu no. 4, Milan: Franco Angeli.

Barbesino, P. and F. Quassoli (1997), *La comunicazione degli immigrati a Milano: Reti comunicative, rappresentazioni dei servizi e modalità di accesso alle risorse pubbliche e del privato sociale di alcuni gruppi nazionali di immigrati in un'area metropolitana*, Quaderni ISMu no 2, Milan: Franco Angeli.

Barjaba, K., G. Lapassade and L. Perrone (1996), *Naufragi albanesi*, Rome: Sensibili alle Foglie.

Barrett, G.A., T.P. Jones and D. McEvoy (1996), 'Ethnic Minority Business: Theoretical Discourse in Britain and North America', *Urban Studies*, 33: 783–809.

Barrett, G., T. Jones, D. McEvoy and C. McGoldrick (2000), 'The Economic Embeddedness of Immigrant Enterprise in Britain', paper given at the Second Conference of the Thematic Network 'Working on the Fringes: Immigrant Business, Economic Integration and Informal Practices', Jerusalem, June.

Barrett, G.A., T.P. Jones and D. McEvoy (2001), 'Socio-economic and Policy Dimensions of the Mixed Embeddedness of Ethnic Minority Business in Britain', *Journal of Ethnic and Migration Studies*, 27: 241–58.

Barthon, C. (1992), 'La Petite Turquie à Strasbourg-Saint Denis: Portrait d'un microcosme à Paris', unpublished MA thesis.

Basson, L. (1988), 'Portuguese Immigration into South Africa', *Familia*, 25: 2–9.

Basu, A. (1998), 'An Exploration of Entrepreneurial Activity among Asian Small Businesses in Britain', *Small Business Economics*, 10: 313–26.

Basu, A. and E. Altinay (2002), 'The Interaction of Culture and Entrepreneurship in London's Immigrant Businesses', *International Small Business Journal*, 20: 373–93.

Basu, D. (1995), *Asian Small Businesses in Britain: An Exploration of Entrepreneurial Activity*, University of Reading, Discussion Paper no. 303, series A, vol. vii.

Bates, T. (1987), 'Self-employed Minorities: Traits and Trends', *Social Science Quarterly*, 68: 539–51.

—— (1994), 'Social Resources Generated by Group Support Networks May Not Be Beneficial to Immigrant-owned Small Businesses', *Social Forces*, 72: 671–89.

—— (1997), *Race, Self-employment, and Social Mobility*, Baltimore: Johns Hopkins University Press.

Battegay, A. (1990), *Références bibliographiques*, Dossiers des Séminaires Techniques, Territoires et Sociétés no. 13, Ministère de l'Equipement et du Logement.

Bauböck, R. (1997), 'Migrationspolitik', in H. Dachs, P. Gerlich, H. Gottweis, F. Horner, H. Kramer, V. Lauber, W. Müller and E. Tálos (eds), *Handbuch des politischen Systems Österreichs: Die zweite Republik*, 3rd edn, Vienna: Manz.

—— and H. Wimmer (1988), 'Social Partnership and "Foreigners Policy"', *European Journal of Political Research*, 16: 659–81.

Bayraktar, O.S. and H. van der Weide (1996), *Kwestie van etniciteit: Kansen voor Turkse ondernemers, kansen voor Rotterdam Noord*, Rotterdam/The Hague: Kybele Consultancy.

BEA (1992), *Illegale confectie-ateliers: Een geïntegreerde bestrijding*, Hoofddorp: BEA.

—— (1994), *De economische betekenis van minderheden voor de arbeidsmarkt*, Hoofddorp: BEA.

Beardsworth, A. and A. Bryman (1999), 'Late Modernity and Quasification: The Case of the Themed Restaurant', *Sociological Review*, 47: 228–57.

Beauftragte der Bundesregierung für Ausländerfragen (2000), *Bericht über die Lage der Ausländer in der Bundesrepublik Deutschland*, Bonn/Berlin: Bundesministerien des Innern.

Bibliography

Beaujot, R., P.S. Maxim and J.Z. Zhao (1994), 'Self-employment among Immigrants: A Test of the Blocked Mobility Hypothesis', *Canadian Studies in Population*, 21: 81–90.

Bechhofer, F. and B. Elliot (eds) (1981), *The Petite Bourgeoisie: Comparative Studies of the Uneasy Stratum*, London: Macmillan.

Becker, G.S. (1995), *Accounting for Tastes*, Cambridge: Harvard University Press.

Becker, H.M. and J.A. de Jong (1987), *Drieëntachtig Rotterdamse etnische ondernemers: Problemen en oplossingen*, Rotterdam: Stichting Buitenlandse Werknemers.

Benner, R. (1998), *Buurtgebonden allochtone detailhandel in Nederland*, The Hague: Hoofdbedrijfschap Detailhandel.

Berg, H., Th. Wijsenbeek and E. Fischer (eds) (1994), *Venter, fabriqueur, fabrikant: Joodse ondernemers en ondernemingen in Nederland 1967–1940*, Amsterdam: Joods Historisch Museum, NEHA.

Bericht der unabhängige Kommission 'Zuwanderung' (2001), *Zuwanderung gestalten: Integration fördern*, Berlin: Bundesministerien des Innern.

Bernasconi, M. (1999), 'L'integrazione degli stranieri nel mercato del lavoro e nel tessuto produttivo', in C.C. di Milan (ed.), *Milano produttiva 1999*, Milan: Camera di Commercio, Industria e Artigianato.

Bernstein, A., L. Schlemmer, C. Simkins, S. Suzman and D. Irvine, assisted by J. Hudson (1997), *People on the Move: A New Approach to Cross-border Migration to South Africa*, Research Series no. 7, Centre for Development and Enterprise, Johannesburg.

Bhana, S. and J. Brain (1990), *Setting Down Roots: Indian Migrants in South Africa*, Johannesburg: Witwatersrand University Press.

Biffl, G., E. Deutsch, H. Lutz and M. Marterbauer (Österreichisches Institut für Wirtschaftsforschung) (1997), *Ökonomische und strukturelle Aspekte der Ausländerbeschäftigung in Österreich*, Vienna: Österreichisches Institut für Wirtschaftsforschung.

Billiet, J. and H. de Witte (1991), 'Naar racisme neigende houdingen in Vlaanderen: Typologie en maatschappelijke achtergronden', *Cultuur en Migratie*, 1: 25–62.

Blainey, G. (1984), *All For Australia*, North Ryde: Methuen.

Blalock, H. (1967), *Toward a Theory of Minority Group Relations*, New York: Wiley.

Blanchflower, D.G. (2000), 'Self-employment in OECD countries', *Labour Economics*, 7: 471–505.

Blaschke, J. and A. Ersöz (1987), *Herkunft und Geschäftsaufnahme türkischer Kleingewerbetreibender in Berlin*, Berlin: Express Edition.

Block, F. (1990), *Postindustrial Possibilities: A Critique of Economic Discourse*, Berkeley, CA: University of California Press.

Bloeme, L. and R.C. van Geuns (1987a), 'Loonkonfektie terug in Nederland? Informele bedrijvigheid in ketens', *Tijdschrift voor Politieke Ekonomie*, 4: 76–98.

Bloeme, L. and R.C. van Geuns (1987b), *Ongeregeld ondernemen: Een onderzoek naar informele bedrijvigheid*, The Hague: Ministerie van Sociale Zaken en Werkgelegenheid.

Blom, E. and T. Romeijn (1981), 'De kracht van traditie: Hoe Chinezen succesvol opereren in het restaurantwezen', *Sociologische Gids*, 28: 228–38.

Blommaert, J. and J. Verschueren (1998), *Debating Diversity: Analysing the Discourse of Tolerance*, London: Routledge.

Body-Gendrot, S. and E. Ma Mung (eds) (1992), 'Entrepreneurs entre deux mondes. Les créations d'entreprises par les étrangers: France, Europe, Amérique du Nord', special issue *Revue Européenne des Migrations Internationales*, 8.

Bögenhold, D. (1989), 'Die Berufspassage in das Unternehmertum', *Zeitschrift für Soziologie*, 18.

— and U. Staber (1990), 'Selbständigkeit als ein Reflex auf Arbeitslosigkeit?', *Kölner Zeitschrift für Soziologie und Sozialpsychologie*, 42.

Boiskin, J. (1993), 'Beinkinstadt's 1903–1993', *Jewish Affairs*, 3: 39–42.

Boissevain, J. (1981), *Small Entrepreneurs in Changing Europe: Towards a Research Agenda*, Work and Social Change no. 4, Maastricht: European Centre for Work and Society.

— (1984), 'Small Entrepreneurs in Contemporary Europe', in R. Ward and R. Jenkins (eds), *Ethnic Communities in Business: Strategies for Economic Survival*, Cambridge: Cambridge University Press.

— (1992), 'Les entreprises ethniques aux Pays-Bas', *Revue Européenne des Migrations Internationales*, 8: 97–106.

— (1997), 'Small European entrepreneurs', in M. Rutten and C. Upadhya (eds), *Small Business Entrepreneurs in Asia and Europe: Towards a Comparative Perspective*, New Delhi: Sage.

— and H. Grotenbreg (1986), 'Ondernemerschap en de wet: Surinaamse zelfstandigen in Amsterdam', *Migrantenstudies*, 2: 2–24.

— and H. Grotenbreg (1987a), 'Ethnic Enterprise in the Netherlands: The Surinamese of Amsterdam', in R. Goffee and R. Scase (eds), *Entrepreneurship in Europe: The Social Processes*, London: Croom Helm.

— and H. Grotenbreg (1987b), 'Survival in Spite of the Law: Surinamese Entrepreneurs in Amsterdam', *Revue Européenne des Migrations Internationales*, 13: 199–222.

— and H. Grotenbreg (1988), 'Culture, Structure and Ethnic Enterprise: The Surinamese of Amsterdam', in M. Cross and H. Entzinger (eds), *Lost Illusions: Caribbean Minorities in Britain and the Netherlands*, London: Routledge.

—, A. Choenni and H. Grotenbreg (1984), *Een kleine baas is altijd beter dan een grote knecht: Surinaamse kleine zelfstandige ondernemers in Amsterdam*, Amsterdam: Universiteit van Amsterdam, Antropologisch-Sociologisch Centrum.

Bonacich, E. (1972), 'A Theory of Middleman Minorities', *American Sociological Review*, 37: 583–94.

— (1993), 'The Other Side of Ethnic Entrepreneurship: A Dialogue with Waldinger, Aldrich, Ward and Associates', *International Migration Review*, 27: 685–92.

— and J. Modell (1980), *The Economic Basis of Ethnic Solidarity: Small Business in the Japanese American Community*, Berkeley and Los Angeles: University of California Press.

—, L. Cheng, N. Chinchilla, N. Hamilton and P. Ong (eds) (1994), *Global Production: The Apparel Garment Industry in the Pacific Rim*, Philadelphia: Temple University Press.

Bonifazi, C. (1998), *L'immigrazione straniera in Italia*, Bologna: Il Mulino.

Bonner, P. (1990), '"Desirable or Undesirable Basotho Women?" Liquor, Prostitution, and the Migration of Basotho Women to the Rand, 1920–1945', in C. Walker (ed.), *Women and Gender in Southern Africa to 1945*, London: James Currey.

Bonnet, A.W. (1980), 'An Examination of Rotating Credit Association among Black West Indian Immigrants in Brooklyn', in R.S. Bryce-Laporte (ed.), *Sourcebook on the New Immigration*, New Brunswick, NJ: Transaction Books.

Borjas, G. (1990), *Friends of Strangers: The Impact of Immigrants on the US Economy*, New York: Basic.

— (1994), 'The Economics of Immigration', *Journal of Economic Literature*, 32: 1667–1717.

— (1996), 'Ethnicity, Neighborhoods, and Externalities', *The American Economic Review*, 85: 365–90.

Borowski, A. and A. Nash (1994), 'Business Migration', in H. Adelman, A. Borowski, M. Burstein and L. Foster (eds), *Immigration and Refugee Policy: Australia and Canada Compared*, vol. I, Melbourne: Melbourne University Press.

Bottomley, G., M. DeLepervanche and J. Martin (eds) (1991), *Intersexions: Gender/class/culture/ethnicity*, Sydney: Allen & Unwin.

Boubakri, H. (1985), 'Modes de gestion et réinvestissements chez les commerçants tunisiens à Paris', *Revue Européenne des Migrations Internationales*, 1: 49–65.

Bouillon, A. (1996), '"New" African Immigration to South Africa', unpublished version of a paper given at the South African Sociological Association Conference, Durban, July.

— (1998), *'New'African Immigration to South Africa*, Cape Town: CASAS.

Bourdet, G. and F. Dams (2000), 'Toeristische profilering van etnische minderheden in steden: Integratiemodel of karikatuur', thesis, Faculty Applied Sciences, University of Ghent.

Bovenkerk, F. (1982a), 'Op eigen kracht omhoog: Etnisch ondernemerschap en de oogkleppen van het minderhedencircuit', *Intermediair*, 8: 1–11.

— (1982b), 'Shylock of Horatio Alger: Beschouwingen over de theorie der handelsminderheden', in *Neveh Ya'akor: Jubilee Volume Presented to Jaap Meijer*, Assen: Van Gorcum.

— (1983), 'De sociologie van de etnische onderneming', *Sociologische Gids*, 30: 264–75.

— and C. Fijnaut (1996), *Georganiseerde criminaliteit in Nederland. Over allochtone en buitenlandse criminele groepen*, Enquête Opsporingsmethoden, TK 1995–1996, 24 072, no. 17.

— and L. Ruland (1984), 'De schoorsteenvegers', *Intermediair*, 51: 23–39.

— and L. Ruland (1992), 'Artisan Entrepreneurs: Two Centuries of Italian Immigration to the Netherlands', *International Migration Review*, 26: 927–39.

—, A. Eijken and W. Bovenkerk-Teerink (1983), *Italiaans ijs: De opmerkelijke historie van de Italiaanse ijsbereiders in Nederland*, Meppel/Amsterdam: Boom.

—, B. den Brok and L. Ruland (1991), 'Meer, minder of gelijk? Over de arbeidskansen van hoogopgeleide leden van etnische groepen', *Sociologische Gids*, 38: 174–86.

—, M.J.I. Gras and D. Ramsoedh (1995), *Discrimination against Migrant Workers and Ethnic Minorities in Access to Employment in the Netherlands*, International Migration Papers no. 4, Geneve: ILO, Employment Department.

Bozorgmehr, M. (1998), 'From Iranian Studies to Studies of Iranians in the United States', *Iranian Studies*, 31: 5–30.

— (2003), 'The New Immigrant Professionals and Entrepreneurs: Iranians in the United States', unpublished manuscript.

—, C. Der-Martirosian and G. Sabagh (1996), 'Middle Easterners: A New Kind of Immigrant', in R. Waldinger and M. Bozorgmehr (eds), *Ethnic Los Angeles*, New York: Russell Sage.

Bradlow, E. (1994), 'The Anatomy of an Immigrant Community: Cape Town Jewry from the Turn of the Century to the Passing of the Quota Act', *South African Historical Journal*, 31: 103–27.

Brassé, P. and W. van Schelven (1980), *Assimilatie van vooroorlogse immigranten: Drie generaties Polen, Slovenen, Italianen in Heerlen*, The Hague: Staatsuitgeverij.

Bremner, L. (2000), 'Re-inventing the Johannesburg Inner-city', *Cities*, 17: 185–93.

Brenner, G.A. and J.-M. Toulouse (1990), 'Business Creation among the Chinese Immigrants in Montreal', *Journal of Small Business and Entrepreneurship*, 7: 38–44.

Breton, R. (1964), 'Institutional Completeness of Ethnic Communities and the Personal Relations of Immigrants', *American Journal of Sociology*, 70: 193–205.

Bronsveld, C. and E. van der Giessen (2000), *Werkgelegenheidsperspectieven op een winkellint in Rotterdam Delfshaven*, Rotterdam: Sociaal Wetenschappelijke Afdeling Dienst Sociale Zaken en Werkgelegenheid gemeente Rotterdam.

Brownell, F. (1985[1977]), 'British Immigration to South Africa, 1946–1970', MA thesis, UNISA, published in *Archives Year Book for South African History*, 48: 1–196.

Brücker, H. (2002), 'Can International Migration Solve the Problems of the European Labour Markets?', paper presented at the United Nations Economic Commission on Europe, Spring seminar in Geneva, 6 May.

Bruderl, J., P. Preisendorf and R. Ziegler (1992), 'Survival Chances of Newly Founded Business Organisations', *American Sociological Review*, 57: 227–42.

Bruin, H.J.E., K. Hellingman and R. de Lange (1997a), *Juridische aspecten van etnisch ondernemerschap*, NISER Working Paper, Utrecht: NISER.

Bruin, M., I. Caljé, A. Gravesteyn, J. de Kuyer and B. van der Putten (1997b), *Imago Chinees Indische bedrijven: Een onderzoek naar het imago van de Chinees Indische restaurants in Nederland*, Maastricht: Hoge Hotelschool, Projectgroep IX.

Brunet, J.R. and H. Palmer (1988), *'Coming Canadians': An Introduction to the History of Canada's Peoples*, Toronto: McClelland and Stewart.

Brussel Th.H.H.F. van, and R.W.M. Veninckx (1997), *Quick scan Koninklijke Horeca Nederland Chinees-Indische bedrijven*, Nederweert: Grande Cuisine.

Buijs, F.J. (1990), *Aan de rand van de arbeidsmarkt: Turkse jongemannen en Nederlandse werkgevers*, Leiden: COMT/Wetenschapswinkel.

Bulck, D. van den (1992), 'De beroepskaart: Een onverantwoorde discriminatie', in I. Vanhoren, S. Bracke, L. Maes and D. van den Bulck, *Cultuur en Migratie*, 2: 87–98.

Burgers, J., G. Engbersen, R. Kloosterman and E. Snel (eds) (1996), *In de marges van de stad*, Research papers no. 8, Utrecht: Onderzoekschool Arbeid, Welzijn en Sociaal-Economisch Bestuur.

Burnley, I. (2000), 'Diversity and Difference: Immigration and the Multicultural City', in J. Connell (ed.), *Sydney: The Emergence of a World City*, South Melbourne: Oxford University Press.

Burton, C., C. Ryall and C. Todd (1995), 'Managing for Diversity', in Industry Taskforce on Leadership and Management Skills, *Enterprising Nation:*

Renewing Australian Managers to Meet the Challenges of the Asia-Pacific Century, vol. 2, Canberra: Australian Government Publishing Service.

Business Week (European edition) (2000), 'Unsung Heroes', 28 February: 20–4.

Byram, M. and J. Leman (eds) (1990), *Bicultural and Trilingual Education: The Foyer Model in Brussels*, Clevedon, Philadelphia: Multilingual Matters.

C

Caestecker, F. (1995a), 'Eigen zelfstandigen eerst: Geschiedenis van de beroepskaart in België', *Bareel*, 59: 7–10.

— (1995b), 'De beroepskaart, discriminatie van etnische ondernemers?', *Bareel*, 59: 12–15.

Calvanese, F. and E. Pugliese (1990), *La presenza straniera in Campania*, Milan: Franco Angeli.

Campani, G., F. Carchedi and A. Tassinari (1994), *L'immigrazione silenziosa: Le comunità cinesi in Italia*, Turin: Edizioni della Fondazione Agnelli.

Campbell, M. and M. Daly (1992), 'Self-employment into the 1990s', *Employment Gazette*, 100: 269–92.

Canak, F. and J. Haanstra (1998), *Migrantenondernemers in Bos en Lommer: Eindrapportage fase I*, Amsterdam: CEO/Annifer.

Candy, G. (1988), 'Italians in Pietermaritzburg', *Natalia*, 18: 70–9.

Capeci, D. Jr. (1985), 'Black-Jewish Relations in Wartime Detroit: The Marsh, Loving, and Wolfe Surveys and Race Riots of 1943', *Jewish Social Studies*, 5: 221–42.

Caritas di Rome (1997), *ImmigrazioneDossier Statistico 1997*, Rome: Anterem.

— (1999), *ImmigrazioneDossier Statistico 1997*, Rome: Anterem.

— (2001), *Immigrazione. Dossier statistico 2001*, Rome: Anterem.

Cassiers, T. (1999), 'Etnisch ondernemen in een transnationale ruimte: De Brabantstraat in Brussel', unpublished BA thesis, Catholic University of Leuven.

Castles, S. and M. Miller (1993), *The Age of Migration*, London: Macmillan.

Castles, S., M. Kalantzis, B. Cope and M. Morrissey (1988), *Mistaken Identity: Multiculturalism and the Demise of Nationalism in Australia*, Sydney: Pluto.

Castles, S., W. Foster, R. Iredale and G. Withers (1998), *Australia and Immigration: A Partnership. A Review of Research and Issues*, St Leonards: Allen & Unwin with the Housing Industry Association Ltd.

Catanzaro, R., D. Nelken and V. Belotti (1997), 'Luoghi di svago luoghi di mercato. Abusivi, commercianti e turisti sulla riviera emiliano-romagnola', *Quaderni di Cittàsicure* 12.

CBS (2000), *Bevolking der gemeenten van Nederland op 1 januari 2000*, Voorburg/Heerlen: CBS.

Centre for Equal Opportunities and Opposition to Racism (Centrum voor gelijkheid van kansen en racismebestrijding) (1997), *Etnische discriminatie bij aanwerving: Belgische deelname aan het internationaal vergelijkend onderzoek van het internationaal arbeidsbureau*, Brussels: FDWTC.

CERC (1999), *Immigration, emploi et chômage, un état des lieux empirique et théorique*, Les Dossiers du CERC-Association no. 3.

Cesarani, D. and M. Fulbrook (eds) (1997), *Citizenship, Nationality and Migration in Europe*, London: Routledge.

Chan, D.W. (1990), 'Emigration: Stress and Adaptation in the 1990s', *Hong Kong Journal of Mental Health*, 19: 2–4.

Chan, J.B.L. and Y.-W. Cheung (1985), 'Ethnic Resources and Business Enterprise: A Study of Chinese Business in Toronto', *Human Organization*, 44: 142–54.

Chevalier, L. (1947), *Le problème démographique nord-africain*, Paris: PUF.

Chin, K.H. (1988), 'Chinese in Modern Australia', in J. Jupp (ed.), *The Australian People: An Encyclopedia of the Nation, Its People and Their Origins*, Sydney: Angus & Robertson.

Choenni, A. (1993), *De allochtone ondernemers van Amsterdam: Een sociaal-geografische inventarisatie*, Amsterdam: Gemeente Amsterdam, Afdeling Economische Zaken.

—— (1997), *Veelsoortig assortiment: Allochtoon ondernemerschap in Amsterdam als incorporatietraject 1965–1995*, Amsterdam: Het Spinhuis.

—— (1998), 'De betekenis van etnisch-culturele factoren: Indiase en Pakistaanse ondernemers', in J. Rath and R. Kloosterman (eds), *Rijp & Groen: Het zelfstandig ondernemerschap van immigranten in Nederland*, Amsterdam: Het Spinhuis.

—— (2000), *Bazaar in de metropool: Allochtone detailhandel in Amsterdam en achtergronden van haar lokale begrenzing*, Amsterdam: Emporium.

—— (2001), *Tussen Toko en Topzaak: Allochtoon ondernemerschap in de detailhandel en de betekenis van herkomstachtergronden*, Amsterdam: IMES.

—— and C. Choenni (1998), 'Allochtoon ondernemerschap', in D.P. Scherjon and A.R. Thurik (eds), *Handboek ondernemers en adviseurs in het MKB*, Deventer: Kluwer Bedrijfsinformatie.

Choi, C.Y. (1975), *Chinese Migration and Settlement in Australia*, Sydney: University of Sydney Press.

CIC (Citizenship and Immigration Canada) (1996), *Business Immigration Division: Program Statistics, 1995*, Ottawa: CIC.

Cinar, D., C. Hofinger and H. Waldrauch (1995), *Integrationsindex: Zur rechtlichen Integration von AusländerInnen in ausgewählten europäischen Ländern*, Reihe Politikwissenschaft no. 25, Vienna: Institut für Höhere Studien.

Clark, P. and M. Rughani (1983), 'Asian Entrepreneurs in Wholesaling and Manufacturing in Leicester', *New Community*, 11: 23–33.

Cobas, J.A. (1985), 'A New Test and Extension of Propositions from the Bonacich Hypothesis', *Social Forces*, 27: 432–41.

— and J. Duany (1997), *Cubans in Puerto Rico: Ethnic Economy and Cultural Identity*, Gainsville, FL: University Press of Florida.

Cockerton, C. (1995), *Running Away from the Land of the Desert: Women's Migration from Colonial Botswana to South Africa, ca. 1895–1966*, unpublished PhD thesis, Queen's University, Kingston, Ontario.

Cohen, Y. and A. Tyree (1994), 'Palestinian and Jewish Israeli-born Immigrants in the United States', *International Migration Review*, 28: 243–55.

Collins, J. (1991), *Migrant Hands in a Distant Land: Australia's Post-war Immigration*, 2nd edn, Sydney and London: Pluto.

— (1992), 'Cappuccino Capitalism: Italian immigrants and Australian business', in Stephen Castles, C. Alcorso, G. Rando and E. Vasta (eds), *Australia's Italians: Culture and community in a changing society*, Sydney: Allen & Unwin, pp. 73–84.

— (1996), 'The Economics of Racism or the Racism of Economics', in George Argyrous and Frank Stilwell (eds), *Economics as a Social Science*, Sydney: Pluto, pp. 41–5.

— (2000), 'Globalisation, Deregulation and the Changing Australian Labour Market', in Santina Bertone and Helen Casey (eds), *Migrants in the New Economy*, Workplace Studies Centre, Victoria University, Melbourne, pp. 13–45.

— and A. Castillo (1998), *Cosmopolitan Sydney: Exploring the World in one City*, Sydney: Pluto.

— and D. Hiebert (2001), 'Ethnic Entrepreneurship and the Suburbanisation of Sydney and Vancouver', paper given at the AAG (Association of American Geographers) Conference, February/March, New York.

—, K. Gibson, C. Alcorso, D. Tait and S. Castles (1995a), *A Shop Full of Dreams: Ethnic Small Business in Australia*, Sydney and London: Pluto.

—, M. Morrissey and L. Grogan (1995b), 'Employment' *1995 State of the Nation: A Report on People of non-English Speaking Background*, Canberra: Federal Race Discrimination Commissioner, Australian Government Publishing Service.

—, C.-L. Sim, B. Dhungel, N. Zabbal and G. Noel (1997), *Training for Ethnic Small Business*, Sydney: University of Technology Sydney (UTS).

— L. Mondello, J. Breheney T. and T. Childs, (2001), *Cosmopolitan Melbourne: Exploring the World in One City*, Sydney: Big Box Publishing.

Cologna, D., L. Breveglieri, E. Granata and C. Novak (2000), *Africa a Milano: Famiglie Ambienti e lavori delle popolazioni africane a Milano*, AIM, Milan.

Colombo, A. (1998), *Etnografia di un'economia clandestina*, Bologna: Il Mulino.

Colombo, M., C. Marcetti, M. Omodeo and N. Solimano (1995), *Wenzhou-Firenze: Identità, imprese e modalità di insediamento dei cinesi in Toscana*, Florence: Pontecorboli.

Confartigianato della Marca Trevigiana (2000), *Un'indagine sul mercato del lavoro della Provincia di Treviso*, Treviso.

Cooke, P. and K. Morgan (1998), *The Associational Economy: Firms, Regions, and Innovation*, Oxford: Oxford University Press.

Cookson, C. and R. Wolffe (1996), 'Young Asians Set to Shun Trade', *Financial Times*, 10 September.

Cooper, C. (1997), 'Immigration Policy: Nationalism, Bilateralism and Regionalism', unpublished briefing paper presented to the Green Paper Task Group on International Migration.

Cornelius, W., P. Martin and J. Hollifield (1994), *Controlling Immigration: A Global Perspective*, Stanford, CA: Stanford University Press.

Cortie, C., M.J. Dijst, R. van Engelsdorp Gastelaars, R. van Kempen and W.P.R. van der Steen (1986), 'Marokkaanse, Surinaamse en Turkse ondernemers in Amsterdam', *KNAG Geografisch Tijdschrift*, 20: 169–82.

Coughlan, J.E. and D.J. McNamara (eds) (1997), *Asians in Australia: Patterns of Migration and Settlement*, Melbourne: Macmillan.

Crang, P., C. Dwyer, S. Prinjha and P. Jackson (2000), 'Transnational Communities and Spaces of Commodity Culture', paper given at the Annual Conference of the Royal Geographical Society (with the Institute of British Geographers), University of Sussex, January.

Crankshaw, O. and C. White (1992), 'Results of the Johannesburg Inner City Survey', unpublished report for the Group for Human Resources, Human Sciences Research Council, Johannesburg.

Cross, M. and R. Waldinger (1992), 'Migrants, Minorities and the Ethnic Division of Labour', in S. Fainstein, I. Gordon and M. Harloe (eds), *Divided Cities: New York and London in the Contemporary World*, Oxford: Blackwell.

Crush, J. (1997), *Covert Operations: Clandestine Migration, Temporary Work and Immigration Policy in South Africa*, Migration Policy Series no. 1, Southern African Migration Project, Cape Town and Kingston.

— (ed.) (1998), *Beyond Control: Immigration and Human Rights in a Democratic South Africa*, Cape Town and Kingston: Idasa and Queen's University.

— (1999), 'Fortress South Africa and the Deconstruction of Apartheid's Migration Regime', *Geoforum*, 30: 1–11.

— and D. McDonald (2000), 'Transnationalism, African Immigration and New Migrant Spaces in South Africa: An Introduction', *Canadian Journal of African Studies*, 34: 1–19.

— and V. Williams (1999), *The New South Africans? Immigration Amnesties and Their Aftermath*, Southern African Migration Project, Cape Town: Idasa.

Cuperus, I. (1999), 'Turks ondernemerschap in Amsterdam: Een regionale analyse naar het functioneren van Turkse ondernemers in Amsterdam en de invloed van het Amsterdamse productiemilieu op de vestigingskeuze en het functioneren van deze ondernemers', MA thesis, University of Amsterdam.

Cyrus, N. (1999), 'Migrants from Poland in the Formal and Informal Labour Markets in Germany and in Berlin', in C. Wilpert (ed.), 'The New Migration and the Informal Labour Market in Germany', TSER project report for the European Commission.

D

Dahan, J. (1985), 'Le fonctionnement du quartier Belzunce', unpublished report, Marseille.

Dahya, B. (1974), 'Pakistani Ethnicity in Industrial Cities in England', in A. Cohen (ed.), *Urban Ethnicity*, London: Tavistock.

Dal Lago, A. (1999), *Non Persone, Non-persone: L'esclusione dei migranti in una società globale*, Milan: Feltrinelli.

Dana, L.-P. (1993), 'An Inquiry into Culture and Entrepreneurship: Case Studies of Business Creation among Immigrants in Montreal', *Journal of Small Business and Entrepreneurship*, 10: 16–31.

Danso, R. and D. McDonald (2000), *Writing Xenophobia: Immigration and the Press in Post-Apartheid South Africa*, Southern African Migration Project, Migration Policy Series no. 17, Cape Town and Kingston.

Davies, W.K.D. and D.T. Herbert (1993), *Communities within Cities: An Urban Social Geography*, London: Belhaven Press.

Deakins, D., M. Majmudar and A. Paddison (1997), 'Developing Success Strategies for Ethnic Minorities in Business: Evidence from Scotland', *New Community*, 23: 325–42.

Delft, H. van, C. Gorter and P. Nijkamp (1988), 'Etnisch ondernemerschap als paspoort voor de stedelijke arbeidsmarkt', *Rooilijn*, 31: 81–6.

Demirçi, K. (1995), 'De onstuitbare opgang van de Turkse ondernemers in België', *Bareel*, 59: 20–3.

Department of Employment, Education and Training and Youth Affairs (1995), 'Evaluation Report: NEIS Pilot Program for Migrants', Canberra: Enterprise Development Section in conjunction with the National NEIS Association.

Der-Martirosian, C. (1996), 'Economic Embeddedness and Social Capital of Immigrants: Iranians in Los Angeles', unpublished PhD dissertation: University of California at Los Angeles.

Dhaliwal, S. and V. Amin (1995), *Profiles of Five Asian Entrepreneurs*, London: Asian Business Institute.

Dicken, P. (1998), *Global Shift: Transforming the World Economy*, 3rd edn, London: Paul Chapman.

Bibliography

Dijk, S. van, R. van Geuns and H. Noordermeer (1993), *Allochtone ondernemers en het Bijstandsbesluit Zelfstandigen*, The Hague: Ministerie van SZW.

Dijst, M.J., M. Hessels, R. van Kempen, A.C. Looman, H.F.J. Nouwens and W.P.R. van der Steen (1984), *Onder de markt: Een onderzoek naar Marokkaanse, Surinaamse en Turkse ondernemers in de oude Pijp*, Publication no. 16, Amsterdam: Universiteit van Amsterdam, SGI.

DILGEA (Department of Immigration, Local Government and Ethnic Affairs) (1991a), *Program Performance Statements 1991–92: Immigration, Local Government and Ethnic Affairs Portfolio*, Budget Related Paper no. 8.9, Canberra, Australian Government Publishing Service.

— (1991b), *Trends in the BMP Monitoring Survey as at 30 June 1991*, Canberra: Business Skills Section, Australian Government Publishing Service.

Dittrich, K. and H. Würzner (eds) (1982), *Nederland en het Duitse exil 1933–1940*, Amsterdam: Van Gennep.

Doctors, S.I. and A.S. Huff (1973), *Minority Enterprise and Presidential Council*, Cambridge, MA: Ballinger and Publishing Company.

Dohse, K. (1981), *Ausländische Arbeiter und bürgerlicher Staat*, Königstein (Ts.): Anton Hain.

Doortmont, M. (1998), 'Britse kooplieden in Rotterdam in de achttiende eeuw', in P. van der Laar, T. de Nijs, J. Okkema and A. Oosthoek (eds), *Vier eeuwen migratie: Bestemming Rotterdam*, Rotterdam: MondiTaal Publishing.

Drijkoningen, G. (1998), 'Etnisch ondernemerschap en een concrete oefening in Genk Noord', unpublished BA thesis, Catholic University of Leuven.

Dubb, A. (1994), *The Jewish Population of South Africa: The 1991 Sociodemographic Survey*, Cape Town: Kaplan Centre of Jewish Studies and Research, University of Cape Town.

Duchenaut, B. (1997), 'Women Entrepreneurs in SME's', report prepared for the OECD conference on 'Women Entrepreneurs in Small and Medium Enterprises: A Major Force for Innovation and Job Creation', Paris, April 16–18.

E

Eitzen, S. (1971), 'Two Minorities: The Jews of Poland and the Chinese of the Philippines', in D. Gelfand and R. Lee (eds), *Ethnic Conflicts and Power: A Cross-national Perspective*, New York: John Wiley and Sons.

Engelen, E. (2001), '"Breaking in" and "Breaking out": A Weberian Approach to Entrepreneurial Opportunities', *Journal of Ethnic and Migration Studies*, 27: 203–23.

Esping-Andersen, G. (1990), *The Three Worlds of Welfare Capitalism*, Cambridge: Polity.

— (1998), *Social Foundations of Postindustrial Economies*, Oxford: Oxford University Press.

European Observatory (1999), 'SYSDEM Trends No. 32', European Commission, Employment and Social Affairs.

F

Fagg, J. (1993), 'Asian Manufacturing Firms in Leicester: A Comparative Analysis', *Leicester Economic Review*, 2: 38–44.

Failla, A. and M. Lombardi (eds) (1993), *Immigrazione, lavoro e tecnologia*, Milan: Etas Libri.

Fairlie, R. (2000), 'The Effects of Immigration on Native Self-employment', Cambridge, MA: National Bureau of Economic Research, Working paper 7561.

— (2001), 'Immigrant Self-employment', University of California, Santa Cruz. Working Paper.

— and B. Meyer (1996), 'Ethnic and Racial Self-employment Differences and Possible Explanations', *The Journal of Human Resources*, 31: 757–93.

Faist, T. (1997), 'International Migration and Transnational Social Spaces: The Bridging Functions of Social Capital in the Economic Realm', paper given at the Second International MigCities Conference, Liège.

Fakiolas, R. (1999), 'Migration and Unregistered labour in the Greek Economy', in R. King, G. Lazaridis and C. Tsardanidis (eds), *Eldorado or Fortress? Migration in Southern Europe*, London: Macmillan, 57–78.

Farina, P., D. Cologna, A. Lanzani and L. Breveglieri (1997), *Cina a Milano: Famiglie, ambienti e lavori della popolazione cinese a Milano*, Milan: AIM.

Faßmann, H. (1993), *Arbeitsmarktsegmentation und Berufslaufbahnen. Ein Beitrag zur Arbeitsmarktgeographie Österreichs*, Vienna: Österreichische Akademie der Wissenschaften.

Feijter, H. de, L. Sterckx and E. de Gier (2001), *Nieuw Amsterdams Peil*, Amsterdamse Sociaal-Culturele Verkenningen no. 1, Amsterdam: SISWO.

Feld, S. and P. Biren (1994), *La main-d'oeuvre étrangère sur le marché du travail en Belgique*, Brussels: Inbel.

Feld, S., P. Biren and A. Manço (1993), *Indépendants d'origine étrangère: Présentation théorique et enquêtes*, Documents de Travail no. 19, Liège: University of Liège.

Fijnaut, C. (1990), 'Ideologie en misdaad in de justitiële beleidsplannen', *Tijdschrift voor Criminologie*, 32: 268–77.

Flap, H., A. Kumcu and B. Bulder (2000), 'The Social Capital of Ethnic Entrepreneurs and Their Business Success', in J. Rath (ed.), *Immigrant Businesses: The Economic, Political and Social Environment*, Basingstoke/ New York: Macmillan/St Martin's.

Flatau, P. and P. Hemmings (1991), *Labour Market Experience, Education and Training of Young Immigrants in Australia*, Canberra: Bureau of Immigration Research, Australian Government Publishing Service.

Fong, E. and L. Lee (eds) (2001), 'The Chinese Ethnic Economy', special issue *Asian and Pacific Migration Journal*, 1.

Forrester, T. (1978), 'Britain's Asians', *New Society*, 23: 420–1.

Foster, L., A. Marshall and L. Williams (1991), *Discrimination Against Immigrant Workers in Australia*, Canberra: Australian Government Publishing Service.

Frayne, B. and W. Pendleton (1998), *Namibians on South Africa: Attitudes towards Cross-border Migration and Immigration Policy*, Southern African Migration Project, Migration Policy Series no. 10, Cape Town and Kingston.

Froschauer, K. (1998), 'Premigration Context and Postmigration Conduct: East Asian and European Entrepreneur Immigrants in British Columbia', research monograph, Department of Sociology and Anthropology, Simon Fraser University: Burnaby, Canada.

Fuchs, B. (1992), 'Freundlich lächelnde Litfaßsäulen: Zeitungskolporteure-Typisierung und Realität', MA thesis, University of Vienna.

— (1997), 'Ethnischer Kapitalismus: Ökonomie der Südasiaten in Wien', PhD thesis, University of Vienna.

G

Gächter, A. (1995), 'Integration und Migration', *SWS-Rundschau*, 35: 435–8.

— (1998), 'Rechtliche Rahmenbedingungen und ihre Konsequenzen', in: AMS Österreich, *AusländerInnen in Österreich: Migrationspolitik und Integration*, AMS Report no. 6, Vienna: AMS.

Gaoyu, R. (1996), 'A Sociological Study of Street Traders in Pretoria', unpublished PhD thesis, University of Pretoria.

Garson, J.-P. and M.E. Mouhoud (1989), 'Sous traitance et désalarisation formelle de la main d'oeuvre dans le BTP', *La note de l'IRES*, 19: 36–47.

Gastelaars, M. (1985), *Een geregeld leven: Sociologie en sociale politiek in Nederland 1925–1968*, Amsterdam: SUA.

Gema, G.H. (2001), 'The Social and Economic Integration of Ethiopian Asylum-seekers', unpublished MA thesis, University of Natal, Durban.

Geuns, R. van (1992), 'An Aspect of Informalisation of Women's Work in a High-tech Age: Turkish Sweatshops in the Netherlands', in S. Mitter (ed.), *Computer-aided Manufacturing and Women's Employment: The Clothing Industry in Four EC Countries*, London/Berlin: Springer Verlag.

Geyevu, S.A. (1997), 'The Socio-economic Impact of Ghanaian Non-professional Illegal Aliens on Durban Metropolitan Area', unpublished MA thesis, University of Durban-Westville, Durban.

Giffinger, R. and U. Reeger (1997), 'Turks in Austria: Backgrounds, Geographical Distribution and Housing Conditions', in: S. Özüekren and R.

van Kempen (eds), *Turks in European Cities: Housing and Urban Segregation*, Utrecht: ERCOMER.

Gitmez, A. and C. Wilpert (1987), 'A Micro-society or an Ethnic Community? Social Organization and Ethnicity amongst Turkish Migrants in Berlin', in J. Rex, D. Joly and C. Wilpert (eds), *Immigrant Associations in Europe*, Aldershot: Gower.

Glezer, L. (1988), 'Business and Commerce', in J. Jupp (ed.), *The Australian People: An Encyclopedia of the Nation, Its People and Their Origins*, Sydney: Angus & Robertson.

Gold, S. (1994), 'Chinese-Vietnamese Entrepreneurs in California', in P. Ong, E. Bonacich and L. Cheng (eds), *The New Asian Immigration in Los Angeles*, Philadelphia: Temple University Press.

— and I. Light (2000), 'Ethnic Economies and Social Policy', *Research in Social Movements, Conflicts and Change*, 22: 165–91.

Goldberg, A. and F. Şen (1997), 'Türkische Unternehmer in Deutschland: Wirtschaftliche Aktivitäten einer Einwanderungsgesellschaft in einem komplexen Wirtschaftssystem', in H. Häußermann and I. Oswald (eds), *Zuwanderung und Stadtentwicklung*, Sonderheft Leviathan no. 17: 63–84.

Goldberg, A. and F. Şen (1999), 'Türkische Unternehmer in Deutschland', *IZA-Zeitschrift für Migration und soziale Arbeit*, 1: 29–37.

Goossens, L. (1988), 'Belgium', in H. Kroes, F. Ymkers and A. Mulders (eds), *Between Owner-occupation and Rented Sector: Housing in Ten European Countries*, De Bilt: NCIV.

Gowricharn, R.S. (1985), *Etnisch ondernemerschap: Werkgelegenheid en economische politiek*, Discussienota Arbeidsproblematiek, Rotterdam: Stichting KROSBE.

Granovetter, M. (1994), 'Business Groups', in N. Smelser and R. Swedberg (eds), *Handbook of Economic Sociology*, Princeton: Princeton University Press.

— (1995), 'The Economic Sociology of Firms and Entrepreneurs', in A. Portes (ed.), *The Economic Sociology of Immigration: Essays on Networks, Ethnicity, and Entrepreneurship*, New York: Russell Sage Foundation.

Guillon, M. (1992), 'Etrangers et immigrés en Ile-de-France', unpublished PhD thesis, Université de Paris 1.

— and E. Ma Mung (1986), 'Les commerçants étrangers dans l'agglomération parisienne', *Revue Européenne des Migrations Internationales*, 2: 105–34.

Gunter, A. (2001), 'Experiences of Xenophobia by Foreigners in South African and Perceptions of National Identity', unpublished paper, Department of Geography, University of the Witwatersrand.

Gutstein, A. (1990), *The New Landlords: Asian Investment in Canadian Real Estate*, Victoria: Porcepic.

H

Haberfellner, R. (2000a), 'Ethnische Ökonomien als Forschungsgegenstand der Sozialwissenschaften', *SWS-Rundschau*, 40(1): 43–61.

— (2000b), 'Unternehmerisch aktive ImmigrantInnen in Wien: Ein Leben zwischen Emanzipierung und Marginalisierung', *Isotopia* 24: 116–30.

— and F. Betz (eds) (1999), *Geöffnet! Migrantinnen und Migranten als Unternehmer*, Vienna/Mühlheim: Guthmann-Peterson.

— and M. Böse (1999) '"Ethnische" Ökonomien: Integration vs. Segregation im Kontext der wirtschaftlichen Selbständigkeit von MigrantInnen', in: H. Faßmann, H. Matuschek and E. Menasse (eds), *Abgrenzen, ausgrenzen, aufnehmen: Empirische Befunde zur Fremdenfeindlichkeit und Integration*, Klagenfurt/Celovec: Drava Verlag.

Hall, P. (1977), 'The Inner Cities Dilemma', *New Society*, 3: 223–5.

— (1998), *Cities in Civilization*, New York: Pantheon.

Hallsworth, A.G. (1999), 'Waiting for WalMart?', *Environment and Planning A*, 31: 1331–6.

Halter, M. (2000), *Shopping for Identity: The Marketing of Ethnicity*, New York: Schocken.

Hardill, I. and P. Raghuram (1998), 'Diasporic Connections: Case Studies of Asian Women in Business', *Area*, 30: 255–61.

Harney, R.F. (1977), 'The Commerce of Migration', *Canadian Ethnic Studies*, 9: 42–53.

Harris, K. (1994), 'The Chinese in South Africa: A Preliminary Overview to 1910', *Kleio*, XXVI: 9–26.

Hartog, J. and A. Zorlu (1999), *Turkish Confection in Amsterdam: The Rise and Fall of a Perfectly Competitive Labour Market*, Amsterdam: Tinbergen Institute.

Harvey, D. (1990), *The Condition of Postmodernity: An Enquiry into the Origins of Cultural Change*, Oxford: Blackwell.

Hatz, G. (1997), 'Die Märkte als Chance für Ausländer: Ausländer als Chance für die Märkte', in: H. Häußermann and I. Oswald (eds), *Zuwanderung und Stadtentwicklung*, Sonderheft Leviathan no. 17: 170–91.

Hawkins, F. (1989), *Critical Years in Immigration: Canada and Australia Compared*, Kingston and Montreal: McGill-Queen's University Press.

Hawthorne, L. (1994), *Labour Market Barriers for Immigrant Engineers in Australia*, Canberra: Bureau of Immigration and Population Research, Australian Government Publishing Service.

Heek, F. van (1936), *Chineesche immigranten in Nederland*, Amsterdam: J. Emmering's Uitgevers Mij.

Held, D., A. McGrew, D. Goldblatt and J. Perraton (1999), *Global Transformations: Politics, Economics and Culture*, Cambridge: Polity.

Henkes, B. (1995), *Heimat in Holland: Duitse dienstmeisjes, 1920–1950*, Amsterdam: Babylon-De Geus.

Hiebert, D. (1994), 'Canadian Immigration: Policy, Politics, Geography', *The Canadian Geographer*, 38: 254–70.

Hillmann, F. (1998), *Türkische Unternehmerinnen und Beschäftigte im Berliner ethnischen Gewerbe*, Berlin: WZB.

— (2000), 'Are Ethnic Economies the Revolving Doors of Urban Labor Markets in Transition?', paper given at the Second Conference of the Thematic Network 'Working on the Fringes: Immigrant Business, Economic Integration and Informal Practices', Jerusalem, June.

Hodenius, B. (1997), 'Weibliche Selbständigkeit: Gratwanderungen zwischen Programmatik und Pragmatik', in M. Thomas (ed.), *Selbständige-Gründer-Unternehmer: Passagen und Paßformen im Umbruch*, Berlin: Berliner Debatte Wissenschaftsverlag.

Hoffer, C. (1998), 'Religieus-medisch ondernemerschap onder moslims: Een contradictio in terminis?', in J. Rath and R. Kloosterman (eds), *Rijp & Groen: Het zelfstandig ondernemerschap van immigranten in Nederland*, Amsterdam: Het Spinhuis.

Hollifield, J.F. (1992), *Immigrants, Markets, and States: The Political Economy of Postwar Europe*, Cambridge, MA/London: Harvard University Press.

Holness, S., E. Nel and T. Binns (1999), 'The Changing Nature of Informal Street Trading in Post-apartheid South Africa: The Case of East London's Central Business District', *Urban Forum*, 10: 284–302.

Holton, R.J. (1988), *Small Business Policy for a Multicultural Australia*, Canberra: OMA Policy Option Paper.

Home Office (1991), 'Ethnic Minority Business Initiative', final report of the Ethnic Minority Business Development Team, London: Ethnic Minority Business Initiative, Home Office.

Hong, M. (1996), *Chinesen in Berlin*, Berlin: Ausländerbeauftragten des Senats von Berlin.

Hosler, A. (1998), *Japanese Immigrant Entrepreneurs in New York City: A New Wave of Ethnic Business*, New York: Garland.

Hough, M. (1995), 'Illegal Aliens in South Africa: Causes and Facilitating Factors', *Strategic Review for Southern Africa*, 17: 1–25.

Hubeau, B. (1997), 'Etnisch ondernemen als (onvoldoende?) voorwerp van onderzoek en beleid', in A. de Muynck, M.C. Foblets, B. Hubeau, A. Martens and S. Parmentier (eds), *Migrantenonderzoek voor de toekomst: Huldeboek Ruud F. Peeters*, Leuven and Amersfoort: Acco.

Hudson, R. (2001), *Producing Places*, New York/London: Guilford.

Hulshof, M.H. and J.W.M. Mevissen (1985), *Starters onder de starters. Onderzoek naar de ondersteuning van allochtone starters, nu en in de toekomst: Eindrapport*, Regioplan-publikatie no. 187, Amsterdam: Regioplan.

Human, L. (1984), *The Chinese People of South Africa: Freewheeling on the Fringes*, Pretoria: University of South Africa.

Human Rights and Equal Opportunity Commission (1991), 'Racist Violence', report of the National Inquiry into Racist Violence in Australia, Canberra: Australian Government Publishing Service.

Human Rights Watch (1998), *'Prohibited Persons': Abuse of Undocumented Migrants, Asylum-seekers, and Refugees in South Africa*, New York: Human Rights Watch.

Hummel, R. (1996), *Krone! Kurier!: Soziale Lage und rechtliche Situation der Zeitungskolporteure*, Vienna: Österreichischer Kunst- und Kulturverlag.

Hurh, W.M. and K.C. Kim (1985), *Korean Immigrants in America: A Structural Analysis of Ethnic Confinement and Adhesive Adaptation*, Madison, NJ: Fairleigh Dickinson University Press.

I

Idiri, A. (1997), 'Les étrangers en Alsace', *Hommes et migrations*, 1209: 12–19.

IfGH (Institut für Gewerbe und Handwerksforschung) (1996), 'Barrieren für potentielle Unternehmensgründer', unpublished report, Vienna.

Inglis, C., S. Gunasekaran, G. Sullivan and C.-T. Wu (eds) (1992), *Asians in Australia: The Dynamics of Migration and Settlement*, Sydney: Allen & Unwin.

INSEE (1995a), *French Annual of Statistics*, Paris: INSEE.

— (1995b), *French Annual of Statistics*, SUSE file, Paris: INSEE.

— Première (2000), *INSEE Première* no. 748, Paris: INSEE.

IReR (1994), *Tra due rive: La nuova immigrazione a Milano*, Milan: Franco Angeli.

Israel, J. (1989), *Dutch Primacy in World trade 1585–1740*, Oxford: Clarendon.

J

Jansen, P.A.A.M. (1999), 'Allochtone ondernemers in Nederland', in *Handboek Minderheden*, Houten: Bohn Stafleu Van Loghum.

Janssens, G. (1999), 'A Social-economic Analysis of Ethnic Entrepreneurschip in Flanders', research proposal VIONA 1999, theme 4.13, Leuven: HIVA.

Jeleniewski, M. (1984), *Etnisch ondernemerschap en de stadsvernieuwing*, Planologisch Memorandum no. 3, Delft: Technische Hogeschool Delft, Vakgroep Civiele Planologie.

— (1987), *Waar vestigt zich de etnische ondernemer?*, The Hague: Seinpost, Centrum voor Stedelijke Processen.

Jennings, R., R. Hirschowitz, Z. Tshandu and M. Orkin (1995a), 'Our Daily

Bread: Earning a Living on the Pavements of Johannesburg. Part 1: The Census', report for the Community Agency for Social Enquiry (CASE), Johannesburg.

Jennings, R., K. Segal, R. Hirschowitz and M. Orkin (1995b), 'Our Daily Bread: Earning a Living on the Pavements of Johannesburg. Part 2: The Survey', a report for CASE, Johannesburg.

Jensen, R. (1999), *The Dream Society: How the Coming Shift from Information to Imagination Will Transform Your Businesses*, New York: McGraw Hill.

Jones, T. and D. McEvoy (1992), 'Ressources ethniques et égalités des chances: Les entreprises indo-pakistanaises en Grande-Bretagne et au Canada', *Revue Européenne des Migrations Internationales*, 8: 107–26.

Jones, T., J. Cater, P. De Silva and D. McEvoy (1989), 'Ethnic Business and Community Needs', report to the Commission for Racial Equality, Liverpool: Liverpool Polytechnic.

Jones, T.P., D. McEvoy and G.A. Barrett (1992), 'Small Business Initiative: Ethnic Minority Business Component', End of Award Report W108 25 1013 to the Economic and Social Research Council, Liverpool: Liverpool John Moores University.

Jones, T., D. McEvoy and G. Barrett (1994), 'Labour Intensive Practices in the Ethnic Minority Firm', in J. Atkinson and D. Storey (eds), *Employment, the Small Firm and the Labour Market*, London: Routledge.

Jones, T., G. Barrett and D. McEvoy (2000), 'Market Potential as a Decisive Influence on the Performance of Ethnic Minority Business', in J. Rath (ed.), *Immigrant Businesses: The Economic, Political and Social Environment*, Basingstoke/New York: Macmillan/St Martin's Press.

Jong, J.A. de (1988), *Kredietverschaffing aan Rotterdamse etnische onderne-mers*, Tweedelijnspublikatie no. 3, Rotterdam: Stichting Buitenlandse Werknemers Rijnmond.

Joske, S. (1989), 'The Economics of Immigration: Who Benefits?', background paper from the Legislative Research Service, Canberra: the Parliament of the Commonwealth of Australia.

Jupp, J., A. McRobbie and B. York (1991), *Metropolitan Ghettoes and Ethnic Concentration*, Working Papers on Multiculturalism no. 1 (2 vols), Wollongong: Office of Multicultural Affairs and the University of Wollongong.

K

Kallen, E. and M. Kelner (1983), 'Ethnicity, Opportunity, and Successful Entrepreneurship in Canada', research monograph, Ethnic Research Programme, Institute for Behavioural Research, York University.

Kamer van Koophandel Rotterdam (2001), *Marokkaanse ondernemers in Rotterdam en Gouda*, Rotterdam: Kamer van Koophandel Rotterdam.

Kansen krijgen (1998), 'Kansen krijgen, kansen pakken', Policy memorandum of the Dutch Ministry of Interior Affairs, The Hague.

Kaplan, M. (1986), *Jewish Roots in the South African Economy*, Cape Town: David Philip.

Kapphan, A. (1997), 'Russisches Gewerbe in Berlin', in H. Häußermann and I. Oswald (eds), *Zuwanderung und Stadtentwicklung*, Sonderheft Leviathan no. 17: 120–37.

Kehla, J., G. Engbersen and E. Snel (1997), *'Pier 90': Een onderzoek naar informaliteit op de markt*, The Hague: Ministerie van SZW/VUGA.

Kermond, C., K. Luscombe, K. Strahan and A. Williams (1991), *Immigrant Women Entrepreneurs in Australia*, Wollongong: Centre for Multicultural Studies, University of Wollongong for the Office of Multicultural Affairs, Department of Prime Minister and Cabinet.

Kerrou, M. (1987), 'Du colportage à la boutique: Les commerçants maghrébins en France', *Hommes et migrations*, 1105: 26–34.

Kessner, T. (1977), *The Golden Door: Italian and Jewish Mobility in New York City, 1880–1915*, New York: Oxford University Press.

Kesteloot, C. and C. Cortie (1998), 'Housing Turks and Moroccans in Brussels and Amsterdam: The Difference between Private and Public Markets', *Urban Studies*, 35: 1835–53.

Kesteloot, C. and P. Mistiaen (1995), 'Les restaurants turcs de la Chausée de Haecht à Bruxelles: Niches ethniques, exotisme et assimilation', *Revue Belge de Géographie*, 119: 369–80.

Kim, D.Y. (1999), 'Beyond Co-ethnic Solidarity: Mexican and Ecuadorean Employment in Korean-owned Businesses in New York City', *Ethnic and Racial Studies*, 22: 583–607.

Kim, I. (1981), *New Urban Immigrants: The Korean Community in New York*, Princeton, NJ: Princeton University Press.

Kim, K.C., W.M. Hurh and M. Fernandez (1989), 'Intra-group Differences in Business Participation: A Comparative Analysis of Three Asian Immigrant Groups', *International Migration Review*, 23: 73–95.

King, R. (1999), 'Southern Europe in the Changing Global map of Migration', in R. King, G. Lazaridis and C. Tsardanidis (eds), *Eldorado or Fortress? Migration in Southern Europe*, London: Macmillan, 1–25.

Klein, N. (2000), *No Logo*, London: Flamingo.

Kloosterman, R.C. (1994), 'Amsterdamned: The Rise of Unemployment in Amsterdam in the 1980s', *Urban Studies*, 31: 1325–44.

— (1996), 'Mixed Experiences: Post-industrial Transition and Ethnic Minorities on the Amsterdam Labour Market', *New Community*, 22: 637–54.

— (1997), 'Immigrant Entrepreneurship and the Welfare State: A Comparison from an International Perspective', paper given at the First International

MigCities Conference, Warwick University.

— (2000), 'Immigrant Entrepreneurship and the Institutional Context: A Theoretical Explanation', in J. Rath (ed.), *Immigrant Businesses: The Economic, Political and Social Environment*, Basingstoke/New York: Macmillan/St Martin's Press.

— (2002), 'Mixed Embeddedness and Postindustrial Opportunity Structures: Trajectories of Migrant Entrepreneurship in Amsterdam', in W. Salet (ed.), *Amsterdam Human Capital*.

— and B. Lambregts (2001), 'Clustering of Economic Activities in Polycentric Urban Regions: The Case of the Randstad', *Urban Studies*, 38: 717–32.

— and J.P. van der Leun (1999), 'Just for Starters: Commercial Gentrification by Immigrant Entrepreneurs in Amsterdam and Rotterdam Neighbourhoods', *Housing Studies*, 14: 659–77.

— and J. Rath (1996), 'Gangsta's Paradise in Holland?', *Migrantenstudies*, 12: 94–100.

— and J. Rath (2000), 'Mixed Embeddedness: Markets and Immigrant Entrepreneurs. Towards a Framework for Comparative Research', paper given at the Second Conference of the Thematic Network 'Working on the Fringes: Immigrant Business, Economic Integration and Informal Practices', Jerusalem, June.

— and J. Rath (eds) (2001a), 'Immigrant Entrepreneurship', special issue *Journal of Ethnic and Migration Studies*, 2.

— and J. Rath (2001b), 'Immigrant Entrepreneurs in Advanced Economies: Mixed Embeddedness Further Explored', *Journal of Ethnic and Migration Studies*, 27: 189–201.

—, J. van der Leun and J. Rath (1997a), *De economische potenties van het immigrantenondernemerschap in Amsterdam*, Amsterdam: Gemeente Amsterdam, Afdeling Economische Zaken/Universiteit van Amsterdam, IMES.

—, J. van der Leun and J. Rath (1997b), *Over grenzen: Immigranten en de informele economie*, Amsterdam: Het Spinhuis.

—, J. van der Leun and J. Rath (1998), 'Across the Border: Economic Opportunities, Social Capital and Informal Businesses Activities of Immigrants', *Journal of Ethnic and Migration Studies*, 24: 239–58.

—, J. van der Leun and J. Rath (1999), 'Mixed Embeddedness: Immigrant Entrepreneurship and Informal Economic Activities', *International Journal of Urban and Regional Research*, 23: 253–67.

—, J. Rath and E. Razin (eds) (2003), 'Immigrant Entrepreneurship', special issue of *International Journal of Urban and Regional Research*.

Knotter, A. (1995), 'Vreemdelingen in Amsterdam in de 17e eeuw: Groepsvorming, arbeid en ondernemerschap', *Historisch Tijdschrift Holland*, 27: 219–35.

Kontos, M. (1997), 'Von der Gastarbeiterin zur Unternehmerin: Biographie-analytische Überlegungen zu einem sozialen Transformationsprozeß', *Deutsch lernen*, 4: 275–90.

Kraut, A. (1982), *The Huddled Masses: The Immigrant in American Society: 1880–1921*, Arlington Heights, IL: Harlan Davidson.

Kroniek (1984), *Kroniek van het Ambacht/Klein- en Middenbedrijf*, 38: 1–34.

Kruyt, A. and J. Niessen (1997), 'Integration', in H. Vermeulen (ed.), *Immigration Policy for a Multicultural Society: A Comparative Study of Integration, Language and Religious Policy in Five Western European Countries*, Brussels and Amsterdam: MPG and IMES.

Kumcu, A. (2001), *De fil en aiguille: Genèse et déclin des ateliers de confections turcs d'Amsterdam*, Amsterdam: Thela Thesis.

—, J. Lambooy and S. Safaklioglu (1998), 'De financiering van Turkse onderne-mingen', in J. Rath and R. Kloosterman (eds), *Rijp & Groen: Het zelfstandig ondernemerschap van immigranten in Nederland*, Amsterdam: Het Spinhuis.

Kwong, P. (1987), *The New Chinatown*, New York: Hill and Wang.

L

Ladbury, S. (1984), 'Choice, Chance, or No Alternative: Turkish Cypriots in Business in London', in R. Ward and R. Jenkins (eds), *Ethnic Communities in Business: Strategies for Economic Survival*, Cambridge: Cambridge University Press.

Lampugnani, R. and R.J. Holton (1989), *Ethnic Business in South Australia: A Sociological Profile of the Italian Business Community*, Adelaide: Centre for Multicultural Studies, Flinders University.

Langlois, A. and E. Razin (1989), 'Self-employment among Ethnic Minorities in Canadian Metropolitan Areas', *Canadian Journal of Regional Science*, 12: 335–54.

Langlois, C. and C. Dougherty (1997), 'The Longitudinal Immigrant Data Base (IMDB)', paper given at the CERF-CIC Conference on 'Immigration, Employment and the Economy', Richmond, BC, October.

Lautard, H. and N. Guppy (1990), 'The Vertical Mosaic Revisited: Occupational Differentials among Canadian Ethnic Groups', in P.S. Li (ed.), *Race and Ethnic Relations in Canada*, Toronto: Oxford University Press.

Lee, J. (1999), Retail Niche Domination among African American, Jewish and Korean Entrepreneurs: Competition, Coethnic Advantage and Disadvantage', *American Behavioral Scientist*, 42: 1398–1416.

Leman, J. (ed.) (1995), *Sans document. Les immigrés de l'ombre: Latino-améri-cains, polonais et nigérians clandestins*, Brussels: De Boeck Université.

— (1997), *Etnisch ondernemerschap: Meerwaarden voor het etnisch ondernemen*, Leuven and Amersfoort: Acco.

Leslie, D., S. Drinkwater and N. O'Leary (1998), 'Unemployment and Earnings among Britain's Ethnic Minorities: Some Signs for Optimism', *Journal of Ethnic and Migration Studies*, 24: 489–506.

Leun, J. van der, and K. Rusinovic (2001), 'B2B: "Mixed Embeddedness" of Immigrant Entrepreneurs in a Booming Sector in Two Dutch Cities', paper prepared for the ISA Conference on 'Social Inequality, Redistributive Justice and the City (RC21)', Amsterdam, 15–17 June.

Lever-Tracy, C., D. Ip, J. Kitay, I. Phillips and N. Tracy (1991), *Asian Entrepreneurs in Australia*, Canberra: Australian Government Publishing Service.

Ley, D. (2000), *Seeking Homo Economicus: The Strange Story of Canada's Business Immigration Program*, Vancouver, Research on Immigration and Integration in the Metropolis (RIIM) Working Paper Series no. 00–02.

Li, P.S. (1976), 'Ethnic Businesses among Chinese in the US', *Journal of Ethnic Studies*, 4: 35–41.

— (1979), 'A Historical Approach to Ethnic Stratification: The Case of the Chinese in Canada, 1858–1930', *Canadian Review of Sociology and Anthropology*, 16: 320–32.

— (1988), *Ethnic Inequality in a Class Society*, Toronto: Wall and Thompson.

— (1992), 'Ethnic Enterprise in Transition: Chinese Business in Richmond, BC', *Canadian Ethnic Studies*, 24: 120–38.

— (1993), 'Chinese Investment and Business in Canada: Ethnic Entrepreneurship Reconsidered', *Pacific Affairs*, 66: 219–43.

— (1994), 'Self-employment and Its Economic Return for Visible Minorities in Canada', in D.M. Saunders (ed.), *New Approaches to Employment Management*, vol. 2, Stanford: Jai.

— (1997), 'Asian Capital and Canadian Business: The Recruitment and Control of Investment Capital and Business Immigrants to Canada', in W.W. Isajiw (ed.), *Multiculturalism in North America and Europe: Comparative Perspectives on Interethnic Relations and Social Incorporation*, Toronto: Canadian Scholars Press.

Liepe, L. (1997), 'Vietnamesische Migrantenökonomie im Ostteil Berlins', in *Berlin: Eine Stadt im Zeichen der Migration*, Berlin: Verlag für wissenschaftliche Publikationen.

Light, I. (1972), *Ethnic Enterprise in North America: Business and Welfare among Chinese, Japanese, and Blacks*, Berkeley and Los Angeles: University of California Press.

— (1979), 'Disadvantaged Minorities in Self-employment', *International Journal of Comparative Sociology*, 20: 31–45.

— (1980), 'Asian Enterprise in America: Chinese, Japanese, and Koreans in Small Business', in S. Cummings (ed.), *Self-help in Urban America*, Pt. Washington, NY: Kenikart.

— (1984), 'Immigrant and Ethnic Enterprise in North America', *Ethnic and Racial Studies*, 7: 195–216.

— (2000), 'Globalisation and Migration Networks', in J. Rath (ed.), *Immigrant Businesses: The Economic, Political and Social Environment*, Basingstoke/New York: Macmillan/St Martin's Press.

— and E. Bonacich (1988), *Immigrant Entrepreneurs: Koreans in Los Angeles 1965–1982*, Berkeley: University of California Press.

— and S.J. Gold (2000), *Ethnic Economies*, San Diego: Academic Press.

— and E. Roach (1996), 'Self-employment: Mobility Ladder or Economic Lifeboat', in R. Waldinger and M. Bozorgmehr (eds), *Ethnic Los Angeles*, New York: Russell Sage.

— and C. Rosenstein (1995), *Race, Ethnicity, and Entrepreneurship in Urban America*, Hawthorne, NY: Aldine de Gruyter.

— and A. Sanchez (1987), 'Immigrant Entrepreneurs in 272 SMSAs', *Sociological Perspectives*, 30: 373–99.

—, I.J. Kwuon and D. Zhoing (1990), 'Korean Rotating Credit Associations in Los Angeles', *Amerasia*, 16(1): 35–54.

—, G. Sabagh, M. Bozorgmehr and C. Der-Martirosian (1993), 'Internal Ethnicity in the Ethnic Economy', *Ethnic and Racial Studies*, 16: 581–97.

—, G. Sabagh, M. Bozorgmehr and C. Der-Martirosian (1994), 'Beyond the Ethnic Enclave Economy', *Social Problems*, 41: 65–79.

—, R. Bernard and R. Kim (1999), 'Immigrant Incorporation in the Garment Industry of Los Angeles', *International Migration Review*, 33: 5–26.

Lijphart, A. (1975), *The Politics of Accommodation: Pluralism and Democracy in the Netherlands*, 2nd edn, Berkeley: University of California Press.

Live, Y.-S. (1991), 'La diaspora chinoise en France: Immigration, activités socio-économiques, pratiques socio-culturelles', unpublished PhD thesis, Ecole des Hautes Etudes en Sciences Sociales, Paris.

Lo, L., V. Preston, S. Wang, K. Reil, E. Harvey and B. Siu (1999), *Immigrants' Economic Status in Toronto: Rethinking Settlement and Integration Strategies*, Working Paper no. 15, Toronto: Joint Centre of Excellence for Research on Immigration and Settlement.

Loeffelholz, H.D. von, H. Buch and A. Gieseck (1994), *Ausländische Selbständige in der Bundesrepublik unter besonderer Berücksichtigung von Entwicklungsperspektiven in den neuen Bundesländern*, Berlin: Duncker und Humblot.

Lof, E. (1997), 'Etnische elite: Allochtonen voorzien in toekomstige arbeidsbehoefte', *Management Team*, 5: 33–41.

Loucky, J., M. Soldatenko, G. Scott and E. Bonacich (1994), 'Immigrant Enterprise and Labor in the Los Angeles Garment Industry' in E. Bonacich, L. Cheng, N. Chinchilla, N. Hamilton and P. Ong (eds), *Global Production: The*

Apparel Industry in the Pacific Rim, Philadelphia: Temple University Press.

Lovell-Troy, L.A. (1980), 'Clan Structure and Economic Activity: The Case of Greeks in Small Business Enterprise', in S. Cummings (ed.), *Self-help in Urban America*, New York: Kenikart.

Lowen, J. (1971), *The Mississippi Chinese: Between Black and White*, Cambridge, MA: Harvard University Press.

Lucassen, J. and R. Penninx (1994), *Nieuwkomers, nakomelingen, Nederlanders: Immigranten in Nederland 1550–1993*, Amsterdam: Het Spinhuis.

Lucassen, L. (1998), 'Het voordeel van de ambulant: Zigeuners als etnische ondernemers in Nederland (1868–1940)?', in J. Rath and R. Kloosterman (eds), *Rijp & Groen: Het zelfstandig ondernemerschap van immigranten in Nederland*, Amsterdam: Het Spinhuis.

— and F. Vermeulen (1999), *Immigranten en lokale arbeidsmarkt: Vreemdelingen in Den Haag, Leiden, Deventer en Alkmaar (1920–1940)*, Amsterdam: Centrum voor de Geschiedenis van Migranten.

Lutz, H. (1992), 'Integreert arbeid? Migranten, arbeidsmarkt en beleid in Nederland', *Migrantenstudies*, 8: 3–13.

M

Ma Mung, E. (1992), 'Dispositif économique et ressources spatiales: Éléments d'une économie de diaspora', *Revue Européenne des Migrations Internationales*, 8: 175–93.

— (1994), 'L'entreprenariat ethnique en France', *Sociologie du Travail*, 1.

— (1996), 'Relation économique et appartenance ethnique', *Revue Européenne des Migrations Internationales*, 12: 211–33.

— (1998a), 'Territorialisation marchande et négociation des identités: Les Chinois à Paris', *Espaces et Sociétés*, 95: 65–81.

— (1998b), 'Ethnic Economy and Diaspora', in Z. Guotu and Alii (eds), *Shiji zhijiau de HaiwawHuaren*, vol. I and II, Fujian Renmin Chubanshe.

— and G. Simon (1990), *Commerçants maghrébins et asiatiques en France*, Paris: Masson, Coll. Recherches en Géographie.

Magatti, M. and F. Quassoli (forthcoming), 'Immigrant Businesses in the Small Firm's Motherland', *International Journal of Urban and Regional Research*.

Maharaj, B. and V. Moodley (2000), 'New African Immigration to the Durban Region', *Canadian Journal of African Studies*, 34: 149–60.

Maharaj, B. and R. Rajkumar (1997), 'The "Alien Invasion" in South Africa: Illegal Immigrants in Durban', *Development Southern Africa*, 14: 61–9.

Majodina, Z. and S. Peberdy, with the Somali Association of South Africa (2000), 'Finding a New Home: A Report on the Lives of Somali Refugees in Johannesburg', Forced Migration Studies Programme, University of the Witwatersrand.

Mak, A.S. and H. Chan (1995), 'Chinese Family Values in Australia', in R. Hartley (ed.), *Families and Cultural Diversity in Australia*, Sydney: Allen & Unwin.

Mantzaris, E. (1978), 'Greek Immigrants in South Africa', unpublished PhD thesis, University of the Witwatersrand, Johannesburg.

Marger, M. (1989), 'Business Strategies among East Indian Entrepreneurs in Toronto: The Role of Group Resources and Opportunity Structure', *Ethnic and Racial Studies*, 12: 539–63.

— and C.A. Hoffman (1992), 'Ethnic Enterprise in Ontario: Immigrant Participation in the Small Business Sector', *International Migration Review*, 26: 968–81.

Marie, C.-V. (1992), 'Les étrangers non-salariés en France: Symbole de la muta-tion économique des années 80', *Revue Européenne des Migrations Internationales*, 8.

Markus, A. (1994), *Australia's Race Relations 1878–1993*, Sydney: Allen & Unwin.

Mars, G. and R. Ward (1984), 'Ethnic Business Development in Britain: Opportunities and Resources', in R. Ward and R. Jenkins (eds), *Ethnic Communities in Business: Strategies for Economic Survival*, Cambridge: Cambridge University Press.

Martens, A. and F. Caestecker (2001), 'De algemene beleidsontwikkelingen sinds 1984', in J. Vrancken, C. Timmerman and K. Van der Heyden (eds), *Komende generaties: Wat weten we (nog) niet over allochtonen in Vlaanderen?*, Leuven and Amersfoort: Acco.

Martens, E.P. and J. Veenman (1999), 'De sociaal-economische positie van etnische minderheden', in H.M.A.G. Smeets, E.P. Martens and J. Veenman (1999), *Jaarboek minderheden 1999*, Houten/Lelystad: Bohn, Stafleu Van Loghum/Koninklijke Vermande.

Martin, J. (1978), *The Migrant Presence: Australian Responses 1947–77*, Sydney: Allen & Unwin.

Martin, V.M. (1986), 'Mauritian Settlement in South Africa: A Study in Population Geography', unpublished MA thesis, University of the Witwatersrand, Johannesburg.

— (1987), 'The Integration of the Franco-Mauritian Community into South African Society', *South African Geographer*, 14: 77–87.

Martina, J. (1999), *Etnisch ondernemerschap in Gelderland Deel 2: Studie naar de knelpunten van het etnisch ondernemen in Arnhem en de behoefte aan ondersteuning*, Arnhem: Stichting Osmose.

Martiniello, M. (1994), 'De communautaire kwestie en het migrantenvraagstuk in België', in R. Detrez and J. Blommaert (eds), *Nationalisme: Kritische opstellen*, Berchem: Epo.

— (ed.) (1995), *Migration, Citizenship and Ethno-national Identity in the European Union*, Aldershot: Avebury.

Massey, D. (1995), 'The New Immigration and Ethnicity in the United States', *Population and Development Review*, 21: 631–52.

— (2000), 'Why Does Immigration Occur: A Theoretical Synthesis', in C. Hirschman, P. Kasinitz and J. DeWind (eds), *The Handbook of International Migration: The American Experience*, New York: Russell Sage.

Masurel, E., P. Nijkamp, M. Tastan and G. Vindigni (2001), *Motivations and Performance Conditions for Ethnic Entrepreneurship*, Tinbergen Institute Discussion Paper no. 48/3, Amsterdam: Vrije Universiteit Amsterdam, Department of Spatial Economics.

Matlou, P. (1999), 'The Making of a National Refugee Policy', unpublished seminar paper presented to a seminar of the Forced Migration Programme, School of Graduate Studies and Humanities, University of the Witwatersrand.

Mattes, R., D. Taylor, D. McDonald, A. Poore and W. Richmond (1999), *Still Waiting for the Barbarians: SA Attitudes to Immigrants and Immigration*, Migration Policy Series no. 14, Southern African Migration Project, Cape Town and Kingston.

Matuschek, H. (1985), 'Ausländerpolitik in Österreich 1962–1985: Der Kampf um und gegen die ausländische Arbeitskraft', *Journal für Sozialforschung*, 2: 159–99.

Mauco, G. (1932), *Les étrangers en France: Leur rôle dans l'activité économique*, Paris: Armand Colin.

Maxim, P.S. (1992), 'Immigrants, Visible Minorities, and Self-employment', *Demography*, 29: 181–98.

Mbaya, L. (1999), 'The Presence of Senegalese Informal Traders in Johannesburg', unpublished paper, Department of Politics, University of the Witwatersrand.

McAll, C. (1990), *Class, Ethnicity, and Social Inequality*, Montreal and Kingston: McGill-Queen's University Press.

McDonald, D. (ed.) (2000), *On Borders: Perspectives on International Migration in Southern Africa*, Southern African Migration Project, New York: St. Martin's Press.

—, L. Zinyama, J. Gay, F. de Vletter and R. Mattes (1998), *Challenging Xenophobia: Myths and Realities about Cross-border Migration in Southern Africa*, Southern African Migration Project, Migration Policy Series no. 13, Cape Town and Kingston.

McEvoy, D. and T. Jones (1993), 'Relative Economic Welcomes: South Asian Retailing in Britain and Canada', in H. Rudolph and M. Morokvasic (eds), *Bridging States and Markets*, Berlin: Edition Sigma.

McGoldrick, C. and D.E. Reeve (1989), 'Black Business in Kirklees: A Survey of Afro-Caribbean and South Asian Businesses in the Kirklees Metropolitan District', report prepared for the Employment Development Unit, Kirklees Metropolitan Council, Huddersfield: Huddersfield Polytechnic.

McKay, J. and T. Batrouney (1988), 'Lebanese Immigration until the 1970s', in J. Jupp (ed.), *The Australian People: An Encyclopedia of the Nation, Its People and Their Origins*, Sydney: Angus & Robertson.

McNamara, D.J. (1997), 'Overview of Asian Immigration, 1982–95', in J.E. Coughlan and D.J. McNamara (eds), *Asians in Australia: Patterns of Migration and Settlement*, Melbourne: Macmillan.

Mehrländer, U., C. Ascheberg and J. Ueltzhöffer (1996), *Situation der ausländischen Arbeitnehmer und ihrer Familienangehörigen in der Bundesrepublik Deutschland*, Bonn: Bundesministerium für Arbeit.

Merens, A. (1996), 'De integratie van Italianen en Chinezen in Nederland in de twintigste eeuw: Een vergelijking', in M. 't Hart, J. Lucassen and H. Schmal (eds), *Nieuwe Nederlanders: Vestiging van migranten door de eeuwen Heen*. Amsterdam: Stichting Beheer IISG/SISWO.

Metcalf, H., T. Modood and S. Virdee (1996), *Asian Self-Employment: The Interaction of Culture and Economics in England*, London: Policy Studies Institute.

Meulen, A. van der, and W. Heilbron (1995), 'The Rise and Drives of Surinamese and Turkish Entrepreneurs of Both Sexes in an Amsterdam Neighbourhood: The Case of Mustafa', *Journal of Social Sciences*, 2: 63–78.

Miellet, R.L. (1987), 'Immigratie van katholieke Westfalers en de modernisering van de Nederlandse detailhandel', *Tijdschrift voor Geschiedenis*, 100: 374–93.

Miles, M. (1991), 'Missing Women: A Study of Swazi Female Migration to the Witwatersrand, 1920–1970', unpublished MA thesis, Queen's University, Kingston, Ontario, Canada.

Min, P.G. (1984a), 'From White-collar Occupations to Small Business: Korean Immigrants' Occupational Adjustment', *The Sociological Quarterly*, 25: 333–52.

— (1984b), 'A Structural Analysis of Korean Business in the United States', *Ethnic Groups*, 6: 1–25.

— (1987), 'Factors Contributing to Ethnic Business: A Comprehensive Synthesis', *International Journal of Comparative Sociology*, 23: 195–218.

— (1988), *Ethnic Business Enterprise: Korean Small Business in Atlanta*, Staten Island, NY: Center for Migration Studies.

— (1989), 'Some Positive Functions of Ethnic Business for an Immigrant Community: Koreans in Los Angeles', final report submitted to the National Science Foundation.

— (1990), 'Problems of Korean Immigrant Entrepreneurship', *International Migration Review*, 24: 436–55.

— (1996), *Caught in the Middle: Korean Communities in New York and Los Angeles*, Berkeley and Los Angeles: University of California Press.

— and M. Bozorgmehr (2000), 'Immigrant Entrepreneurship and Business Patterns: A Comparison of Koreans and Iranians in Los Angeles', *International Migration Review*, 34: 707–38.

— and A. Kolodny (1994), 'The Middleman Minority Characteristics of Korean Immigrants in the United States', *Korea Journal of Population and Development*, 23: 179–202.

Minaar, A. and M. Hough (1995), 'Causes, Extent and Impact of Clandestine Migration in Selected Southern African Countries with Specific Reference to South Africa', unpublished report Human Sciences Research Council, Pretoria.

Minaar, A. and M. Hough (1996), *Who Goes There? Perspectives on Clandestine Migration and Illegal Aliens in Southern Africa*, Pretoria: Human Sciences Research Council.

Minaar, A., S. Pretorius and M. Wentzel (1995), 'Who Goes There? Illegals in South Africa', *Indicator SA*, 3: 33–40.

Minghuan, L. (2000), *'We Need Two Worlds': Chinese Immigrant Associations in a Western Society*, Amsterdam: Amsterdam University Press.

Mingione, E. and M. Magatti (1994), 'The Informal Sector: Follow-up to the White Paper', unpublished paper.

Mingione, E. and F. Quassoli (1999), 'The Insertion of Immigrants in the Underground Economy in Italy', in R. King, G. Lazaridis and C. Tsardanidis (eds), *Eldorado or Fortress? Migration in Southern Europe*, London: Macmillan.

Mintel (2001), *CTN Retailing*, London: Mintel International Group Limited.

Modood, T., R. Berthoud, J. Lakey, J. Nazroo, P. Smith, S. Virdee and S. Beishon (1997), *Ethnic Minorities in Britain: Diversity and Disadvantage*, London: Policy Studies Institute.

Montagné-Villette, S. (1991), *Espaces et travail clandestins*, Paris: Masson.

Morokvasic, M. (1987), 'Immigrants in the Parisian Garnment Industry', *Work, Employment and society*, 4: 441–62.

— (1988), *Minority and Immigrant Women in Self-employment and Business in France, Great Britain, Italy, Portugal and the Federal Republic of Germany*, Paris: EEC.

— (1993), 'Immigrants in Garment Production in Paris and Berlin', in I. Light and P. Bhachu (eds), *Immigration and Entrepreneurship: Culture, Capital, and Ethnic Networks*, New Brunswick, NJ/London: Transaction.

—, R. Waldinger and A. Phizacklea (1990), 'Business and Ragged Edge: Immigrant and Minority Business in the Garment Industries of Paris, London, and New York', in R. Waldinger, H. Aldrich, R. Ward and Associates (eds), *Ethnic Entrepreneurs*, Newbury Park, CA: Sage.

Morris, A. (1998), '"Our Fellow Africans Make Our Lives Hell": The Lives of Congolese and Nigerians Living in Johannesburg', *Ethnic and Racial Studies*, 21: 116–36.

— (1999), *Bleakness and Light: Inner-city Transition in Hillbrow, Johannesburg*, Johannesburg: Wits University Press.

Mort Subite (1990), *Barsten in België: Een geografie van de Belgische maatschappij*, Berchem: EPO.

Mottura, G. and P. Pinto (1996), *Immigrazione e cambiamento sociale: Strategie sindacali e lavoro straniero in Italia*, Rome: EDS.

Moulier-Boutang, Y., J.-P. Garson and R. Silberman (1986), *Economie politique des migrations clandestines de main d'oeuvre*, Paris: Publisud.

Multiculturalism Canada (1986), *Highlights of Self-employment of Ethno-cultural Groups in Canada*, Ottawa: Multiculturalism Canada.

Mushonga, H. (2000), 'Local Government Intervention in the Informal Sector: A Case Study of the Yeoville Market', unpublished MA thesis, Rand Afrikaans University, Johannesburg.

Muus, Ph. (2000), *SOPEMI-Netherlands 2000. Migration, Immigrants and Policy in the Netherlands: Recent Trends and Developments*, Utrecht: ERCOMER.

N

Nascimbene, B. (1995), *Da Schengen a Maastricht: Apertura delle frontiere, cooperazione giudiziaria e polizia*, Milan: Giuffrè.

— (1997), *La condizione giuridica dello straniero: Diritto vigente e prospettive di riforma*, Padua: Cedam.

Nash, A.E. (1987), *The Economic Impact of the Entrepreneur Immigrant Program*, Studies in Social Policy, Discussion Paper no. 84B.1, Ottawa: Institute for Research on Public Policy.

— (1996), 'Ethnic Entrepreneurs: The Case of Canada's Business Immigrants', paper given at the American Association of Geographers Annual Meeting, Charlotte, North Carolina, March.

National Statistics (2000), 'Labour Market Spotlight', *Labour Market Trends*, 108: 253.

Nethengwe, N. (1999), 'Cross-border Dynamics in Southern Africa: A Study of Informal Cross-border Trade between South Africa and Zimbabwe', unpublished MA thesis, University of the Witwatersrand, Johannesburg.

Nienhuis, A., M. Brander and S. Alta (2001), *Effectiviteit van ondersteuning door STEW*, Den Haag: B&A Groep Beleidsonderzoek & -Advies.

NIS (National Institute for Statistics) (1999), *Bevolkingsstatistieken*, Brussels: NIS.

O

Oc, T. and S. Tiesdell (1998), 'Training and Business Support for Ethnic Minority Groups in City Challenge Areas', *Local Economy*, 13: 71–7.

Oc, T. and S. Tiesdell (1999), 'Supporting Ethnic Minority Business: A Review of Business Support for Ethnic Minorities in City Challenge Areas', *Urban Studies*, 36: 1723–46.

OECD (Organization for Economic Co-operation and Development) (1985), 'Employment in Small and Large Firms: Where Have the Jobs Come From?', *Employment Outlook*, Paris: OECD.

— (1992), *Employment Outlook 1992*, Paris: OECD.

— (1995), *Labour Force Statistics 1973–1993*, Paris: OECD.

— (1999), *Wirtschaftsberichte: Österreich*, Paris: OECD.

— (2000), *Fostering Entrepreneurship*, Paris: OECD.

Olds, K. (1996), *Developing the Trans-Pacific Property Market: Tales from Vancouver and Hong Kong*, Research on Immigration and Integration in the Metropolis (RIIM) Working Paper Series no. 96–02, Vancouver.

— and H. Yeung (1999), *(Re)shaping Chinese Business Networks in a Globalization Era*, Research on Immigration and Integration in the Metropolis (RIIM) Working Paper Series no. 99–12, Vancouver.

One Nation (1998), 'Pauline Hanson's One Nation Policy Document Immigration Population and Social Cohesion', http://www.gwb.com.au/onenation/policy/immig.html (27 August).

Onselen, C. van (1982), *Studies in the Social and Economic History of the Witwatersrand, 1886–1914*, 2 vols, Johannesburg: Ravan Press.

Ostrow, R. (1987), *The New Boy Network*, Richmond: William Heinemann Australia.

Oucho, J., E. Campbell and E. Mukamaambo (2000), *Botswana: Migration Perspectives and Prospects*, Southern African Migration Project, Migration Policy Series no. 19, Cape Town and Kingston.

Owen, D. (1996) 'Size, Structure and Growth of the Ethnic Minority Populations', in D. Coleman and J. Salt (eds), *Ethnicity in the 1991 Census. Volume One: Demographic Characteristics of the Ethnic Minority Populations*, London: HMSO.

— (1997), 'Labour Force Participation Rates, Self-employment and Unemployment', in V. Karn (ed.), *Ethnicity in the 1991 Census. Volume Four: Employment, Education and Housing among the Ethnic Minority Populations of Britain*, London: The Stationery Office.

P

Pairault, T. (1995), *L'intégration silencieuse: La petite entreprise chinoise en France*, Paris: L'Harmattan.

Palidda, S. (1992), 'Le développement des activités indépendantes des immigrés en Europe et en France', *Revue Européenne des Migrations Internationales*, 8: 83–96.

— (2001), *Devianza, criminalità e vittimizzazione dei migranti*, Milan ISMU/Franco Angeli.

— and E. Reyneri (1995), 'Immigrazione e mercato del lavoro', in A.M. Chiesi, I. Regalia and M. Regini (eds), *Lavoro e relazioni industriali in Europa*, Rome: La Nuova Italia Scientifica.

Palmer, M. (1957), *The History of Indians in Natal: Natal Regional Survey*, vol. 10, Cape Town: Oxford University Press.

Pang, C.L. (1993), *Tussen inpassing en identiteit: De Chinese gemeenschap in België*, Leuven: HIVA.

— (1994) 'Chinese migratiestromen naar België', *Bareel* 57: 31–4.

— (1998), 'Invisible Visibility. Intergenerational Transfer of Identity and Social Position: Chinese Women in Belgium', *Asian and Pacific Migration Journal*, 7: 433–52.

— (1999), 'To "Chinese" as a Verb: Interplay between Ethnic Food and Local Taste', paper given at the Workshop 'Chinese Immigrant Food: Identity and Change' of the 51st Annual Meeting of the AAS (Association of Asian Studies), Boston, March.

— (2000), 'Strategies of Diaspora Formations: The Case of the Chinese', paper given at the Summer School in Ceccina, Tuscany, July.

— (2003) 'Beyond Authenticity: Reinterpreting Chinese Immigrant Cuisine in Belgium', in T. Döring, M. Heide and S. Mühleisen (eds), *Eating Culture: The Politics and Poetics of Food*, Heidelberg, Winter.

Parker, D. (1995), *Through Different Eyes: The Cultural Identities of Young Chinese People in Britain*, Aldershot: Avebury.

Parliament of the Commonwealth of Australia (1991), *Business Migration Program*, Canberra: Australian Government Publishing Service.

Parnreiter, C. (1994), *Migration und Arbeitsteilung: AusländerInnenbeschäftigung in der Weltwirtschaftskrise*, Vienna: Manz.

Parsley, J. (1998), 'Free Markets, Free Women? Changing Constructions of Citizenship and Gender Relations among Cross-border Women Traders in Contemporary Southern Africa', unpublished MA thesis, University of the Witwatersrand, Johannesburg.

Pascoe, R. (1988), *Buongiorno Australia: Our Italian Heritage*, Melbourne: Greenhouse Publications and the Vaccari Italian Historical Trust.

— (1990), *Open for Business: Immigrant and Aboriginal Entrepreneurs Tell Their Story*, Canberra: Australian Government Publishing Service.

Pastore, M. (1995), *Produzione normativa e costruzione sociale della devianza e criminalità tra gli immigrati*, Quaderni ISMu no. 9, Milan: Franco Angeli.

Peberdy, S. (1997a), 'A History of South Africa's Immigration Legislation', unpublished briefing paper for the South African Government's Green Paper Task Group on International Migration, Cape Town, South Africa.

— (1997b), 'Street Traders and Cross Border Trade', unpublished briefing paper submitted to the South African Government's Green Paper Task Group on International Migration, Pretoria, South Africa.

— (1998), 'Obscuring History? Debating Regional Immigration Policy in South Africa', in D. Simon (ed.), *South Africa in Southern Africa: Reconfiguring the Region*, London and Cape Town: James Currey and D. Phillips, Ohio University Press.

— (1999a), 'Selecting Immigrants: Nationalism and National Identity in South Africa's Immigration Policies, 1910–1998', unpublished PhD thesis, Queen's University, Kingston, Ontario, Canada.

— (1999b), 'Shopping and Street Trading: Informal Sector Cross-border Trade between South Africa and Mozambique', unpublished paper for the Southern African Migration Project, Cape Town.

— (2000a), 'Mobile Entrepreneurship: Informal Cross-border Trade and Street Trade in South Africa', *Development Southern Africa*, 17: 201–19.

— (2000b), 'Border Crossings: Small Entrepreneurs and Informal Sector Cross-border Trade between South Africa and Mozambique', *Tijdschrift voor Economische en Sociale Geographie*, 91: 361–78.

— (2001), 'Exclusive Immigration Policies and Inclusive Identities in Post-1994 South Africa', *Africa Today*, 48(3), Fall: 15–34.

— and J. Crush (1998a), 'Rooted in Racism: The Origins of the Aliens Control Act', in J. Crush (ed.), *Beyond Control: Immigration and Human Rights in a Democratic South Africa*, Cape Town and Kingston: Idasa and Queen's University.

— and J. Crush (1998b), 'Trading Places: Cross-border Traders and the South African Informal Sector', Migration Series no. 6, South African Migration Project, Cape Town and Kingston.

— and J. Crush (2001), 'Invisible Trade, Invisible Travellers: The Maputo Corridor Spatial Development Initiative and Informal Cross-border Trading', *South African Geographical Journal*, 83(2): 115–23.

— and Z. Majodina (2000), '"Just a Roof over My Head?" Housing and the Somali Refugee Community in Johannesburg', *Urban Forum*, 11: 273–88.

— and C.M. Rogerson (2000), 'Transnationalism and Non-South African Entrepreneurs in South Africa's Small, Medium and Micro-enterprise (SMME) Economy', *Canadian Journal of African Studies*, 34: 20–40.

—, B. Cavel, J. Caetano and Z. Ombe (2000a), 'The Maputo Corridor Spatial Development Initiative and Informal Sector Cross-border Trade between Mozambique and South Africa', report submitted to the Canadian

International Development Research Centre.

—, S. Sakhau, B. Makovere and S. Elsey (2000b), 'Women from Botswana, Swaziland and Zimbabwe and Informal Sector Cross-border Trade in Southern Africa', report for the Canadian International Development Research Centre.

Peeters, L., E. de Bruyn and K. Demirçi (1996), 'New Perspectives, New Horizons', interim report of the project 'Horizon', ESF, Genk: Stebo (Steunpunt Buurtopbouwwerk, Limburg).

Peeters, R. and M. de Muynck (1997), 'De zorg voor allochtonen: De aandacht voor Marokkanen en Turken in de Vlaamse gezondheidszorg', in M.C. Foblets, B. Hubeau and A. de Muynck (eds), *Migrantenonderzoek voor de toekomst*, Leuven and Amersfoort: Acco.

Penninx, R. (1979), 'Naar een algemeen etnisch minderhedenbeleid', in WRR, *Etnische minderheden*, Rapporten aan de Regering no. 17, The Hague: SDU.

— (1988), *Minderheidsvorming en emancipatie: Balans van kennisverwerving ten aanzien van immigranten en woonwagenbewoners 1967–87*, Alphen aan den Rijn: Samsom.

Pe-Pua, R., C. Mitchell, R. Iredale and S. Castles (1996), *Astronaut Families and Parachute Children: Hong Kong Immigrants in Australia*, Canberra: Bureau of Immigration, Multicultural and Population Research, Australian Government Publishing Service.

Péraldi, M. (1999), 'Marseille: Réseaux migrants transfrontaliers, place marchande et économie de bazar', *Cultures et conflits*, 33–4.

Perrone, L. (1991), 'Immigrati nel Salento: Costumi stili di vita e adattamento nel mercato del lavoro', *Politiche del Lavoro*, 12–13: 38–64.

Peters, N.I. (1999), *Trading Places: Greek, Italian, Dutch, and Vietnamese Enterprise in Western Australia*, Perth: University of Western Australia.

Piard, M.F., J.J.L. van Dijk and S. Dermijn (1988), *Etnisch ondernemerschap in Gelderland Deel 1: Inventarisatie van kerncijfers*, Rapportreeks Osmose no. 5, Arnhem: Stichting Osmose.

Pichler, E. (1997), *Migration, Community-Formierung und Ethnische Ökonomie: Die italienischen Gewerbetreibenden in Berlin*, Berlin: Edition Parabolis.

Pieke, F. (1987), 'De restaurants', in G. Benton and H. Vermeulen (eds), *De Chinezen*, Migranten in de Nederlandse Samenleving no. 4, Muiderberg: Coutinho.

Piore, M. (1983), *Birds of Passage*, Cambridge: Cambridge University Press.

— and C. Sabel (1984), *The Second Industrial Divide: Possibilities for Prosperity*, New York: Basic.

Poinard, M. (1992), 'L'insaisissable objet d'une "recherché à problèmes"', *Migrants-Formation*, 90: 6–20.

Pollard, J., J. Bryson, N. Henry and C. McEwan (2000), 'Globalisation from

Below: Birmingham – Postcolonial Workshop of the World', paper given at the Annual Meeting of the Association of American Geographers, Pittsburgh, April.

Pool, C. (2003), *Dossier Y-markt: Relaas van een mislukt Amsterdams prestige-proiect*, Amsterdam: IMES.

Porter, J. (1965), *The Vertical Mosaic: An Analysis of Social Class and Power in Canada*, Toronto: University of Toronto Press.

Portes, A. (1987), 'The Social Origins of the Cuban Enclave Economy in Miami', *Sociological Perspectives*, 30: 340–72.

— (ed.) (1995), *The Economic Sociology of Immigration: Essays on Networks, Ethnicity, and Entrepreneurship*, New York: Russell Sage Foundation.

— and R. Bach (1985), *Latin Journey: Cuban and Mexican Immigrants in the United States*, Berkeley and Los Angeles: University of California Press.

— and R.G. Rumbaut (1990), *Immigrant America: A Portrait*, Los Angeles: University of California Press.

Power, D. (2001), 'Power: The Spatial and the Economy', *Review of International Political Economy*, 8: 548–56.

Price, C. (1963), *Southern Europeans in Australia*, Canberra: Australian National University Press.

— (1974), *The Great White Walls Are Built: Restrictive Immigration to North America and Australasia 1836–1888*, Canberra: Australian National University Press.

Putnam, R.D. (1998), 'Foreword', *Housing Policy Debate*, 1: v-viii.

— (2000), *Bowling Alone: The Collapse and Revival of American Community*, New York: Simon & Schuster.

Putten, M. van, and N. Lucas (1985), *Made in Heaven: Vrouwen en de veranderende internationale arbeidsverdeling*, Amsterdam: Evert Vermeer Stichting.

Q

Quassoli, F. (1999), 'Migrants in the Italian Underground Economy', *International Journal of Urban and Regional Research*, 23: 212–31.

— and C. Venzo (1997), *La formazione linguistica per lavoratori stranieri: Dare voce ai diritti e alle risorse*, Milan: Franco Angeli.

R

Raes, S. (1996), 'De Nederlandse kledingindustrie en het mediterrane gebied: Migrerende bedrijven en migrantenondernemers', *Sharqiyyât*, 8: 143–65.

— (2000a), *Migrating Enterprise and Migrant Entrepreneurship: How Fashion and Migration have Changed the Spatial Organisation of Clothing Supply to Consumers in The Netherlands*, Amsterdam: Het Spinhuis.

— (2000b), 'Regionalization in a Globalizing World: The Emergence of Clothing Sweatshops in the European Union', in J. Rath (ed.), *Immigrant Businesses: The Economic, Political and Social Environment*, Basingstoke/ New York: Macmillan/St Martin's.

—, J. Rath, M. Dreef, A. Kumcu, F. Reil and A. Zorlu (2002), 'Amsterdam: Stitched up', in J. Rath (ed.), *Unravelling the Rag Trade: Immigrant Entrepreneurship in Seven World Cities*, Oxford: Berg.

Rager, J.J. (1950), *Les Musulmans algériens en France et dans les pays islamiques*, Paris: Belles Lettres.

Ram, M. (1992), 'Coping with Racism: Asian Employment in the Inner City, *Work, Employment and Society*, 6: 601–18.

— (1994), *Managing to Survive: Working Lives in Small Firms*, Oxford: Blackwell.

— (1996), *African-Caribbean Enterprise and Business Support: Views from Providers*, Birmingham: Small Business Research Centre, University of Central England.

— (ed.) (2002), 'Ethnic Minority Enterprise: Policy in Practice' in M. Ram and D. Smallbone (eds), special issue, *Entrepreneurship and Regional Development*, 15(2), April–June.

— and G. Hillin (1994), 'Achieving "Break-out": Developing Mainstream Ethnic Minority Business', *Small Business Enterprise and Development*, 1: 15–21.

— and T. Jones (1998), *Ethnic Minorities in Business*, Milton Keynes: Small Business Research Trust.

—, T. Abbas, B. Sanghere, G. Barlow and T. Jones (2001), '"Apprentice Entrepreneurs"? Ethnic Minority Workers in the Independent Restaurant Sector', *Work, Employment and Society*, 15: 353–72.

—, T. Jones, T. Abbas and B. Sanghere (2002), 'Ethnic Minority Enterprise in its Urban Context: South Asian Restaurants in Birmingham', *International Journal of Urban and Regional Research*, 26(1): 24–40.

—, T. Jones, D. Deakins and D. Smallbone (in preparation), 'Funding the Ethnic Minority Firm'.

Ramakers, J. (1996), *Bakens of valkuilen: Migranten in onderzoeksperspectief*, Leuven: HIVA.

— (1997), 'The Challenges of Refugee Protection in Belgium', in Ph. Muus (ed.), *Exclusion and Inclusion of Refugees in Contemporary Europe*, Utrecht: ERCOMER.

Rath, J. (1991), *Minorisering: De sociale constructie van 'etnische minder-heden'*, Amsterdam: SUA.

— (1993), 'La construction sociale des minorités ethniques aux Pays-Bas et ses effets pervers', in M. Martiniello and M. Poncelet (eds), *Migrations et*

Bibliography

minorités ethniques dans l'espace européen, Brussels: De Boeck.

— (1995), 'Beunhazen van buiten: De informele economie als bastaardsfeer van sociale integratie', in G. Engbersen and R. Gabriëls (eds), *Sferen van integratie: Naar een gedifferentieerd allochtonenbeleid*, Meppel/Amsterdam: Boom.

— (1997), 'Ein ethnisches Bäumchen-wechsel-dich-Spiel in Mokum? Immigranten und ihre nachkomen in der Amsterdamer Wirtschaft', in J. Brech and L. Vanhué (eds), *Migration: Stadt im Wandel*, Darmstadt: Verlag für Wissenschaftliche Publikations/Wohnbund Publikationen.

— (1998), 'Een etnische stoelendans in Mokum: Over de economische incorporatie van immigranten en hun nakomelingen in Amsterdam', in A. Gevers (ed.), *Uit de Zevende: 50 jaar Sociaal-Culturele Wetenschappen aan de Universiteit van Amsterdam*, Amsterdam: Het Spinhuis.

— (1999a), 'The Informal Economy as Bastard Sphere of Social Integration', in E. Eichenhofer (ed.), *Migration und Illegalität*, IMIS-Schriften no. 7, Osnabrück: Universitätsverlag Rasch.

— (1999b), 'The Netherlands: A Dutch Treat for Anti-social Families and Immigrant Ethnic Minorities', in M. Cole and G. Dale (eds), *The European Union and Migrant Labour*, Oxford: Berg.

— (2000a), 'A Game of Ethnic Musical Chairs? Immigrant Businesses and Niches in the Amsterdam Economy', in S. Body-Gendrot and M. Martiniello (eds), *Minorities in European Cities: The Dynamics of Social Integration and Social Exclusion at the Neighbourhood Level*, Basingstoke: Macmillan.

— (2000b), 'Immigrant Businesses and Their Embeddedness in the Economic, Politico-institutional and Social Environment', in J. Rath (ed.), *Immigrant Businesses: The Economic, Political and Social Environment*, Basingstoke/New York: Macmillan/St Martin's.

— (ed.) (2000c), *Immigrant Businesses: The Economic, Political and Social Environment*, Basingstoke/New York: Macmillan/St Martin's.

— (2001), 'Eigen bouwvakkers eerst: Over de uitzonderlijke situatie dat in Nederland zo weinig immigranten werkzaam zijn in de bouwnijverheid', in F. Lindo and M. van Niekerk (eds), *Dedication and Detachment: Essays in Honour of Hans Vermeulen*, Amsterdam: Het Spinhuis.

— (2002a) 'Needle Games: A Discussion of Mixed Embeddedness', in J. Rath (ed.), *Unravelling the Rag Trade: Immigrant Entrepreneurship in Seven World Cities*, Oxford: Berg.

— (2002b) 'Sewing up Seven Cities', in J. Rath (ed.), *Unravelling the Rag Trade: Immigrant Entrepreneurship in Seven World Cities*, Oxford: Berg.

— (ed.) (2002c), *Unravelling the Rag Trade: Immigrant Entrepreneurship in Seven World Cities*, Oxford: Berg.

— (2002d), 'Immigrants and the Tourist Industry: The Commodification of

Cultural Resources', paper prepared for the Research Committee Sociology of Migration RC31 Sessions 10 and 11 on 'Immigrant and Ethnic Entrepreneurship' in the XVth World Congress of Sociology, 7–13 July 2002, Brisbane.

— (2002e), 'Do Immigrant Entrepreneurs Play the Game of Ethnic Musical Chairs? A Critique of Waldinger's Model of Immigrant Incorporation', in A. Messina (ed.), *West European Immigration and Immigrant Policy in the New Century*, Westport, CT: Praeger.

— (2002f), 'A Quintessential Immigrant Niche? The Non-case of Immigrants in the Dutch Construction Industry', *Entrepreneurship & Regional Development*, 14: 355–72.

— and R. Kloosterman (1998a), 'Bazen van buiten: Naar een nieuwe benadering van het zelfstandig ondernemerschap van immigranten', in J. Rath and R. Kloosterman (eds), *Rijp & Groen: Het zelfstandig ondernemerschap van immigranten in Nederland*, Amsterdam: Het Spinhuis.

— and R. Kloosterman (1998b), 'Economische incorporatie en ondernemerschap van immigranten', in R. Penninx, H. Münstermann and H. Entzinger (eds), *Etnische minderheden en de multiculturele samenleving*, Groningen: Wolters Noordhoff.

— and R. Kloosterman (eds) (1998c), *Rijp & Groen: Het zelfstandig ondernemerschap van immigranten in Nederland*, Amsterdam: Het Spinhuis.

— and R. Kloosterman (1998d), 'Een zaak van buitenstaanders: Het onderzoek naar immigrantenondernemerschap', in K. Geuijen (ed.), *Multiculturalisme*, Utrecht: Lemma.

— and R. Kloosterman (1999), 'The Netherlands', paper given at the First Conference of the Thematic Network 'Working on the Fringes: Immigrant Businesses, Economic Integration and Informal Practices', Amsterdam, October.

— and R. Kloosterman (2000), 'Outsiders' Business: A Critical Review of Research on Immigrant Entrepreneurship', *International Migration Review*, 34: 657–81.

Raulin, A. (1986), 'Mise en scène des commerçants maghrébins parisiens', *Terrain*, 7: 24–33.

— (1988), 'Espaces marchands et concentrations urbaines minoritaires', *Cahiers Internationaux de Sociologie*, LXXXV: 225–42.

Ray, J. (1937), *Les Marocains en France*, Paris: Edition Sirey.

Razin, E. and A. Langlois (1996), 'Metropolitan Characteristics and Entrepreneurship among Immigrants and Ethnic Groups in Canada', *International Migration Review*, 30: 703–27.

Razin, E. and I. Light (1998), 'Ethnic Entrepreneurs in America's Largest Metropolitan Areas', *Urban Affairs Review*, 33: 332–60.

Rechberger, H. (1992), 'Die arbeitsrechtliche Stellung der Zeitungskolporteure', MA thesis, University of Salzburg.

Rees, S., G. Rodley and F. Stilwell (eds) (1993), *Beyond the Market: Alternatives to Economic Rationalism*, Leichhardt: Pluto.

Reil, F. and T. Korver (2001), *En meestal zijn het Turken: Arbeid in de Amsterdamse loonconfectie-industrie*, Amsterdam: Het Spinhuis.

Reitz, J.G. (1980), *The Survival of Ethnic Groups in Canada*, Toronto: McGraw-Hill Ryerson.

— (1990), 'Ethnic Concentrations in Labour Markets and Their Implications for Ethnic Inequality', in R. Breton, W.W.Isajiw, W.E. Kalbach and J. Reitz (eds), *Ethnic Identity and Equality: Varieties of Experiences in a Canadian City*, Toronto: University of Toronto Press.

Reitzes, M. (1995a), *Insiders and Outsiders: The Reconstruction of Citizenship in South Africa*, Policy: Issues and Actors Monography no. 8 (1), Centre for Policy Studies, Johannesburg.

— (1995b), *Divided on the 'Demon': Immigration Policy Since the Election*, Policy: Issues and Actors Monography no. 8 (9), Centre for Policy Studies, Johannesburg.

— (1996), *Mindsets and Migrants: Conceptions of State, Sovereignty, Citizenship and Human Rights in South Africa*, Policy: Issues and Actors Monography no. 9 (4), Centre for Policy Studies, Johannesburg.

—, Z. Tamela and P. Thulare (1997), *Strangers Truer than Fiction: The Social and Economic Impact of Migrants on the Johannesburg Inner City*, Research Report no. 60, Centre for Policy Studies, Johannesburg.

Rekers, A.M. (1993), 'A Tale of Two Cities: A Comparison of Turkish Enterprises in Amsterdam and Rotterdam', in D. Crommentuyn-Ondaatje (ed.), *Nethur School Proceedings 1992*, Utrecht: Nethur.

Revesz, J. and R. Lattimore (1997), *Small Business Employment*, Canberra: Industry Commission Staff Research Paper, Industry Commission.

Reyneri, E. (1998a), 'The Role of the Underground Economy in Irregular Migration to Italy: Cause or Effect?', *Journal of Ethnic and Migration Studies*, 24: 313–31.

— (1998b), 'Addressing the Employment of Migrants in an Irregular Situation', paper given at the Technical Symposium on International Migration and Development, organized by the United Nation ACC Task Force.

— (2000), 'L'integrazione nel mercato del lavoro', in G. Zincone (Ed.), *Secondo rapporto sull'integrazione in Italia*, Bologna: il Mulino.

— and M. Baganha (1998), 'New Migrants in South European Countries and Their Insertion in the Underground Economy', in E. Reyneri (ed.), 'Migrants' Insertion in the Informal Economy, Deviant Behaviour and the Impact on Receiving Societies', final report for the CE/DGXII, TSER program.

Rifkin, J. (2000), *The Age of Access: The New Culture of Hypercapitalism, Where All of Life Is Paid-for Experience*, Los Angeles: Torcher Los Angeles.

Rijkschroeff, B. (1998), *Etnisch ondernemerschap: De Chinese horecasector in Nederland en de Verenigde Staten van Amerika*, Capelle a/d IJssel: Labyrinth.

Rimmer, S.J. (1991), *The Costs of Multiculturalism*, Bedford Park: Flinders Press.

Rinder, I. (1959), 'Strangers in the Land: Social Relations in the Status Gap', *Social Problems*, 6: 253–60.

Rogerson, C. (1986), 'Third World Multinationals and South Africa's Decentralization Programme', *South African Geographical Journal*, 68: 132–43.

— (1996), 'Urban Poverty and the Informal Economy in South Africa's Economic Heartland', *Environment and Urbanisation*, 8: 167–81.

— (1997), *International Migration, Immigrant Entrepreneurs and South Africa's Small Enterprise Economy*, Migration Policy Series no. 3, Southern African Migration Project, Cape Town and Kingston.

— (1998), '"Formidable Entrepreneurs": The Role of Foreigners in the Gauteng SMME Economy', *Urban Forum*, 9: 143–53.

— (1999a), *Building Skills: Cross-border Migrants and the South African Construction Industry*, Migration Policy Series no. 11, Southern African Migration Project, Cape Town and Kingston.

— (1999b), 'New Enterprises for Johannesburg Inner-city: The Role of African Immigrant Entrepreneurs', unpublished report for the Johannesburg Inner-City Task Team, Johannesburg.

— (1999c), 'Johannesburg's Clothing Industry: The Role of African Migrant Entrepreneurs', unpublished report for BEES Consulting Group, Johannesburg.

— (2000a), 'SMME Infrastructure and Policy in South Africa', in M. Khosa (ed.), *Infrastructure Mandate for Change 1994–1999*, Pretoria: Human Sciences Research Council.

— (2000b), 'Emerging from Apartheid's Shadow: South Africa's Informal Economy', *Journal of International Affairs*, 53: 673–95.

— and J. Rogerson (1997), 'The Changing Post-apartheid City: Emergent Black-owned Small Enterprises in Johannesburg', *Urban Studies*, 34: 85–103.

— and J. Rogerson (1999), 'Industrial Change in a Developing Metropolis: The Witwatersrand 1980–1984', *Geoforum*, 30: 85–9.

Rogerson, J. (1995), 'The Changing Face of Retailing in the South African City: The Case of Inner-city Johannesburg', *Africa Insight*, 25: 163–71.

Roofey, B., A. Stranger, D. Forsaith, E. McInnes, E. Petrone, C. Symes and M. Xydias (1996), *Women in Small Business: A Review of Research*, Canberra: Department of Industry Science and Tourism, Australian Government Publishing Service.

Roosens, E. (1989), *Creating Ethnicity: The Process of Ethnogenesis*, Newbury Park, London, New Delhi: Sage.

— (1998) *Eigen grond eerst? Primordiale autochtonie: Dilemma van de multiculturele samenleving*, Leuven and Amersfoort: Acco.

Rosvelds, S., Y. Ben Abdeljelil, A. Martens and P. Arryn (1993), *Zelfde zweet, ander brood: Onderzoek naar de arbeidsmarktpositie van Belgen en migranten op twee lokale arbeidsmarkten, Antwerpen en Gent*, Brussels: Dienst voor Programmatie van het Wetenschapsbeleid.

RSA (Republic of South Africa) (1998), 'Population Census, 1996: The People of South Africa. Census in Brief', report no. 03–01–11 (1996), Pretoria: Government Printer.

RSVZ (Rijksdienst voor de Sociale Verzekeringen der Zelfstandigen) (1996), *Statistieken van de personen van vreemde nationaliteit van het sociaal statuut van de zelfstandigen*, Brussels: RSVZ.

Rubenstein, W. (1988), 'Jewish Contribution to Australian Elites', in J. Jupp (ed.), *The Australian People: An Encyclopedia of the Nation, Its People and Their Origins*, Sydney: Angus & Robertson.

Rudolph, H. and F. Hillmann (1997), 'Döner contra Boulette: Berliner türkischer Herkunft als Arbeitskräfte und Unternehmer im Nahrungsgütersektor', in H. Häußermann and I. Oswald (eds), *Zuwanderung und Stadtentwicklung*, Sonderheft Leviathan no. 17: 85–105.

Rumbaut, R. (1995), 'Origins and Destinies: Immigration, Race, and Ethnicity in Contemporary America', in S. Pedraza and R. Rumbaut (eds), *Origins and Destinies: Immigration, Race, and Ethnicity in America*, Belmont, CA: Wadsworth.

Rutland, S.D. (1988), 'Early Jewish Settlement 1988–1880', in J. Jupp (ed.), *The Australian People: An Encyclopedia of the Nation, Its People and Their Origins*, Sydney: Angus & Robertson.

S

Salem, G. (1981), 'De Dakar à Paris. Des diasporas d'artisans et de commerçants: Etude socio-géographique du commerce sénégalais en France', MA thesis, EHESS, Paris.

Sanders, J. and V. Nee (1996), 'Immigrant Self-employment: The Family as Social Capital and the Value as Human Capital', *American Sociological Review*, 61: 231–49.

Saron, G. and L. Hotz (eds) (1955), *The Jews in South Africa*, Cape Town: Oxford University Press.

Sassen, S. (1991), *The Global City: New York, London, Tokyo*, Princeton: Princeton University Press.

— (2001[1991]), *The Global City: New York, London, Tokyo*, 2nd edn,

Princeton/London: Princeton University Press.

Saunders, P. (1994), *Welfare and Inequality*, Cambridge: Cambridge University Press.

— and A. King (1994), *Immigration and the Distribution of Income, Bureau of Immigration and Population Research*, Canberra: Australian Government Publishing Service.

Saxenian, A. (1999), *Silicon Valley's New Immigrant Entrepreneurs*, San Francisco: Public Policy Institute of California.

Scarman, Lord (1986), *The Brixton Disorders 10–12th April 1981*, London: HMSO.

Schama, S. (1991), *The Embarrassment of Riches: An Interpretation of Dutch Culture in the Golden Age*, London: Fontana Press.

Schmidt, D. (ed.) (2000), 'Ethnisierung und Ökonomie', special issue *Prokla, Zeitschrift für kritische Sozialwissenschaft*, 3.

Schor, R. (1985), *L'opinion française et les étrangers, 1919–1939*, Paris: Publications de la Sorbonne.

Schrover, M. (1996), 'Omlopers in Keulse potten en pottentrienen uit het Westerwald', in M. 't Hart, J. Lucassen and H. Schmal (eds), *Nieuwe Nederlanders: Vestiging van migranten door de eeuwen heen*, Amsterdam: Stichting Beheer IISG/SISWO.

— (1998), 'Gescheiden werelden in een stad: Westfaals ondernemerschap in Utrecht in de negentiende eeuw', in J. Rath and R. Kloosterman (eds), *Rijp & Groen: Het zelfstandig ondernemerschap van immigranten in Nederland*, Amsterdam: Het Spinhuis.

— (2001), 'Immigrant Business and Niche Formation in Historical Perspective: The Netherlands in the Nineteenth Century', *Journal of Ethnic and Migration Studies*, 27: 295–312.

Schuleri, U.K. (1982), *Ausübung eines Gewerbes oder Handwerks durch Ausländer*, Berlin: Verwaltungsakademie (Mimeo).

Schuman, J. (1999), 'The Ethnic Minority Populations of Great Britain: Latest Estimates', *Population Trends*, 96: 33–43.

Schumpeter, J. (1974), *Capitalism, Socialism and Democracy*, 4th edn, London: Unwin.

Scidà, G. and G. Pollini (1993), *Stranieri in città*, Milan: Franco Angeli.

Sciortino, G. (2000), *L'ambizione della frontiera*, Milan: Franco Angeli.

Scott, A. (1998), *Regions and the World Economy: The Coming Shape of Global Production, Competition, and Political Order*, Oxford: Oxford University Press.

Seidel-Pielen, E. (1996), *Aufgespießt: Wie der Döner über die Deutschen kam*, Hamburg: Rotbuch-Verlag.

Sengenberger, W., G.W. Loveman and M.J. Piore (eds) (1990), *The Re-emer-*

gence of Small Enterprises: Industrial Restructuring in Industrialised Countries, Geneva: International Institute for Labour Studies.

Sengstock, M. (1982), *Chaldean-Americans: Changing Conceptions of Ethnic Identity*, Staten Island, NY: Center for Migration Studies.

SER (Sociaal-Economische Raad) (1998), *Etnisch ondernemerschap: Advies 98/14*, Den Haag: SER.

Setzpfand, R.H., W.M.C. Engels and P.F.A.M. Linssen (1993), *Inventarisatie van allochtone ondernemers in Nederland*, Utrecht: Coopers & Lybrand.

Sheth, M. (1995), 'Indian Americans', in P.G. Min (ed.), *Asian Americans: Contemporary Trends and Issues*, Thousand Oaks, CA: Sage.

Shibutani, T. and K. Kwan (1965), *Ethnic Stratification: A Comparative Approach*, New York: Macmillan.

Simon, G. (1976), 'Une approche du petit commerce en France: l'Exemple des commerçants tunisiens', *Recherches sur les Migrations, ERMI-CNRS*, 1: 21–31.

— (1993), 'Immigrant entrepreneurs in France', in I. Light and P. Bhachu (eds), *Immigration and Entrepreneurship*, New Brunswick, NJ: Transaction.

Simone, A.M. (1997), 'Urban Development in South Africa: Some Critical Issues from Johannesburg', in R. Burgess, M. Carmona and T. Kolstee (eds), *The Challenge of Sustainable Cities: Neoliberalism and Urban Strategies in Developing Countries*, London and New Jersey: Zed.

— (1998a), 'Between Ghetto and Globe: Remarks on Urban Life in Africa', unpublished paper given at the 'Associational Life in African Cities: Urban Governance in an Era of Change Conference' organized by the Nordic Africa Institute and the Chr. Michelsen Institute, Bergen, Norway, August.

— (1998b), *Changing Cities: Challenges to Urban Governance in an Era of Globalization*, Occasional Paper no. 1, Graduate School of Public and Development Management, University of the Witwatersrand.

Sloan, J. and S. Kennedy (1992), *Temporary Movements of People To And From Australia*, Canberra: AGPS.

Sly, F., T. Thair and A. Risdon (1998), 'Labour Market Participation of Ethnic Groups', *Labour Market Trends*, 106: 601–15.

Sly, F., T. Thair and A. Risdon (1999), 'Trends in the Labour Market Participation of Ethnic Groups', *Labour Market Trends*, 107: 631–9.

Small Business Deregulation Task Force (1996), 'Time for Business', report of the Small Business Deregulation Task Force, Canberra: Australian Government Publishing Service.

Smit, M. (1994), *Illegale confectie-ateliers in Nederland en België: Een actualisering*, Amsterdam: SOMO.

— and L. Jongejans (1989), *C&A, de stille gigant: Van kledingmultinational tot thuiswerkster*, 2nd rev. edn, Amsterdam: SOMO.

SMO (Stichting Maatschappij en Onderneming) (1972), *Gastarbeid in Nederland*, The Hague: SMO.

Solomon, H. (1996a), 'Who is an Illegal Immigrant?', *African Security Review*, 6: 43–7.

— (1996b), 'Strategic Perspectives on Illegal Immigration into South Africa', *African Security Review*, 4: 9–10.

Song, M. (1997a), '"You're Becoming More and More English": Investigating Chinese Siblings' Cultural Identities', *New Community*, 23: 343–62.

— (1997b), 'Children's Labour in Ethnic Family Businesses: The Case of Chinese Take-away Businesses in Britain', *Ethnic and Racial Studies*, 20: 690–716.

— (1999), *Helping Out: Children's Labor in Ethnic Businesses*, Philadelphia, PA: Temple University Press.

Soni, S., M. Tricker and R. Ward (1987), *Ethnic Minority Business in Leicester*, Birmingham: Aston University.

SOPEMI (1998), *Trends in International Migration: Annual Report 1998*, Paris: OECD.

Sorkin, M. (1994), *Variations on a Theme Park: The New American City and the End of Public Space*, New York: Hill and Wang.

Soysal, Y. (1994), *Limits of Citizenship: Migrants and Postnational Membership in Europe*, Chicago/London: University of Chicago Press.

Spanoudes, R.N. (1982), 'The Shop down the Road: A Preliminary Study of Greek Cafes in South Africa', unpublished BA Hons. thesis, University of the Witwatersrand.

Srinivasan, S. (1995), *The South Asian Petty Bourgeoisie in Britain*, Aldershot: Avebury.

Statistics Canada (1997), *Labour Force Update: The Self-employed*, Ottawa: Statistics Canada.

Statistisches Bundesamt (s.y.), 'Excerpts from the Micro-census', Bonn: Statistisches Bundesamt.

Stavrinoudi, A. (1991), *Das ethnische Kleingewerbe in Berlin am Beispiel der griechischen Gastronomie*, Berlin: Edition Parabolis.

— (1992), *Struktur und Entwicklung des Gastgewerbes und Lebensmittel-handels in der Bundesrepublik Deutschland*, Berlin: Edition Parabolis.

Steenkamp, F. (2000), *Winst is de broer van verlies: Kwalitatief onderzoek naar de invloed van contacten op de economische en sociale positie van Turkse en Nederlandse ondernemers in Nijmegen*, Arnhem: Stichting Osmose.

Steinberg, S. (1981), *The Ethnic Myth*, Boston, MA: Beacon.

Stichting Opstand (1993), *De zwarte draad*, Amsterdam: Stichting Opstand.

Stone, J. (1973), *Colonist or Uitlander? A study of the British Immigrant in South Africa*, Oxford: Clarendon.

Stoop, R. and K. Neels (1998), 'Social Mobility and Equal Opportunities: The Case of Turkish and Moroccan Minorities in Belgium', *IPD Working Papers*, 3: 1–19.

Storey, D. (1994), *Understanding the Small Business Sector*, London: Routledge.

Storper, M. (1997), *The Regional World: Territorial Development in a Global Economy*, New York/London: Guildford.

Strahan, K. and K. Luscombe (1991), *Immigrant Access to Small Business Support Services*, Wollongong: Centre for Multicultural Studies, University of Wollongong, Australia.

Strahan, K. and A. Williams (1988), *Immigrant Entrepreneurs in Australia*, Wollongong: Centre for Multicultural Studies, University of Wollongong, Australia.

Stromback, T. and R. Malhotra (1994), *Socioeconomic Linkages of South Asian Immigrants with Their Country of Origin*, Canberra: BIPR/Australian Government Publishing Service.

Sungkekang, M. (1998), 'Cameroon as a Case Study in International Migration', unpublished paper, Department of Geography and Environmental Studies, University of the Witwatersrand, Johannesburg.

Suyver, J.F. and J.A. Lie A Kwie (1998a), *Allochtoon ondernemerschap in de detailhandel: Inventarisatie en mogelijkheden tot positieverbetering*, Zoetermeer: EIM/Handel en Distributie.

Suyver, J.F. and J.A. Lie A Kwie (1998b), *Professioneler ondernemen door allochtonen*, Zoetermeer: Hoofd Bedrijfschap Detailhandel, EIM.

Swinkels, K. (1991), *Beleid ten aanzien van allochtone bakkers*, The Hague: Nederlandse Bakkersorganisatie.

Swyngedouw, E. (1998), *De wederopstanding van de feniks: De regie van de steden*, Rotterdam: NAI.

T

Tálos, E. (1997), 'Sozialpartnerschaft: Kooperation, Konzertierung, politische Regulierung', in H. Dachs, P. Gerlich, H. Gottweis, F. Horner, H. Kramer, V. Lauber, W. Müller and E. Tálos (eds), *Handbuch des politischen Systems Österreichs: Die zweite Republik*, 3rd edn, Vienna: Manz.

—, K. Leichsenring and E. Zeiner (1993), 'Verbände und politischer Entscheidungsprozess: Am Beispiel der Sozial- und Umweltpolitik', in E. Tálos (ed.), *Sozialpartnerschaft: Kontinuität und Wandel eines Modells*, Vienna: Verlag für Gesellschaftskritik.

Tap, L.J. (1983), 'Het Turkse bedrijfsleven in Amsterdam', MA thesis, University of Groningen.

Tarrius, A. (1995), 'Naissance d'une colonie: Un comptoir commercial à Marseille', *Revue Européenne des Migrations Internationales*, 11: 21–52.

— and L. Missaoui (1995), *Arabes de France dans l'économie mondiale souterraine*, Paris: Ed. de l'Aube.

Taylor, J. (1992), *Occupational Segregation: A Comparison between Employed Aborigines, Torres Strait Islanders and Other Australians*, Centre for Aboriginal Economic Policy Research, Discussion Paper no. 33.

Teixeira, C. (1998), 'Cultural Resources and Ethnic Entrepreneurship: A Case Study of the Portuguese Real Estate Industry in Toronto', *The Canadian Geographer*, 42: 267–81.

Tepper, E.L. (1988), *Self-employment in Canada among Immigrants of Different Ethno-cultural Backgrounds*, Ottawa: Employment and Immigration Canada.

Tesser, P.T.M., F.A. van Dugteren and A. Merens (1996), *Rapportage minderheden 1996: Bevolking, arbeid, onderwijs, huisvesting*, Rijswijk: SCP.

The Economist (2002), 'Who Gains from Immigration?', 29 June: 37–8.

Thompson, R.H. (1979), 'Ethnicity versus Class: An Analysis of Conflict in a North American Chinese Community', *Ethnicity*, 6: 306–26.

— (1989), *Toronto's Chinatown: The Changing Social Organization of an Ethnic Community*, New York: AMS Press.

Tillaart, H. van den (1993), 'Zelfstandig ondernemerschap van etnische groepen', in R. Gowricharn (ed.), *Binnen de grenzen: Immigratie, etniciteit en integratie in Nederland*, Utrecht: De Tijdstroom.

— (2000), *Diversiteit in de Rotterdamse markt: Inventarisatie en analyse van de ontwikkelingen in het ondernemerschap van allochtonen in Rotterdam*, Ubbergen: Uitgeverij Tandem Felix.

— (2001), *Monitor allochtone ondernemers in Rotterdam: Ontwikkelingen in het ondernemerschap van allochtonen in Rotterdam in de periode 1990–2000*, Nijmegen: ITS.

— (2002), *Monitor etnisch ondernemerschap 2000: Zelfstandig ondernemerschap van etnische minderheden in Nederland in de periode 1990–2000*, Nijmegen: ITS.

— and E. Poutsma (1998), *Een factor van betekenis: Zelfstandig ondernemerschap van allochtonen in Nederland*, Nijmegen: ITS.

— and T.J.M. Reubsaet (1988), *Etnische ondernemers in Nederland*, Nijmegen: ITS.

— M. Olde Monnikhof, S. van den Berg and J. Warmerdam (2000), *Nieuwe etnische groepen in Nederland: Een onderzoek onder vluchtelingen en statushouders uit Afghanistan, Ethiopië en Eritrea, Iran, Somalië en Vietnam*, Nijmegen/Ubbergen: ITS/Uitgeverij Tandem Felix.

Timngum, D.A. (2001), 'Socio-economic Experiences of Francophone and Anglophone Refugees in South Africa: A Case Study of Cameroonian Urban Refugees in Johannesburg', unpublished MA thesis, University of the Witwatersrand, Johannesburg.

Tinnemans, W. (1989), 'Doorzetters: Immigranten in hogere functies', *Intermediair*, 7: 39–49.

Titlestad, B.M. (1991), 'Eating-houses on the Witwatersrand, 1903–1979', unpublished MA thesis, University of the Witwatersrand, Johannesburg.

Tomlinson, R. and C. Rogerson (1999), 'An Economic Development Strategy for the Johannesburg Inner City', unpublished report prepared as part of the UMP City Consultation Process on behalf of the Inner City Section 59 Committee, Johannesburg.

Torre, E.J. van der (1998), 'Marokkaanse harddrugshandelaren', in J. Rath and R. Kloosterman (eds), *Rijp & Groen: Het zelfstandig ondernemerschap van immigranten in Nederland*, Amsterdam: Het Spinhuis.

Tseng, H. (1991), 'The Adaptation of Taiwanese Immigrants in the Republic of South Africa', unpublished PhD thesis, University of Pretoria.

Tseng, Y.-F. (1995), 'Beyond "Little Taipei": The Development of Taiwanese Immigrant Businesses in Los Angeles', *International Migration Review*, 29: 33–58.

Turner, J. and E. Bonacich (1980), 'Toward a Composite Theory of Middleman Minorities', *Ethnicity*, 7: 144–58.

Turpin, T. (1986), *Migrant Workers in Victoria: Perceptions of Barriers and Change*, Melbourne: Victorian Ethnic Affairs Commission.

U

Uneke, O. (1996), 'Ethnicity and Small Business Ownership: Contrasts Between Blacks and Chinese in Toronto', *Work, Employment & Society*, 10: 529–48.

US Bureau of the Census (1960), *Historical Statistics of the United States, Colonial Time to 1957*, Washington, DC: US Government Printing Office.

— (1975), *Historical Statistics of the United States, Colonial Time to 1970*, Washington, DC: US Government Printing Office.

US Immigration and Naturalization Service (1950–1978), *Annual Reports*, Washington, DC: US Government Printing Office.

— (1979–2001), *Statistical Yearbook*, Washington, DC: US Government Printing Office.

V

Vanhaverbeke, J.M. and J. Leman (1988), 'De gastarbeider als zelfstandige: Knelpunten en mogelijke oplossingen', *Gids op maatschappelijk gebied*, 79: 3–19.

Vanhoren, I. and S. Bracke (1992), *Etnisch ondernemerschap in het Brusselse Hoofdstedelijk Gewest*, Leuven: HIVA.

Velde, V. van de (1997), 'De doorstroming van allochtone leerlingen in het Vlaamse onderwijs: Enkele illustratieve cijfers', paper given at 'The Staten

Generaal voor gelijkheid van kansen en voor racismebestrijding',
November.

Vellinga, M.L. and W.G. Wolters (1973), 'De Chinezen', in H. Verwey-Jonker
(ed.), *Allochtonen in Nederland: Beschouwingen over de gerepatrieerden,
Molukkers, Surinamers, Antillianen, buitenlandse werknemers, Chinezen,
vluchtelingen en buitenlandse studenten in onze samenleving*, 2nd rev. edn, The
Hague, Staatsuitgeverij.

Veraart, J. (1987), 'Turkse koffiehuizen in Nederland', *Migrantenstudies*, 3:
15–27.

— (1996), *In vaders voetspoor: Jonge Turken op de arbeidsmarkt*, Amsterdam:
Thesis.

Verhoeven, H. (2000), *De vreemde eend in de bijt: Arbeidsmarkt en diversiteit*,
Leuven: Steunpunt Werkgelegenheid, Arbeid en Vorming.

Verlot, M. (2001), 'Van een beekje naar een stroom: Vijftien jaar onderzoek naar
onderwijs aan migranten in Vlaanderen (1985–1999)', in J. Vranken, C.
Timmerman and K. Van der Heyden (eds), *Komende generaties: Wat weten we
(nog) niet over allochtonen in Vlaanderen?*, Leuven and Amersfoort: Acco.

— and S. Sierens (1997), 'Intercultureel onderwijs vanuit een pragmatisch
perspectief', *Cultuurstudies*, 3: 130–78.

Vermeulen, H. (ed.) (1991a), 'Handelsminderheden', special issue *Focaal*, 15.

— (1991b), 'Handelsminderheden: Een inleiding', *Focaal*, 15: 7–28.

— (ed.) (1997), *Immigration Policy for a Multicultural Society: A Comparative
Study of Integration, Language and Religious Policy*, Brussels and
Amsterdam: MPG and IMES.

—, M. van Attekum, F. Lindo and T. Pennings (1985), *De Grieken*, Migranten in
de Nederlandse Samenleving no. 3, Muiderberg: Coutinho.

Verweij, A.O., E.J. Latuheru, A.M. Rodenburg and Y.M.R. Weijers (1999),
*Jaarboek 1998 Grotestedenbeleid Deel 1: Situatie en ontwikkelingen in de
steden*, Rotterdam: ISEO.

Verwey-Jonker, H. (ed.) (1973), *Allochtonen in Nederland: Beschouwingen over
de gerepatrieerden, Molukkers, Surinamers, Antillianen, buitenlandse werknemers, Chinezen, vluchtelingen en buitenlandse studenten in onze samenleving*,
2nd rev. edn, The Hague: Staatsuitgeverij.

Villiers, R. de, and M. Reitzes (eds) (1995), *Southern African Migration:
Domestic and regional policy implications*, Workshop Proceedings no. 14,
Centre for Policy Studies, Johannesburg.

Vink, J. (s.a.), *To Sang Fotostudio*, Amsterdam: Basalt.

Vogels, R., P. Geense and E. Martens (1999), *De maatschappelijke positie van
Chinezen in Nederland*, Assen: Van Gorcum.

W

Waldinger, R. (1984), 'Ethnic Enterprise in the Garment Industry: Latin Americans in New York City', *Social Problems*, 32: 60–71.

— (1985), 'Immigration and Industrial Change in the New York City Apparel Industry', in G. Borjas and M. Tienda (eds), *Hispanics in the US Economy*, Orlando, FL: Academic Press.

— (1986a), *Through the Eye of the Needle: Immigrants and Enterprise in New York's Garment Trades*, New York: New York University Press.

— (1986b), 'Immigrant Enterprise: A Critique and Reformulation', *Theory and Society*, 15: 249–85.

— (1989), 'Structural Opportunity or Ethnic Advantage? Immigrant Business Development in New York', *International Migration Review*, 23: 48–72.

— (1996), *Still the Promised City? African-Americans and New Immigrants in Postindustrial New York*, Cambridge, MA: Harvard University Press.

— (2001), 'The Immigrant Niche in Global City-regions: Concept, Patterns, Controversy', in A. Scott (ed.), *Global City-regions: Trends, Theory, Policy*, Oxford: Oxford University Press.

—, H. Aldrich, R. Ward and Associates (1990a), *Ethnic Entrepreneurs: Immigrant Business in Industrial Societies*, Newbury Park, London, New Delhi: Sage.

—, H. Aldrich, R. Ward and Associates (1990b), 'Opportunities, Group Characteristics, and Strategies', in R. Waldinger, H. Aldrich, R. Ward and Associates (eds), *Ethnic Entrepreneurs: Immigrant Business in Industrial Societies*, Newbury Park, CA: Sage.

Walton-Roberts, M. and D. Hiebert (1997), 'Immigration, Entrepreneurship, and the Family: Indo-Canadian Enterprise in the Construction Industry of Greater Vancouver', *Canadian Journal of Regional Science*, 20: 119–40.

Wang, S.-W. (1988), 'Chinese Immigration 1840s-1890s', in J. Jupp (ed.), *The Australian People: An Encyclopedia of the Nation, Its People and Their Origins*, Sydney: Angus and Robertson.

Wanzenböck, H. (1998), *Das österreichische Gründungsgeschehen*, Vienna: Institut für Betriebswirtschaftslehre der Klein- und Mittelbetriebe.

Ward, R. (ed.) (1986), 'Ethnic Business and Economic Change', special issue *International Small Business Journal*, 3.

Ward, R. (1987) 'Ethnic Entrepreneurs in Britain and Europe', in R. Goffee and R. Scase (eds), *Entrepreneurship in Europe*, Beckenham: Croom Helm.

— (1991) 'Economic Development and Ethnic Business', in J. Curran and R.A. Blackburn (eds), *Paths of Enterprise: The Future of the Small Business*, London: Routledge.

— and R. Jenkins (eds) (1984), *Ethnic Communities in Business: Strategies for Economic Survival*, Cambridge: Cambridge University Press.

Watson, J. (1975), *Emigration and the Chinese Lineage*, Berkeley: University of California Press.

— (1977), 'The Chinese: Hong Kong Villagers in the British Catering Trade', in J.L. Watson (ed.), *Between Two Cultures: Migrants and Minorities in Britain*, Oxford: Blackwell.

Watson, R., K. Keasey and M. Baker (2000), 'Small Firm Financial Contracting and Immigrant Entrepreneurship', in J. Rath (ed.), *Immigrant Businesses: The Economic, Political and Social Environment*, Basingstoke/New York: Macmillan/St Martin's.

Weerd, J. van der (2001), 'Allochtone ondernemers moeten naoorlogse wijk redden', *Geografie*, 4: 19–21.

Weiss, L. (1988), *Creating Capitalism: The State and Small Business Since 1945*, Oxford: Basil Blackwell.

Werbner, P. (1980), 'From Rags to Riches: Manchester Pakistanis in the Textile Trade', *New Community*, 8: 84–95.

— (1984), 'Business on Trust: Pakistani Entrepreneurship in the Manchester Garment Trade', in R. Ward and R. Jenkins (eds), *Ethnic Communities in Business: Strategies for Economic Survival*, Cambridge: Cambridge University Press.

— (1990), 'Renewing an Industrial Past: British Pakistani Entrepreneurship in Manchester', *Migration*, 8: 17–41.

Wermuth, M. (1998), 'Zwaai je handen: Immigranten in de wereld van de (populaire) muziekindustrie', in J. Rath and R. Kloosterman (eds), *Rijp & Groen: Het zelfstandig ondernemerschap van immigranten in Nederland*, Amsterdam: Het Spinhuis.

Whitley, R. (2000), *Divergent Capitalism: The Social Structuring and Change of Business Systems*, Oxford: Oxford University Press.

Willems, J. (1996), 'Etnisch ondernemen', unpublished BA thesis, LUC Diepenbeek.

Williams, A.J. (1992), 'Employment Patterns and Practices in Small Firms in Australia: An Assessment of Skill Deficiencies and Training Needs', in Bureau of Industry Economics, *Small Business Review 1992*, Canberra: Australian Government Publishing Service.

Williams, L. and T. Batrouney (1998), 'Immigrants and Poverty' in R. Fincher and J. Nieuwenhuysen (eds), *Australian Poverty: Then and Now*, South Carlton: Melbourne University Press.

Wilpert, C. (1980), *Die Zukunft der zweiten Generation*, Königstein (Ts.): Anton Hain.

— (1988), *Entering the Working World: Following the Descendants of Europe's Immigrant Labour Force*, Aldershot: Gower.

— (1998a), 'Migrant Insertion in the Informal Economy: Deviant Behaviour and the Impact on Receiving Societies', TSER report for the European Commission.

— (1998b), 'Migration and Informal Work in the new Berlin: New Forms of Work or New Sources of Labour?', *Journal of Ethnic and Migration Studies*, 24: 269–94.

— (1999a), 'Die Initiative Selbständiger Immigrantinnen (ISI): Ansatz und Erfahrungen', in Frauenhochschule Kassel (ed.), *ORTSveränderungen: Perspektiven weiblicher Partizipation und Raumaneignung*, Königstein (Ts.): Ulrike Helmer Verlag.

— (ed.) (1999b), 'The New Migration and the Informal Labour Market in Germany', TSER project report for the European Commission.

—, F. Helten and H. Mainer (1999), *Neue Berliner Zielgruppen für haushaltsnahe Dienstleistungen*, Berlin: Zukunft im Zentrum.

Wilson, K. and W.A. Martin (1982), 'Ethnic Enclaves: A Comparison of the Cuban and Black Economies in Miami', *American Journal of Sociology*, 88: 135–68.

Wilson, P. and J. Stanworth (1985), *Black Business in Brent*, London: Small Business Research Trust.

Wilton, J. and R. Bosworth (1984), *Old Worlds and New Australia*, Ringwood: Penguin.

Wimmer, H. (1986), 'Zur Ausländerbeschäftigungspolitik in Österreich', in: H. Wimmer (ed.), *Ausländische Arbeitskräfte in Österreich*, Frankfurt/Main: Campus.

Wisniewski, J. (1982), 'Artisans étrangers en France', *Hommes et Migrations*, 1028: 27–33.

Wit, P.B.P. de (1999), *Allochtoon ondernemerschap in de horeca: Rapportage 1998*, Zoetermeer: Bedrijfschap Horeca en Catering.

Witte, E. de (1997), 'Ruimtelijk-economische analyse van etnisch ondernemerschap in Ghent: Met toepassing op de Turkse gemeenschap', unpublished BA thesis, Department of Applied Economic Sciences, Catholic University of Leuven.

Wolff, R. and R. Penninx (1993), *De ontwikkeling van de positie van minderheden op de Nederlandse arbeidsmarkt 1979–1992*, The Hague: SDU/DOP.

Wolff, R. and J. Rath (2000), *Centen tellen: Een inventariserende en verkennende studie naar de financiering van immigrantenondernemingen*, Amsterdam: Het Spinhuis.

Wollner, E. (1996), 'Auf dem Weg zur sozialpartnerschaftlich regulierten Ausländerbeschäftigung in Österreich', MA thesis, University of Vienna.

Wong, B. (1998), *Ethnicity and Entrepreneurship: The New Chinese Immigrants in the San Francisco Bay Area*, Boston: Allyn and Bacon.

Wong, L. (1993), 'Immigration as Capital Accumulation: The Impact of

Business Immigration to Canada', *International Migration*, 31: 171–90.

— (1995), 'Chinese Capitalist Migration to Canada: A Sociological Interpretation of Its Effect on Canada', *Asian and Pacific Migration Journal*, 4: 465–92.

— and N.S. Netting (1992), 'Business Immigration to Canada: Social Impact and Racism', in V. Satzewich (ed.), *Deconstructing a Nation: Immigration and Racism in '90s Canada*, Halifax: Fernwood.

— and M. Ng (1998), 'Chinese Immigrant Entrepreneurs in Vancouver: A Case Study of Ethnic Business Development', *Canadian Ethnic Studies*, 30: 64–85.

Woo, E. (1997), 'The New Entrepreneurs and Investors from Hong Kong: An Assessment of the Business Program', in E. Laquian, A. Laquian and T. McGee (eds), *The Silent Debate: Asian Immigration and Racism in Canada*, Vancouver: Institute for Asian Research, UBC.

Woodard, M.D. (1997), *Black Entrepreneurs in America: Stories of Struggle and Success*, New Brunswick, NJ: Rutgers University Press.

Wooden, M., R. Holton, G. Hugo and J. Sloan (1994), *Australian Immigration: A Survey of the Issues*, 2nd edn, Canberra: Australian Government Publishing Service.

Wrigley, N. (1996), 'Sunk Costs and Corporate Restructuring: British Food Retailing and the Property Crisis', in N. Wrigley and M. Lowe (eds), *Retailing, Consumption and Capital*, Harlow: Longman.

Wubben, H.J.J. (1986), *'Chineezen en ander Aziatisch ongedierte': Lotgevallen van Chinese immigranten in Nederland, 1911–1940*, Zutphen: De Walburg Pers.

Y

Yancy, R.J. (1974), *Federal Government and Black Business*, Cambridge: Ballinger.

Yap, M. and D. Man (1996), *Colour, Confusion and Concessions: The History of the Chinese in South Africa*, Hong Kong: South African Chinese History Project and Hong Kong University Press.

Yoo, J.K. (1998), *Korean Immigrant Entrepreneurs: Networks and Ethnic Resources*, New York and London: Garland.

Yoon, I.-J. (1991), 'Changing Significance of Ethnic and Class Resources in Immigrant Business: The Case of Korean Businesses in Chicago', *International Migration Review*, 25: 303–31.

— (1997), *On My Own: Korean Business and Race Relations in America*, Chicago: University of Chicago Press.

Younge, G. (1999), 'Britain Bites the Hand that Feeds It', *The Guardian*, 10 August.

Yuan, C.M. (1988), 'Chinese in White Australia 1901–1950', in J. Jupp (ed.),

The Australian People: An Encyclopedia of the Nation, Its People and Their Origins, Sydney: Angus and Robertson.

Z

Zanfrini, L. (1998), *Leggere le migrazioni: I risultati della ricerca empirica, le categorie interpretative i problemi aperti*, Milan: Franco Angeli.

— (1999), *La discriminazione nel mercato del lavoro*, Milan: Franco Angeli.

Zeldenrust, I. and J. van Eijk (1992), *Op zoek naar schone kleren: Strategieën voor het verbeteren van de arbeidssituatie in de confectie-industrie*, Amsterdam: SOMO.

Zenner, W. (1991), *Minorities in the Middle: A Cross-cultural Analysis*, Albany, NY: State University of New York Press.

Zentrum für Türkeistudien (1989), *Türkische Unternehmensgründungen: Von der Nische zum Markt? Ergebnisse der MAGS-Untersuchung bei türkischen Selbständigen in Dortmund, Duisburg und Essen*, Studien und Arbeiten no. 5, Opladen: Leske und Budrich.

— (ed.) (1991), *Ausländische Selbständige in Nordrhein-Westfalen*, Opladen: Leske und Budrich.

— (ed.) (1998), *Türken als Unternehmer: Eine Gesamtdarstellung und Ergebnisse neuerer Untersuchungen*, Opladen: Leske und Budrich.

Zhang, K. (1999), *Problems and Strategies of Chinese Immigrants: A Study of the Restaurant Sector in the Dutch Labour Market*, Burnaby, BC: Simon Fraser University/Shanghai Academy of Social Sciences.

Zhou, M. (1992), *Chinatown: The Socioeconomic Potential of an Urban Enclave*, Philadelphia: Temple University Press.

Zincone, G. (ed.) (1999), *Primo rapporto sull'integrazione in Italia*, Bologna: Il Mulino.

Zinopoulos, L. (1992), *Women and TAFE: Education and Training Needs of Women from Non-English Speaking Backgrounds*, Sydney: Women's Co-ordination Unit, NSW TAFE Commission.

Zorlu, A. (1998), 'Goedkope arbeid als wondermiddel? Hoe immigrantenondernemers in de Amsterdamse confectie-industrie hun personeel werven', in J. Rath and R. Kloosterman (eds), *Rijp & Groen: Het zelfstandig ondernemerschap van immigranten in Nederland*, Amsterdam: Het Spinhuis.

Zucchetti, E. (1995), 'L'imprenditorialità etnica', in Fondazione Cariplo-ISMu, *Primo rapporto sulle migrazioni 1995*, Milan: Franco Angeli.

Index